THE IMPACT OF FILM

THE IMPACT
OF Film

HOW IDEAS ARE COMMUNICATED THROUGH CINEMA AND TELEVISION

Roy Paul Madsen

Macmillan Publishing Co., Inc.
New York
Collier Macmillan Publishers
London

AAK4596

To the American Film Industry
Sire of an Art Form

Contents

vii

Preface

Cinema began some three quarters of a century ago as a dramatic novelty, a moment's escape from banality. From its beginning as a brief diversion, the medium evolved into an art form and means of communication that so permeates our lives that we can scarcely escape its sights and sounds. Moreover, film is no longer one medium, but the fusion of two: cinema and television. And cinema-television no longer speaks only in the language of drama, but assumes a tremendous variety of forms and concepts according to its utilization in American society.

This book represents a first attempt to define how film and television programs are organized for idea communication in their major areas of use. Its central purpose is to provide a source work to which laymen, students and professionals alike may turn to understand how the medium of cinema-television can be effectively utilized to achieve a specific purpose in drama, teaching and persuasion. And it may, moreover, enable the average viewer to realize on sight when the medium and its message are being manipulated to influence his opinions.

The work contains four major divisions: the first deals with the syntax of cinema-television and the means by which ideas are expressed through techniques unique to the language of the medium. The second section reveals the basic dramatic forms for cinematic development of plot and character, and the forms and concepts which have evolved in major film and television genres. The third segment deals with the uses of cinema-television in effecting political, social and economic changes. And the fourth division treats the proved teaching and research techniques used in schools and industries.

This book is not necessarily concerned with communication theory. The content is a synthesis of ideas and techniques that have proved their worth in practice. What is new and truly effective is included as being of enduring value. What is new and unproved is so stated. Zealots who advocate one approach to the exclusion of others may be dismayed to find their commitment placed in perspective, or may be eager to point out exceptions in this film or that director, but my concern is to emphasize what is essentially true in communication by cinema-television.

This work is written on the premise that the characteristics of the target audience must be an integral part of every aspect of cinema-television, regardless of whether the production takes a dramatic, documentary or educational form. The viewer, the key to success or failure in media communication, is often ignored or lightly treated in most books about film and television. It is apparently assumed by most producers that if the filmmaker is creative in his ideas and competent in his craft that the reaction of the viewer to the film can only be favorable. The viewer's underlying motives for selecting a film or television program to watch—age, sex, level of formal education, socio-economic milieu, and life space—are unmentioned in most of the literature treating cinema-television. And such crucial considerations as selective exposure, perception, retention, and the "boomerang effect" are ignored as if they did not exist. This attitude may account for the failure of so many films and television programs to achieve their intended purposes, and for the vacuous rhetoric which fills so much of the professional literature.

In writing this book I drew extensively upon material which has appeared in research journals, books, theses, dissertations, newspapers and other periodicals. Some originated in obscure research studies and some in little magazines long out of print. Much of it was widely dispersed and required long (happy) hours of digging in libraries through related but relatively unfamiliar fields. The great bulk of the content, however, derives from my own professional and research experiences, and from the contributions of outstanding individuals and studios of the American film and television industry.

The brevity of treatment given to certain areas should be explained. Technical material has been included only when necessary to clarify the communication aspects of some ramification of cinema-television.

Such abstruse specialties as aerospace cinematography, deep-sea cinematography and medical cinematography are so complex technically that large volumes have been devoted to each purview. I have sought primarily to illuminate the principles governing their use as art and communication, and those of other genres treated in this book.

The media communications industry is being transformed by a synthesis of film and television technologies, techniques and ideas. Dramas recorded in a studio on videotape are being combined with filmed sequences photographed on location. Theatrical films are frequently produced with television reruns in mind and contain dramatic breaks for the later insertion of television commercials. Moreover, the slam-bang opening of the television adventure program, to prevent the viewer from switching channels, has now transformed the once sedately begun theatrical film. The first dramatic films have recently been recorded entirely on videotape and transferred to film for theater projection. And the development of video discs and the computer-based Random Access Videotape Editor, now make it possible to combine filmed and videotaped scenes as if they were one, and to electronically edit them all in the cinematic time and tempo of pure cinema.

The same fusion of cinema-television forms and concepts also holds true in nontheatrical genres. Documentary films, photographed and edited as pure film, are being introduced at the beginning and summarized at the end by spokesmen recorded on videotape, in the traditional interview format of television. Classroom lectures are recorded in videotape and the substance of the lectures given visual form by the inclusion of live action and animated film sequences. One need look no further for the conceptual synthesis of cinema-television forms and concepts than the much laureled education television series, *Sesame Street*.

This work takes cognizance of film and television as separate media of communication, and as cinema-television, a synthesized medium of communication. The effects of this cross-pollenation on individual productions, and the reactions of viewers, have been defined as far as the state of the art and proved research permits.

I hope this book will be of value to the reader in clearing up the sometimes murky waters of cinema-television as art and communication.

Acknowledgments

I am pleased to acknowledge the contributions, assistance and cooperation freely offered by many generous persons and organizations during the writing of this book.

Mr. Desi Arnaz, executive producer of many television network series, has my sincere appreciation for his goodwill in obtaining illustrations, research material and the cooperation of others.

Mr. Joseph Bluth, president of the Vidtronics Division of the Technicolor Corporation, took time from his tight schedule to offer information and illustrations, and to proofread the videotape segments of the manuscript.

I am indebted to Mr. Floyd Crosby, Academy Award–winning cinematographer, for his careful editing and constructive criticism of the filmmaking chapters.

Mr. Jay McMullen, award-winning CBS television producer, has my sincere appreciation for his ruthless use of the blue pencil on the documentary chapters, and for his constructive suggestions.

I wish to thank Dr. Leo Persselin, Assistant Director of the Special Education Instructional Material Center Network, of the Council for Exceptional Children, for rigorously editing the chapters on education.

Dr. Clarence Stephenson, playwright and director, deserves thanks for his incisive criticism of the chapters on drama.

At Station KPBS-TV, San Diego, my sincere appreciation is extended to Mr. Chris Rager, chief engineer, for his critique of those chapters relating to electronic systems.

I should like to thank those executives who took much time from their busy schedules to assist me in obtaining all necessary information, illustrations and permissions: *Arjo Productions*: Norman Corwin. *California State University, San Diego*: Dr. Hayes Anderson, Elizabeth Heighton, Robert E. Lee, and Dr. K. Charles Jameson. *CBS News*: Charles Steinberg and James Byrnes. *CBS Television Network*: Robert A. Daly. *Computer Image Corporation*: Lee Harrison, III, and Carl Hedberg. *Faces, Inc.*: John Cassavetes. *Hanna-Barbera Productions*: Joe Barbera, William Hanna and John Michaeli. *KOGO-TV, San Diego*: Dale Schwartz. *KPBS, Public Broadcasting*: Jack Summerfield. *Walt Disney Productions*: Roy Disney and George Sherman. *Lucille Ball Productions*: Lucille Ball and Howard Rayfiel. *Metro-Goldwyn-Mayer*: David Jacobson and Norman Kaphan. *Murakami-Wolf*: Jerry Good. *The National Association of Broadcasters*: Paul Comstock. *National Film Board of Canada*: Gerald Graham, T. L. Johnston and David Novek. *National Geographic Society*: David Arnold, Marta M. Marschalko and Dennis B. Kane. *Paramount Pictures Corporation*: Arthur N. Ryan, Hal Wallis, John Wayne, Joseph Hazen and Ralph Kamon. *Roger, Cowan & Brenner, Inc.*: Dale Olson. *Scripps Institute of Oceanography*: John Isaacs, Richard A. Schwartzlose, Richard Schutz and Sargun Tont. *Twentieth Century Fox*: George Stephenson. *Universal City Studios*: Arline Conklin, E. Goodman, M. Sattler and J. Mann. *University of California, San Diego. School of Medicine*: Dr. Roger Marchand. *Wolper Productions*: David Wolper. I should also like to thank producers Dennis Sanders and Robert Fresco.

Many talented dramatic artists receive my gratitude for their cooperation in the use of their pictures as illustrations: the *Andromeda Strain*: James Olson and George Mitchell. *Bedknobs and Broomsticks*: Angela Lansbury, David Tomlinson, Roddy McDowall, Sam Jaffe and John Erickson. *Butch Cassidy and the Sundance Kid*: Paul Newman, Robert Redford and Katharine Ross. *Faces*: Audrey Caire, Lynn Carlin, Seymour Cassel, John Marley, Gena Rowlands and Dennis Patrick. *I Love Lucy*: Desi Arnaz and Lucille Ball. *Joe*: Peter Boyle, K. Callan, Patrick McDermott, Dennis Patrick and Susan Sarandon. *Lonely Are the Brave*: Kirk Douglas and William Raisch. *Lust for Life*: Again, Kirk Douglas. *Mary Poppins*: Julie Andrews and Dick Van Dyke. *M.A.S.H.*: Sally Kellerman. *Norman Corwin Presents*: Lloyd Bochner and John Gardiner. *Patton*: George C. Scott and Paul Stevens. *Ryan's Daughter*: Robert Mitchum and Sarah Miles. *Thoroughly Modern Millie*: Again, Julie Andrews. *True Grit*: Kim Darby and John Wayne. Others I should like to thank include Paul Lynde, Anita Mann and Michael Sarrazin.

Officials in other organizations and institutions also cooperated in obtaining illustrations and permissions. Those I wish to acknowledge include Richard A. Purser of *Appleton-Century-Crofts*, Rebecca Auerbach of the Cannon Group, Robert Montague of the *Convair Aerospace Division: General Dynamics*, A. I. Murray of *Crawley Films, Ltd.*, John Cassavetes of *Faces*, Mr. Charles Adams of *Pyramid Films,* Walter Reade and Paul Baise of the *Walter Reade Organization*, Alan Morris of *Group W Productions*, Alan Wood of the *Jet Propulsion Laboratory*, Leo Dratfield of *Contemporary Films/McGraw-Hill*, Richard Spence of *Great Plains National Instructional Television Library*, Dr. Wolfram von Hanwehr of the *University of Southern California*, Captain John Reilly and Frederick Roessler of the *United States Navy*, and Ron Garrison of the *San Diego Zoo*.

I should like to thank Elizabeth Jordan for her astute care in editing and criticizing the manuscript, and Nina Lott for her cheerful assistance in research.

Others I should like to acknowledge include Evelyn Camp, Kay Church, Betty Jackson, Tony O'Donnell and Dorothy Woodyard.

Mansour Emami has my appreciation for his special photography, and Glen Shimada for his line drawings.

I especially wish to express my deep appreciation to Barbara, my wife, for her long hours spent in editing, proofreading and retouching photographs, and for her infinite patience.

The
Concepts of
Cinema-Television

PATTON. *20th Century-Fox.*

1

Cinema-Television and the Viewer

Film is so much a part of our growing up that it seems fatuous to say we must learn how to watch motion pictures and interpret their meanings, or to assert that we each view and interpret the same film differently in the light of our individual values, education and life experiences. But we are not born with a knowledge of film forms and concepts, and we have no innate grasp of the languages of cinematography and editing. Film literacy is a language we have learned, but learned at so early an age that it was acquired in much the same way we learned to speak, without conscious effort or cognizance of the learning process, from our media-drenched society. Babies ingest television programs with their mothers' milk. Children are shown educational films and television programs as core content in their classroom studies. Teenagers and adults attend neighborhood theaters to escape their mundane worlds for a few hours, to vicariously live other lives presented on the screen. And the senior citizen is connected to the unrelenting world again through television. From cradle to grave we are offered a steady diet of motion pictures.

We live in a pluralistic, multiracial, multiethnic, multireligious society, however, and are not exposed to the same kinds of films, nor do we bring to a film viewing the same life experiences; we perceive selectively, as through a filter, only those things we recognize as being important to us. A film or television program may present content of supreme

MARY POPPINS. Theater entertainment. © *Walt Disney Productions.*

importance to the viewer, but unless it is presented in terms of the viewer's perceptions, values and capacity to understand, he will not willingly watch the screen. If the viewer is forced to watch in a captive-audience context, such as a classroom, he may distort the meaning of what he sees to make it fit into his preconceptions, or, more likely, he may daydream through the presentation until awakened by the flare of room lights. Many well-intended films of genuine merit and importance are not watched by their intended audience because the producers were solely concerned with the quality of the films, and took no cognizance of the relationship between film forms and content and the characteristics of their target audience. The producer who makes his film without learning the characteristics of his viewers may waste his investment of time, money and talent.

The relationship between film and the viewer is twofold: first, there are the characteristics of the film medium as perceived by the viewer, those to which he most readily responds. These elements are *visual primacy, visual context, reinforcement of existing attitudes and knowledge* and *content relevance*. Second, there are those characteristics of the viewer himself which affect his perception and response to that film. These elements are *age, sex, intelligence, level of formal education, social attitudes and opinions* and *life space*.

Film Characteristics

Visual Primacy

Visual primacy is the essence of film communication. The human eye has a direct link to the brain and is the primary means by which the

Television News.
CBS News.

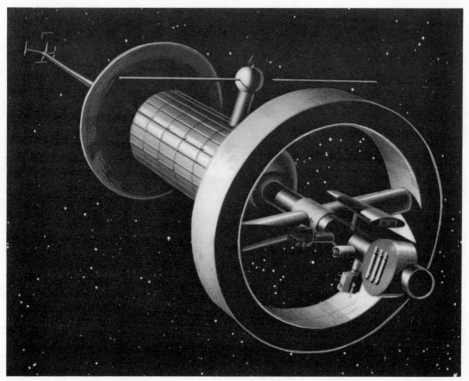

LIFELINE IN SPACE. Visual Primacy. *Graphic Films/Pyramid.*

physically normal person learns about and relates to his environment. Seeing provides the most direct communication to the mind, and images do not need to be translated to be understood. Sound is secondary in film communication because its content reaches the brain through the ear in the form of a symbols system—words—which needs translation by the mind to be understood. Furthermore, spoken words tend to be more easily forgotten. The eye remembers, the ear forgets.

The implications of visual primacy are these: The content of a motion picture or television program should be ninety percent visual in order to make good use of the medium. The remaining ten percent may be given over to narration or dialogue to clarify what is shown on the screen, or to relate the visuals to what has gone before. The sound track should play a supportive role; if the content is so verbal in nature that it requires having someone stand before the cameras to make a purely verbal statement, the medium is being improperly used. Content which is essentially verbal ought to be published or broadcast over the radio, not put in a motion picture or television program. Many well-intentioned educational producers ignore the principle of visual primacy and offer programs which are little more than radio with pictures. In that case the medium adds nothing to the message, and may actually detract from it. The compelling reason for communicating ideas in film or television form should be the graphic nature of their content, not their importance.

VISUAL CONTEXT

Visual context refers to identification by the viewer with what is taking place on the screen, and is achieved in part by including in the film things that are familiar to the viewer. The average person is a subjective creature who perceives and responds selectively to those things in a film that he finds significant for himself. In dramatic pro-

THE THINGS I CANNOT CHANGE. Viewer empathy. *National Film Board of Canada.*

grams he identifies with the people caught up in a conflict and feels, "There, but for the grace of God, go I." In educational films he looks for content that relates to the subject he is studying and asks, "What can I use?" In documentary films he looks for those things that impinge upon his life or environment and asks, "How does this affect me?" The degree to which film and television programs present content in a familiar visual context may affect the degree to which the viewer takes an interest in the show and accepts what is being presented.

Visual context has these implications in film communication: Content should be cast in as familiar a mold as is practicable. Since people tend to identify with other people rather than with objects or ideas, most subjects are more effectively presented in terms of human consequences. A documentary film bristling with statistics on poverty will not have nearly the motivational impact of one scene presenting a starving child—a subject with whom the viewer can empathize. Next best are environmental situations that the viewer recognizes, or symbols with which he has ego involvement. Least effective is new content in a new context, because it appears to lack relevance. Whatever is not recognized as important by the viewer may tend to be ignored, regardless of its real value, unless it is presented in terms of or paired with the familiar and significant. The more apperceptive factors and cues that can be included in a film or television program, the more likely it is that the viewer will relate to and accept what is being shown.

REINFORCEMENT

Reinforcement is nearly equal in importance to visual primacy among the factors to be considered in film communication. Reinforcement refers to the fact that a film has its greatest influence when its content extends and confirms previous knowledge and attitudes held by the viewer, and has the least influence when its content is outside the viewer's purview of knowledge or is antagonistic to his existing attitudes. Rarely does a single film revolutionize the established attitudes of its audience; far to the contrary, a film presenting content strongly incompatible with the bias of the viewer may anger him and leave him more convinced than ever of the rightness of his original opinion, a result referred to as the "boomerang effect." Under most circumstances a viewer will refuse to look at such a film, and if forced to do so, will tend to selectively perceive only that which supports his original point of view. Most children and many adults tend to accept without cavil all presumably factual information in film and television programs and to retain such information remarkably well, while failing to draw the intended conclusions from the facts. The weight of research to date points to two general conclusions: Film and television programming may successfully transmit a barrage of facts about an issue and yet be ineffectual in influencing the opinion or attitude of the viewer whose mind is made up. Explicit material (facts) is readily accepted, while implicit material (ideas) is resisted or distorted when the viewer already has an opinion on the subject.

When the viewer has no opinion on an issue, however, a single film may create an opinion and be of unshakable importance. "The first word to the world is always right," said Joseph Goebbels, and subsequent research has confirmed his belief in the efficacy of getting to the audience first with a media presentation. The first point of view expressed on an issue tends to prevail in the mind of the viewer in a way that later communications cannot expunge, particularly if it is reinforced by films. Media recognition confers prestige and status on ideas, persons, organizations, public issues and social movements. Social standing and respect come to those who merely receive attention on the screen, quite apart from the validity of their views. The first person to present his point of view on film and television programs may get his way for a long time, for once a point of view on a new subject is established, viewer characteristics of selective exposure and selective perception will come into play to protect and reinforce it.

The reinforcement relationship between the "first film" and the viewer may have crucial implications in public affairs. Times of social unrest and revolution, when the pat answers of the past no longer suffice, create enormous potential for opinion formation on new issues by the media. Not only may film and television present and reinforce revolutionary views, but they may introduce and define ideas to which many viewers have given little or no attention. And once the audience has been instilled with an opinion, however ill-founded, it tends to be inoculated against later programming which presents evidence to the contrary. In this way, therefore, the thrust and focus of a nation permeated by the media may be shaped by film and television programming on those new issues about which the people are unlikely to have opinions. And little by little, a nation's character may be changed by the film and television programming to which it is exposed, for good or ill.

The principle of reinforcement, however, may also inadvertently act as a censor. Television advertisers and producers depend for their life-blood on attracting and holding a vast and varied audience, and they are careful to avoid espousing any point of view that might alienate a commercially significant minority. This tends to restrict serial film and television programming to views and values to which there is virtually no objection, and acts to reinforce dominant cultural values. Some current television dramas do deal circumspectly with subjects that were previously taboo, such as drug addiction, extramarital relations, homosexuality and miscegenation, and occasional prime time is also given now to topics formerly relegated to the Sunday afternoon intellectuals' ghetto. But for the most part, content analyses of television dramas consistently reveal that their conflicts stem essentially from individual inadequacies and seldom from social forces, and that deviations from culturally approved behavior lead to catastrophe. Theatrical film producers, incidentally, have capitalized on the censorship effect of reinforcement on television programming by presenting daring topics in their rawest forms to lure patrons from their sets into the theaters.

The censorship generalization does not apply to the occasional newscast or documentary film broadcast, some of which do attempt to present controversial issues courageously. But these are one-shot presentations seldom designed to influence public opinion. Nor does it apply to some serial newscasts and news commentaries when the network had a covert policy on a public issue and tries very quietly to shape public opinion by presenting film clips whose content supports its policy. But it does apply to educational film and television programming, in a strict sense, because of the sensitivity of educators to pressures from public organizations concerned with the content being taught in the schools.

The principle of reinforcement carries these practical implications: Every film and television program intended to achieve specific objectives should be preceded by careful research on the present beliefs and knowledge of the target audience, and then attempt to achieve only modest results by extending and reinforcing present knowledge and attitudes when introducing new material. The absence of preestablished opinions on a subject, of course, gives the producer full discretionary powers. And finally, films and television programs are far more effective when they are planned and used as a progressive, cumulative series, all segments of which function to achieve common objectives. Those who work in television advertising recognize the importance of repetition in reinforcement and plan their campaigns conceptually as a series of programs all designed to motivate one behavioral response in the viewer— buy the product. And those (worth their salt) in educational film and television production must also present their ideas as progressive extensions of reinforcement if they wish to motivate their students to the desired behavior goal—learn the subject.

CONTENT RELEVANCE

Content relevance is an important communication concept because the effect of a film or television program is more specific than general. This means, very simply, that the producer should decide in advance of production exactly what he wants the audience to do as a result of having seen the film, and include only that content in the film which is relevant to achieving this goal. If a bill is pending in Congress which will require a segment of industry to desist from some kind of pollution of the environment, and the filmmaker is producing a documentary film on this subject intended to persuade the viewer to write his Congressman to support this legislation, the content of the documentary should include only that information relevant to persuading the viewer to write his Congressman. If the documentary producer cannot resist the temptation to pontificate, and introduces material unrelated to the specific issue under consideration, on other kinds of pollution, for example, the focus of the audience will be diffused and the individual viewer may fail to take pen in hand.

The principle of content relevance has these implications: A narrow "rifle" approach to a given subject with a given target audience is more apt to succeed than the "shotgun" approach of many vaguely defined objectives intended for a mass audience. The film or television program should be defined in terms of its behavior-stimulation purpose—what the producer wants the viewer to learn or do as a result of seeing the communication—and not in terms of subject matter. The objectives of the film should determine the content, not the converse. The producer should weigh every aspect of his production to determine whether it states or implies only that which enhances the film's message, and delete everything that detracts. Those juicy little "extras," that marvelous scene with the superb photography which is not quite relevant to the film's goals but seems too good to waste, must be ruthlessly pruned, because whatever does not advance the film's purposes subtracts from its success by distracting the viewer's attention from what is important.

Viewer Characteristics

The relationship between the film and the viewer is affected as much by what he brings to the film experience as it is by the film itself. First is the factor of selective exposure: the average person seeks out those films whose points of view corresponds to his own, and avoids those that do not. Second is the factor of selective perception: if forced to view a film whose content runs counter to an established opinion or attitude, the average person tends to perceive only what reinforces his existing viewpoint, ignoring what does not, or to react in anger by distorting the film's content to justify and reaffirm his convictions—the boomerang effect. Third is the factor of selective retention: the average viewer will remember those things in a film or television program that he considers of value according to his *age, sex, intelligence, level of formal education, socioeconomic values* and *life space.*

AGE

Age as a factor of film perception relates primarily to film literacy and selection of content. In most industrialized nations the individual now begins to develop film literacy from the time he is able to sit up and watch television, and he continues to learn through school presentations and viewing of entertainment films in local theaters. His ability to interpret cinematography and editing techniques matures at an early age and continues to develop for as long as he continues to view films. The ability to perceive and retain content, however, is another matter. The capacity to learn from films grows until it reaches a peak in the late teens and early twenties, and then declines, never again to reach this height in the average individual. This decline in receptivity has been attributed to either of two causes, but is probably a combination of both. The first is "adult discount"—the skepticism and resistance to excitability that comes with maturity. The individual has learned to take what he sees and hears with a grain of salt, and by this process of discrimination, he tends to filter out what he might have learned if the new information conflicts with what he has already learned or wants to believe. The second is simply the decline in human physiological reactions after a certain age; anyone over twenty-two years old is over the hill in terms of his peak response capabilities.

Film and television programming have the documented ability to influence young viewers' concepts of adult subjects in which they are interested and about which they have few other sources of information. Television soap-opera emphasis on adults in personal conflict tends to produce in children an early awareness of the complexity and essential unfairness of life and anxieties about leaving school, finding work and making a place for themselves in the world. Many viewers—thirteen- to fourteen-year-old girls in particular—expressed fear about growing up, based upon their viewing of adult films and television programs. Boys of the same age tended to become more materialistic in proportion to their degree of media exposure, more interested in the things they would like to own than in the work they would like to do. And there is research to indicate that boys who are constantly exposed to violence in films and television programs tend to regard the unrealistic dramatic characters as realistic, and to judge real-world adults in terms of stereotypes learned from the media.

Age is the chief operant factor in reactions to scenes of love and sex, staple elements in many entertainment films. Under twelve years of age, the physiological response is negligible. The index of reaction rises in the twelve-to-fifteen age group, and reaches its peak in the sixteen-to-nineteen age group. From the age of nineteen through the early twenties the reaction to love scenes declines to the level of the twelve-to-fifteen age group, and after twenty-five it drops still further, perhaps due to the discovery that there is no substitute for the real thing. It is worth noting, however, that greater differences in intensity of response to love scenes may appear between two individuals within one age group than between the response averages of two age groups, and that excitability decreases with repeated viewings of the same kind of film.

Violence is another element common to dramatic film and television programming that has profoundly moving and lasting effects on the young. The reactions to situations portraying tragedy, conflict and danger are most intense under the age of twelve; stories about kidnapping, in particular, are apt to trigger reactions of fear and excitement which may last for days, or longer, and engender nightmares. The intensity of response to depictions of violence on film reaches its peak near the age of nineteen and sharply decreases thereafter. Interest in war and adventure films and westerns is stronger among males than females at all ages.

Attention span is an important factor when presenting films intended to teach hard content. In educational presentations to children in the first three elementary grades, film length should be held to five to ten minutes. Youngsters in the intermediate grades can absorb content from films eleven to fourteen minutes long, and those in junior high and high school—when the innate capacity to learn from films reaches its peak—may be able to absorb hard content from films as long as twenty-two minutes. In programs longer than twenty-two minutes, even the brightest students may begin to forget what was presented at the beginning. Films have their maximum communication effectiveness with students; the reliability of effective communication reaches the level of probable certainty in senior high school and college populations, and drops off thereafter because of adult discount.

An important factor with increasing age is the growing tendency to react with a "boomerang effect" toward films that challenge emotionally rooted beliefs. If a film or television presentation runs directly counter to cherished beliefs on subjects such as politics, race and religion, and if the viewer is over twenty-five years old, the chances are that he will turn it off; or, if he sits through it, he will become angry and more set in his beliefs, leaving the film convinced that the presentation was mere propaganda. Circumstances in his immediate world would have to change, shaking his beliefs in past answers, before he could become amenable to media influence.

SEX

Sex, in terms of the perceptions people bring to film viewings, refers primarily to the activities, values and occupations assigned by our culture to males and females, and secondarily to depictions of love and sexual activity. Men and women respond differently to film and television presentations through the factor of identification with the male and female roles portrayed. And each viewer takes an interest in film subjects to the degree that they concern that viewer's sex role in American society. Men are interested in politics and occupation-related subjects in documentary and educational films. In viewing dramatic films, they tend to identify with subjects who display aggressive, dominant, heroic characteristics, with male leads who defend themselves and others, by force if necessary, against predatory forces that threaten them. Men show far greater preference for stories dealing with crime, violence and thrilling adventure than do women.

Women perk up when presented with film topics that relate to their assigned concerns; child-rearing, homemaking and personal attractiveness. Sex identification is the key factor in the addiction of so many housewives to daytime television soap operas. The typical heroine is home-and-family centered, neurotic, and a moral bastion in an amoral world. The female viewer can identify with soap opera situations because the stories are a (carefully researched) compendium of the typical gripes, fears and resentments of the average American housewife presented as protracted dramatic anguish. Many housewives are addicted to soap operas because these programs offer a chance to cry over situations similar to their own, vicarious participation in tragedies greater than their own, the comfort of knowing they are not alone in their wifely woes, indirect advice in the handling of their own domestic crises, and the reassurance of knowing that if they remain serenely passive in the face of catastrophe, everything will come out in the wash—and be replaced by another problem.

Response to scenes of romance and sexual activity are a function of age, as discussed earlier, and identification. This is partly instinctive, through emotional identification in dramatic films. Sex in the form of romance is made an integral part of entertainment films in order to attract both men and women, and is depicted far more graphically than ever before in theatrical films.

The long-term effects of constant exposure to sexually stimulating films has not been established by research in the United States at this time. But if an inference may be drawn from the Danish and Swedish experience with legalized pornography, it would appear that films depicting sexual activity, without good stories and character development, soon pall and become a bore. The film and magazine pornographers in those two countries are staying in business primarily through the export of their products to other countries where the sale of pornography is illegal. This evidence seems to indicate that pornography ought to be legalized, but for one fact: Sweden and Denmark have the highest rate of illegitimate births in the twelve-to-fifteen-year-old age group of any nations in the world. It may be that the open display of sexual activity in films and magazines motivates boys and girls to identify and experiment before they have the maturity to control conception.

There is one additional factor of sex identification. Because ours is a male-dominated culture, there is a willingness on the part of females at certain ages to identify with a male lead, while males may tend not to identify with a female lead at any age. The Feminist Revolution may change this, but for the present that is the way it is. A typical example is the willingness of young girls to identify with the typical blond, adolescent boy of the Disney films, used to represent youthful viewers of both sexes. In educational films and television programs for the very young, it is now common practice to include a representative boy and girl as an identification vehicle for viewers of each sex. But in those subjects unique to each sex, or assigned by our culture as the function of either sex, it is advisable to include a representative appropriate to the subject to preclude reduction of the viewers' willingness to accept the content of the film.

INTELLIGENCE

Intelligence as a factor relates primarily to educational films and television programs, and secondarily to dramatic presentations. "Intelligence" is a dubious term, however, because it is measured by culture-bound tests which are closely correlated with peer-group aspirations, occupation, status in the community social structure and level of formal education.

Conventional wisdom holds that dull students learn more from and are more easily influenced by films than are intelligent students, and that films may be a waste of time in teaching the mentally gifted. This is a misconception, however, because the value of film lies in its capacity to present those forms of content, processes and ideas which require vision in motion in order to be understood. And the more intelligent the viewer, the proportionately greater will be his learning from the film experience.

The unique advantage of educational films lies in the ability of dull or disadvantaged students to learn difficult concepts from film presentations which they otherwise might not learn at all. Through animation, for example, a film may give substantive form to abstract ideas, simplify complex processes and structures, depict processes which cannot be visualized through live-action cinematography, make visual generalizations, and provide visual cues for the purpose of clarification. These and other special film techniques may enable even quite retarded children to learn from visualized examples, thereby enhancing their ability to keep up in school and eventually to compete successfully in our complex, technological society.

Higher intelligence figures most importantly as a factor when the content itself is intrinsically difficult to understand, and the film presentation must depart from readily recognizable forms in order to graphically depict relationships. The higher the intelligence quotient of the target audience, the greater the quantity of information that may be included in the film, the more rapidly the information may be presented, and the more abstract may be the presentation in terms of verbal, mathematical and diagrammatic symbols. Explicitness is also a function of intelligence; the lower the intelligence of the viewer, the less one may expect from him in the degree of insight and rational thinking required to interpret the presentation on the screen, and the more the content will need to be clearly and graphically demonstrated.

An indirect factor of motivation derives from intelligence: the more useful the viewers perceive the content to be, the more apt they are to learn from the presentation. The more intelligent viewers seem better able to project the long-term usefulness of relatively abstract content that is unrelated to their present daily lives. Those who are less intelligent may sometimes ignore content of crucial importance to them as irrelevant because of their inability to perceive and project its importance.

Two additional factors are a function of intelligence: Highly intelligent persons who suspect that their opinions are being manipulated in a film presentation are less likely to shift their opinions as a result of a viewing experience; intelligent people seem to acquire adult discount at an early age. And while the ability to learn concepts and factual information is consistently higher among these fortunates, their opinions and attitudes are sometimes inoculated against change by the quickness of their minds to protect their original points of view.

In one area only does there seem to be no measurable difference in the learning ability of those with high and low intelligence, and this is in the learning of manipulative skills from a film or television presentation.

EDUCATION

Level of formal education and intelligence are closely correlated. Their importance depends upon whether the film is being produced for entertainment, educational or documentary purposes. In entertainment films the appeal is to the emotions and the purpose to offer escape from the tedium of daily life; the content, therefore, may be presented at a level understandable to all viewers of normal or higher intelligence, regardless of their formal education.

In educational and documentary films, however, the effectiveness of the communication is dependent upon a tight correlation with the curriculum. Such films are produced to be integrated with the study program in content and vocabulary at a given level of formal education, so that the students will gain a valuable learning experience from the film at the time a given subject is taught. The same film presented a grade earlier than it should be may be incomprehensible; a grade later, repetitious. The more advanced and intrinsically difficult the subject, the more carefully the content of any film or television production must be related to the level of formal education of its target audience. Production of communications presenting hard-content subjects, such as chemistry, physics or mathematics, in which animated film is used to depict abstract relationships, must be preceded by the most careful research on the preparedness of intended viewers to understand the content of the film. Moreover, a film properly utilized in the classroom is dependent upon the teacher's introduction, contingent upon subsequent class discussions to clarify the new content, and related to later activities which will reinforce what has been learned.

Formal education in the United States is increasingly a matter of lifetime learning; adults must continue to study in order to keep up with the information explosion and to compete successfully in a technological society. As the number of college-educated persons increases (now the highest in proportion to population of any nation in the world), documentary film and television producers will be able to undertake subjects of higher and higher levels of sophistication, thereby bringing more abstruse but important subjects to the attention of the educated segment of the public. But this increase in the number of college graduates also means widening spread between the haves and have-nots of higher education, with a concomitant need to relate documentary films to different levels of formal education.

SOCIAL ATTITUDES AND OPINIONS

Social attitudes and opinions—political, religious and economic— are learned primarily from the people among whom the individual grows up, and secondarily from viewing film and television programs. "Attitude" is here defined as the tendency to react in a favorable or unfavorable way to events which impinge upon politics, religion or economics, or any other subject producing a gut reaction. A basic attitude is very resistant to change because it is rooted in a person's whole outlook, conditioned by a lifetime of experiences.

"Opinions," while related to attitudes, are concerned with specific localized issues and do not necessarily produce reactions which are favorable or unfavorable. For example, an opinion on "Who will win the Rose Bowl football game?" would be without great emotional commitment for most persons because the issue does not impinge upon a basic social attitude. Opinions are, for the most part, concerned with changes of belief which do not affect an attitude and are readily subject to modification by film and television programming. Only by careful research can the producer determine whether the subject and interpretation of this film will impinge upon an attitude or an opinion held by his target audience and thereby anticipate the possibility of boomerang effect.

Most ostensibly "individual" opinions and attitudes are actually the norms of groups to which the individual belongs or wishes to belong. Since people tend to join groups whose values are congenial to their own, they in a sense seek out those who will confirm and reinforce what they want to believe, and their continued association in good standing tends to act as a deterrent against opinion changes (unless they are opinion changes by the group). Group members intensify their point of view by intragroup discussions and by selected viewings of film and television programs.

Friends tell friends about films they may have missed; this common social habit tends to reinforce the selective viewing habits of individuals within a group. By shared interests, by friendship and by shared conversation, the decision to view a given film or television program ripples

THE JOURNEY OF ROBERT F. KENNEDY. Opinion leader influence. *Wolper Productions.*

through a group and reinforces its opinions by common exposure to a selected communication which is sympathetic to its established point of view. The degree of individual resistance to influence by group-approved film and television programs depends upon how much an individual values his membership in the group and believes in the validity of its point of view.

There are two contexts in which group-norm allegiances break down and the individual becomes vulnerable to the influences of the media. The first is when group answers to a situation are clearly not believable in the face of personal experiences. An example of this is the cohesion of an armed forces unit in war; as long as the individual soldier believes

Ethiopia: The Hidden Empire. Mixed reactions. *National Geographic Society.*

in his cause and eventual victory, he will listen only to the propaganda of his own side—discounting enemy propaganda—and fight bravely. But if the tide of battle turns and the soldier sees his own military units shattered by enemy forces, the promises of victory may lose their credibility and he may then be persuaded by enemy propaganda to surrender with the rationalization that, since defeat is inevitable, he might as well save his own skin.

The second context of group change comes when a peer-group leader appears in person, or on a film or television program, to announce a change of policy on a given issue. The group may then change its attitude to correspond to the new position of its leader, or split up into new factions or groups, some of which may be sympathetic to further film influences as they seek out communications to reinforce their point of view. An example of this is the controversy within the Catholic Church over the issue of birth control, in which the traditional position was taken by the Pope. Both sides made fullest use of the media to sway the undecided.

There is a two-step level of film and television influence through group opinion leaders. Leaders tend to be more effective than films or television programs in influencing followers on a public issue, such as a voting decision, because most group members simply accept a leader's opinion and tend not to watch the kind of programming directed to the issue. But the opinion leaders themselves watch such public affairs film and television programming, and pass their interpretations and decisions along to their followers, most of whom apparently accept them at face value. Ideally, a public information program on the issues should be watched by the public as a whole with each citizen coming to an independent decision. Unfortunately, the public as a whole prefers to watch entertainment programs, and the average citizen is willing to reach his political, religious and economic decisions secondhand. The implication of this two-step level of communication effectiveness is clear: When dealing with a cohesive group, structure the film to influence the opinion leaders on a given issue.

The filmmaker is well advised to do careful research on what the group attitude of his target audience may be on a given social issue before undertaking the production of a communication intended to change that attitude, and to do research on whether that group is undergoing the kind of internal stresses that will tend to make the individual member susceptible to media influence. A head-on challenge to the convictions of a cohesive group is apt to result in either of two consequences: The film will not be willingly viewed by those it is intended to influence because the word will permeate the group that this is a "bad film." Or, if it is viewed in a captive-audience context, it may have a boomerang effect and reinforce the attitudes it is intended to change. Research seems to indicate that cohesive groups are best influenced by reaching the opinion leaders, and unstable groups are best reached by appeals to the individual.

The family is the most cohesive group of all and its values are seldom completely outgrown. As each person matures he tends to acquire the political, religious and economic attitudes of his family, which he learns to accept as "right" and "normal." These social attitudes permeate the fibre of the individual's being because they are learneu gradually, rather than suddenly, from family experiences that are cumulative rather than single. (Sometimes a social attitude may develop from a single traumatic experience, either felt or witnessed, but this is an exception.) Strong attitudes frequently grow without guidance, thoughtful judgment or critical analysis. They are often created by the necessity of the individual to conform to the social norms of the religious, political and economic groups with which the family identifies itself. Conformity is rewarded by acceptance, approval and enhanced status for the individual within the family, while nonconformity is penalized.

Many viewers adhere to a given point of view for no other reason than that it is family-anchored. For example, television viewing is a family group activity, with the selection of programming a matter of common agreement, which tends to reinforce the attitudes of each individual within the family and make him an unlikely subject for conversion. Despite talk about the generation gap and publicity about revolutionary youth, so strong is the tendency toward family homogeneity that in one study only four percent of those interviewed claimed that someone in the family had voted differently from the other members. The degree of deviation is closely related to the degree to which the individual values membership in his family. A person who is kicking over the traces is apt to act in a manner contrary to the wishes of his family and be susceptible to influences by the media.

It is worth noting that the strongest attitude reactions to media presentations come from an audience of adolescents drawn from families of various socioeconomic statuses and different racial descents. Adolescence is the age of the most intense reactions to films (and to everything else), and a subject or theme that impinges upon the political, religious and economic views held by a youth's family will evoke a response which depends, in part, upon the nature and strength of that individual's conditioning to the subject prior to viewing the film. This means that a film shown to a class of mixed racial and socioeconomic backgrounds is likely to engender mixed reactions.

LIFE SPACE AND SUBJECTIVITY

Life space and subjectivity refer to those things which impinge upon an individual in an intimate, direct, personal way—one's hopes, fears, aspirations, job security, draft status, personal attractive-ness, etc. Life space relates closely to the four basic postulates of motivation: self-preservation, self-realization, self-identification, and self-regard. American and Western European cultures, shaped by the Judeo-Christian ethic, value the preservation of the integrity of the individual and his fullest development above that of the development of a super-state or super-group of any kind. Given the ethos of this culture, it is difficult to induce viewers to sacrifice their personal well-being for the public interest when the content is couched in abstractions; it is com-paratively easy to influence their behavior when the content is presented to the viewer in terms of: "What's in it for me?"

Concern for life space in filmmaking means recognizing that a given communication should take cognizance of everything relating to film and the viewer treated to this point—age, sex, intelligence, level of formal education, social attitudes and opinions—plus, where possible, the personal stake the individual viewer may have in the subject of the film. For example, a young woman who is taking birth control pills, and who normally never takes the slightest interest in scientific subjects, may avidly watch a film treatise on the side effects of the pill if it is presented in terms of its effects on the average young woman—because it affects her "life space." Another example: a young man of draft age will be extremely attentive to changes in government policy on the draft be-cause it affects his life space, while a man too young, too old, or too infirm to be drafted will be relatively indifferent because his life space is unaffected (unless, of course, a member of his family is subject to the draft, when it then becomes part of his life space, but to a lesser de-gree).

Life space means, in practical terms, identifying the *existing* needs and desires of the individual viewer, relating them to the subject of the film, and pointing out how acting on the purpose of the film will enable the viewer to satisfy his wants.

Recognition of life space is the essence of advertising: television commercials do not sell soap, but sex appeal; not breakfast food, but vitality; not alkalizers, but comfort; not beer, but gusto. In each instance the product is demonstrated in terms of its experienced effects on the personal life of the viewer—what he will taste, feel or gain as a conse-quence of using the product. Advertising actually creates life space in American society by defining wants the viewer may never have been consciously aware of, and then functions to keep these needs and wants insatiable. Virtually all of advertising plays upon some aspect of the three-point essence of our aspirations—health, wealth and popularity. The basis of persuading a viewer to switch from one brand to another is not a matter of reason, logic and proved superiority, but of life-space sensual appeals to greater satisfaction ("Double your pleasure, double your fun"), or scare appeals to loss of popularity ("Don't be half-safe"), or bandwagon appeals to majority acceptance ("Four out of five doctors recommend"), or incomplete comparisons of product gratification ("You can be sure, if you buy—").

The family, important as it is to social attitudes and opinions, is even more important to the concept of life space. Most Americans are members of a family, and as such are susceptible to film influence when an issue is presented in terms of its human consequences to a family. Among the most effective documentary films in achieving social change —*Harvest of Shame, The Battle of Newburgh, Superfluous People*— have been those cast largely in terms of the consequences to the family, an approach which cuts across all strata of American society in a common-denominator appeal.

Life space has a strong effect on the interpretation given to dramatic content in such television formats as the family situation comedy. Because the housewife is the buyer of products in the American family, the comedy content is slanted to flatter and emphasize the importance of the wife, while taking sly swipes at other members of the family, in particular the husband. The wife is usually portrayed as gentle, wise, all-knowing, patient, kind and understanding. The husband—a nonpurchaser of detergents—is frequently portrayed as a buffoon given to temper tantrums, wild dreams of impossible success, timidity before his employer, unreasonable tightness with money and indolence in the face of dripping faucets and uncut lawns. The children are, of course, charming, irresponsible, helter-skelter idiots who could not survive a day without her loving attentiveness. These appeals have a grain of truth in the life space of the housewife (or, at least she believes they do), or they would not be used as the bases of appeal. Should the day come when the husband buys the household products, the appeals to life space will presumably be reversed and tap the reservoir of grudges accumulated by the typical man of the house.

Subjectivity is crucially important in the success of a dramatic film. The viewer tends to lose consciousness of self and identify with the lives being lived on the screen to the degree that he can empathize with the role of the protagonist or principal characters, the personalities of the actors, the conflicts of the dramatic situations, the crises and climax of the story, and the successful realization of the dramatic theme.

Of all the viewer characteristics concerned with communications effectiveness, none is more important than life space and subjectivity.

2

The Language of Cinema-Television

Film and the Other Arts

The written and spoken word has historically been the primary means of media communication in Western civilization, followed by still art-work and sculpture. Ideas unsuitable for transmission through one of these media died unmarked.

Film and television, children of technology, born of the twentieth century, now offer forms of communication emancipated from the cul-ture-bound concepts of the printed word or immobile art. Visual mean-ings, expressed in movement, may now be sent from mind to mind through the eyes. The human face, subtle to the flicker of an eyelash in its expressions, can speak of inner experience and nonrational emo-tions. A man may be unable to express his ideas or emotions in words, yet be overflowing with things to say that others may understand. Through his facial expressions, gestures, movements and actions, he can convey ideas which have no means of expression in graphic or written languages.

The cinema has evolved a language having syntax, grammar and modes of expression, which, like written language, reveals whether the filmmaker is literate or illiterate. The cinematic counterpart of words, phrases, sentences, paragraphs, chapters, and punctuation are scenes, sequences, scene sizes, camera and lens movements, editing tempos and concepts, and optical effects. Each cinematic concept and technique has acquired, through usage, its own set of functions and connotations. The filmmaker must understand how cinematic concepts function in order to say what he means in a sense comprehensible to the viewer.

Cinematic Communication

Motion pictures and television communicate ideas and generate emotions by their perceptual appeals to the eyes and ears of the viewer. Their appeals are made in three modes: the vision-in-motion of *cinematography*; the *editing* of lengths of film to present a logical sequence of events, to imply meanings not inherent in the original content, and to create a time and distance relationship only peripherally related to reality; and the *sound track* presentation of narration, dialogue, music and sound effects to contribute exposition and realism and enhance the emotional impact of the edited motion picture.

These three areas—cinematography, editing and sound—will be analyzed in detail in succeeding chapters. This chapter presents an overview of the three cinematic elements to introduce their salient characteristics, and to explore how they communicate ideas in the language of film.

The illusion of motion pictures is made possible by a weakness of the human eye called *persistence of vision*. The retina, because of this defect, retains the image of a subject for a fleeting instant after the subject has moved. If a series of still pictures depicting the progressive phases of a single movement is presented rapidly to the viewer, the human eye, unable to perceive the gaps between the still photographs, perceives the subject as moving in a single, continuous flow of motion. Film and television programs are no more than a series of still images fused into apparent moving images through the persistence of vision.

Cinematography

MOVEMENT

Movement is the essence of cinematography, and takes two primary forms: *movements by the subject before the camera*; and *movements by*

MEN OF THE SERENGETI. Pan after action. *National Geographic Society/Wolper Productions.*

the camera or its lenses over the subject. Later, under "Editing," we will treat the matter of movements created by the implied relationships of the spliced film footage.

Movements by the subject within the scene is the first form. So strong is the attraction of the human eye to movement within a scene that it largely nullifies the laws of artistic composition. A scene may be composed with very strong directional lines and massive shapes and forms, yet if there is one small man in the scene—moving—the viewer's gaze will dart to him. A solitary person walking through the concrete canyons of New York's skyscrapers would attract the first attention of the viewer.

Movement by the camera or its lens over the subject, or to follow the subject's actions, is the second form. The movements may be those of the camera itself, as it follows horses, vehicles or moving people. Or the movements may be implied by a change of focus, from one subject to another, or a change of focal length, such as a zoom-in to a closeup of a woman's eyes. An extensive array of camera-movement and lens-movement concepts has evolved, each having a specific name and generally accepted usage within the language of film. The camera-movement concepts are the "pan," "swish pan," "tilt," "trucking shot," "dolly shot," "crane shot" and "hand-held shot." The lens-movement concepts are the "zoom" and the "shift focus."

A "pan" is a horizontal scan of the camera from a pivotal point, usually that of a tripod. The pan is used for three main purposes: to follow the actions of a moving subject, such as a soldier rising from his foxhole to attack an enemy position, racing horizontally across a field of fire; to relate two subjects having an important content relationship, such as a man's discovery of a burglar in his room, within one single continuous roll of the camera; and to create a first-person point-of-view of someone looking out over an area, studying a landscape, such as that of a sheriff scanning the cliffs of a mountain wilderness for a glimpse of an escaped convict, an effect that would have the viewer looking through the eyes of the sheriff.

The pan is second only to the zoom in its abuse by novices. All too frequently it is used to provide specious excitement to a dull scene, or to imply meanings where none exist.

The "swish-pan" is a panning camera movement, but the movement is so fast as to reduce the images to flashing blurs, in effect smearing the subjects to abstraction. The swish-pan is not used to follow a subject, but primarily as a transitional device to imply a change of time or location.

A "tilt" is a vertical version of the pan, an up-or-down scanning movement by the camera from a pivotal point. The tilt also has three main purposes: to follow the ascending actions of a subject, such as a hunted man fleeing up the ladders of an oil refinery; to relate two subjects having an important content relationship, such as a scientist watching the blast-off of his missile project, within one continuous filming of the scene; and finally, to let the viewer experience the rising gaze of a screen character, such as a policeman peering up at the windows of a building in his search for a sniper.

The term "trucking shot" derives from the silent-film practice of mounting a camera on a truck to enable the cinematographer to keep pace with the man on the white horse at the head of the posse. The trucking shot is used to follow those fast and far-ranging horizontal actions of a subject that would exceed the scope of a pan—running, riding, driving—and to photograph detailed reactions of the moving performers. In *Phoebe* a pregnant teenager mentally fantasized scenes in which she told her parents and boy friend about her condition. Her wish to flee was visually expressed by repeated trucking shots in which her boy friend ran away, yelling, "You're not going to wreck my life," or as she ran away from the problem down endless, sterile, concrete corridors, preceded by a truck-mounted camera.

The "dolly shot" is an in-studio variant in which the camera is moved on wheels from one position to another, used in feature films and in three-camera television productions. Its purpose is simply to move the camera closer to a subject, usually to frame it in a tighter scene size, while another camera is actively recording the subject from another angle. In cinematography, a dolly shot may be used to follow the walk of a subject down a corridor when a crane is unavailable or cannot be used.

The "crane shot" consists of mounting the camera (with director and cameraman) to the height of a highly mobile crane, to change heights, directions and movements in a continuous fluid manner—in one long roll of the camera. The crane is used when an infinite variety of heights is needed for an establishing shot, or during times of confrontation between two persons when the feelings of suspense may be enhanced by revealing the changing relationships between them through fluid cinematography. In *Love Story* the exchange of nonreligious marriage vows between the boy and girl was solemnized by a crane shot that circled around them, expressing their "oneness" cinematically.

The "hand-held camera" is an excellent technique for portraying the subjectively unsteady feelings of a person in an emotionally distraught condition—drunk, frightened, psychotic, afraid, fleeing from an assailant. A hand-held camera scene, when cut into a scene portraying a child fleeing wildly, may subjectively render her feelings of a panic in a way that could scarcely be equaled by any other mobile camera technique.

A "zoom-in" creates the illusion of a continuous approach by the camera to the subject, with a concomitant reduction of the area being photographed, an effect made possible by the variable focal-length or "zoom" lens. The zoom-in is used primarily to draw attention to a detail having special meaning while enabling the viewer to remain aware of the detail's relationship to the whole context. The speed of a zoom-in depends upon its use. In dramatic film, in those situations where impact is more important than information, a zoom-in is usually fast for a shock effect on the viewer. On the other hand, when a growing sense of horror or realization is intended, a fairly slow zoom-in is used, alterting the viewer to look for information or exposition. In educational films and television programs, which usually offer content to be studied carefully, the zoom-in is done slowly to maintain viewer orientation.

In dramatic film a series of zooms coming one after another can be used to convey a sense of indecision or obsession. In the film *You're No Good* the growing temptation of a teenager to steal a flashy motorcycle parked at the curb was implied by repeated zoom-ins to the boy's face, to the motorcycle, to the imagined faces of family and friends reacting to his theft, and culminated in his decision to grab it and run—dramatized by a smashing zoom-in.

The "zoom-out," the reverse of the zoom-in, is a progressive retreat from the subject, gradually expanding the area being photographed. It is used in both dramatic and educational productions to relate a detail to a greater context. Again, the speed of the move depends upon its uses: slow moves for exposition or a growing sense of realization, fast moves for emotional impact. A slow zoom-out creates some suspense.

"Shift focus" is a change of lens focus from a nearer subject to a farther one, or vice versa, with no change of image size. The shift focus is used (sparingly) to imply a meaningful relationship between two subjects at a given moment and may be considered functionally as a "pan in depth." In the film *You're No Good* the filmmaker communicated the boy's interest in stealing the motorcycle by a shift focus from the boy to the motorcycle. The shift focus technique is sometimes combined with a slow pan or tilt.

The motion picture camera is the means of capturing movement. The lens is the eye of the camera, but it differs from the human eye in that it is unselective, rendering everything within its scope and depth of field with equal emphasis—dishes, furniture, beautiful women and discarded gum wrappers.

To compensate for these shortcomings, and to break the shackles of time and distance, the filmmaker photographs only that aspect of a subject that he wants the viewer to look at during a given phase of the motion picture. With the evolution of the language of cinema, the viewer has come to infer certain meanings from the way a subject is composed, framed, cropped and lighted for cinematography. An extreme closeup, for example, is analogous to the use of an exclamation point in written language for emphasis. Other forms and concepts have their unique meanings and terminology, as follows:

SCENE, SEQUENCE AND SETTING

The term *scene* has a cinematic meaning quite different from its popular associations with the theater. A scene is defined as that length of film footage exposed in one uninterrupted roll of the camera, unbroken by any change to another visual. Theoretically, a scene may be as brief as one frame, or as long as the roll of film that may be practicably photographed. Alfred Hitchcock once created a cinematic tour de force when he produced a feature-length film, *The Rope*, consisting of one uninterrupted scene.

A *sequence* in cinema corresponds conceptually to an act in the theater, or a chapter in a book, and consists of a series of scenes constituting a complete dramatic action within the film, containing a beginning, a middle and an end. Theoretically, there is no limit to the number of scenes a sequence may contain, nor to the maximum number of sequences in a film. Pragmatically, the tolerable length of a film is defined by human sitting endurance, usually a maximum of four uninterrupted hours.

A *setting* is where dramatic events occur, and refers not only to the location and physical properties of the environment, but to its mood and atmosphere.

SCENE SIZES

Subjects may be photographed in a wide variety of scene sizes, ranging from a wide-angle shot that seems to encompass half the world to extreme closeups that reveal only the iris of an eye. In between are a wide array of scene sizes, many of which, in the evolution of the language of film, have acquired general connotations for the viewer. Scene sizes have meanings relating to the subjects they frame, and the functional use of scene size is an expression of film literacy.

An *establishing shot*, sometimes called a "long shot," is an introductory scene used at the beginning of a film, or at the start of a sequence within it, to reveal where the following action will take place, and to indicate something of the mood and character of the story. The establishing shot is most often a wide-angle view which reveals a relatively wide expanse of locale. The classic use of the establishing shot is in the western, which traditionally opens with a view of an immense spread of rugged terrain, and the figure of a lonely horseman riding under the fervid stare of the sun.

The establishing shot is an exposition concept, however, and the wide-angle technique is not mandatory; a detail may be used if it somehow introduces the story and gives the flavor of what is to follow. Some form of an establishing shot is usually needed within the film whenever there has been a major change of time or location in the dramatic action.

A *full shot* is a full-length figure shot equivalent to the screen height of a man and is used primarily to introduce a new character or object to the viewer. The introduction of a new character at the beginning of a film or a sequence within it is customarily done with a full shot, followed by closer scenes to reveal his face and his other physical characteristics. Within the context of the film, a full shot of the chief character often follows an establishing shot when there has been a major change of time or location, and a full shot is frequently used in ensemble scenes to show the comparative sizes of the different characters.

A *medium shot* is a waist-up view of a character, and is most often used to show him doing something with his hands. Since a medium shot of a character will automatically draw the viewer's gaze down to the subject's hands, if they offer nothing to develop the story or character it will tend to distract the viewer's attention.

Television dramatic films make extensive use of the medium shot because its scope of action is large enough to permit movements and gestures to be readily seen on the small screen. The medium shot serves narrative functions formerly performed by full shots when films were seen only on the large screens of theaters and classrooms. Moreover, this scene size is cinematically flexible; the performer can easily move toward the camera into a closeup, or away into a full shot. Because of the television rerun factor, even wide-screen theatrical films are often photographed with more medium shots than was once the case.

The *tight two-shot* is a variant of the medium shot, and presents two

TRUE GRIT. Establishing shot. *Paramount Pictures Corp.,* © *1969.*

THE ANDROMEDA STRAIN. Full shot. © *Universal City Studios, Inc.*

Joe. Medium shot. *Cannon Films*.

FACES. Tight two shot. *John Cassavetes, FACES*.

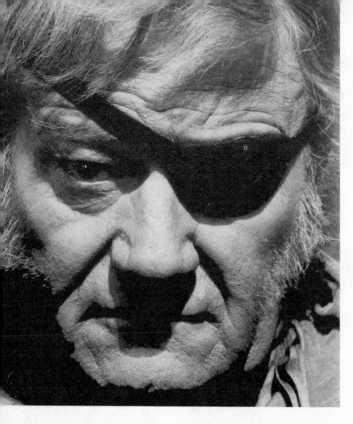

TRUE GRIT. Closeup.
Paramount Pictures Corp.,
© *1969.*

FACES. Tilted camera angle.
John Cassavetes, FACES.

subjects together in a scene, implying a relationship between them. Two persons quarreling, loving, conversing or conspiring are invariably photographed in some variant of the tight two-shot. If the filmmaker inadvertently presents two persons, or a person and an object, in a tight two-shot when no relationship is implied or intended, the viewer may become momentarily confused.

The *closeup* is equivalent to a head shot of a person, and is used for dramatic emphasis of a detail whose meaning is important at that point in the film: the stunned reaction of a middle-aged man cashiered from his job with a corporation to which he has devoted his professional life; the anguish of a woman who suddenly realizes she has alienated the man she loves; the martini glass containing a murderous dose of LSD. A closeup alerts the viewer and says, "Look at this carefully—it's important." If closeups are used casually when no emphasis is intended, the device may be deprived of its power at a time when the drama cries out for it.

In educational films and television programs the closeup serves a different function. Whenever a skill or a process is being taught, a closeup should be used to demonstrate a changing physical relationship. For example: If a film or videotape is made to demonstrate safety techniques in operating underwater scuba-diving equipment, a closeup would be mandatory whenever the manipulation of a device as critical as an oxygen valve was shown. The life of the person learning scuba-diving safety techniques from the film may be jeopardized unless this crucial function is portrayed and emphasized by the proper use of the closeup.

An *extreme closeup* is the cinematic equivalent of an exclamation point. The extreme closeup is used at those points of greatest importance or emotional crescendo in dramatic films. A classic use of the extreme closeup was in Hitchcock's film *The Man Who Knew Too Much*, when the lips of a dying man trying to whisper his precious secret spread a macabre thirty feet across a wide theatrical screen—an extreme closeup with a vengeance, but an excellent use of the scene size to hammer home an important dramatic point.

A *tilted camera angle*, in which the subjects and their background are slanted on the screen, may be used to imply that something is awry. The tilted camera angle is most often used at times of emotional confrontation between two persons, or when some individual is behaving irrationally—drunk, frightened, on drugs—to let the viewer know that

JOE. Low-key tonality. *Cannon Films.*

the subject, like the horizon line, is off balance. The tilted camera angle is also used during scenes portraying disasters of war, earthquake, riot and shipwreck, to add another dimension to the turbulence of the scene.

TONALITY

Tonality, the proportions of light to dark in a scene, is an important factor in creating mood and atmosphere and interpreting the subject to the viewer. Tonality is a function of lighting, and emotional connotations are created according to whether the scene is lighted with a *low-key, high-key* or *narrative* tonality.

I LOVE LUCY. Narrative tonality. *CBS Television Network.*

MARY POPPINS. High-key tonality. © *Walt Disney Productions.*

Low-key tonality means that more than half the image area is devoted to darks and halftone values. Low-key tonality is used to create an aura of ominous foreboding, of implied menace, a connotation born of man-imagined fears of the night. Or, given a man and a woman as camera subjects, it may offer the suffused mystery of romance.

High-key tonality means that more than half the image area is committed to light, bright values. High-key tonality most often implies cheerfulness and gaiety, and this is the tonality that characterizes most comedies and musicals. When carried to extremes, however, high-key tonality may be used to create a sense of barrenness and sterility, as in a desert scene or a science-fiction film about the antiseptic world of a technological tomorrow.

In both low-key and high-key lighting the illumination of the subject remains at the same level of intensity, except in a night scene. The illusions of low-key and high-key lighting are created by the proportions of the image area given over to darks, halftones and lights, not by changing the levels of illumination of the subject. Reducing the light level on a subject in a low-key scene would make it appear underexposed; increasing the light level in a high-key scene would make it appear overexposed.

Narrative tonality falls between the other two extremes in its allocation of light and dark tonalities. As the term implies, narrative tonalities are used in straightforward action devoid of extreme emotional overtones, in which the subjects are illuminated simply so that the viewer can easily follow the action.

The three foregoing classifications are necessarily simplistic, and do not pretend to cover the subtleties and ramifications of the extremely complex and sophisticated art of lighting for emotional connotations.

Editing

Editing is the second major dimension of media communication in motion pictures and television. Unedited film footage, stacked in cans, is like single words selected from the dictionary, offering little more than their intrinsic meaning—raw material. Only when scenes are edited into sequences to communicate ideas, like words arranged into a sentence, do they take on real meaning and become cinema. All the filmic elements that precede editing—writing, directing, acting, cinematography, special effects, set design, lighting, sound recording—are brought to fruition when orchestrated into a motion picture by editing.

The physical act of splicing two pieces of film or videotape together is not editing. Film editing, as art and communication, is defined by the relationships between the content of two scenes, their internal movements, the screen directions of their subjects, their associated image shapes and the lengths of each scene used to create tempo.

Each scene is selected and edited into the film for what it says about the subject and the story at that point in the film. And a single dramatic action is photographed as many bits of action in different scene sizes, later to be edited into one movement, because its psychological impact may be heightened in editing by eliminating the superfluous and emphasizing first one detail and then another to make the edited action more vivid than the original action.

TRANSITION

The average viewer has been conditioned to understand that certain ways of changing from one scene to another carry with them, like punctuation, distinct meanings in terms of continuity and transitions of time or location. These continuity and transitional concepts are the *cut,* the *fade*, the *dissolve*, the *wipe* and the *superimposure.*

The *cut* is an instantaneous change from one scene to another—the basic technique of film editing. The cut is used to portray *a continuous flow of action within an uninterrupted span of time*, usually within a sequence. For example: A dramatic sequence presenting two persons engaged in a quarrel would be edited with a series of cuts from one person shouting, to the other person reacting, to represent a continuing flow of action in an uninterrupted flow of time.

The *fade-in* is the gradual appearance of a scene from the black, darkened screen. The fade-in is universally used at the beginning of every motion picture—theatrical, nontheatrical and television—to introduce the film, and serves as the rising curtain of motion pictures. The length of the fade-in implies the emotional flavor of the film to follow: a heavy drama may be introduced by a fade-in as long as a minute to connote a foreboding quality; a comedy or television commercial (where time is money) may have a fade-in as brief as a snappy six frames—little more than a soft cut.

The *fade-out*, conversely, is the gradual disappearance of a scene to a black, darkened screen, an effect used to end a scene, a sequence or the film itself. As with the fade-in, the longer the fade-out, the more emotionally laden the effect.

Fades may be used within the central body of the film to separate major sequences. In this context, their occurrence is reversed: first a fade-out, then a fade-in. Viewers have been conditioned to accept the fade-out/fade-in as connoting *a major change of time or location*, from one sequence to the next. Again, the briefer the fade, the lighter its implications. The longer the fade, the heavier its overtones.

A *dissolve* combines the fade-out of an outgoing scene with the fade-in of an incoming scene—simultaneously—within the same length of film. The images of the first scene gradually yield and phase out as the images of the second scene materialize and take possession of the screen. Dissolves are most often used as a transitional device within the body of the film to connote a *minor change of location* or a *short lapse of time*.

A long, long dissolve is sometimes used in dramatic films to create the effect of a slow awakening to reality. In *The Diary of Anne Frank* the two lovers become aware only gradually of the approach of the jack-booted Gestapo, an implication made through the use of a dissolve several minutes long.

In animated films long dissolves are frequently used between a series of related still pictures to create the illusion of continuous growth, as a kind of poor man's substitute for high-cost animation. The dissolve is also used in animation to create pulsating effects between two static positions, such as the beating of a heart.

The substitution of a cut for a dissolve or a fade when making a change of time or location is a recent vogue among dramatic filmmakers, which originated on television as a time-saver. The effect on the viewer may be an instant of confusion as he finds himself thrust into a new sequence without warning, unless the new setting is so clearly established that he can immediate reorient himself. Using a cut instead of a dissolve as a transitional device is analogous to writing a new sentence without putting a period to the old, and then starting the second sentence without a capital letter. The technique has justifiable uses as an occasional shock device, but consistent use may exact the price of confusion.

A *wipe* is a transitional device in which the outgoing scene is physically displaced on the screen by the incoming scene, with both scenes sharply visible on the screen for the length of the effect. The wipe is used in a manner similar to the dissolve, to connote a minor change of time or location, but it does so with certain liabilities. First, the wipe is a kind of split-screen effect, with two centers of attention, forcing the viewer to move his eyes back and forth to keep track of them both for the length of the effect. Second, because the wipe effect is clearly contrived, it draws attention to itself as a trick effect, sometimes distracting the viewer from the content of the film. Any effect that breaks the viewer's absorption in the content of the film, and belief in the film, tends to detract from its credibility.

Superimposition is the simultaneous printing of two or more scenes

Superimposition. *United States Navy.*

in the same length of film, usually to connote stream-of-consciousness. Most often, the effect will present the closeup of a person with the superimposure of another scene revealing what that person is thinking. In *Midnight Cowboy* Joe Buck attended a drug party in New York, popped a cube of LSD into his mouth, and the viewer was treated to the kaleidoscopic fantasy of colors and effects passing through Joe's mind, through superimposition.

THE THIRD MEANING

The edited position of any scene, in relation to the scenes that come before and after, is what gives that scene its cinematic meaning. When two related scenes are edited they take on a third meaning not inherent in either of the scenes. This third meaning may be *narrative*, seen visually on the screen, or *implicit*, created in the mind of the viewer.

Narrative editing in its simplest sense means telling a story in a continuity order. If the film editor presents a closeup of a man looking intently at something, and then splices that scene to one portraying a T-bone steak, the narrative third meaning would be: "a hungry man about to eat." If the same closeup of the man were followed by a scene presenting a hypodermic needle and a packet of white powder, the narrative third meaning would be: "a heroin addict about to take a fix." In each example, the two related scenes, when spliced together, acquired a third narrative meaning not inherent in either of them, and each scene assumed a different connotation in the presence of the other.

Implicit editing means presenting two scenes together to create a symbolic meaning in the mind of the viewer that is not intrinsic to either of the scenes or to the narrative continuity.

If the same closeup of the man were followed by a brief scene of lava bubbling in a volcano—when a New York City setting had been established—the implicit third meaning would be that he is smouldering with inner rage, not that a natural disaster had come to Times Square. If our closeup of the man were followed by a scene showing a hawk soaring up on a thermal—in the context of a prison cell on Death Row—the implicit meaning would be a wish for freedom.

The third meanings created by implicit editing are not necessarily narrative, but expressive of the inner feelings of the subject. The extent to which implicit editing may be used depends upon the film literacy of the viewer and his familiarity with the symbolism intended by the filmmaker. Implicit editing is exciting editing for a film's own generation of viewers, but it is the surest way to date a film. One generation's meaningful symbols often become the next generation's objects of derision. Narrative editing, while sometimes less electrifying, often better stands the test of time.

CINEMATIC TIME AND CINEMATIC DISTANCE

The first dramatic films were photographed stage plays in which each actor's movements were photographed in their entirety. Presenting dramatic actions in real time and real distance, however, was soon found to be the dullest of film forms, so dull that people soon tired of watching and would not pay to attend such films. Only when the dramatic actions were broken up into small bits of action and edited together to create an action more exciting than reality was film born as an art form.

The essence of this change of cinematic thinking and technique was the selection of only those phases of dramatic action that were most graphic and meaningful, and the discarding of all those that were dull or insignificant, to create what is called *cinematic time* and *cinematic distance*.

Real time and *cinematic time* are often two different concepts. Real time in film or videotape form would present a full-length visual record of an event that would require as long a time for the viewer to watch as the event took to occur. When used in film and television production, it yields a presentation only as exciting as the event staged before the cameras, and little more. Real time is used primarily when the subject is of such intrinsic interest that the medium provides only an instrument to record the happening, or when the artistry is before rather than behind the camera, such as television panel shows, news reports and variety shows. But real time makes pedestrian use of the medium compared to the stimulating product of edited cinematic time.

Cinematic time consists of holding a scene on the screen only long enough to reveal character, develop the plot, make a dramatic point—and then moving on to the next scene before the viewer loses interest. The real time of the events being dramatized is almost irrelevant. The relevant concern is that the viewer be shown the significant and dramatic aspects of an event only long enough for him to understand the scene and remain interested, and then change to another scene. The next scene is then held on the screen for only as long as it takes to make its dramatic point, and so on, to the end of the film. In this way, events that take days, weeks, months or years to occur in real time may be compressed into hours or even minutes in cinematic time.

Cinematic time is also emotional time, and as such may be longer or shorter than the real time of the event. For example: The headlong dash of a soldier changing a machine-gun nest lying across fifty feet of open meadow, a matter of seconds in real time, may be lengthened to minutes in cinematic time to reveal the emotional eternity it seems to the soldier having to make the charge. An ambush of the same soldier and his platoon, lasting several minutes but springing as it does from nowhere, may be cinematically rendered as over in seconds, because that is how quickly it may seem to happen in the confused melee of combat. And the instant of death, in which the hopes, dreams and aspirations of a man become nothing, may be edited as an event of majesty, or a snuffing out of no consequence, by its extension or compression in cinematic time.

Real distance and *cinematic distance*, like real time and cinematic time, are not necessarily synonymous. In real distance, for example, a filmed sequence of a businessman leaving his office for the day would depict him clearing his desk, donning his coat, giving last-minute instructions to his secretary, joking with his associates, riding down the elevator to the ground floor, walking across the foyer and through the revolving door to the street—rendered every inch of the way by the camera.

In cinematic distance, however, only those events needed to tell the viewer that the businessman was leaving his office would be rendered, and the less important the departure, the fewer the actions that would be photographed. If the man's departure for home was only incidental to other dramatic elements, there would probably be a scene of him arising from his desk, followed by his arrival home, with the intervening distance eliminated in favor of cinematic distance, implied by a dissolve.

Failure to transform real time into cinematic time and real distance into cinematic distance is primarily what separates many videotape productions and most home movies from quality cinema.

TEMPO

Tempo is controlled in film and television editing by the length of time a scene is held on the screen. As a rule, the longer the scene is held on the screen, the more relaxed the tempo; the shorter the scene, the more exciting. Each extreme, and those in between, have their proper uses. The classic method of building suspense in dramatic films is to start with long scenes and gradually shorten them in order to accelerate the tempo as the film proceeds toward the climax. A climactic finish having a great deal of movement is usually cut in very short scenes, almost a kaleidoscope of movement, in which movement itself becomes the subject. Conversely, an extremely long scene, within the context of a dramatic film, is used as a suspense device because the viewer is conditioned to expect a change on an average of one every ten to twenty seconds. If a scene is held on the screen for much longer than that, an inner tension begins to rise in the viewer and a visceral feeling cries out *"Cut!"*

The emotional quality of the content in a sequence determines the length of the scenes used in editing it. A sequence having a mood of ennui, boredom or dreariness would probably be cut with long slow-moving scenes to reflect, in the tempo of the editing, the mood of the story. A sequence of high-content excitement, such as the shoot-out ending of *Butch Cassidy and the Sundance Kid*, would be rendered in short scenes of frenetic action to imply in the editing tempo the desperate excitement of life-or-death combat.

OTHER EDITING CONCEPTS

The concept of time and distance may also be treated through editing in the *flashback*, *flashforward*, *montage* and *visual simile and metaphor*.

The *flashback* is an expositional device used to portray an event that occurred at an earlier time than the present dramatic action happening on the screen. Traditionally, a screen character begins to narrate what happened at that earlier time, a long dissolve or ripple-wipe apprises the viewer that he is being transported to another time and place, and the story of the earlier event is then told as if occurring in the present. When the flashback incident has been told—in the past-present tense—another cinematic transition returns the viewer to the original time dimension, and the dramatic action picks up the story where it left off when the flashback began.

At each time transition in a flashback the viewer struggles to reorient himself to the only time-tense that film really has—the present. A flashback is simply action made artificially "now" by a cinematic convention. It is essentially a crutch to compensate for the inability of cinema—a perceptual form—to change its time dimension from present to past to future, as may easily be done in the novel. Flashbacks tend to disrupt continuity, disorient the viewer and weaken the dramatic build toward the climax of the film.

The *flashforward* is used to portray an event that may occur in the future. Again, a cinematic device, such as the dissolve, is used to apprise the viewer that he is being whisked away into tomorrowland, and he is then presented with a sequence that may occur in the future as if it is transpiring in the present. The flashforward is used to render events imagined or fantasized by a screen character, to project future consequences of present industrial or scientific actions, and to create a science-fiction context. The flashforward disrupts the continuity in a manner similar to the slugged-in quality of the flashback, but in compensation, sometimes adds zest by giving the viewer something to look forward to.

A *montage*, as defined in American film, is a series of relatively short scenes, which, when viewed as a whole, convey a single unified meaning. A montage may be used to connote the passage of a long period of time, such as the duration of a war, when that period of time is something that has to be accounted for in the story but is not to be emphasized. The montage concept is actually an extension of implicit editing, with the difference that the scenes within it are usually connected by dissolves rather than cuts to further imply the passage of time. It is also used for a stream-of-consciousness effect, such as in dreams and fantasies.

In Russian film the montage is used to portray events of great importance rather than as a fill-in for episodes that cannot be accounted for in straight dramatic continuity. In *War and Peace*, for example, the climactic Battle of Borodino was more than an hour long and perhaps the most magnificent montage of the sound-film era.

In the rest of Europe and in many other parts of the world "montage" is used in the same sense that Americans used the term "editing." For the purposes of this book, however, "montage" is used in the restricted American sense, while "editing" is used broadly to define that phase of film production concerned with the selection, cutting and splicing of scenes into a motion picture.

Visual similes and metaphors, an edited visual comment on one subject made by intercutting it with a scene of another subject, was

widely used during the silent film days. During one sequence of the
Russian film *October* the strutting portrayal of Kerensky, then premier
of the provisional government, was intercut with scenes of a peacock
spreading its tail, to reveal his allegedly preening vanity. Visual commentary of this kind (related to implicit editing) fell into general disuse
in America with the coming of the sound film, because the technique is
cinematically slow and reflective rather than quick and narrative, lacks
dramatic momentum and tends to seem self-consciously arty in a medium characterized by realism. Visual similes and metaphors are still
widely used by a number of European directors in their sound films.

Sound Track

The sound track, consisting of *voices, sound effects* and *music*, is
the third major dimension of communication in film and television. The
sound track enables the viewer to complete his understanding of what
he sees on the screen.

VOICE

Voice on film takes the two forms of dialogue and narration, with
these differences between them:

Dialogue is lip-synchronous; the viewer sees the player speak his
lines and simultaneously hears the words, in the closest possible approximation to earthy realism in the picture-sound relationship. Dialogue is
used in dramatic films because it adds credibility to see the characters
speak. Dialogue in drama is not truly realistic, however, but is used
functionally to develop character, to offer plot information or to get a
laugh, when these things cannot be done visually.

Narration refers to the voice of an unseen speaker who comments
upon the visual events being presented on the screen. Narration is most
often used in documentary films, educational films and television programs, because the narrator can freely explain and offer information to
the viewer—in a straightforward factual manner—without being concerned about the emotional identification needed in drama. The functions of narration are to add verbal information to the visual content on
the screen, to relate what is presently being seen to what has been

presented previously, and to summarize the major points in a factual presentation.

On television newscasts the voice track frequently changes from lip-synchronous dialogue to voice-over narration. It begins as the reporter is seen reading the news, or introduces film clips in a lip-synchronous manner, and then discusses the following footage content in voice-over narration as the film clip is broadcast. This whole newscast concept is properly considered narration, lip-synchronous or not, because no attempt is made to elicit the identification of the dramatic form.

SOUND EFFECTS

Sound effects are used primarily as elements of realism by providing the sounds we normally associate with whatever is being portrayed on the screen: the image of a police car racing down the street is usually accompanied by the sounds of an automobile motor, a screaming siren and squealing tires. At a more sophisticated level, sound effects may be used to imply a nonexistent location. A soldier wading through a shallow pond in a city park may be implicitly placed in a tropical jungle by including the sounds of monkeys and exotic birds.

MUSIC

Music, on the other hand, is used more for emotional reinforcement than for exposition, an element to be felt rather than heard in dramatic films other than musicals. Music is commonly used at moments of crisis or suspense, as a transitional device when slipping from one sequence to another, and as thematic music intended to be identified with a character or location in the mind of the viewer. "Lara's Theme" from *Dr. Zhivago* is a case in point; whenever Dr. Zhivago thought about Lara, the screen revealed a closeup of him, while the sound track carried the music of "Lara's Theme."

Cinema-Television

Motion pictures and television are frequently discussed as if they were two entirely different media, each communicating with the viewer on different terms. Inasmuch as most of the dramatic programming created for television is produced in motion picture form, or if created for theatrical release, reappears eventually on the *Late, Late Show* much of the high-octane rhetoric about "hot medium" and "cool medium" seems to be an academic strawman. The differences between them relate to screen size, viewing environment and story continuity, not to differences of media. Films viewed in theaters or classrooms are shown on a large screen, in a darkened room having few distractions, with an uninterrupted presentation. Films viewed on television, on the other hand, are seen on a small screen, in a semi-lighted room having many distractions, with a presentation frequently interrupted by commercials or other breaks.

These differences in viewing circumstances may result in the same film having greater emotional impact on the viewer when seen in a theater than when seen on television, but the assertion that they are two different media with two different modes of communication is unsupportable. Film and television communicate by essentially the same modes, concepts and forms, despite the differences in their viewing environments. For the purposes of this book, the communication concepts of cinematography, editing and sound are considered essentially the same for television as for motion pictures, subject to certain modifications for the small television screen.

3

The Grammar of Cinematography

Cinematography has emancipated the spectator from the bondage of a single location or point of view. Every scene on the screen presents him with a new position or angle from which he sees through the roving eye of the camera. Fundamental to understanding the nature of film is the realization that the mobile camera *keeps the viewer always in motion.* Although he may be comfortably seated on a fixed chair, he can nevertheless fly from an aerial view of a battlefield to a closeup of an actor's face, to an object at which the actor is peering, to a parallel race with a vehicle in which he shares the emotions and experiences of its riders. He is carried along to see the action instantly from the best points of view, whether it is the creep of a microbe, the kiss of a woman, the gallop of a horseman or the silent trajectory of a spaceship hurtling through intergalactic time.

The viewer's attention should be focused on the subject most important to the story at any given moment—this is the essence of cinematography. The subject most important in any given scene, at any given point in time and space, may be a performer, an object, a setting, a landscape or even a mood, but the filmmaker must decide in advance what dramatic point he wants to make to the viewer, before he sets up the camera.

The previous chapter, "The Language of Cinema-Television," introduced some fundamental concepts of cinematography: movements by the subject before the camera; movements by the camera or its lens

53

over the subject; the meanings of scene sizes and sequences; screen directions; settings; and optical transitions. The present chapter deals more specifically with the cinematography concepts and techniques by which the filmmaker renders and interprets his subjects for the viewer.

There are essentially two ways to photograph a subject at a given scene size. The first is to set up the camera at a suitable distance from the subject to crop the subject to the desired proportion with that particular lens. The second is to change lenses on the camera, selecting a focal-length lens that will use its optical characteristics to create the desired image size of the subject on film, without changing the camera-to-subject distance. The second alternative is obviously the easier means, but the lenses offer problems of optical distortions from reality, as the normal eye perceives it.

The camera lens differs from the human eye in that it is undiscriminating; it cannot see true depth, distorts perspective, gives false emphasis, and has only a fraction of a normal person's scope of vision. The human eye, on the other hand, tends to perceive only what the person is interested in—a subjective value judgment—and tends not to notice anything considered unimportant.

The filmmaker must therefore use the lenses of the camera, within the limitations of each lens, to approximate the selectivity of the human eye, making the value judgment of what is important to see in a given scene. Then, movements by the subject, the camera and the lens are fused to approximate human selective perception—and feel psychologically true. The filmmaker's need to approximate normal human vision, and use optical distortions for emotional effects, has led to the development of a wide array of lenses, each having unique properties and uses.

The Lens

Lenses are generally grouped into four categories according to their *focal length*, a term relating to a len's magnification power, depth of field (focus) and scope of vision. The four categories are: the *wide-angle lens* (under 25 mm.); the *normal lens* (25 mm. to 65 mm.); the *long focal-length lens* (65 mm. to 100 mm.); and the *telephoto lens* (100 mm. and longer). Each of these focal lengths has an unique set of optical distortions which may be used to simultaneously photograph and

Fisheye lens. *United States Navy.*

interpret the subject to the viewer. In 16-mm. cinematography the zoom
lens now seems to be superceding fixed focal-length lenses.

THE WIDE-ANGLE LENS

The wide-angle lens has the widest scope of vision, the greatest
depth of field (focus) and the strongest proclivity to bend the lines and
distort the proportions of the subject. At its shortest focal-length extreme, the 5-mm. "fisheye" lens presents a wildly distorted view of the
world, with all lines bowed and all subjects grotesquely warped in their
relative proportions, perspectives and relationships. The fisheye lens is

used when distortion is psychologically desirable, as when presenting the point of view of a person drunk, drugged or mentally disturbed. At the other extreme of the wide-angle focal length, 25 mm., the optical distortions are reduced nearly to the point of normality, but still warp the images enough to hint that something is awry.

The excellent focusing depth of the wide-angle lens makes it useful whenever two subjects at different distances are to be kept in focus simultaneously. Another use relates to its tendency to exaggerate the feeling of distance. A small room may appear much deeper on film when photographed with a wide-angle lens, and any movements by a subject from foreground to background will tend to be exaggerated.

THE NORMAL LENS

The normal lens is so called because it most nearly approximates the perceptions of a normal human eye as it sees the relative proportions of people and objects in perspective. Its depth of field and ability to resolve content before and behind the subject roughly approximate normal human vision.

When changing from a wide-angle to a normal lens, the effect is that of moving closer to the subject, narrowing the scope of vision, revealing the subject in greater detail and softening the focus on the foreground and background. Linear distortion does enter in, subtly, at both ends of the normal spectrum. At the short focal-length end there is a slight tendency to warp and distort all subjects in the image area. At the long focal-length end there is a slight tendency to flatten perspective, localize the subject and reduce apparent movements in depth. For most narrative filming intended primarily to tell a story or reveal a process without strong emotional implications, *the 40-mm. lens*—right in the middle—is possibly the most commonly used of all the focal lengths.

THE LONG FOCAL-LENGTH LENS

A long focal-length lens begins to distort many visual elements in a way different from their perception by the normal human eye. When changing from a normal to a long focal-length lens, the effect is that of moving even closer to the subject, narrowing the scope of vision, revealing more minute details and further reducing the depth of field.

One effect of the long focal-length lens is to make those subjects in focus appear crowded together as apparent perspective becomes shallower. Television news cameramen who wish to make a small crowd loosely gathered around a speaker resemble a multitude crushing into him often use this focal-length lens. A second effect is to diffuse those visual elements that lie before and beyond the subject's depth of field, tending to lift the subject out of context. This technique is used in dramatic films to make young lovers appear in focus only to each other, and oblivious to the busy but diffused world. A third effect is to flatten out apparent movements in depth, making them appear slower than they are, an effect familiar to anyone who has watched a newsreel of racehorses rounding the far turn with their hooves pounding the turf without perceptible progress.

THE TELEPHOTO LENS

A telephoto lens is at the far extreme in focal length from the wide-angle lens, and offers, of all the focal lengths, the narrowest scope of vision, the shallowest depth of field, the strongest crowding of visual elements and the sharpest reduction of apparent movement in depth.

The telephoto lens seems to bring the viewer so close to the subject that he can see fine details which are barely perceptible to the unaided eye. Those visual elements surrounding the subject in the immediate foreground and background appear to be packed so densely that it often appears as a two-dimensional picture to the viewer. Foreground and background are diffused. Apparent movements in depth are flattened to the degree that a person may appear to be running for a long period of time without making any apparent progress. Foreshortening is visually reduced to one-half or two-thirds of its real distance. In *The Graduate* a young man, Benjamin, was running to the church to prevent the marriage of his sweetheart to another man. To reveal Ben's inner feeling of running his heart out, but getting nowhere, the director used an extremely long telephoto lens to photograph his desperate race against time. Ben's arms and legs churned furiously, but he was apparently suspended in time and space.

The optical distortions created by lenses of different focal lengths—linear distortion of perspective, definition control of foreground and background visual elements, and manipulation of apparent movements in depth—are important cinematic considerations. The decision of when to use a lens in a straightforward narrative fashion and when to

Long focal length lens at 20 feet. *Mansour Emami.*

use distortion for its interpretive value and emotional impact on the viewer is a matter of artistic judgment by the filmmaker. So important is the interpretive value of a lens, however, that a professional filmmaker may select his lens first, and then compose and light the scene.

Control of the Viewer's Attention

The gaze of the viewer should be drawn to the inintended subject or center of interest in every scene through design of its visual elements.

Telephoto lens at 20 feet. *Mansour Emami.*

Given the enormous scope of today's theatrical screen, the viewer's attention can easily be left dangling twenty feet from the subject when the film cuts from one scene to another, unless his gaze is controlled compositionally, with a concern for the proved factors of visual perception. The factors of visual perception known to draw attention are as follows: *Movement; dominance of the lightest area; sharply defined over softly defined subjects; perspective lines and composition in depth; dominance of moving lips or eyes; foreground activity over background activity; larger subjects over smaller; the design of background shapes;*

the rule of thirds; brighter color over duller color; lighting; and *dominance.*

MOVEMENT

Movement is itself a powerful compositional element, one that may supercede all others if forcible enough. In contrast to still photographs, in which all visual elements are frozen into one stationary image, the motion picture is a flow of ever-changing images as the subject, or the camera, or both, *move.* So attractive is movement to the viewer's eyes, that it alone may obscure a host of other compositional sins if its thrust is powerful.

In most scenes the subject moving the quickest in a horizontal direction across the screen will first attract the viewer's attention. The same holds true of a subject moving diagonally from background to foreground, thereby growing in image area on the screen. If the two movements are occurring simultaneously in two subjects, the more dynamic subject in mass and speed will tend to dominate, or the viewer's attention may be divided between the two. Exceptions to the dominance of movement occur when the subject is static and all about him are in motion, or when the subject is moving against a countervailing tide, such as a person pushing his way through a crowd going the opposite direction.

The shapes of movements are as important in cinematic composition as the shapes of the subjects and their backgrounds. An exquisitely composed static scene may become a shambles when the performer and cameras begin to move unless the scene is composed in terms of *where the subjects' movements will begin and end within the scene*, and the intervening path of movement is plotted across the screen.

When photographing quickly moving subjects intended to be edited together into one movement, such as a long shot and a closeup of a flying bird, there should be a good deal of overlap, because the viewer's eye is following a trajectory path across the screen and will tend to keep on going at the end of the first scene. The subject in the second scene should be approximately where the viewer's gaze is traveling at the point of transition, in a cut or a dissolve.

Insignificant movements should be avoided anywhere in the scene. So dominant is a moving subject that the viewer's gaze may be easily

distracted by the undesired movement of an unimportant object or performer. The quieter the scene, the more readily minor movements will
catch the eye.

The mobility of the camera itself, through pans, tilts, trucking and
dolly shots, hand-held, on a crane, and with the zoom lens, may add
dynamic movements to a scene. But a camera movement should always
be motivated by the dramatic action of the story—what is happening to
the subject at that time—and not be added for its own sake.

Dominance of the Lightest Area

The dominance of the lightest area on the screen is reflected in the
old Saturday afternoon serial-western practice of putting the cowboy
under a white hat or over a white horse. No matter how large the posse
or how much dust it raised, the audience full of yelling boys was trans-
fixed by that white spot thundering across the screen.

The same principle of light-dominance holds true at more sophisticated levels. Given a scene with a normal range of values from light to
dark, the viewer's gaze will go quickly to the lightest point. And the
darker the tonality of the scene, the more quickly the viewer will see the
lightest value. The exception occurs when the story is taking place in a
light environment, such as a snowy winter scene, in which a dark subject will attract the eye. The danger here is that any secondary dark
subject may distract the viewer's attention; he may look first at the
background forest, second at a stone outcropping and third at the subject of the scene. Light environments with a dark subject are more
vulnerable to distraction than are dark or halftone settings with a light
subject.

Sharply Defined over Softly Defined Subjects

Sharply defined subjects tend to dominate over softly defined subjects, primarily because they are easier to see and understand. Trying to
perceive a fuzzy subject is hard work, and if there is another subject on
the screen that is easier to understand, the viewer will probably look at
that.

Controlling the viewer's gaze by sharpness of focus may be approached in several ways. When the subject is among several persons

composed in depth, the use of a long focal-length lens will define the subject in focus quite sharply, while those standing before and behind him are progressively softened.

The shift-focus technique, discussed earlier as a pan in depth, may be used to focus first on one subject, as he speaks, and then shift to a second subject, as she reacts, with each subject taking a turn at being in and out of focus according to his or her dramatic dominance.

Television news cameramen have developed a special lens which presents only the central area of a scene in sharp lateral focus, while progressively vignetting the focus of the peripheral areas. This lens is used primarily in closely crowded scenes to focus on one person being interviewed, while putting into soft focus those sitting beside him.

PERSPECTIVE LINES AND COMPOSITION IN DEPTH

Perspective lines and composition of subjects in depth is important in controlling the viewer's gaze and enhancing the quality of cinematic realism. Cinematic depth is realized in five principal ways:

By placing subjects in a foreground-middleground-background depth relationship, using their real diminution of size to create the cinematic illusion of three dimensions on a two dimensional screen.

By selecting camera angles that will emphasize natural perspective lines, such as those of buildings, streets and landscapes. A three-quarters view of a subject, or even a slight angle, will produce the diagonal perspective lines in the objects, settings and backgrounds and strong modeling in the players that will eliminate the two-dimensional flatness and dullness that characterizes head-on cinematography.

By having people or other mobile subjects move from background to foreground or foreground to background, thereby expanding or reducing their mass area on the screen and effecting an apparent change of distance.

By photographing over-the-shoulder shots of objects as well as people to emphasize depth.

And by the selection of lenses whose optical properties expand or contract apparent depth.

The viewer's perceptions of the dramatic horizon may also be implicitly enlarged beyond the limits of the image area. For example, by having the hand of a performer outside the scope of the lens intrude into the foreground the impression is given that an entire figure, an entire

THE ANDROMEDA STRAIN. Dominance of perspective lines. © *Universal Pictures.*

world, exists just beyond the limits of the screen. With the enhancement
of off-screen voices, music and sound effects, the viewer may be made
to feel that there are no physical boundaries to the screen world.

DOMINANCE OF MOVING LIPS OR EYES

The dominance of moving lips or eyes seems to derive from some
voyeur instinct in the viewer. He wants to know what people are saying, even it is none of his business. The filmmaker may put a screen

character in the darkest recess of the composition, and fill the rest of the screen with psychedelic color, yet the viewer will strain to read the moving lips of the character, while ignoring the rest of the cinematic fireworks. In application, this means that only the central figure of a given scene should, under most circumstances, be shown with moving lips. The exception occurs when everyone on the screen is talking at once, except for the central subject, at which time the viewer will watch his lips and await his words.

Moving eyes are second in dominance only to moving lips. The eyes are called the windows of the soul because they reveal so much about the inner feelings of the person and may be used to interpret his spoken words. We are accustomed to "reading the eyes" of other people to determine whether they are saying what they mean, or just the opposite. We interpret the communication of others not so much by what they say, but how they say it through the expression in their eyes. A complete dramatic sequence, fully revealing the relationships between people, may be presented without a single spoken word—through the meanings expressed in their eyes.

FOREGROUND ACTIVITY OVER BACKGROUND ACTIVITY

As a rule, foreground activity is dominant over background activity. The viewer's gaze will tend to go first to the nearest object in motion primarily because of its large mass area on the screen. This generalization is subject to some compositional "ifs." If the foreground subject is out of focus, the viewer may glance beyond to a more clearly defined subject. If the nearer subject is heavily cropped, while the farther subject stands in the clear, the viewer's eye may drift to the farther subject because it is more easily comprehensible. For the most part, however, foreground activity, because of its mass and the grossness of its movements across the screen, tends to dominate over background activity.

LARGER SUBJECTS OVER SMALLER

Larger subjects tend to dominate over smaller subjects, because of their intrinsic size on the screen. This rule may be modified compositionally: If the larger subject is cropped, while the smaller subject stands in the clear, the viewer's gaze may go to the smaller subject. If the smaller subject is in motion, while the larger subject is static, the smaller subject will attract the eyes. If both large and small may be clearly seen, however, the larger subject of the two will tend to dominate the scene.

BACKGROUND SHAPES

The design of background shapes to direct the eye is important to keeping the attention of the viewer on the subject, but the degree of its importance depends upon the scene size. A closeup reveals little context, in most cases, and the background is relatively unimportant. As the scene size increases in scope, however, design of the background shapes becomes increasingly important.

Wide establishing scenes, involving sweeping mountain landscapes or swarming city streets, are backgrounds in which the subject may be difficult to see unless the compositional lines of the mountains or the

LONELY ARE THE BRAVE. Dominance of foreground activity. © *Universal Pictures*.

buildings lead to or near the subject. In scenes having strong perspective lines the compositional thrust may carry the viewer's gaze irresistibly toward the horizon. In all such cases the subject should be placed so that the compositional thrust is toward or near him, not away or past him. Crowd scenes, in particular, require that the people be arranged so that the abstract shape of each group provides graphic directional lines leading directly to the subject, or he may be hard to distinguish.

RULE OF THIRDS

The rule of thirds relates to planning cinematography with consistently located centers of interest so that the footage may be edited smoothly and the viewer will not be forced to consciously search for the center of interest. The center of attention at the end of one scene should be located in approximately the same one-third of the image area in the succeeding scene, enabling the viewer to make a smooth and unaware transition from one scene to the next. If, to the contrary, the center of attention leaps from one extreme of the screen to the other, from scene to scene, the viewer may be constantly jolted by jump cuts. The wider the viewing screen, the more important becomes the rule of thirds. In the case of the wide theatrical screen the viewer's gaze should not be left dangling at screen left in one scene, and then be expected to leap thirty feet to screen right in order to keep up with the dramatic flow of action.

The television screen is far less affected by the rule of thirds because of the small image area. Medium shots and closeups tend to dominate in the broadcast medium, and when larger scene sizes are used it requires little effort to locate the subject.

BRIGHTER COLOR OVER DULLER COLOR

Brighter color is dominant over duller color in most circumstances. The viewer's eye will tend to gravitate toward whatever is the lightest and brightest area on the screen. The linking of "lightest" with "brightest" is intentional and important, because color has intrinsic values of light to dark, in addition to having the intensity of chroma. A person wearing a bright red shirt which has the same value as his background will be more difficult to perceive than if there were a wide difference between the values of the shirt and the background.

The factors affecting the image quality of color are these: the validity of its black, halftone and white values; the verity of its color chroma value; and the lines, masses and textures emphasized in illumination.

LIGHTING

Lighting a subject for cinematography is governed by four factors of viewer recognition: *line, mass and value, texture* and *color*.

Lines and outlines tell the viewer most about the subject. The configuration of a woman with a given hair style and clothing style may enable a friend to recognize her a long distance away, simply through the familiarity of her outline. Let that woman adopt a radical change of hair style or a differing mode of dress, and the friend may fail to recognize her until she is close enough for her face to be seen. The first consideration in lighting a subject for quick recognition, an important consideration in a film with a large cast, is to light the subject in a way that will emphasize its most significant lines and outlines.

Mass and value, next in importance, are related factors that involve lighting the subject with good plastic modeling and a range of values (shades of gray) from light to dark that will emphasize the three-dimensional form of the subject. The illusion of depth in a scene may be enhanced by progressively reducing the fullness of the lighting of each subject as it recedes in the distance, lighting foreground subjects with a strong sense of mass, middleground subjects with a flatter rendition and background subjects with nearly a one-dimensional silhouette. Or, the reverse technique of dark-halftone-light may create depth. Recognition is made easier by maintaining distinct contrasts in composition; that is, by composing subjects in terms of light against dark, and so forth, to maintain line recognition while modeling masses and values.

Texture is important as a recognition factor because of what may be termed the culinary appeal of realism. Emphasis on the textures of a subject can make it seem so real the viewer can almost touch it, feel it, taste it. The texture of a subject may be emphasized by three-quarter back-angle cross-lighting, or deemphasized by illumination from a high angle. The more intimate the dramatic mood, the closer the scene size, the more important becomes the factor of textures. The more exciting scenes visually are those in textures that range from silk on a woman's skin to mud caked on a soldier's boots.

Color is an eye-catching element that may contribute greatly to the film's enrichment and the viewer's enjoyment. Color as communication, however, tends to be "extra," because the average viewer perceives people and objects primarily in terms of black-and-white relationships —line, masses and values—and only secondarily in color. Some dramatic films, such as musicals, historical films and others requiring pageantry, are given an emotional shot in the arm by color. And some educational films, such as those using schematic forms, may be clarified by color codes. These are exceptions, however, to the black-and-white basis of the viewer's recognition of meaningful forms.

Low color chroma, approaching the tenors of black-and-white, is preferable when a sense of contemporary realism is desired. The garish color saturation of many color film stocks used in the past tended to detract from the credibility of the film. Color has pushed many otherwise believable films into the realm of fantasy and, in some cases, the stories might have been more effectively rendered in black and white. For somber mood films, color may be a serious detraction. Color has now become standard in the film and television industry, needed or not, and is universally used, appropriate or otherwise. Nevertheless, color films intended to mirror the moods of reality are better produced as black-and-white films—in color.

The *key-to-fill lighting ratio*—the proportionate amount of light falling on the subject from the primary source as compared to the amount coming from the secondary source—affects the mood of the scene and the interpretation of the subject. The more harshly lighted a face is, from light to dark values, the more turgid will seem its expression. Faces contorted with fear or anger in a quarrel are often harshly lighted to reflect the emotions of the confrontation. If a person's face is illuminated fully, with little plastic modeling, the lighting may create an impression of candor, good will, gaiety. Move the direction of the key light around toward the rear of the subject, throwing the person's face into a shadowed low-key tonality, and the subject may acquire an aura of mystery or menace.

The *height of the key light* also affects the viewer's interpretation of the subject. The normal direction of illumination is by overhead lighting from the sun. Any lowering of this height to eye level or below may begin to give the person an unnatural appearance. In psychodramas in which surface normality is underlain with mental aberrations or evil abnormality, the subject is frequently key-lighted at shoulder level, in a setting otherwise lighted from a normal direction, to make the viewer feel uneasy about that particular person. In horror films, such as Dracula and Frankenstein monster movies, the monster is frequently lighted from below—the reverse of the normal direction—to imply that this individual draws its life from some lower world of sulphurous evil.

DOMINANCE

Dominance in cinematography composition means giving dramatic emphasis to one of the performers in a two-shot or three-shot composition. The most obvious example is an over-the-shoulder composition, which makes dominant the person who is standing nearly full-face to the camera and subordinates the person whose face is turned away from the camera. The principle of full-face dominance holds true even as the two-shot composition swings around to a profile angle on both subjects. The face turned slightly toward the camera tends to dominate over the pure profile, given equal lighting emphasis on both subjects. The more into profile a subject turns, the more it becomes subordinate.

JOE. Implied weakness through high camera angle. *Cannon Films.*

Dominance may also be created in a two-shot by manipulating the mass, height and lighting relationship between two subjects. Dominance may be given to one subject and subordination to the other by placing a large figure opposite a small one, a standing figure over a seated figure, and a brightly lighted subject over one dimly lighted. Dominance may be shifted from one subject to the other by having the performers change positions in relation to the camera lens, by using a crane-mounted camera to swing around to a different angle and by reversing the actor's positions.

Triangular compositions are useful for creating dominant and subordinate dramatic relationships when dealing with groups of players. Having the vulnerable character sit or lie down while the others stand is sufficient to interpret their power relationship in the dramatic conflict. Triangular compositions are infinitely variable and serve the added function of containing the viewer's gaze tightly within the screen area.

The height of the camera in relation to the subject has other implications. A simple eye-level view of the subject is essentially neutral and narrative, used to render the subject in scenes that are without heavy dramatic overtones. Lower the camera in relation to the subject—looking up at her—and she will appear increasingly strong and aggressive. Raise the height of the camera angle in relation to the subject—looking down at her—and she will appear increasingly weak and defenseless.

Planning Cinematography

The professional filmmaker plans his cinematography by asking himself certain working questions:

Will a given camera angle tell the story at that point in the film, rendering the action and expressing the mood of the script? This is the primary creative function of the director and his cinematographer.

How large a scene size should be used to reveal the dramatic or expositional point desired at that time in the film?

Will the planned camera position and angle yield scenes that will edit properly with the scenes that precede and follow it? This consideration brings into play such factors as consistent screen direction, scene-to-scene centers of interest and so forth.

Does the importance of the scene to the sequence and the story justify the time it will require technically to set it up for cinematography?

The professional filmmaker plans his cinematography with an eye to how the film footage will be edited. Some directors, such as John Ford and Alfred Hitchcock, have planned their scenes and sequences of cinematography so carefully that they almost literally edit the film in the camera, leaving the editor with little option but to splice the scenes together according to the dictates of the film footage. While these are extreme cases of advance planning, no professional worth his salt will shoot a film without planning consistent screen directions and interpreting his subjects in terms of camera *viewpoints*.

Points-of-View

The filmmaker may interpret the subject from any of three viewer relationships to the life on the screen. These are the *objective*, the *subjective*, and the *performer's viewpoint*.

OBJECTIVE VIEWPOINT

In the objective viewpoint relationship the viewer takes no part in the action, but views it as a spectator from the outside throughout the length of the film, eavesdropping, as it were, on the lives of others. He is a bystander who is given a choice position from which to watch, through every camera angle and scene size, what is taking place within the story. When a scene has been presented long enough for the viewer to get the point, the filmmaker presents him with another, and so on to the end of the film. The objective viewpoint is by far the most widely used in film because of its greater flexibility in presenting the best possible view of every action, angle, movement and interpretation— anything goes.

SUBJECTIVE VIEWPOINT

The subjective viewpoint places the viewer in the position of a screen character, seeing as he sees, through the lens of the camera. This changes the viewer's relationship to the screen story from the third-person point-of-view to the first-person, and his role from that of spectator to that of participant.

The subjective camera technique is used in dramatic films at points

LONELy Are the Brave. Objective viewpoint. © *Universal Pictures.*

of high emotional intensity—when the romantic lead is about to receive a kiss from a lovely woman or a fist in his face from an adversary—changing the emotional impact on the viewer from impersonal to personal.

Whenever a subjective viewpoint by one of the performers is to be shown within an otherwise objectively photographed film, the subjective scene is usually preceded by a closeup of the face of the actor, looking off-screen. This alerts the viewer to what character's eyes he is supposed to be seeing through; if there is only one performer in the scene there would probably be little confusion if the closeup were omitted, but the grammar of film technique is such that the viewer has been conditioned to expect a closeup as an alerting cue to a subjective scene. The use of the subjective shot within an objective context adds sudden dramatic zest.

Flashback sequences are often photographed entirely in the subjective viewpoint as a performer relates an event that has happened to him. The cinematic concepts are then limited to what would be experienced by a single person: the image may be handled erratically, if the performer's mental or physical condition in the story so justifies—shaken, blurred or unsteady—and a sudden blow or fall would then affect the viewer almost as if he were undergoing the experience.

The most extreme application ever made of the subjective camera technique was the feature film *Lady in the Lake*, in which all of the dramatic action was seen through the eyes of the protagonist. The puckered lips of lovely women, the kindly handshakes of friends, the flying fists of enemies, all came straight at the viewer through the eyes of the chief character. The only time the actor was ever seen in the traditional third-person relationship of cinema was when he stood before a mirror and saw his reflection through his own eyes. Novel and interesting as this subjectivity was, most viewers felt uneasy seeing through the eyes of a film character for the entire length of a feature film, as if the relationship were unnatural.

The subjective camera approach offers editing difficulties in a long dramatic sequence, television episode or feature-length film. The events that may be cinematically presented to the viewer are limited to those an earthbound individual would normally be able to see and experience. The flexibility and omniscience of the objective viewpoint which presents, through editing, what is going on in several locations contemporaneously, must be discarded, and with it much of the excitement of a motion picture. Moreover, the insights into the motivations of characters revealed through closeups must also be discarded in the subjective approach, unless the performer through whose eyes the viewer is looking approaches another performer to look closely into his face. The subjective camera approach becomes unwieldy when used at length, and serves better as a dramatic highpoint within an objectively photographed film.

The second application of the subjective camera technique lies in teaching a skill in a film or television program. Whenever the film is supposed to teach some kind of manual process, such as the assembling of a piece of machinery, it is advisable to use the subjective camera technique, presenting the process on film to the student as he would see it while doing the work, to minimize transfer errors in the applications of his knowledge.

Television provides a third application of the subjective concept of eye contact between performer and viewer. A typical example is that of the commercial in which the man or woman who is making the sales pitch looks directly into the camera lens to make eye-to-eye contact with the viewer, and, brimming with sincerity, confidence and integrity, appeals to the potential customer personally. Another example is that of the television newscaster, who addresses himself directly to the lens to establish a personal relationship between himself and the viewer.

A television variant of the subjective drama concept consists of having a host, or one of the performers who may appear later in the story, step forward to introduce the episode to follow, interpreting the events and their characters as if he were relating a personal anecdote. Sometimes the same personality may appear at the end of the program to provide a subjective summing up.

Performer's Viewpoint

The performer's viewpoint is a hybrid of the objective and subjective viewpoints. The performer's viewpoint is in part an objective angle in the sense that it keeps the viewer outside the dramatic action, looking in, and he never has the direct participation effect of eye-to-eye contact. The camera is placed so close to one of the performers, however, that the viewer sees the dramatic action very nearly as the performer does. While the viewer remains a spectator, he comes to identify strongly with a given player by looking, quite literally, over his shoulder. During a buildup of emotional intensity, a filmmaker may progressively change from an objective viewpoint to a performer's viewpoint to a subjective viewpoint, to make the dramatic action progressively more heightened and personal to the viewer.

Master Scene Technique

The master scene technique consists of photographing a dramatic action in segmented scene sizes—full shot, medium shot, closeup, etc.—

LONELy ARE THE BRAVE. Peformer's viewpoint. © *Universal Pictures.*

so the individual scenes may be edited later into a complete sequence of dramatic action. One reason for segmenting the action is that scenes of different sizes may be edited into a dramatic composite whose action would be more exciting than if it were photographed in a single scene size with one roll of the camera. Another reason is that scenes of different sizes convey.different meanings, and the filmmaker is always concerned with interpreting the subject to the viewer. The component elements of master scene technique are control of *screen directions, matching the action, matching the look,* the *continuity line* and *dramatic progression.*

SCREEN DIRECTIONS

Consistent screen direction, by movements of the subject or the camera, should be maintained from one scene to another, or the changed direction should be explained visually. An establishing shot of a man driving his car into a lot to park, followed by a medium shot of him getting out of his car, followed by a closeup of his hand locking the door, should have consistent scene-to-scene screen direction in order to reveal the action logically. Any change in the screen direction not explained visually will tend to confuse the viewer, and the instant he asks "What's happening?" the film has lost its grip.

Changes of directional continuity may be explained visually by any of three cinematic techniques. The first means is that of having the subject change direction within the scene.

The second is that of photographing a scene having a neutral direction—the subject moves directly toward the viewer in a head-on shot, or directly away in a tailaway shot. A neutral direction permits the subject to subsequently begin anew in either screen direction. It is a wise filmmaker who photographs a neutral direction scene as a transitional device, or to take the curse off a possible jump cut.

A third means of changing screen direction is through the use of a cutaway. A cutaway is a subject having a logical but not visual relation to the main dramatic action. A cutaway is presented long enough for the viewer to forget what the screen direction was, or long enough for the screen direction of the dramatic action to have plausibly changed. For example: If a cinematic fight is being photographed in which two men are struggling for possession of a gun lying on the floor, and the director has inadvertently flipped the screen direction while directing the scene, the film editor could cover up the error by presenting a closeup of the gun long enough to make it plausible that the fight being heard on the sound track had changed its screen direction.

When two separate but contemporaneous actions are planned and intended to be intercut later in editing for dramatic buildup, each dramatic action should have a consistently different screen direction. An example of this would be two armies marching toward each other to battle; one army should be consistently moving from left to right, the other from right to left, so when the two parallel actions are intercut in editing, the viewer may instantly understand, from its directional movement, which army he is watching. Another example would be the hunter and the hunted, in which both may be moving in one direction, but the hunted is always looking back at his pursuer.

MATCHING THE ACTION

Matching the action consists of photographing the component scenes of a dramatic action so that the resulting footage may be edited into a single smooth flow of action. For example: If a dramatic action consisted of one man lunging forward to wrest a gun from the hand of another, his movements would probably be photographed in their entirety in four scene sizes: an establishing shot of the two men as one leaped forward and tore the gun from the hand of the other; a medium shot of the aggressor as he lunged forward and seized the gun; a tight two-shot as they struggled for possession of the weapon; and a closeup of the gun as it was wrenched from the hand of the second man. Each of these scenes would record the same complete movements, but only short lengths of each scene would be used to edit a composite dramatic action that would appear, to the viewer, as a single continuous flow of action. By progressively intercutting the different scene sizes to create a composite form of the struggle for the gun, the edited sequence becomes more realistic than reality, more exciting than life.

The dramatic action thus photographed must be repeated four times, or photographed simultaneously with several cameras, in order to have overlapped action in the four scenes suitable for proper editing. Any failure to match the action smoothly when photographing the four scene sizes may be detected immediately by the viewer as a "jump cut." The main reason the action must be duplicated is so that during the editing stage certain phases of the dramatic action may be overlapped for a few frames, when cutting from one scene to the other, in order to extend the drama of the fight.

MATCHING THE LOOK

Matching the look refers to having people look in the correct direction when photographing medium shots and closeups out of context, so that when the resulting film footage is edited together, the subjects will appear to be gazing at each other.

During dramatic cinematography it is not uncommon for two subjects of the same sequence to be photographed at different times, and

You're No Good. Matching the look (a). *National Film Board of Canada.*

their interactions created entirely by the film editor. The first subject in a quarrel, for example, may be photographed all alone as he argues and snarls and gesticulates, while the second subject, the person he is arguing with, is home puttering in his garden. Then the second party to the quarrel may come onto the set to argue his half before the camera while the first goes home. The resulting two lengths of film footage are then sent to the film editor, who intercuts the words and gestures of the two subjects into an interactive "quarrel."

Matching the look is particularly important in a continuing television dramatic series. The star of the series frequently prefers to have all of his appearances in all of the episodes of the television season photographed out-of-context in three hellish months, so he can spend the rest of the year playing golf. When each episode is subsequently photographed and edited, his part is cut into the film as if he had participated fully in its production. Photographing all of the star's appearances out of context, before any of the context episodes are photographed, requires clear understanding by the director of what direction the star must be looking in the yet-to-be-photographed episode.

CONTINUITY LINE

The continuity line is an invisible stage line within whose 180-degree arc all the scenes of a sequence having a consistent screen direc-

YOU'RE NO GOOD. Matching the look (b). *National Film Board of Canada.*

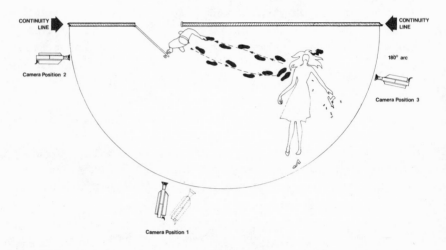

Continuity line. *Drawing by Glen Shimada.*

tion should be photographed. Camera positions may be set up anywhere within this 180-degree continuity line and the resulting film footage may be properly edited in terms of screen direction. Whether there is one subject or a hundred, whether the action is a single character walking across the room or a rampaging mob swarming through the city, whether the scenes are photographed from a tripod or a mobile crane, the resulting footage can be edited with the right relationships between the subjects if the filmmaker remembers this continuity line.

Make the mistake of photographing one scene *beyond that continuity line, however, and edit it into the sequence photographed within* the action line, and the viewer will be instantly confused. His orientation to the whole dramatic sequence will suddenly be reversed. Establishing a new action line for a new confrontation may be perfectly acceptable, and desirable, but only after using a neutral shot as a transition to the new action line.

Three or four camera positions, within the 180-degree arc of the continuity line, are usually enough to photograph a complete dramatic action. If the cinematography has been carefully planned, the resulting film footage should comprise a complete range of scene sizes from establishing shot to closeup, with matching action, ready for editing.

DRAMATIC PROGRESSION

Changing lenses in each basic camera position is the principal means of obtaining the range of scene sizes from no more than four camera positions. By planning in advance how the film footage will be action-matched in editing, the filmmaker can decide which of the camera positions will photograph any given portion of the dramatic action in any given scene size. This means, in effect, that the filmmaker must edit the sequence in his mind before he sets up his camera.

The following dramatic sequence presents an elementary example of the master scene technique, using no more than three camera positions to photograph it properly for editing.

A man enters through a door and is surprised to discover the body of a woman lying across the room, with a pistol near her hand. He walks quickly across the room, kneels beside the woman and touches her to confirm that she is dead. Then he picks up the pistol and examines it, suddenly panics and drops the pistol, and rises to flee out the door.

In the above dramatic action, the filmmaker would be concerned with making the following dramatic and narrative points:

(1) Establishing for the viewer the setting in which the dramatic action will take place.

(2) Presenting the man who walks into the room, and his reaction to the discovery of the body of the woman.

(3) The action of the man as he walks over and kneels beside the body.

(4) His confirmation of death, and his reaction.

(5) His discovery of the weapon, and his sudden panic.

(6) His flight to the door, his glance back, and the slam of the door.

The foregoing dramatic sequence could be photographed as follows in master scene technique, illustrated by the top-view schematic drawing. Notice that the scenes are not photographed in the same order in which the dramatic action occurs, but in the order that will minimize the number of needed lighting and camera setups.

1. Camera position number one would be used to photograph three scenes of the dramatic sequence. An *establishing shot* of the room, and complete cinematography of the whole dramatic action from beginning to end, *panning* after the subject as he walks *toward the body* and *away from the body*. This provides the film editor with a covering master scene

to which he can cut if he has trouble editing any of the other scenes.

From the same camera position number one the filmmaker would probably photograph a *medium shot* of the man as he picked up the gun near the body and looked over his shoulder in panic.

Also from camera position number one, the filmmaker would photograph a *closeup* of the man's face as he paused on his way out the door to look back at the body.

2. Camera position number two would be used to photograph two scenes of the dramatic sequence: a *subjective camera shot*, through the eyes of the man as he discovers the woman, probably followed by a *zoom-in* to a *full shot* of her body.

Furthermore, from camera position number two there would be a *full shot* of the man as he rises from the woman's body and runs toward the camera into a *medium shot* as he opens the door.

Camera position number three would be used for four scenes: a *low-angle shot*, looking past the woman's body to a *full shot* of the man standing at the door, *slipping focus* as *he walks forward* and *kneels beside the woman*, and is reframed with her in a *tight two-shot*.

A complete dramatic sequence has been photographed from three camera positions, with controlled screen directions, matching action, matching looks, a full range of lens and camera movements and a full spectrum of eleven scene sizes—from establishing shot to extreme closeup—with all visual elements pulling their weight in editing.

The master scene technique has some disadvantages: Actors must memorize their movements while they are performing in order to repeat them for retakes with other lenses, and subsequently be able to match those movements perfectly for other scene sizes. The movements and actions photographed in the original master scene, covering the entire dramatic action, must be duplicated by each player in his full shot and closeups. Moreover, any apparel worn or objects held in the hand must be draped or manipulated in the same identical way, or a cut from one scene to another will reveal the error as a jolting jump cut. Also, the need to repeat actions perfectly in the master scene technique tends to discourage improvisation and spontaneity.

Multicamera Technique

The alternative to the master scene technique is the use of the multi-camera setup, in which the actor performs his long dramatic scenes without interruption, while being photographed by two or three cameras running simultaneously, each equipped with a different focal-length lens. The disadvantage of this technique, however, is that the lighting of the scene may be ideal from the point of view of one camera position but substandard from another, and this can result in film footage whose inconsistent lighting quality will become conspicuous in editing.

The dramatic progression to be used in editing should be planned carefully in cinematography, so that the scenes will be photographed as needed. Only by thinking in advance how a sequence should be edited can a filmmaker decide how a scene should be photographed. In a film entitled *I Want to Live!* the interpretation of a woman was progressively changed by gradually raising the average height of the camera as the drama progressed. The story concerned a woman who lived the high life with gangsters, became embroiled in their crimes and ended by facing execution. The film started with low camera angles, looking up at her during her days of handsome living. The angles were gradually raised as her fortunes sank until, at the end, the camera looked down on her from a very high angle—appearing small, weak and defenseless—on Death Row.

The professional filmmaker has certain practical, mundane considerations to think about when directing a scene that do not necessarily relate to the purely cinematic quality of his film.

How can each sequence be photographed most effectively with a minimum number of lighting and camera setups? As discussed earlier, most dramatic confrontations may be photographed from three or four basic camera positions, providing the director understands how the footage is to be edited and to what effect. Expense is the imperative consideration. The cost of producing and lighting an interior set is very high, and the importance of the sequence to the film should be weighed before undertaking the expense of its production. And the low cost of lighting an exterior (thanks to the great light in the sky) is offset by the expense of taking the cast and production crew out on location.

Is the sequence covered to excess? This consideration relates to budget as well as dramatic exigency. It is all very well to have a magnificent first half of the film in the can, but there must be a few dollars left with which to shoot the second half. Filmmakers sometimes become so enamored of certain dramatic situations that they go into a creative frenzy from which they do not recover until they are broke. Sometimes, too, a director may fail to bear in mind the relationship of a given sequence to the whole picture and have more angles photographed than are needed to properly edit the film footage.

Is the dramatic action blocked in a way that will obtain the best performance from the actors? A performer often becomes popular with the public because of his excellence in a certain kind of dramatic action; many viewers may attend a film to enjoy his kind of excellence, and may be disappointed if they don't see it. Actors on the whole are wildly insecure creatures, and are exquisitely sensitive to how they appear on the screen. If the director does not block the dramatic action in a way that reveals the actor at what he considers his best, the more dramatic performances may occur off-screen.

4

The
Syntax of
Editing

Cinema is a multifaceted medium, but if one phase of motion picture production were to be singled out as the essence of cinematic technique, it would be editing.

Only when the film editor sits down to the Moviola with his photographed scenes and begins to create a continuity order, with actions and reactions and a tempo to which the viewer responds at an almost subliminal level, does the film begin to come alive as cinema. The best-directed, best-photographed film footage may be intrinsically beautiful, but it is not a living motion picture that will hold the viewer's interest for long unless it has been creatively and dynamically edited. Conversely, good footage mundanely directed may sometimes be transformed into an excellent film by a fine film editor. Editing is the heart of cinema art, and more than one fiasco has been elevated to the Academy Award level through the imagination and artistry of its editor.

Some fundamental concepts of editing—screen directions, narrative and implicit editing, cinematic time and distance, tempo, flashback and flashforward, montage, visual simile and metaphor—were introduced in the broad overview presented in "The Language of Cinema-Television." The present chapter deals more specifically with the concepts and techniques by which the film editor communicates ideas and arouses emotions in the viewer.

Functional Editing

Every scene and sequence in a film should be there for a functional reason: to contribute to the development of a character, tell the story, provide humor, give exposition, develop mood and atmosphere or imply meanings. Any scene not serving some contributory function to the film story should be discarded, no matter how succulent the cinematography, for any scene that does not add to the substance of the film detracts from it.

A professional dramatic filmmaker usually photographs his scenes with the editing phase clearly in mind. This is particularly true of dramatic films in which the director must be careful to maintain a logical screen direction, match the performers' looks and gestures, and maintain a consistent emotional tenor, while directing scenes and sequences which are frequently photographed out of context with each other.

Selecting Scenes

Given the complexity of editing film footage, the editor's first job is to eliminate unusable footage by culling the film rushes for bad takes, duplicated actions, poorly acted closeups, muffed lines of dialogue and all superfluous scenes.

If several scenes are acceptable from a technical point of view, the selections are narrowed on the basis of three visual criteria:

1. The content should graphically reveal the script's desired action, with economy of viewpoint and simplicity of expression.

2. The photographic quality should be excellent in terms of composition, exposure, focus and smoothness of camera and lens movements.

3. The continuity relationship of a scene should work editorially in relation to those which precede and follow it in terms of consistent screen directions and matching action.

When the film editor is concerned with lip-synchronous sound, and has narrowed his selection of scenes according to the above visual criteria, he makes his final selection according to the following considerations: the best sound takes in terms of clarity, rate of delivery, and naturalness of expression.

Sometimes a scene which is good visually will have poor recorded sound quality, or a good sound recording may have a poor visual counterpart; it then becomes a matter of making the editorial best of a bad bargain. The editor often resolves the dilemma by playing the good sound-recorded voice over some alternative scene that can plausibly be cut into the dialogue—such as another person's reaction.

The dramatic film is photographed from a written script, the reference point in cinematography, and the dramatic film editor is less concerned with correcting errors of camera technique and directing than his documentary counterpart.

Documentary films, on the other hand, in which the action is often improvised or uncontrolled, are sometimes photographed without a script, creating serious problems in editing. Such films are not always photographed with editing requirements in mind, but the final edited films are judged as if they were. Many television documentaries are created in the cutting room from film footage photographed in different parts of the world by several cameramen functioning independently. Their footage is made coherent only through the concerted efforts of an editor-writer team and cutaways to the ever-ready television commentator who fills in the holes in continuity with explanations.

Editing Techniques

Some of the cinematic techniques of editing that contribute to the substance and development of the film story deal with: *logical continuity, motivation, suspense, cutting on movement, lip-synchronous sound, cutaways,* the *insert, expanded* and *contracted cinematic time* and *cross-cutting*.

LOGICAL CONTINUITY

Logical continuity is the essential framework for narrative editing in most films, because the viewer must be oriented at all times to follow the story and be absorbed in the life on the screen. Breaks in continuity are breaks in believability. For simple storytelling the classic editing approach is: long shot—medium shot—closeup—long shot. The long shot establishes the player and his setting. The medium shot introduces the player and presents him doing something typical to reveal his character and personality. A closeup gives the viewer an intimate look at his face.

And then, once more, a full shot to reveal a new character or begin a new dramatic action.

MOTIVATION

Motivation is an equally important basis for a change of scene. Each cut should be motivated by something occurring in the preceding scene. If a woman turns her head to look at something, it is followed by a scene of what she is looking at. If what she sees is frightening, it is followed by a reaction shot revealing her emotions. If her emotion is that of panic, her reaction may be that of flight, and this should be shown in action. In each instance a cut to another scene is motivated by what has preceded it—motivated visually, emotionally and logically.

SUSPENSE

Suspense is created largely by the editor who, like a magician, manipulates the interests and emotions of the viewer by the way he presents some scenes and holds back others. The film editor selects and arranges the scene sizes as much for their flavor and impact as for their narrative content.

For a slow tempo, to gradually quicken the viewer's interest in a person or a subject, the change in scene sizes is slow and progressive: full shot—medium long shot—medium shot—medium closeup—closeup. This editing concept is useful in crowd sequences when the intent is to slowly single out one person for the viewer's attention without the rigorous impact of a zoom or a radical change of scene size. This slow-tempo approach is often used to plant clues to the existence of a minor character who may become important later in the story.

For suspense leading to shock, an efficient technique is: closeup—closeup—closeup—long shot. The series of closeups alerts the viewer to the importance of a pending event, while the similar scene sizes lull his visual perceptions, then the long shot startles him by its contrast, with the added shock value of the dramatic action. In *Wait Until Dark* a blind girl was trapped in a night-blackened apartment with a psychopathic killer. Repeated closeups revealed her frightened face as she crept around to evade him in the dark. Then a wide-angle shot was cut in just as the killer leaped at her from a doorway—an editing trick that made the audience scream with terror as one.

The principles of building suspense to a shock effect through the repetition of scene sizes to lull the viewer, followed by a radical change, applies to almost any scene size. The progression may be: long shot— long shot—long shot—closeup, to the same effect.

Suspense may be increased by delaying the scene of the inevitable. Adding extra scenes before the dramatic highpoint, or having a character make an elaborate ritual of what he is about to do, or staging unexpected delays—like the ringing of the telephone—can arouse suspense within the viewer to a degree that he is literally sitting on the edge of his seat. Another suspense technique is to run the scene on the screen for a long, long time—far beyond the time when one would normally expect a cut to another scene—thereby building a sense of rising tension in the viewer.

For fast-paced editing and excitement the scenes should vary radically for staccato effect: long shot—closeup—full shot—extreme closeup—medium shot, and so forth. Any viewer who has ever seen the portrayal of a cattle stampede, with its rapid cuts from a full shot of the entire herd to a closeup of horses' hooves, from a sea of horns to cowboys' spurs, will recognize this fast-tempo editing technique.

Television has changed the concept of progressive tempo because of the need to pique the viewer's interest in the story before he can switch channels. And because feature films are now produced with an eye to reruns on the *Late, Late Show*, theatrical dramas also are now frequently photographed with a fast-action beginning. If the traditional slow tempo has been used, the editor frequently creates a montage of the high crises of drama, selected from the film itself, to use as the television shirttail. This is intended to capture the viewer's interest and preclude his switching to another channel.

The content of the story should determine the editing concepts and techniques used in every sequence in a dramatic film. Out-of-character editing, such as a snappy tempo in a sequence with lanquid or pensive overtones, tends to mislead the viewer, unless the intended effect is that of comedy or satire.

Cutting on Movement

Cutting on movement is one of the uses made of the master scene technique. Because the same dramatic action may be photographed as a full shot, medium shot and closeup, the film editor may use all three scenes to create a dramatic action, cutting from one to the other at any point along the movement.

An important principle exists here: The film editor creates one movement out of many scenes. He selects only those phases of the movements from each component scene that are most graphic in depicting the action, and discards those phases that are dull or superfluous. He thus creates a cinematic action more exciting than reality. Moreover, cutting during a subject's movements softens the jolt of physical changes in scene sizes and thereby enhances the sense of continuity.

When making a cut during rapid dramatic action, such as a fight, an important illusionary principle comes into effect: the cut on movement is *not* made at the same phase of the movement in both scene sizes. The first few head frames of the second scene are either deleted or overlapped according to whether the cut is made from a larger scene size to a smaller, or from a smaller to a larger.

If the cut is being made from a larger scene size to a smaller, such as a long shot to a closeup, several frames of movement at the head of the second scene are *deleted*. The edited action skips a few frames when cutting from a larger to a smaller scene size because the shock value of an abrupt move closer carries with it the cinematic illusion of edited movement. The viewer's eyes will perceive the rapid actions—with closeup frames deleted—as a continuous flow of motion. If such a cut were made without removing a few head frames from the second scene, the action would appear to jump in mid-movement.

Conversely, when a cut is made from a smaller scene size to a larger, such as a closeup to a full shot, several frames at the head of the second scene *overlap the tail action* of the first. The edited action briefly duplicates the movement at the head of the second scene because of the disorienting effect of moving suddenly from a smaller to a larger scene size. There is an instant of confusion which must be compensated for by briefly duplicating the action for the reorientation of the viewer. If the editing is handled artfully, the viewer's eyes will then perceive the action as a continuous flow of motion. If a direct cut were made on the same phase of action in both the closeup and the full shot, there would appear to be several frames missing, even though the action matched exactly.

During purely visual action sequences—fights, chases, montages—almost anything goes, if motivated, but certain working principles have emerged from the welter of experience. For an important visual action, cut to the most graphic viewpoint just before the action occurs. If the action is significant in terms of *story content*, play the entire dramatic action in full, without cutting it. If, on the other hand, the dramatic action is unimportant to the story, cut on irrelevant but eye-catching action.

Directional cutting, whereby the movement of the subject in one scene is picked up in the following scene, has important continuity uses. First, it is used to maintain screen direction in editing scenes photographed with the master scene technique, when creating one subject movement out of many scenes. Second, it is used on a grander scale to reflect the sweep of mobs or armies, or the gigantic movements of unnatural disasters, by intercutting rapidly between subjects that are moving in one direction ever more quickly, and intercutting radically between scene sizes, so that the screen seems swollen with wildly moving images.

In most dramatic sequences the viewer should be shown the next subject he expects to see or hear—but not in the way he expects. A cut to an unusual angle, a camera movement or a radical change in scene size will add the zest of surprise to the fulfillment of expectation. Combining surprise with fulfillment in every scene is the essence of good editing.

After each action, cut to a reaction. After each reaction, cut to an action. A unique characteristic of dramatic action in film, in contrast to the stage play, is that the most cinematic actions emphasize the *reactions* to dialogue or events rather than the stimuli actions themselves.

It is axiomatic that great screen actors are reactors; that is, their cinematic acting is done in reaction to a crisis, usually in a closeup. At times of great emotional crisis the attention of the viewer is most often directed to the screen character being subjected to the dialogue or dramatic actions. This is the reverse of the stage play, in which the actor speaking the lines holds the center of interest. Moreover, if a film actor is given a long span of dialogue to speak, he may appear stagey and pretentious—an unexplained phenomenon of acting for the cinema. It requires an actor with masterly low-key control to speak long passages of dialogue on film without becoming a shade laughable.

LIP-SYNCHRONOUS SOUND

Lip-synchronous sound has an inhibiting effect upon editing tempo. A dramatic film is most earthbound when the actors are speaking lip-synchronous sound, because the editing is then bound to real time. Dialogue scenes are difficult to infuse with editing tempo as long as the filmmaker allows himself to be enslaved by a locked-in picture and sound relationship. The intuitive filmmaker knows this, and emancipates his art by emphasizing visual reactions in editing. Again, experience has evolved some editorial techniques to leaven the spoken word.

Show the speaker before he talks. In most dramatic sequences the picture should precede the spoken word to alert the viewer. In virtually all educational film and television programs, the image should precede the description or valuable content may slide by unobserved before the viewer has been alerted.

Use closeups during crucial dialogue, and use medium shots and full shots for less important conversation. Save the closeups for dramatic emphasis.

A lip-synchronous sentence may be broken visually to show a reaction shot. The sentence may be cut visually in the middle of the speaker's line to show the reaction of the listener to what is being said. Then the listener would dominate the dramatic action, accompanied by the voice-over sound of the speaker. This is an important editing technique, because it is one way of skirting the earthbound quality of lip-synchronous dialogue.

This technique is also a valuable way of reducing production costs. A dramatic sequence may begin with a few words of lip-synchronous dialogue, and then be edited with reaction shots, over the shoulder and at angles, then conclude with a few words of lip-synchronous dialogue. The viewer will be left with the impression that he has viewed a completely lip-synchronous scene. Between the first few words and the last, there may be a sequence of great cinematic excitement, with the "dialogue" presented voice-over.

The cut may come between ideas or sentences for many kinds of casual conversation. This is the easiest, weakest way to present dialogue. Heavy-handed cutting from one person speaking to another person speaking was common in the early days of the sound film, and is ponderously prevalent today in educational television productions. If the editor has the option of cutting independent picture and sound tracks, he may create far more exciting relationships by thinking in terms of independent actions, reactions, counterpoint and contrast in his two tracks.

The Cutaway

Cutaways are those scenes which have no visual continuity with the previous scene, but have a *logical continuity*. A cutaway shifts the viewer's attention away from the main action to a secondary action occurring at the same time elsewhere, but a secondary action related in some way to the main story line. The cutaway has an immense variety of uses.

Time, suspense and tempo may be controlled through the use of cutaways. In tense dramatic situations, such as a chase or a pending disaster with lives at stake, cutaways to more peaceful places—"back at the ranch"—may postpone the climax and raise the emotional temperature of the film. Cutaways are often inserted at the moment something very exciting is about to happen: an airplane is about to crash, an escapee is about to be captured, a woman is about to say "yes" or "no" to a crucial proposal.

Dramatic events too expensive or dangerous to stage and photograph may be skirted by a cutaway to the reaction of a spectator. The crash of a jet airline might be rendered by first showing a plane coming down at a dangerous angle, then intercutting short scenes of the pilot's face as he desperately tries to control the aircraft, then cutting to details of the failing jet engines, a rush of approaching earth, and just as the jet crashes—a cutaway to the reaction of a bystander, accompanied by sounds of screaming metal, shattering glass and an explosion.

The emotional meaning of an event may also be created by a cutaway to the reaction of a bystander. An explosion can have a wide variety of emotional meanings—tragedy, humor, mystery, heroism, cowardice —according to the reactions of the screen characters who witness the cinematic event. A cutaway to the reaction of bystanders cues the viewer to the desired emotional response.

Undramatic and time-consuming actions may be completed more quickly through the use of a cutaway than if portrayed in full on the screen. During a recent war movie, for example, a soldier began to change clothes from his mud-caked battle fatigues to civilian garb, talking all the while to a second soldier. After showing the first soldier sitting down to unlace a boot, the film editor played the rest of the scene on the silent reactions of the second, and then cut back to the first soldier, combed, washed, shaved and clad in civilian garb—within fifteen seconds. The cutaway to the second soldier, played over the words of the first, eliminated the real time and motions necessary for the sartorial transformation.

Actions too complex to be revealed cinematically, or actions inaccessible to the lens of the camera, may in a dramatic film be covered simply by a cutaway to some person explaining what is happening. In *The Andromeda Strain*, for example, the mutations of the deadly viruses brought back from outer space on the projectile were explained in a cutaway to a scientist because the mutation process itself could not be depicted in a meaningful way to the lay viewer.

Cutaways have been used for satirical commentary almost since the birth of film. War films that portrayed soldiers fighting and dying in trenches and jungles would frequently include a cutaway to reveal other men wallowing in luxury, or deserting to escape combat, by way of comparison.

The cutaway may be used to distract the attention of the viewer from the filmmaker's mistakes. If the horseman in a western has been shown going from screen left to screen right, and then from right to left—an illogical reversal of screen direction—the error may be masked by a cutaway to the face of a person supposedly watching the horseman change directions. The cutaway may also be used as a crutch to cover up mismatched actions, inconsistent lighting tonality, jumps in the centers of interest from scene to scene and a host of other cinematic blunders.

The Insert

The insert is related to the cutaway. This is usually an extreme closeup of some detail, such as a light switch or a newspaper headline, intended to be a disorienting scene. The insert is often used as a cutaway to separate serious cinematic discrepancies; because of its extreme disorientation properties, it should not be held on the screen too long or it may disrupt the continuity more than the error it is intended to correct.

Expanded and Contracted Cinematic Time

The emotional qualities of a dramatic event may be reflected in the time it takes to occur on the screen, in expanded and contracted cinematic time.

Expanded time is the cinematic expansion of apparent time, created by overlapping the scenes of a movement to make the action appear much longer than it takes in real time. Expanded time was used in a classic way in the documentary film *The River*. The felling of a giant Douglas fir was an event of great symbolic importance to the theme of the film: the beginning of the wanton destruction of forests and watershed. The filmmaker set up cameras from several different sides to photograph the tree's felling. Then, in editing, he repeatedly overlapped the scenes depicting its fall to expand time and made it seem as if an eternity were passing during the conifer's majestic collapse to the ground. The cutting of that Douglas fir was too important an event to be photographed simply from one position with one roll of the camera.

Contracted time is the cinematic reduction of apparent time by the elimination of frames and scenes—symbolically—to make time seem to pass more quickly than it would in real time. In the same film, *The River*, the passage of years was symbolically contracted to minutes by following the path of one drop of water from its drip on an eroded hillside to its fusion with a rivulet, to its joining with a gully stream, and so forth, until it grew to a rampaging flood that ravaged the Mississippi Valley, destroying farms, towns and lives, leaving hundreds of thousands of people homeless.

CROSS-CUTTING

Cross-cutting in dramatic film refers to the intercutting of two parallel dramatic actions occurring simultaneously, and implies a plot relationship between the two events that will pay off eventually in a confrontation. Typical examples are the marching of armies against each other, a race for an objective, or pursuers and pursued in a chase sequence. Consistent screen directions in both actions are important because the viewer must immediately know which side he is watching every time a cross-cut is made.

Cross-cutting may be used to maintain interest by switching to the action on the second side when the first side begins to lag in excitement. It may be employed to heighten suspense by showing one side with its guard down while the other pushes forward. And cross-cutting may be used to compare two events separated in time, such as a portrayal of combat techniques in World War II and some future war in space.

In nontheatrical films—documentary, educational, industrial and process—the cross-cutting technique is used to show cause and effect relationships and to make comparisons. It may reveal the relationship between new forms of technology and their economic benefits to the nation, or their pollution of natural resources. Or it may reveal how a family's life style differs in various parts of the world according to its race and socioeconomic milieu. Cross-cutting may be used in any film or videotape program to relate an event occurring anywhere, at any time and place, with any other event that occurs at any other time and place, for the purposes of creating suspense, advancing the story, making a comparison or heightening the viewer's interest.

The Jump Cut and Its Cures

A jump cut is any noticeable failure to bridge a flow of action when cutting from one scene to another. This visual aberration is a distraction from the viewer's absorption in the film and may result from any of several discrepancies.

Failure to match the subject's dramatic actions during master scene cinematography may leave the film editor with no way to cut directly on movement from one scene size to another because there is no overlapping of filmed action. His only options are to play out the action in full with one scene or to use a cutaway reaction shot.

The cinematographer may have changed lenses in the same identical camera position and height, producing a visual shock of sameness. The editor's alternatives are to use a less desirable scene from another angle, or the master scene.

The director may have failed to account for consistent screen directions during the dramatic actions, or to provide a neutral shot to cover a change of screen direction, leaving the film editor with no logical way to account for the subject's abrupt change of direction. The editor's alternatives are the perennial cutaway to a reaction shot, to a neutral scene, or a cross-cut to another contemporaneous dramatic action.

Inconsistent lighting of differing scenes within an interior sequence will become obvious in editing through constant jumps from low-key to high-key tonality. The editor's option here may require the grouping of scenes having similar tonality—in effect rewriting the sequence of dramatic actions—and introducing each group with an establishing shot that logically accounts for the tonality to follow. When all else fails— the cutaway.

A jump in the center of attention from one part of the screen to another, from scene to scene, may, in a wide-screen theatrical presentation, force the viewer to swivel his head back and forth like a spectator at a tennis match. Each time the viewer has to search for the center of interest, part of the dramatic action may slip away before he can find it. The bigger the screen, the more important becomes the matter of consistency in centers of interest from scene to scene. The rule of thirds, discussed in the previous chapter, comes into play—the cinematographer should shoot so as to ensure that in the editing phase the film may be spliced in a way that will direct the viewer's gaze to approximately the same one third of the screen from one scene to the next.

Audible distractions are one means of taking the curse off a jump cut. A loud noise, a sudden off-screen shout, a crescendo of music or dialogue may—if dramatically plausible—momentarily make the sound track dominant over the image. If done cleverly, the visual jump may slide by before the viewer has recovered from the shock and the image is once again dominant.

Atypical Editing Concepts

A number of ancillary editing concepts have evolved during the growth of cinema which often add sophisticated elements of art and communication to the finished film, elements which, in a few films, have become major concepts. These editing concepts are the *shock-attraction principle*, the *flutter cut, associative editing, metric montage, tonal editing, dialectical editing of movements* and *linkage*.

THE SHOCK-ATTRACTION PRINCIPLE

The shock-attraction principle holds that when two scenes are spliced together they take on a third emotional meaning not inherent in either of the scenes, a concept related to implicit editing. An example of this would be a sequence from the Canadian film *You're No Good*. A high school dropout was employed to deliver sandwiches to the plush offices of an architectural firm; when he entered to deliver the food he inadvertently tracked mud on the slick white floors and the receptionist glared at him with an expression that oozed contempt. The boy was humiliated. The filmmaker, to portray the boy's inner feelings of resentment, cut first to a closeup of his angry eyes, then to an extreme closeup

of a hand holding and then throwing a hand grenade, then to the mush-
rooming cloud of an atomic explosion, and then back to a closeup of
the boy's sullen face. Obviously, the filmmaker did not intend the grenade and atomic explosion to be interpreted literally by the viewer; the
sequence expressed the sum total "third meaning" of the boy's anger,
based on the shock-attraction principle.

The shock-attraction concept presents some danger of being mis-
understood, or not being understood at all by the viewer. First, the film
literacy of the viewer must be high enough so he does not expect everything to be rendered literally. Second, the content of the scenes used
must be intrinsically meaningful to the viewer or he will be unable to
draw the intended third-level inferences.

THE FLUTTER CUT

The flutter cut is a subjective editing technique in which very short
clips of film from different scenes are quickly intercut, either to provide
a transition from one sequence to another, or to render the subjective
feelings of a character.

When the flutter cut is used in lieu of a dissolve to connote a change
of time or location, short clips from the incoming sequence are cut into
the outgoing sequence. These incoming clips are progressively increased
in length until the outgoing sequence is itself reduced to short clips—
and then phased out—and the incoming sequence is in full possession of
the screen. The flutter-cut transition gives a staccato visual effect which
draws attention to itself and is best used as a transitional device when
there is a change of dramatic action to a second location whose appearance is very similar to the first. The change of location must be emphasized to avoid confusion in the mind of the viewer.

The flutter cut may be used to bring subjective memories of the past
into dramatic actions whose setting is the present. In *The Pawnbroker*
an old Jewish man watched a gang of hoodlums beating up a boy who
attempted to flee by climbing a fence, and this triggered remembrance
of a time when the old man had himself attempted to escape from Nazi
soldiers by climbing a fence. This memory was rendered in the present
tense by flutter-cutting short scenes of his past in the concentration
camp with closeups of the old pawnbroker. The flutter cut, if carried far
enough, can be extended into a flashback to tell another story whose
setting is rooted in the past.

ASSOCIATIVE EDITING

Associative editing is the splicing of two scenes in sequence whose subject images have similar shapes, such as a cut from the round mouth of a cannon to the rim of a champagne glass. Associative editing is most often used as a transitional device, in lieu of a dissolve or a wipe, to bridge a change of time or location. At other times this editing technique is used to connote other meanings: In *Psycho*, for example, a woman was stabbed to death while taking a shower. One scene presented a slow zoom-in to an extreme closeup of the iris of her eye, then cut to a closeup of the round drain with whorls of water running down, a symbol of her life draining away.

METRIC MONTAGE

Metric montage refers to an editing technique in which scenes are cut to the beat of a metronome to create a mathematical undercurrent to the overall tempo. Metric montage does not mean, obviously, that a scene is cut on each and every beat. But when a scene is cut, at whatever length, the cut is made right on the beat of the metronome. However long or short a sequence cut to metric montage, its rhythms and progressions are given a mathematical relationship to which most viewers respond with a feeling of suspense.

The classic use of metric montage was in the western *High Noon*. The sheriff of a small town was destined to face three outlaws arriving on the noon train, who had sworn to kill him. The tick of the clock counted the fleeting hours, minutes and seconds as even his friends deserted him. The inexorable march of time was reflected in the editing of the film—cut from beginning to end to the beat of the metronome—whose tempo was gradually increased as the story progressed. *High Noon* was probably the first American sound film edited to the rhythms of metric montage, and its effect on the average viewer in the United States was electrifying.

TONAL EDITING

Tonal editing is actually a lighting concept in which succeeding scenes are gradually lightened or darkened to correspond to an improving or deteriorating situation in the story. In Eisenstein's film *October* the deteriorating condition of the workers under the Czarist regime was reflected in the gradual darkening of the tonality of each succeeding scene until there came the fury of revolution. After the revolution the workers' alleged joy was reflected in an immediate lightening of tonality.

DIALECTICAL EDITING

Dialectical editing originated as an attempt by the Russians to impose philosophical principles upon cinematic form. Dialectical editing presents a series of mass movements from scene to scene in a given direction, which is visually opposed by a single thrust of opposition, to yield a third meaning of "conflict." This is, of course, the Marxian-Hegelian principle of thesis, antithesis, synthesis. In Eisenstein's "Odessa steps sequence" in *Battleship Potemkin* the relentless march of the murdering cossacks down the stairs was countervailed by a pleading woman holding up her child, and other brief flurries of opposition, to create an emotional third meaning of the futility of appeals to humane feeling under the Czarist regime. The principles of dialectical editing are universally used in war films to reflect the sweep, ebb and flow of mass battle between opposing armies.

LINKAGE

Linkage as an editing concept was developed by another Russian director, V. I. Pudovkin. Linkage defines the individual scene in a film as being analogous to the bricks in a building—without intrinsic meaning until assembled by the film editor. When edited, however, the scenes acquire a *cumulative meaning*, a concept related to the montage. The theory of linkage further holds that symphonies of visual beauty may be edited together regardless of the ugliness of the scenes used to create that beauty. Linkage is the montage concept carried to the extreme, the antithesis of narrative editing, and is most often used today in tone-poem and experimental films, or in dreamy montage sequences within a narrative film.

5

The Punctuation of Sound

Sound accompanied films long before the advent of sound tracks. The early silent dramatic flickers were often released with a musical score for piano and orchestra: soft melodies to accompany the love scenes, minor-key tremolos to warn of a nearby villain, and great crescendos to bolster the hero as he raced toward the climax. And if the theater was equipped with a Mighty Wurlitzer organ, the patter of raindrops, the clatter of horses' hooves, the rumble of lightning and thunder, could be suggested by a touch upon the organ's keys and pedals. Further attempts to link sound with image were made by recording voices and music on records and attempting to synchronize them manually, attempts that proved impracticable. Then, in 1927, Warner Brothers released *The Jazz Singer*, the first dramatic film with an optical sound track that physically integrated dialogue, music and sound effects, synchronized with the images on the screen, and a new dimension was created that has steadily grown in importance to film and television.

Although the art of the film is essentially visual, the need for sound to enhance and complement the images on the screen—for emotional enrichment and realism—seemed present from the outset in the viewer.

The first dramatic sound films were "All-talking, All-singing, All-dancing"—a cacophony of raw sounds that soon proved as dull as photographing the complete dramatic actions of a stage play. Moreover, the unselective reproduction of reality in sound had as unreal an effect in cinema as raw, unedited scenes. Sounds, it was gradually realized, had to be selected and recorded for the roles they were to play at a given point in the film. Voices, music and sound effects should be included or left out according to their importance to the dramatic action they were intended to accompany, and superfluous or uninteresting sound, like unwanted film footage, should be dropped in the cutting room.

The possibilities of sound in film are infinitely variable because each of the component sound tracks—voices (dialogue and narration), music and sound effects—may be recorded separately and then "mixed" into one track afterwards. For example: The voice tracks may be recorded first under ideal circumstances in each dramatic scene, with control over sound perspective and movement. Then music tracks may be recorded, to match the cinematography and editing, under optimum circumstances for music. And then sound effects tracks, such as the squeal of tires or the bark of guns, may be recorded on location under the most realistic circumstances.

Later, in a sound mixing studio having maximum controls for each track, with electronic filters and other devices to modify the sound quality, the voice, music and effects tracks are combined into one sound track. The "sound mixer" controls the relative proportions and intensities of each track at each given point in the dramatic action to complement the image track. Although the cinema is a visually-dominant medium, its emotional and communication impact is the result of an orchestration of sight and sound, with each sound element taking its turn to fuse with the moving pictures, and becoming crucial at different phases of the film story. The artistic judgment of when one or the other of the sound elements will be accented is a matter of seasoning the sound stew to taste.

Sound Characteristics

All of the three basic sound tracks have uses and considerations in common which are of concern to the filmmaker. These are *fidelity, sound in character with the subject, perspective, sound movements, indistinct sounds* and *sound montages*.

FIDELITY

Fidelity is of primary importance in sound recording, particularly when recording voices and music. The average viewer may be influ-

TOYS ARE FUN IN '71. Dialogue sound recording. © *Hanna-Barbera Productions.*

enced to like or dislike a screen personality according to the properties of his voice. Where music is concerned, nearly everyone with normal hearing is exquisitely sensitive to tone quality; distortions of music intended to complement visuals may be almost physically painful to hear, and may ruin an otherwise excellent film. Sound effects are less critical, in most cases, but even here fidelity of recording can only be a virtue. The sound mixer may subsequently decide to depart from realism through distortions of faithfully recorded sounds, but if the original recording is itself distorted, he may be out of luck.

SOUND IN CHARACTER WITH THE SUBJECT

Sounds should have audio textures in character with the subject. Rooster Cogburn of *True Grit* growled, rumbled and spat his way through every human relationship like the rough-hewn gunfighter he was. Jenny Cavalera in *Love Story* spoke in low, soft, mellifluous tones, even when she swore, to reflect the gentle womanly human being she really was. Rooster's voice never had a soft edge, and Jenny's voice was never raspy. The mixer in a sound studio can manipulate the audio textures of the dialogue of each person to reflect his role in the film, through the use of electronic filters and other devices.

PERSPECTIVE

Perspective is as much an element of sound as of picture. A full shot of a man speaking ten feet from the camera must not have the sound quality of a voice spoken ten inches from the camera or it may lose its credibility. Whether the scene records a subject in extreme closeup or from the distance of an establishing shot, the perspective of the sound should be proportionate to the distance of the subject from the camera.

SOUND MOVEMENTS

Sounds move with their subjects. As a screen character moves toward or away from the camera, or laterally across the screen, the sounds of his voice must seem to progressively move in relation to the camera. Moreover, the sound movements should reflect the environment through which the subject is moving. If two persons are trying to talk while walking through a crowd at a football game as the quarterback is passing for a touchdown, the two must be seen and heard as if trying to speak up over the shouts of the spectators. If they are talking in normal conversational tones while the background shouts are merely turned down in volume, the effect will be patently false to the viewer.

INDISTINCT SOUNDS

Indistinct sound is intended to reflect the realism of life itself. Indistinct sound is acceptable when presenting unimportant dialogue in distant perspective, evocative music or atmospheric sound effects. Dialogue or narration that carries important content, however, should be distinct enough to be clearly understood without straining. Any time the viewer has to consciously work at trying to perceive some aspect of the presentation, his reservoir of patience begins to drain away. Indistinct sound plays a functional role in supportive sound, but in communicative dialogue and narration the words should ring out clearly.

SOUND MONTAGES

The sound montage is the audio counterpart of the visual montage: a sound montage comprises snatches of dialogue, narration, music and sound effects whose sum total meaning is different from its component elements. In *The Magnificent Ambersons*, for example, the confusion of the great family upon the death of the grandfather was reflected in a sound montage containing snatches of worried phrases, weeping, shouting, recriminations, slamming doors, running footsteps and so forth, none of which had intrinsic value, yet the third meaning of the sound montage was understandable—pandemonium. The sound montage is most often used in this way to a stream-of-consciousness effect.

Each of the major sound elements—*narration, dialogue, music* and *sound effects*—has acquired certain usages in the language of cinema.

Narration

Narration is a voice-over-visuals concept in which an unseen speaker discusses and explains what the viewer sees on the screen. Narration is most often used in documentary and educational films because it is a straightforward informational technique that is inexpensive, easy to do and may be added to the visuals after the film has been edited. Narration is added to the edited film primarily to serve the following functions:

To add relevant, verbal information to the visual information seen on the screen. A documentary film about refugees from Pakistan being fed in India might include such verbal information that the food was contributed by the United Nations.

To clarify some visual relationship that requires verbal interpretation. A sequence showing an oceanography vessel with a drilling rig, sonar equipment and computers—all three operating in split-screen unison—would require narration to explain that they are not drilling for oil, but are core drilling the surface of the sea bed to measure its age.

To relate what the viewer is looking at to what he has already seen. A how-to-do-it film on the assembly of a jet engine might, near the conclusion of the film, refer back to a technique introduced earlier, to explain the relationship between past and present visual processes.

When one of these three functions is not being served, the sound track is better given over to music or sound effects. Garrulous narration tracks often permeate educational film and television presentations, primarily because the producers cannot stand to let the visuals speak for themselves. The result is that many viewers turn off the programs; or, if trapped in a classroom, their minds depart for happier places and leave an unoccupied body to stare with glazed corneas at the babbling screen.

Visual presentation of an educational or documentary subject should *precede* the narration. The viewer must see what the subject is before he hears any explanations, or the words may slide in one ear and out the other with scarcely a pause. Viewers tend to forget what they hear unless they can relate it to something they *see* or already know. Some filmmakers feel that they will pique the interest of the viewers by feeding them information before presenting the content visually. If the intent is only that of transitional entertainment to arouse their interest, and the content of the introductory information is unimportant, fine. But if the content is to be remembered—the picture should precede the narration.

Narration should be written to be heard, not read. It is the ear, not the eye that counts, and narration should be tried aloud and revised until it comes trippingly on the tongue and is easily understood when heard. The active voice is preferable to the passive, and simple declarative sentences make the best sense. Certain forms common in written prose ought to be scrupulously avoided: convoluted sentence structure; highly involved clauses; exotic words and obscure phraseology; and language style that is out of character with the film, such as iambic pentameter in a film about welding. Simplicity, lucidity and euphony are the hallmarks of good narration. The words and sentences should be revised until they are easy to speak, pleasant to hear, and simple to understand.

Labeling what the viewer can see for himself is a bane of narration that seems to haunt educational film and television programs. One film about Mexico currently being distributed to elementary schools included the following gem: The opening scene revealed a little Mexican boy leading his donkey through an adobe village. The narrator said, "This is a little Mexican boy leading his donkey through an adobe village."

Other mistakes to avoid in writing narration are these: bleeding copy, in which content belonging exclusively to a given sequence is allowed to slop over into a following sequence which introduces something new; statistical information, in which facts and figures are shot into the air to ricochet off the viewer's eardrums and be remembered by virtually no one; verbal descriptions of subjects that never appear visually on the screen; purple prose, in which a humble subject is treated with verbal majesty; humorous remarks made by someone who is not a humorist; extravagant claims and statements unsupported by corroborating visual evidence; the trumpeted finale, a summary repeated ad nauseum after the film has reached its logical conclusion; and the loaded sound track, saturated with more information than a viewer can absorb at a sitting, because the sponsor or educator is determined to get his money's worth.

Narration Styles

Narration can take any of several stylistic forms to complement the subject and the intended behavioral purpose of the film. The major kinds of narrative style that have evolved include *lyric free verse, personal narrative, subjective microphone, direct appeal, descriptive* and *instructional forms.*

LYRIC FREE VERSE

The lyric free verse style is best suited to subjects with an epic or poetic quality. But it must be used only at a time when the people are in the right emotional state to receive it. If used during a period when the mood of the people is coldly pragmatic, lyric free verse is likely to evoke laughter. A good example of lyric free verse narration used in the right kind of film at the right time in history was *The River*, the classic documentary produced during the pit of the Depression in the thirties. This film told the history of the erosive rape of the soil in the Mississippi

Valley and made a passionate appeal to save the land and the people living on it with ringing lyric free verse. It began:

> From as far West as Idaho,
>> Down from the glacier peaks of the Rockies—
> From as far East as New York,
>> Down from the turkey ridges of the Alleghenies—
> Down from Minnesota, twenty-five hundred miles,
>> The Mississippi River runs to the Gulf.
> Carrying every drop of water that flows down two-thirds the
>>> continent,
>> Carrying every brook and rill,
>> Rivulet and creek,
> Carrying all the rivers that run down two-thirds the continent,
>> The Mississippi runs to the Gulf of Mexico.

Lyric free verse narration finds other uses in sentimental tone poem films, experimental films and historical films having an epic quality.

PERSONAL NARRATIVE

The personal narrative form harkens back to the *minnesinger* and storyteller. The narrator speaks as if the film presented on the screen were a projection of his own memories of things past. Some dramatic films begin with a voice-over narrative to fill in background on the story to follow, and then change to dialogue. In *The Summer of '42* the recounting of a boy's introduction to sexual love in the arms of a suddenly widowed woman began with the voice of the boy, now grown to manhood, reminiscing about those bygone summer holidays in the buttery sun of the island.

The personal narrative form is also used in documentary and educational films to give history the feeling and intimacy of personal experience, as in the Indian legend of *The Loon's Necklace*:

> One year snow and bitter winds ushered in the coldest
> winter the village had ever known.
> Our hunters returned with empty hands.
> They told of much hunting, but little game.
> And so it was day after day.
> The women mourned their starving children.

SUBJECTIVE MICROPHONE

The subjective microphone technique is a kind of voice-over sound montage in which several points-of-view are expressed by different persons who chime in, one after another, to present a cross-section of opinion. This technique originated during the great days of radio and carried over into the sound tracks of documentary films produced during World War II. *The True Glory*, an epic historical film which recounted the Allied assault on Hitler's Festung Europa, used the subjective microphone technique throughout to allow soldiers, sailors, marines, pilots, officers and enlisted men—those who did the fighting—to express their feelings about the invasion and the war. They joked, laughed and swore in words and phrases, snips of sentences, which added up to a montage of courage, humor and high resolution.

DIRECT APPEAL

The direct appeal is essentially a call for action directed at the viewer, usually in terms of his life space. This narrative form is a one-to-one message from the narrator to the viewer asking that he do something immediately. Anyone who has ever watched a television commercial and listened to fear appeals ("Don't risk the lives of your loved ones by driving with worn-out wiper blades") or reassurance appeals ("You can trust your car to the man who wears the star") will not fail to recognize the one-to-one relationship of the direct appeal. During wartime the direct appeal may be used in documentary films as a clarion call to arms. This is the most commonly used narration form when trying to evoke a simple behavioral response: Join the army. Vote for Proposition A. Contribute to the college of your choice.

DESCRIPTIVE NARRATION

The descriptive narration style is used to add ancillary verbal information to the visual statement on the screen. A documentary film about the business of heroin may show a scene of an "ounce man" walking down the street, while describing his relationship to the smuggling syndicate and explaining how he cuts the drugs to smaller proportions, seals them in their typical white plastic packets and wholesales them to the street pusher. An educational film about forest genetics would employ descriptive narration in a similar way, adding verbal information to the images of the animated film sequence:

> Traits of interest in forest genetics are sometimes governed by a single gene pair—one gene being received on a chromosome from each parent. . . . The dominant color gene A-1, A-1 causes the pine seedling on the left to be dark green.

INSTRUCTIONAL NARRATION

Instructional narration consists of unabashedly nuts-and-bolts directions on how to implement some process—weld stainless steel, do a chemistry experiment, assemble a jet engine, thread a film chain, light a television studio. This form of narration is the purview of those filmmakers who have a student audience willing to sit through anything to learn the skill or process being taught by the film or television presentation. The desired virtue in instructional narration is clarity.

Dialogue

Dialogue is the second sound mode. Dialogue is lip-synchronous, simultaneously seen and heard, and intended to be credible as realistic conversations between the characters living out a dramatic story. In screen dialogue the viewer usually remains a third party to the story, eavesdropping into other lives, and is seldom addressed directly on a one-to-one basis, as in television narration.

Dialogue is intended to be acceptable to the viewer as true to real life. Real-life conversations, however, seldom have dramatic quality or content, but are filled with superfluous comments, jokes, complaints, and are peppered with incomplete phrases and sentences, many of which would not make sense in a dramatic film. "Realism" in screen terms means reducing dialogue to the absolute minimum by saying as much as possible with visuals. Only those concepts that are intrinsically verbal and cannot readily be said with images are expressed as dialogue.

Screen dialogue has three important functions, which are the same as those given in August Thomas' dictum about stage dialogue: "A line must *advance the story, develop character*, or *get a laugh*." One additional function of film dialogue is to enhance *continuity*.

STORY ADVANCEMENT

Advancing the story means using dialogue as exposition. In the *Andromeda Strain* a deadly virus accidentally brought back to earth from outer space suddenly began to mutate, a process of change that would make no sense visually to a lay viewer unless explained in dialogue, as it was, by one of the scientists in the story. The daily soap operas on television are drenched with exposition carried in dialogue so that housewives may go about their daily tasks while listening to, rather than watching, them. (These serial dramas are really radio with pictures rather than cinema.)

Dialogue exposition is usually heaviest at the beginning of a drama in order to present the theme of the story, to explain the events that lead up to joining of the conflict and to give a brief history of the protagonist. In *Lust for Life* Norman Corwin summed up in expository dialogue the history of failures by Vincent Van Gogh, when that creative soul tried to become a missionary, his last attempted career before becoming an artist. The opening sequence depicts his rejection by the missionary board in two minutes of dialogue that reveal ten years of failures:

DULL GRAY-YELLOW OF A MANILA FOLDER:
Lay Missionary Committee
Application of:
VINCENT VAN GOGH
October 1878
CAMERA STARTS TO PULL BACK, as we hear—

BOKMA (O.S.)
This is the case I mentioned to you . . .

PIETERSEN'S VOICE (O.S.)
He's been waiting all day. . . . In fairness to him, I don't think we should put it off any longer.

By now, CAMERA HAS PULLED BACK to disclose a conference table, around which sit four lay members of the Belgian Committee of Evangelization: DE JONG and VAN DEN BRINK: DR. BOKMA, a small wiry man sitting opposite them; and PIETERSEN, obviously chairman of the group.

PIETERSEN
(*to Bokma, indicating the folder*)
Dr. Bokma, are you going to stand by this report?

BOKMA
(*with conscientious care*)

I'm afraid I must. His classwork is wholly unsatisfactory.
His speech is poor; his dress is careless. He is arrogant
and headstrong; he resents criticism . . .

VAN DEN BRINK

What's his history?

DE JONG
(*consulting the folder*)

Discharged from a clerkship in Paris . . . failed at teaching
in England . . . left a job in a bookstore . . .

BOKMA
(*summing it up*)

A wanderer . . .

Dialogue exposition may serve a number of other purposes. It may
be used to explain the movements of characters not present in a given
scene, to describe other locales, other times, other places and other
events, although these expository functions are often served by the cutaway or the flashback.

CHARACTER DEVELOPMENT

The development of character is a second function of dialogue.
Until a person speaks, the viewer does not really know what to make
of him in terms of his personality, attitudes, occupation, educational
background and socioeconomic milieu. This is particularly true in judging males. The old axiom, "A man may look like a bum and be a
gentleman, but if a woman looks like a tramp, she's a tramp," may no
longer hold true with regard to women; but in sizing up a man, appearance *is* less important than his qualities revealed in actions and dialogue. What a screen character says in his interrelationships with other
screen characters reveals what kind of person he is at the beginning, and
what kind of person he becomes at the end.

Moreover, dialogue reveals the emotional condition of a character
at any point in the drama. The histrionics of emotional expression used
during the silent-film days have been replaced by the eloquence of a
few, and sometimes a single word. A simple "yes" or "no" may be
spoken with a range of expression that renders the gamut of human

emotions, and explains the relationship of one character to all other characters. A single word, used in conjunction with a graphic visual, may reveal who a character is, what he wants and where he is going at that point in the dramatic film. All speech is shaped by the person's emotional state. When happy, he speaks buoyantly. When sad, he speaks quietly and hesitantly. When angry, he speaks with staccato rapidity. When composed, he speaks quietly, with complete sentences.

GETTING A LAUGH

Getting a laugh in dialogue is a third function of drama. Humorous dialogue, which is difficult to write because humorists are born and not made, is needed in a dramatic film to relieve tension in the viewer. If a long suspense film is produced without occasional comic relief, inner tension may build up in the viewer to the point where he will laugh hilariously when a character is skewered with a stilleto or a man and woman are tenderly making love. Getting a laugh in humorous films will be discussed at length in the chapter on "The Comedy and the Musical."

CONTINUITY

Continuity may be enhanced through the use of the *dialogue hook*. A dialogue hook consists of repeating a key word or phrase in character-to-character exchanges to subtly impress an important clue upon the viewer. These verbal echoes may be as long as a sentence or as short as a single word:

"I will never sell this place."
"Never sell?"
"Never."

The use of repeated questions is a variant of the dialogue hook used to enhance interest, a technique that plays upon the curiosity of the viewer:

"Where have you been until two in the morning?"
" Out."
"Out where?"

"Out visiting a friend."
"What friend?"
"An old friend."
"A male friend or a female friend?"

If the question is answered with a question, it adds the element of confrontation, a touch of defiance:

"Where have you been until two in the morning?"
"What business is that of yours?"
"Don't you think I have a right to know?"
"What makes you think you have the right to know?"
"Aren't you playing verbal games to be evasive?"

The *soliloquy*, a long delivery of solitary dialogue, was early attempted in dramatic sound films, usually in closeup, but was generally discarded as pretentious and destructive of cinematic time—an attempt to impose the conventions of the theater on the cinema.

The television soliloquy, however, seems to have a slightly different impact on the viewer. A filmed soliloquy that aroused impatience when seen in the movie theater may become acceptable on its television rerun. In *Guess Who's Coming to Dinner* long passages of windy dialogue laden with social significance (tolerable primarily because its content was on the side of the angels) became credible when seen on television, in flat contradiction to its effect in the large-screen theater. The difference in acceptability may be simply a matter of screen size. A face in closeup on a forty-foot theatrical screen is gigantic, often repelling, while on a television screen it nearly approximates life size. It appears that dramatic films and videotapes made solely for television release may sustain far more dialogue, including soliloquies, than can their theatrical forms.

The function of dialogue in motion pictures is to reveal dramatic facts that cannot be rendered visually. Dialogue must have the effect of realism in telling the story, revealing character, arousing humor and enhancing continuity, but must do so selectively. If it wanders from its lean and functional role to become an end in itself, or to become truly "realistic"—a mishmash of mumbles and verbiage—it may stop the flow of drama dead in its tracks. Dialogue should contain only the words and phrases needed to implement the cinematic story and all else should be ruthlessly blue-penciled. Edited screen dialogue should be weightless and move as lightly and swiftly as all other elements of cinema.

Music

Music is a third sound mode. Completed musical scores are less readily manipulated than are dialogue and sound effects. For this reason, music is usually composed after the editing of the film to complement the moods and tempo of the story, the cinematography and the editing. The practice is to carry a film to the fine-cut stage, then bring in a composer.

Two exceptions to the rule of images first and sound afterwards are the animated film and the musical. In animation the music is composed and recorded first. The music is then measured in terms of frames of film and the information written down on bar sheets. The animators work from the written bar sheets, and the finished animated film matches the music to the frame. In musicals, of course, the characters are filmed singing and dancing to the rhythms of the music, which requires the precedence of completely recorded musical scores.

Original music for films is unique in the sense that it is conceived and composed to support the cinematography, editing and story content, and is not intended to stand alone as music. This has not prevented many film themes and scores from becoming widely popular and being recognized as fine music on their intrinsic merits, but this is seldom the intent at the time of genesis. Music is composed for film to make such dramatic contributions as development of *character themes, locale themes, moods, tempo, continuity, dramatic emphasis, premonition, commentary, satire, humor, transitions*, and to add *information*.

CHARACTER THEMES

Character themes are widely used to identify a certain person in a film, such as the now-famous "Lara's Theme" in the historical film *Dr. Zhivago*. Once the strains of a theme have been identified with a given character, it may be played in almost any setting and circumstance in the film to arouse a haunting memory. Whenever Dr. Zhivago rode to meet his mistress, remembered her, wrote about her, won her, lost her, suffered a heart attack at a glimpse of her in the crowd, the music track swelled with "Lara's Theme." The same principle applies to less savory characters: Komarovsky, in the same film, had a minor-key theme with a harshly grating quality to echo his existence, visually present or not. The use of a minor chord to imply a menacing presence is, of course, universal.

Locale Themes

Locale themes orient the viewer and evoke memories of things past in a certain setting. The Texas western has its harmonica rendition of "Red River Valley," and the New York eastern has its rollicking strains of "Lullaby of Broadway." Once music has been introduced as relating to a given locale, it may be played again later in the film, usually over a melancholy closeup, to echo the memories of other times, other places, other people.

Moods

The mood of a sequence or an entire film may be created by its music. The coronation of a king may be rendered as a farce or an event of majesty by its musical accompaniment. Laughter and joy on the screen may be chilled by an undercurrent of implied musical menace. The death of a man may be made hilarious if accompanied by jolly music, as in Hitchcock's macabre jest *The Trouble with Harry*. An exquisite use of mood music was Burt Bacharach's "Raindrops Keep Fallin' on My Head" in *Butch Cassidy and the Sundance Kid*, in which the essentially childlike and charming character of Butch was dramatized in mood music as he clowned around on that symbol of the encroachment of civilization, the bicycle.

The moods of music sometimes go far afield and exist almost independent of the image track, yet affect it, if only through counterpoint. Some Europeans, such as Ingmar Bergman, are given to using classical music to accompany the major sequences of their films. The dignity of the music enhances the dignity of the film and transfers a degree of its prestige, regardless of the intrinsic cinematic merit of that film. Communist filmmakers in general, and the East Germans in particular, make a fetish of using classical music to dignify ideological concepts.

TEMPO

The tempo function, an extension of mood music, is intended to complement fast-moving dramatic actions seen on the screen. The confused sequences of desperate aerial combat in *The Blue Max*, the hot pursuits of a thousand and one westerns, the pratfalls of comedians from Mack Sennett to the present, have been accompanied by fast-moving music. Climactic sequences seem to be those in which dynamic music can contribute most to the dramatic impact without drawing attention to itself. And the editing of these scenes is frequently done in close conjunction with the sound track in order to carefully play picture against sound for heightened tempo.

BUTCH CASSIDY AND THE SUNDANCE KID. Raindrops keep falling. *20th Century-Fox.*

CONTINUITY

Continuity music may tie together a series of unrelated scenes, such as a montage depicting travel, a search or a long period of time. The music then reflects the spirit of the dramatic action, and proceeds continuously and more or less independently of the subjects' movements. In *Butch Cassidy and the Sundance Kid* the relentless pressures of the law and the tightening grip of civilization drove the two main characters to a decision to take their girl and go to Bolivia, which was still primitive enough for them to live the old outlaw life. Mr. Bacharach's continuity music tied together the travel sequence as they fled the Old West to New York, through the boat trip to South America, to Bolivia—eight thousand miles covered in a few minutes, tied together with music of immense charm.

DRAMATIC EMPHASIS

Dramatic emphasis is the most pervading use of music in a theatrical film. A single word or phrase in the story, or even a noise, may be loaded with content significance that could be missed by some of the viewers if not underscored with an orchestral crescendo. This was once done to excess in Hollywood films. The heavy-handed use of music to complement each and every crisis, typical of many tear-jerking motion pictures made around World War II, is far less common today; the television reruns of these older films are often accompanied by derisive laughter from viewers at the way each turn of the head was accompanied by violins. Recently the trend has been away from the insipid slathering of music over an entire film; in most dramas, dialogue and sound effects are used throughout and the musical emphasis is saved for intense crises.

Music for dramatic emphasis may be used in documentary and educational films. In *Thursday's Children* a moment of achievement occurred when a deaf-mute boy managed to speak a word he had never heard—"bath." As he deserved, the victory was commemorated by a triumphant trill on the flute.

PREMONITION

Premonition music warns of things to come. The doomed sweethearts of *The Diary of Anne Frank* talked happily about their prospects for a postwar future, while heavy Teutonic premonition music promised only the gas chambers of a concentration camp. Almost every war and western film signals impending battle with the enemy by premonition music commonly recognized by the viewer as identified with a national or racial entity. And virtually every film in which a doomed character makes plans for the future seems to have a menacing chord to punctuate his dreams, pluck the heartstrings of the viewer and announce that his hopes can never be.

COMMENTARY

Commentative music is a ballad whose words give expression to feelings and ideas having no visual counterpart. It is most often used to introduce the theme of a film, to express the inner thoughts of a character or to make a satirical comment on one of the characters. The cynical theme of the comedy-western *Waterhole #3* was expressed in a song whose refrain chanted, "Do *it* unto others, before they do *it* unto you." In *I Walk the Line*, in which a middle-aged sheriff was torn between his passion for a nubile young woman and his duty to a dowdy wife, his inner thoughts were crooned softly in a ballad sung to accompany his pensive face. Satirical commentary reached a new high in *The Graduate* when a chorus jeered its contempt at the middle-aged woman having an affair with Benjamin: "Mrs. Robinson." Commentative music is increasingly used in lieu of stream-of-consciousness dialogue spoken over a silent closeup.

SATIRE, HUMOR, TRANSITIONS, INFORMATION

Music may be used in several other ways: for *satire*, as when scenes of Hitler's armies resting beside a road in a documentary film were accompanied by the distorted strains of Brahm's "Lullaby"; for *humor*, to mimic the walk or pretensions of a screen character, for example; for *transitions* from one related sequence to another; for *information*, as when using authentic Navajo music in an educational film or television program about some aspect of that Indian culture. No description can encompass all the nuances and ramifications of the contributions that a skilled film composer can make to a film. Except for the musical, however, or sequences in which music becomes an end in itself, this element of the cinema carries only one stricture—music should be felt rather than consciously heard.

Realism is better served in some documentary and dramatic films with a minimal use of music, and that reserved for emotional crescendos. In *Murphy's War*, a story of one man's revenge on a German submarine, virtually the entire film story was told in the cold realism of dialogue and sound effects. Only the two emotional high points of the film—the machine-gunning of a helpless British crew in the water (the first conflict), and Murphy's sinking of the submarine, while killing himself (the climax)—had musical accompaniment to reinforce their dramatic magnitude. The lack of music in other parts of the film gave it multiple impact at those two points.

Sound Effects

Sound effects are the fourth sound mode and serve the primary function of enhancing realism, complementing and completing the viewer's understanding of what he sees on the screen. The sight of a door slamming shut is fused with the sound of a door slamming shut. The sight of a dog barking is synchronized with the sounds of a dog barking. Sound effects can serve many other functions, however, that transcend realism. Some of these are *to extend the limits of what is seen, to create mood, to imply nonexistent locations, to create sound effects montages* and *to "create" silence.*

EXTENDING VISUAL LIMITS

Sound effects may be used to imply all kinds of activities happening just beyond the periphery of the screen. A scene of a housewife working in a small kitchen may be expanded through the sounds of children running and toys banging in an unseen playroom, a television set droning in the family room, the hammer of pipes as a plumber repairs a leak in the basement, and the distant roar of a lawnmower, certifying that the man-of-the-house is implementing his wife's orders—all extensions of reality created by sound effects. The viewer is led by sound to believe that what he sees on the screen is only a small part of a big screen world just beyond.

CREATING MOOD

The mood function of sound effects is important in suspense films: the maniacal cry of a loon streaking over a mist-shrouded lake; the quiet tread of footsteps and the creak of an opening door in a supposedly empty house; unexplained noises and objects rattling; wind shrieking like a calliope as it plays over the rusted metal screen runners of an abandoned factory; the bark of a distant fox heard from the warm fringe of a campfire. The unexplained sounds of the unseen seem to touch some atavistic fear of the unknown; an unidentified sound must be seen and certified as harmless before we can relax. This human survival instinct can be manipulated by the clever filmmaker to create mood and suspense.

IMPLYING NONEXISTENT LOCATIONS

Nonexistent locations may be implied by the clever use of sound effects, a common practice in dramatic film to obviate the need for expensive filming with a crew and cast on distant locations. For example: There is a small pond on the MGM production lot which is fringed by rushes and surrounded by trees, with a small sand beach. That pond has been the "tropical location" for productions ranging from the Tarzan films of the thirties to the jungle warfare films of the seventies, with the locale implied by the sound effects of exotic birds and howler monkeys, machine-gun fire and the curses of the enemy shouted in foreign tongues. That pond, conveniently located in Los Angeles, has seen more marine assaults than any beachhead of any war in the world.

This use applies also to interiors. A "factory sequence," for example, may be set up in one corner of a sound stage and equipped with a workbench, tools, blueprints, etc. By adding a sound track with the throb and rattle of punch presses, drill presses, lathes—all conveniently recorded at a real factory with a light portable tape recorder—that sequence will appear to be authentically produced at a factory, without incurring the high costs of location filming.

CREATING SOUND EFFECTS MONTAGES

The sound effects montage is tied to memories, fears, emotions. In *I Never Sang for My Father* a middle-aged man ruminated over the political career of his near-great father, now old and forgotten by the city whose mayor he had been; and as he talked with the young woman who was his bedroom playmate, the effects track carried the faraway sounds of parades, shouts, unintelligible speeches and applause, the cacophony of a last hurrah expressed through a sound effects montage saturated with ineluctable nostalgia.

"CREATING" SILENCE

Silence, too, is sound, and sometimes a blessing. If a dramatic film has been orchestrated throughout, as was the romantic film *Dr. Zhivago*, high points of drama are sometimes prefaced by a moment of total silence. The contrast of dead quiet to the previous busyness of the sound track alerts the viewer to the imminence of an important dramatic action. Silence finds a similar expressive use in documentary films. In *Thursday's Children*, an exquisite British film about the education of deaf children, their disability was given cinematic form by presenting a closeup of their teacher's lips as she spoke to her class, while gradually turning the volume of her voice down to nothingness as her lips continued to speak. After a moment of silence, the narrator said, "But the children do not hear—"

6

Videotape and Film: The New Synthesis

Magnetic tape recording has been used for decades for professional and personal sound recording, but few persons at first considered the possibility that a strip of opaque, oxide-coated, rust-colored material could be used to render a visual image. Then, in the early 1950s, Bing Crosby Enterprises startled the communications world by announcing that they had developed a method of tape-recording visual signals that could be played back on a television monitor; they used eleven video signals and a tape that moved at the high speed of 100 inches per second (i.p.s.). Quick to follow was RCA with a videotape unit of simpler recording and playback design, but with an even higher and more impractical speed of 360 i.p.s., which required a reel 17 inches in diameter for 4 minutes of television time.

Meanwhile, the Ampex Corporation was developing a videotape recorder based upon a different principle: the recording and playback head moved in conjunction with the videotape, reducing the need for high-speed tape movements to get a video signal and the necessity for huge reels to record a program. Videotape now offered certain advantages over film: picture and sound could be recorded and played back immediately, without laboratory costs, work prints, processing delays or mishaps in delivery—thus videotape was a practical medium for time-short television.

In November, 1956, CBS presented the first regularly scheduled videotape program: *Douglas Edwards and the News.* Videotape soon began to be adopted for recording television news programs, documentaries, panel discussion shows, comedy hours and musicals, where cinematic editing techniques were unnecessary. Use of the new medium then spread to schools, industries and government agencies where its low material costs and immediate playback capabilities soon proved advantageous. Recent production and technical developments, combining the best of videotape production techniques with the best of cinema, now promise the development of a new medium: Video-Film.

Videotape and the Viewer

It makes little difference to the average television viewer how the program he is enjoying may have been originally produced. He may watch a videotape program and think it is a live performance, a live performance and believe it is videotape, a videotape and think it is film. The average viewer could not care less whether the program he enjoys is live, filmed or on videotape, since it is presented essentially in the language of cinema he has always known. The original form of production, however, makes a great deal of difference to the professional, since the techniques and technology of film and videotape differ in several fundamental ways. The ways in which a videotape production differs from a film production derive from the strictures in technique imposed by electronic production facilities.

Studio Recording Facilities

Television studio production facilities resemble a hybrid of motion picture and radio facilities. In the staging area the production set appears to have the accoutrements of a motion picture studio. Huge lights hang from ceiling grids. Scenery flats, roll drops and traveling curtains surround the area. Huge cameras face the staging area from three directions. Sound control batting covers the studio walls and ceiling. Adjacent to the staging area, however, is a distinctly noncinema control room which resembles a glorified radio control room. There is the usual audio control panel, but in addition there are several television viewing monitors, a communications system between the control room and the staging area, and a video switcher which serves as the means of recording and editing a videotape while the performance is taking place in the staging area.

Videotapes produced in a television studio have certain production characteristics imposed upon them by the nature of the electronic facilities used. The facilities that modify the interpretation of the subject are *electronic cameras, staging areas* and the *control room*, with its camera-switching and monitoring facilities.

Electronic Cameras

From one to four electronic cameras are running continuously during any given program. Each television camera is connected by an electronic cable to the control units in the control room, and to its power supply. Although each camera is mounted on wheels so it can be moved from one camera position to another while the show is in progress, it is mobile only to the limits of its umbilical power cord. Each camera is equipped with a viewing monitor (actually a small television receiver) which enables the cameraman to see the image his camera is viewing and putting out and to compose the images of the subjects. The operator of each camera in the staging area wears a receiving set over his ears which enables him to receive spoken commands from the director (in the control room) instructing him as to what subject he should pick up, where he should position his camera in relation to the performers and how he should compose his subject. In practice, all camera positions are worked out in relation to the performers and marked on the floor of the staging area during rehearsals.

In a studio production involving three cameras it is common today for each camera to be equipped with a variable focal-length or zoom lens. These lenses vary over at least a ten-to-one ratio. The optical properties of these lenses are the same for videotape as they are for motion pictures.

Electronic photography for videotape requires the same principles of composition and perception as does motion picture cinematography. First to catch the viewer's gaze are movements by the subject, the camera and the lens. Light areas are visually dominant over dark areas; sharply defined subjects over softly defined subjects; foreground activity over background activity; brighter over duller colors, and so forth, in both media. Lenses of any given focal length render a subject with the same degree of fidelity or distortion on both videotape and film. And the points-of-view used to interpret a subject—objective, subjective and performer's—are identical in their connotations to those discussed in "The Grammar of Cinematography."

The lighting units for videotape production are essentially the same as those used for film, except that they are hung from battens on ceiling sky hooks in deference to the presence of three cameras (a floor light would surely be exposed by at least one of the cameras). Illumination levels can be set much lower for videotape than for film because of the greater sensitivity of electronic media to light. Often it is possible to do without fill lights to give a subject a rounded form, or rim lights to set forth the subject from his background, because the ambient illumination of the studio lights is sufficient to render the subject legibly. The positioning of lights is important in multiple-camera techniques because a closeup, a medium shot and an establishing shot may be composed respectively on three studio cameras, each of which is facing the subject from a different direction.

A continuing possible complication to the movements of the performers and the cameras is the sound man with his fishpole microphone. In more than one television program the sound man has been revealed through the presence of a microphone shadow, or even the microphone itself, dipping down from the top of the television screen.

STAGING AREAS

The studio staging area of a network videotape production usually has three to four adjacent sets, representing different rooms of a home or office, to provide the illusion of location change from one dramatic sequence to the next. Smaller studios, such as those found in universities and educational television stations, seldom have more than a single set staging area, in which the scenery is changed between every major sequence of a production. In both kinds of setups compositional deference is paid to the presence of three mobile cameras: dramatic movements by the performers must be blocked so that each camera has a clear field of view and freedom to move.

THE CONTROL ROOM

The control room where the program is recorded and edited usually has the following facilities:

Five *viewing monitors*, one for each of the three electronic cameras active in the staging area, plus a master monitor which reveals what is being recorded on videotape and a preview monitor. The preview monitor enables the director to see scenes that come from outside the studio staging area, such as films and slides, or images transmitted from a mobile van. The audio console is similar to that used in a radio control room, and is connected to the extensible fishpole microphone used in the staging area to follow the sounds of actors as they move.

The *video switcher* is the creative control center. It consists of a double row of buttons controlling the "on" or "off" recording relationship of each camera. A direct cut from one image to the other can be

Staging area. *Drawing by Glen Shimada.*

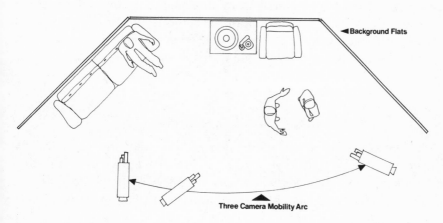

Control room. *Drawing by Glen Shimada.*

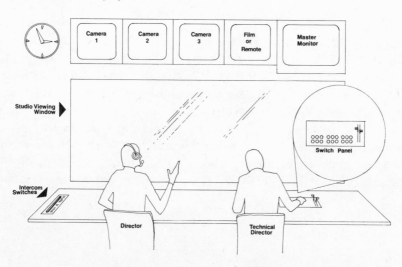

made by punching one of the "on" buttons. A dissolve can be created by using the fader control to change from one image to another. Not only may straight cuts and dissolves be made from one camera to another, but fades, wipes, special effects and superimposures as well. A superimposure may be achieved, for example, by throwing the fader between camera number 1 and camera number 2 only halfway, thereby electronically rendering both images simultaneously to be recorded on videotape.

The video switcher approach requires at least two persons at the video console to make and implement editorial decisions—the director and the technical director. The first is in charge of making creative decisions and issuing commands; the second is responsible for operating the control panel in response to those commands. During a recording session the director is simultaneously directing the moves of the three cameramen and their composition of the subjects and giving commands to the technical director to cut or dissolve from one camera to the other, while watching the five monitors and the performers.

Videotape Staging and Production

Videotape staging and production methods are characterized by *concurrent directing, photography and editing* of the videotape during the performances, and *continuous performances by the actors* during production. This production concept was originated by Desi Arnaz, using films, in the creation of *I Love Lucy*.

CONCURRENT DIRECTING, PHOTOGRAPHY AND EDITING

Concurrent directing, photography and editing of the videotape during the performance is at the heart of the video switcher approach. The production phases of directing, photography and editing, which are separate in cinema, are done simultaneously in videotape. The three studio cameras display their subjects on the monitors in the control room, beside the images of the preview monitor and the recording master monitor, and the director makes his selection of images for recording on videotape. He commands the technical director to cut or dissolve as he makes his artistic decisions. He is, in effect, editing the videotape as he goes along.

Whenever a cut or effect is created by the director and technical director, the effect is shown only on the master monitor. No change is noted on the camera monitor or preview monitor.

The program may be videotaped in dramatic sequences, with changes of scenery between takes, but the segments are essentially edited by the director while the performance progresses.

The dramatic action may move from the living room to the kitchen, for example, and the separate major sequences will later be spliced together. Perhaps the director may discover, during a playback, a closeup he does not like, or a bad reaction shot, and decide to restage and rephotograph that scene to be later edited into the master composite videotape. For the most part, however, the videotape produced by the video switcher approach is edited "on the board" and the master composite recording is essentially completed at the end of the performance.

CONTINUOUS PERFORMANCES

Continuous performances by the actors requires a directing and staging approach more closely resembling theater than cinema, and its advantages are many: The performers can play their parts spontaneously and intuitively, sensing their roles in relation to each other, the dramatic situation, the presence of the cameras and—in the case of comedies—the presence of a live audience. All this gives the performers the rapport and sense of timing found in the theater. For such television situation comedies as *All in the Family*, the natural laughter evoked from the audience is far more credible than any dubbed-in laugh track could ever be. Moreover, performance before a live audience lets everyone know whether he is indeed being funny, and modifications can be made during a second recording session and spliced into the master videotape. Because of the spontaneous rapport between cast and audience, the viewer senses the immediacy of the performance and feels himself a participant.

Careful blocking of action is required of cast and cameramen so that a given performer will be at a given position in the staging area at a time when a selected cameraman will have his electronic camera in the right place to photograph the actor's image. For the staging system to work, everyone associated with the production must memorize the script and the blocked action and learn where every move and pause is marked on the floor. Props are often used in preference to floor marks for the cast so the performer can move freely from point to point without having to glance down at the floor marks.

Dramatic sequences are usually rehearsed and recorded in short segments averaging five to ten minutes in length. If the performances are recorded in longer segments, then everyone has to memorize a great many more moves and positions, in addition to remembering the lines and giving a performance. Longer sequences tend to be error-prone, which leave the director with the options of having an unprofessional product or staging expensive retakes. Short sequences enable cast and crew to quickly make a new arrangement and setup between difficult parts, and to get past clumsy camera-performer relationships. When used properly, this segmented method preserves the spontaneity of the performance while enabling the producers to render an acceptable program on videotape.

NORMAN CORWIN PRESENTS. Blocking camera positions. *Group W Productions.*

IMMEDIATE FEEDBACK CAPABILITY

The immediate feedback capability of videotape offers important advantages during a tight shooting schedule. A given performance of a sequence may be viewed immediately over monitors by the filmmakers and the cast, and the decision made whether another take of the same scene is necessary. During motion picture cinematography, on the other hand, it is common practice to photograph several takes of the same scene to be certain that one of them will be acceptable for editing when the film returns from the laboratory the next day after processing. The immediate feedback capability of videotape is critically important in programs requiring subtle judgment of the actor's spontaneity before the camera.

THE THREE-CAMERA TECHNIQUE

The three-camera electronic approach lends itself to certain kinds of television programs. Such television situation comedies as *All in the Family* are suitable. The dramatic actions occur within the restricted area of a home or a studio with situations that can easily be dramatized with studio sets and rendered continuously with three cameras. The actions of comedy and musical performers involve a good deal of moving within a confined area, which means that most of the scenes are rendered in wide-angle shots, with only a few critical closeups and reaction shots needed as inserts. This kind of show is ideal for the video recording approach because the composition of the scenes and the editing of the footage are less important than the spontaneity of the cast performing before the cameras.

Daytime serial dramas are rendered on videotape by the three-camera video switcher method. In these confessional dramas, however, the cameras are scarcely needed at all. Soap operas are written as radio with pictures, with all the exposition embedded in dialogue, so that the housewife may go about her chores in other rooms while listening to the characters' heart-to-heart talks and confrontations. The visual aspects are utterly subordinate to the verbal; the cameras simply ooze in and out as the characters pour out their souls, telling all.

Other kinds of electronically recorded programs have a different kind of relationship to the viewer than does drama. In interviews, panel shows, variety shows, song and dance numbers, news reports and so forth, there is no attempt to create the illusion that the viewer is peering into the lives of others. The performers talk directly to the television viewers, and to each other, with full consciousness of the millions of viewers. In such programs the immediacy of videotape makes it the preferred medium, and the electronic video approach the most economical means of production.

THE SINGLE-CAMERA TECHNIQUE

There are times when the three-camera video switcher approach is inadequate, because it provides neither the time nor the opportunity to visually interpret the subject with superior dramatic values. In a Norman Corwin videoplay, for example, where the relationship of character to plot has been carefully conceived, where every line of dialogue carries nuances of meaning, and the interpretation of those lines requires a sensitivity by the performers exceeded only by the sensitivity of cinematic interpretation, the creative spirit of the drama cannot be captured by setting up three cameras and letting them roll, while punching buttons in the control room.

There are times when a camera must be placed squarely in the center of the staging area to capture the point-of-view of one character or the reaction of another. At other times the drama may visually require rapid but sensitive cuts from side to side during a confrontation, or a sudden reverse angle. Often the director must capture a particular feeling or a unique mood through the use of a specific lens, a distinctive composition, careful lighting or a dramatic action or reaction by a performer. Cinematic artistry tends to be incompatible with the video switcher approach because there is too much going on at one time, and the contemporaneous presence of three cameras limits where any one of them can be placed in relation to the staging area.

Moreover, in sequences requiring very fast action, such as a fist fight, the single-camera technique is preferable. The editing of such sequences requires overlapped action on the part of the performers in order to create the illusion of matched action during cutting. This kind of dynamic excitement cannot be credibly edited on the spot by the video switcher technique, but must be constructed one scene at a time with the master scene approach of cinema, to be edited in the manner of film, even though recorded on videotape. Dramatic sequences requiring a high order of visual quality are better done with the meticulous approach of the single-camera technique.

THE COMBINED THREE-CAMERA–SINGLE-CAMERA TECHNIQUE

A fine videoplay may be rendered sensitively, however, by combining the three-camera approach of television with the single-camera approach of cinema, within one production. The drama is first staged as a three-camera show, with full blocking of action for cast and crew, and performed. The director in the control room cuts and mixes the input from the three cameras and the preview monitor to obtain a complete master videotape, but does so with full cognizance that some of the more dynamic sequences within it will need to be done all over again.

After this electronically edited program has been completed, with all the wide-angle and medium shots finished and the narrative editing generally stated, then the dramatic crescendos and points of greatest sensitivity are restaged. Those sequences requiring careful composition and camera angles, rapid reversals of angle, unique points-of-view, closeups, reaction shots and cinematic editing are then rendered by the single-camera master scene technique. Once the single-camera sequences have been edited, they are spliced into the longer videotape produced by the three-camera video switcher method. This technique of combining three-camera with single-camera sequences invokes the best of both film and videotape creative methods; it is a true synthesis of the media.

An important advantage offered by the combined three-camera and single-camera technique is that it provides the illusion of sound in perspective. The three-camera approach, with its many wide-angle shots and loose compositions, tends to preclude a close approach by the microphone. All of the dialogue seems recorded at a distance, which it is. By using the single-camera technique, the microphone can be brought as close as necessary to record the dialogue with a degree of perspective consonant with the apparent distance of the subject from the camera.

THE VIDEO SWITCHER TECHNIQUE

Once the performance has been recorded on a master composite videotape, electronic special effects—freeze-frames, skip-frames, polarization, and so forth, may be added by means of the Special Effects Recorder, or video disc recorder.

The techniques of dynamic editing, which are the essence of cinema, have offered problems to those who prefer the video switcher method of producing videotapes. The main editing concept in this three-camera approach is narrative straightforward storytelling. All of the dramatic sequences rendered solely by this method have been photographed and edited at the time of their occurrence, in real time and real distance, exactly as they occurred. Post-production editing consists primarily of deleting bad takes and splicing together good sequences which have the tempo and pacing of the real event.

The nature of the three-camera video switcher approach, edited on the board, fuses real time and real distance with the dramatic events in a way that cannot readily be changed in post-production editing. The editing done while the program is in progress is essentially there to stay. Videotapes produced solely by this approach cannot be changed for cinematic time and distance without creating jumps in continuity; therefore, the kinds of programs most suitable to the video switcher method are those in which real time equals recording time.

Moreover, the tempo of motion pictures is created in part by controlling the length of time a scene is held on the screen to achieve a desired emotional impact on the viewer. As a rule, the longer the scene is held on the screen, the more relaxed the tempo of the drama; the progressively shorter the scenes, the more exciting the drama. The overall principle of building suspense and excitement in a film is to begin with scenes that are long and gradually shorten them as the drama approaches its climax. In the climax, movement itself often becomes the subject.

Editing for tempo by controlling scene lengths becomes a major problem in this electronic recording approach. The director has his hands full making decisions based upon the offerings of the monitors, and giving commands to the three cameramen on the floor and the technical director beside him, without having to think about progressively shortening the lengths of scenes as the drama approaches its climax. Editing scene and sequence lengths to create emotional values is impractical in the video switching approach.

Cross-cutting—intercutting between two separate dramatic sequences occurring contemporaneously—is also impractical, because there would be too much to see and do at the same time. It would require two studios with three cameras each, ten monitors and a director with a dozen eyes and razor-sharp reflexes. Contemporaneous dramatic actions can, however, be rendered separately on videotape and later edited for a cross-cutting effect in the manner of motion pictures.

THE THREE-RECORDER SYSTEM

The three-recorder system is a hybrid variant of studio videotape production which provides the opportunity for both video switcher and cinematic editing techniques. As the name implies, this technique consists of having three electronic cameras feed three separate recorders, providing complete videotape coverage of the performance from three points-of-view. This provides the filmmaker with the equivalent coverage of scenes photographed in the cinematic master scene technique, with footage enabling him to edit videotape exactly as he would edit film—with complete matching action.

In practice, the three-recorder system is combined with the video switcher approach for most productions utilizing this method. The output from each camera is fully recorded on separate videotapes, while simultaneously the images from the three cameras are channeled to a video switcher to be edited by the director while the program is in progress. With the three complete recordings available, the director has the option of reediting the three videotapes as if he were editing film. Obviously, if the director wishes to edit his videotape with the tight action-reaction dynamics of cinema, he can completely dispense with the switcher phase and begin to edit his drama using only the three separately recorded videotapes.

The mechanical aspects of film and television production are generally outside the communications purpose of this book. Two new technical developments, however, promise to combine and transform film and videotape to such a degree that they deserve some discussion here. These new innovations are the *Random Access Videotape Editor* and the *Vidtronic videotape-to-film transfer system.*

The Random Access Videotape Editor

Perhaps the most revolutionary development since the introduction of videotape is a computer-based editing machine called the Random Access Videotape Editor or RAVE. This system can store the scenes of a film or videotape production, photographed out of context in the master scene technique and assembled in chaotic disorder. Upon demand, RAVE instantly calls up any scene requested by the editor, in any order desired, and the editor can electronically produce a finished product in the required continuity order.

The heart of the RAVE system is its ability to make all the scenes and takes of a production (electronically code-numbered) instantly available to the editor. RAVE is a computer-integrated system comprising memory banks, video and digital tape recorders, and magnetic video discs. Sight and sound from film and videotapes are all stored electronically on banks of discs across which recording or playback heads pass in fractions of a second. Because each of the scenes has an electronic code number, the computer system can retrieve the precise scenes wanted in their desired order. These electronic code numbers magnetically measure the frame of every foot of videotape in a manner which is the equivalent of the key numbers that measure foot and frame on motion picture film stock. These electronic numbers are not visible to the human eye, but the computer can readily transfer the reference system from videotape to film, or from film to videotape.

The RAVE system is internally complex, but extremely simple for the filmmaker to operate. It consists essentially of a console with two viewing monitors. There are no knobs to turn or buttons to push. Both monitors are used to display scenes; the monitor on the right presents the outgoing scene, the monitor on the left the incoming scene.

Editing decisions are made on the surface of the monitor on the right, which lists the capabilities of the RAVE system in English terms. The phosphors of the monitor may display a "menu" which lists, for example, SCENE LIST, PLAY and EDIT. The editor gets what he wants by pointing to the term on the monitor with a "light pen." This light pen is a photoelectric device which emits a sharp rectangle of light on the word displayed in phosphors on the tube, which in turn relates to a specific scene or action in the computer's memory. When the editor wants to know what scenes are available for a given sequence, he touches the light pen to SCENE LIST, and the machine responds instantaneously to the command by providing the filmmaker with a list of all the available scenes and takes.

When the filmmaker points the light pen at the number of the desired take, that scene instantly appears for viewing. The menu of scenes disappears, and in its place appears a series of working commands used in editing, such as, SPLICE, EDIT, PLAY and so forth. By pointing the light pen at the appropriate command, the scene can be displayed on the monitor in a variety of ways: forward or reverse, fast or normal speed, frame-by-frame or still-frame.

When the filmmaker has made his decision, he points to the word SPLICE with his light pen, and immediately the last frame of the selected scene will be held in freeze-frame. Then the next scene is called up for editing consideration—or several takes of the same scene may be called up for successive viewing and consideration—and the editing process is repeated. Once the creative decisions are made of where to head and tail splice a given scene, the word SPLICE is again touched, and so on to the end of the film. Optical effects, such as fades, dissolves and wipes, may be obtained during the editing process by pointing to the name of the effect, then to the length of the effect, and the effect will be instantly recorded.

Matching the subject's actions in outgoing and incoming scenes is easily facilitated. Both scenes are visible at the same time; either can be moved a frame at a time in either direction for perfect matching in a matter of seconds. Editing decisions can be reviewed repeatedly—adding a frame here, deleting a frame there—until the filmmaker is satisfied.

Since image and sound are recorded simultaneously on the discs, playback of program material is on both a video and an audio basis. Dialogue is lip-synchronous to the frame. A unique feature of the disc system is that a singer may be held in a visual freeze-frame, and his voice, in playback, will hold the recorded note on that frame without audio distortion. Because of the RAVE's sound-hold capability, there is little difficulty in cutting between words of dialogue, or even in trimming off the sibilance of a word.

The speed and convenience of the RAVE system can scarcely be exaggerated. Every phase of continuity editing may be carried out with a script in one hand and a light pen in the other; the filmmaker never touches scissors or splicers. This instant access to all scenes by a touch of the light pen eliminates hours of rummaging through bins of film or racks of tape for a scene or frame hidden somewhere. Frame-by-frame decisions are practicable; a touch of the pen indicates to the computer's memory the exact frame to start and the exact frame to stop on any scene, with its direction and speed under the filmmaker's complete control. Because the filmmaker can now intercut 16-mm. and 35-mm. film with videotape, all randomly recorded on magnetic disc packs, he can create sequences of story line, characterization and cutting tempo with greater ease and higher cinematic artistry than ever before. And the RAVE system is serenely silent; creative decisions are made completely free of personal or mechanical distractions imposed by a busy control room or the clutter surrounding a Moviola.

The principles of editing electronically are theoretically identical to those governing editing with cellulose triacetate film, because the communication elements of sight and sound are essentially the same. The significant change that has occurred is in a speedup of editing time from an average of twenty minutes to make a decision and cut in film, to two or three minutes to make a decision and cut in videotape on the Random Access Videotape Editor.

When an entire film or television program is completely edited, the computer will automatically print a list of all the scenes in continuity order, complete with edge numbers and the frames used, for the negative cutter. Thus the RAVE machine even does the bookkeeping.

The Random Access Videotape Editor can be used to great advantage in combining three-camera videotape production with single-camera cinema sequences in the manner described earlier. The editor can view the master videotape on RAVE as if he were watching a finished program, and wherever he needs a closeup, or a sequence edited with different dynamics, he can instantly call up those scenes rendered by the single-camera technique and edit them into the videotape.

The original cinematography or electronic photography is shot in the normal way, using either master scene film or video switcher techniques. If the original footage is on film instead of videotape, all the usable scenes may be loaded magnetically into the RAVE machine, just as they come from the laboratory, by running the footage through a telecine camera for transmutation onto the magnetic disks. The scenes need not be loaded into RAVE in the continuity order of the film; the machine will remember where everything is and will retrieve any scene on demand in an average time of less than 13 milleseconds—13/1000 of a second.

Since the RAVE system can accept scenes rendered by either the single-camera master scene technique deriving from cinema or the three-camera video switcher technique deriving from videotape, the question arises, which of the two techniques best lends itself to the capabilities of the RAVE system? Surprisingly, the one-camera technique deriving from film gets the nod, because it renders distinct separate scenes that can be separately identified by number and retrieved upon demand. The three-camera approach, a continuous process in which the director is cutting and dissolving while the program is in progress, results in sequences which are already edited and tend to flow together in a continuum which is somewhat less sharply delineated for separate iden-tification and retrieval.

Transferring Videotapes to Film

Transferring videotapes to film for projection has been attempted since the advent of television. In principle, the method consists of displaying images on a television tube and photographing them with a motion picture camera. The sharpness of resolution in these rephoto-graphed images is dependent upon the number of scan lines used in the television display tube. The American television system has 525 scan lines, which offers softer definition in the transfer process than does the British system of 626 scan lines. In the past, "kinescopes" produced by this method were notorious for their narrow spectrum of light to dark values and the softness of their definition. Color kinescopes were even worse than the black and white versions, and eventually the most sting-ing insult that could be paid to film footage was to say that it looked like a kinescope.

Recent technical developments in the videotape-to-film transfer process have reversed this trend. The first development was the "expan-sion" of the information contained in the phosphors of each scan line, thereby filling in the gaps between the lines that created the softness of definition and narrowness of values. The second development was a three-step process of transferring the colors of a videotape to film.

THE VIDTRONIC SYSTEM

The Vidtronic system for transferring color videotape to film, de-veloped by the Technicolor Corporation, involves three playbacks on a television tube for photography by a motion picture camera. During each playback, one of the three primary colors—red, green or blue—is separated from the maze of other television signals for display and photographed with *black and white* film stock. If red is the signal chosen for display, only those aspects of the subject containing red will be displayed on the television tube. The same principle holds true for the display of the green or blue signal.

Each color signal is sharpened for display on the television tube, with monitored control over edge transition, contrast, brightness and the chroma of the three primary colors—enhancing the red, green and blue signals to make them as sharp, clean and pure as possible.

After the electronic enhancing process, each color image is separately displayed on a monitor and photographed on black and white film. After three passes, there will be three black and white films, one of a red signal, one of a green signal, one of a blue signal.

Each of the black and white films serves as a matrix for one of the three primary colors, and acquires its color by imbibition. The black and white film that has photographed the red signal is immersed in a red solution and the images absorb the red primary color. Then the black and white film that has recorded the green images is similarly immersed in a solution to imbibe the green color, with the same process used to infuse the blue images with a blue color. These three separate films are made into imbibition matrices, and thence to prints. Or, the three separations are combined into an internegative, used to make prints. Thus the Vidtronic process of transferring videotape to film makes possible 35-mm., 16-mm. or Super-8 prints.

The Vidtronic system was used to produce *200 Motels*, the first feature film made on videotape whose resolution and color were good enough in transfer to be projected on a large theatrical screen without the degradation of a kinescope. The only clues to its videotape origin lay in the tendency of highlights on musical instruments to reveal hints of scan lines, and a slight softening trail of phosphors during fast movements.

DEFECTS AND LIMITATIONS

There are certain technical limitations inherent in the electronic media that will, unless scenes are very carefully photographed, tend to inhibit the use of videotape for transfer to feature films. Many of them appear frequently on television but pass unnoticed because of the small screen. In a videotape-to-35-mm.-film transfer, however, electronic production problems may become conspicuous defects when projected on a wide theatrical screen. Some of these problems are *image retention, halo effect, streaking, ghosting, target blemishes, color change, dropout of details* and *portability.*

Image retention is a major problem. The electronic camera tube has a tendency to retain the image of a subject that has been held in focus a long time. This retention trait is further enhanced by high contrast in a subject. As an actor walks before a high-contrast background, it is not uncommon to be able to see through him to the background, as if he were a ghost. A partial solution is the use of plain backgrounds and short scenes.

The *halo effect* in electronic photography is a black flare that develops around a particularly bright highlight, such as a flame or a white shirt. The greater the contrast, the darker and wider the contrast area. The halo effect can be minimized somewhat by restricting the brightness range within the scene and reducing or eliminating highlights. Obviously, in outdoor productions the degree to which this can be done is limited.

An effect called *streaking* is the tendency of the electronic camera to run all horizontal lines that are parallel with the scan lines of the television tube right through the persons standing in front of the horizontal lines. Venetian blinds, for example, will appear to pierce the people standing in front of them, an effect echoed in exteriors by the horizon line and by buildings whose roofs parallel the direction of the electronic scan lines. Streaking can be reduced by never photographing a subject against a background whose lines parallel those of the scan lines.

Ghosting is another effect deriving from the contrast weakness of the electronic videotape system. Whenever a bright subject is seen against a dark background, not only is there a halo effect, but a ghost of the subject's image will appear on the opposite part of the screen. If the subject is placed toward the left, his ghost will be displaced toward the right, and vice versa. There is only one sure way of avoiding ghosting in a high-contrast subject, and that is to place him in the center of the screen. A dead-center composition may be acceptable on the small television screen, but it is a dead composition on the theatrical screen.

Spotting by tiny flecks of lights, called *target blemishes*, sometimes remains on the screen for the duration that a single camera is focused on the subject. There is only one solution: Cut to another camera.

Problems deriving from such contrast-control difficulties, inherent in electronic photography, are controlled primarily by camera movements: movements by the camera over the subject; movements by the subject within the scene; and movement of the scene itself. Long, long static scenes are presently impractical in videotapes intended for transfer to film.

Color change during a zoom shot at low illumination levels can turn the subject a greenish color. This can be compensated for by manipulation of color during the electronic photography, or in a post-production transfer to another videotape. The fact that the green cast appears during the movement of the lens, however, makes color manipulation difficult to avoid. Green skin on a lovely actress means an unhappy actress and a disenchanted viewer.

Dropout of details in long shots is a peculiarity of videotape. Whenever an outdoor scene is photographed with the electronic cameras, the distant images will be rendered as flat as a water-color painting, almost devoid of details. In those videotapes in which the background is important for atmosphere, character development and exposition, the dropout of details in long exterior shots may be a serious handicap for productions intended for theatrical films.

Portability is the last of the major problems, and will probably be the first to be solved. At the present state of art, videotape production is inhibited by its power supply and recording system, and those dramatic actions whose movements extend beyond the limits of a power cable also extend beyond the capabilities of electronic photography. While it is true that there are back-pack electronic cameras whose signals can be radioed or shortwaved back to a recorder, this system is more clumsy, tedious and expensive than the highly mobile motion picture camera. It is easier to photograph moving exterior scenes on film and later mix the footage with videotape on the console.

Transferring Film to Videotape

Transferring film to videotape has also been done since the development of videotape, because film cameras have heretofore been more portable and film editing techniques more practical than their electronic counterparts. With time, videotape has become a synthesizer used to integrate live performances with slides, films, sub-recorded videotapes and commercials produced by whatever means. The old movies seen on late night television are usually transferred to videotape before being broadcast to preclude any possibility of a film break during the broadcast. Film-to-videotape transfers, however, also have their problems.

Although both film and videotape can be played over closed-circuit, cable and broadcast television, there is a subtle but perceptible difference between them when seen on the television tube. Film, when electronically transmitted, suffers a slight degradation in resolution and color richness because its content has been transmuted from optical to magnetic form.

Videotape, on the other hand, looks sharper and richer over television systems because there is no fundamental transmutation of its original electronic form: when a video signal is recorded on tape by electronic means, the tape plays it back as electronic impulses, and the images on the tubes are displayed as electronic impulses. The videotape signals go through no optical systems whatever, and the final living image is just as clear on playback as it was on record. The television system favors all-electronic playback and recording.

Conversely, film is presently superior to a videotape-to-film print in projection. Given a 35-mm. film, photographed at its optimum, and a 2-inch-high-band color videotape, recorded at its optimum and transferred to film—the original film-as-film will appear crisper in most respects when projected. The original film was recorded optically, printed optically and projected optically, and is generally superior for most forms of projection. Motion pictures and videotape are freely interchangeable for both projection and television, yet each serves more brilliantly when displayed in its original medium.

Video-Film: The New Synthesis

The polemic about film versus videotape quality tends to be an academic strawman. There are inherent advantages and disadvantages to each form, and if used appropriately, the two forms can be used to complement each other within the same production. The decision of whether to use film or videotape produced by the switcher technique as the recording and editing medium depends upon the nature of the content, the dramatic intensity of a given situation and the importance of artistic factors. There is one even more critical factor—production costs.

With videotape it is possible to save from ten to fifty percent in production costs if a three-camera technique is employed. The practicability of this technique, in turn, depends upon the nature of the content. A one- or two-set studio drama, a musical review, a panel discussion show, an interview—or any program in which the content is carried in words and music—is obviously suited to the multiple-camera technique. In these kinds of programs, the crucial factor of subject mobility is held to a minimum; editing consists primarily of deleting mistakes and duller moments and is less concerned with producing the action-reaction dynamics of cinema.

Multiple-camera techniques of electronic photography have intrinsic advantages of cost and technique: The filmmaker can see everything being viewed by all three cameras simultaneously and can direct each cameraman, by microphone, as he photographs the action. He can roughly edit the program in progress, cutting or mixing from one camera to the other, according to the dictates of the content. Lighting is less of a problem because it can be done at lower levels of illumination than is required for film; color balance and contrast ranges are clearly seen and adjustable at all times. All guesswork is eliminated because the filmmaker is getting what he sees. There are virtually none of the lighting, editing, time delay and laboratory problems that would exist if the same subjects were photographed on three cameras simultaneously with film stock, because the problems can be seen and corrected at the time of electronic photography. The scenes recorded can be replayed immediately on the monitors so that producers and actors alike can judge their own performance and decide whether another take is necessary.

Whatever saves production time on the set, of course, also saves the producer money. Everyone associated with a production on the set—actors, gaffers, makeup artists, technicians—spends a large part of his time waiting for somebody else to do something, wasted time for which he is being paid. The more the production process can be speeded up, the greater the amount of program material that can be put in the can at the end of a day's production, and the fewer the number of production days required of cast and crew.

The extravagant stock and laboratory costs of film do not exist in videotape. Once motion picture film is photographed, it is consumed. Moreover, film has the attendant costs of processing at the laboratory and the need for a work print, which subjects it to vagaries in laboratory processing and handling. Videotape, on the other hand, may be used, erased and used again until a given take is acceptable. There is no need for processing and striking a work print for editing; moreover, since the tape is rough-edited while the program is in progress, there is little need for handling it at all.

The other side of the coin, however, is that the maintenance of film equipment does not require the constant attention of many skilled, expensive engineers. Even a small studio production center for videotapes requires continuous servicing by many salaried technicians because electronic equipment is inherently fragile and subject to unexpected failures. Any cost comparison between the two media based solely upon the costs of film stock and videotape is, at best, of dubious validity. Videotape offers a genuine savings in cost primarily when there is a high level of continuing productions and very little dead time draining off money in the form of technician's salaries.

It is important for filmmakers who are accustomed to the single-camera master scene technique to learn the short-cut methods of multiple-camera techniques. If a four-week shooting schedule can be brought down to three weeks by means of multiple cameras and mix-and-cut editing, the filmmaker will save money.

Conversely, it is equally important for directors groomed in multiple-camera techniques to learn master scene techniques. Scenes photographed by multiple cameras are earthbound to real time and real distance because it is difficult to incorporate editing techniques for dynamism and excitement when the program has been preedited on the console while in progress. In most film and television programs there are sequences of action requiring exciting editing dynamics which demand master scene techniques, and there are sequences rich in dialogue but quiet in movement that are better served by the multiple-camera technique. The filmmaker who knows both techniques, and when each technique is appropriate, will be far ahead in both economy and quality.

The economics of dramatic film and television production seem destined to drive more and more film producers to use videotape for part or all of their productions in order to reduce production expenses. The major studios and networks have simply been unable to hold down labor costs to the point where they can complete a theatrical production without deficit financing and an extremely high level of risk. If a production has a poor run in the theaters, or if a television program is canceled after thirteen weeks or lacks rerun potential, the filmmakers are forced to write it off as a loss. The consequence in the past has been runaway production to other nations, where filmmakers have special tax benefits as well as lower labor costs. The consequence in the present, with the astonishing new electronic developments, can only be some degree of a turn to videotape.

The language of film will remain the same whether the production is in film or videotape or some combination of the two media. It has been the growing capability of videotape to approximate or duplicate the effects of cinema at a lower cost that makes it worthy of consideration. As far as the viewer is concerned, the change will not make the slightest difference in his viewing pleasure or menu. It is primarily the economics of the fusion that will force the change, not necessarily any desired improvement in program quality. Simply put, the combination of film and videotape techniques and technology seems sure to provide a means of creating economically sound dramatic productions, whose costs may be amortized at the time of sale.

The first type of production to adopt videotape techniques will be the television situation comedy, whose spontaneity lends itself to the three-camera video recording technique. Second will probably be indoor dramas, followed by exterior dramas staged outdoors, but not requiring a great deal of fast subject movements. Last to change will be the action dramas for television and theatrical release. But change they will to some degree in a low-cost combination of the two media into a new synthesis: video-film.

7

Animation: The Eye of the Mind

Origins

The first attempts to draw animated images go back three hundred centuries to the caves of Lascaux and Altimira, where Neanderthal man drew multilegged boars and bears, rampaging to attack, and the blurred multiple hooves of wild bison running in time-swallowed stampedes. The first truly animated-projected image, as we understand the term, was drawn in the form of a turning windmill in 1736 by Pieter van Musschenbroek—antedating the first live-action film by more than two hundred and fifty years. The first animation on film, per se, was created by an unknown artist in the employ of Thomas Edison in 1900, when he drew the face of a tramp who began to billow animated clouds of smoke from his artist-endowed cigar butt. To complete this list of precedents—the first film with an optical sound track was an animated film, produced in 1922 by the engineers of the General Electric laboratory. The animated film may legitimately be called the original film form.

The animated film is an extraordinary creative opportunity for the filmmaker to give full rein to his imagination in defiance of the laws of gravity and reality. Whatever he can think of, and give graphic visual form to, may be expressed in the animated film. Until recently that potential has been exploited primarily for entertainment, in forms that

147

ranged from the zany extravaganzas of theatrical short subjects and Saturday morning television shows, to feature-length films done with the exquisite taste of *The Yellow Submarine* and *Fantasia*. The television advertising industry seized upon animation to make their cereals go snap, crackle, pop, and filled the tube with caricatured potato chips and aerosol cans. Outside the limelight of the theatrical and advertising industry, however, the animated film has spread steadily through the artistic coteries of experimental film and permeated educational film and television programs to express visually nonrealistic ideas that could not otherwise be given graphic perceptual form. The use of animated film to give visual form to ideas—as art and communication—is the substance of this chapter.

Live-Action Film and Animation

Live-action film and animation represent radically different approaches to cinema, differences that should be explored in order to understand the effective use of each form. They are: *subject matter, photography concepts, production techniques, interpretive values, selection of visual content* and *imaginative freedom*.

SUBJECT MATTER

Subjects are dissimilar. The live-action subject is usually alive and in motion at the time of cinematography, and the filmmaker's concern is to photograph scenes of the subject's actions suitable for editing. In animation, however, the subjects are traditionally still artwork, objects or puppets, which are seldom alive or in motion at the time of photography.

PHOTOGRAPHY CONCEPTS

Photography concepts are reversed. Live-action cinematography is photographed with long sustained runs of the camera, often recording scenes that may number thousands of exposed frames. Animated film, on the other hand, is *single-frame photography on motion picture film*. The film is exposed one frame at a time; only when it is projected does it become cinema. Because the essence of the animation technique is the single-frame exposure, each move of the subject before the camera, between exposures, must be planned almost microscopically.

Production Techniques

Production techniques are totally different. Live-action cinematography is extremely mobile, with the camera capable of being turned in any direction and moved to any location, on land, sea or air, to achieve a desired effect. Live-action dramatic scenes are customarily photographed from several different camera positions in order to obtain a variety of scene sizes and movements, with an infinite variety of lenses and lighting. Traditional animation cinematography is just the opposite: the camera is mounted rigidly on a column, pointed toward the inanimate artwork, and can only move toward or away from the subject. The traditional animation camera can view the subject only from a right angle; it cannot pan or tilt or change its angle of view. The illusion of a pan or tilt is created by moving the compound on which the artwork is mounted in the desired direction, but apparent lateral moves are no more than a cinematic illusion.

Interpretive Values

Interpretive values are different. Live-action cinematography, because of the great flexibility afforded by changes of lenses and lighting and camera mobility, can provide an infinitely variable range of interpretations of a single subject engaged in almost any action. Moreover, the resulting scenes may then be edited narratively and implicitly to provide meanings and evoke emotions that transcend the intrinsic content of the scenes. The broad, flexible methods of live dramatic actions, with the possibilities of much improvisation and free interpretation, are at the opposite pole of cinema from the tight, precise methods of the animated film.

Animated film can offer only the interpretive values of the subjects presented to the one lens and one angle of the camera, with the subject lighted with a fixed relationship. Moreover, the resulting footage is not edited, unless a mistake has been made, and the visual images of an animated film are photographed at one time, in one location and in exactly the order in which the animated sequence will appear on the screen. Every move of an animated (actually static) subject before the

THE ARISTOCATS. Realism
in animation. © *Walt
Disney Productions.*

THE ARISTOCATS. Stylized
realism. © *Walt Disney
Productions.*

camera is plotted almost microscopically and implemented by small shifts of minutely calibrated controls.

SELECTION OF VISUAL CONTENT

Selection of content is an important contrast between live-action and animated film. The live-action director must in some degree photograph things as he finds them and accept the limitations of reality. He can stage props and block performers' actions, but his creativity is nevertheless constricted by the forms of things as they are. The animator, on the other hand, may select any visual element from life that he wishes to use, without regard to the limitations of reality.

IMAGINATIVE FREEDOM

If live-action cinematography is so flexible and animation generally so rigid and difficult, why, then, make animated films at all? The reason lies in their final, fundamental difference: The live-action camera corresponds to the human eye and can photograph only what already exists in physical reality—you cannot photograph a thought. The animated film is an extension of the human imagination and can give graphic form to anything the mind can imagine through the artwork presented before the camera. Live action can reproduce anything that physically exists. Animation can reproduce any idea that can be visually conceived. The animated filmmaker has the total freedom and flexibility to express any idea he may have on film, whether it be totally nonobjective in form, combinations of live-action cinematography, animation and special effects, or realism itself. Paradoxically, the animated film, the most inflexible of film techniques, is the most infinitely variable in its film forms and concepts.

Animation Styles

Animated film styles have evolved into a variety of forms and formats to suit the intended uses of the films and the characteristics of the target audiences. Stylistically, they constitute a continuous spectrum, but for practical purposes may be considered in terms of *realism, caricature, decorative form, schematics, symbols* and *nonobjective animation.*

REALISM

Realism, or some derivative thereof, is the most effective form for communicating ideas to the greatest number of people. Recognizable forms are meaningful even to those with a low level of film literacy and formal education, and therefore realism is the most widely used style in educational, industrial and sales films. The realistic style, however, does not preclude the use of strongly designed shapes and distortions when dramatically appropriate to the visual concept.

On the other hand, any attempt to invade live action's field of fac-simile naturalism with animation is a misapplication of the medium: Naturalistic animation usually fails to approximate what live-action cinematography can do better, costs far more to do, and ends by losing both the charm of animation and the naturalism of live-action cinema-tography—at times bordering on the macabre. The rightful world of the animated film is that of the imagination, a realm wide enough to wan-der, one should think, without attempting the certain failure of fool-the-eye naturalism. Nevertheless, it may be worth remembering that every step away from recognizable forms narrows the size of the target audi-ence and the communication effectiveness of the animated film. Recog-nition of content is mandatory in any form of universal communication.

CARICATURE

Caricature animation presents recognizable forms, but is a step to-ward formal art values. This decorative approach emphasizes the basic shapes of objects in nature, but rejects irrelevancies of detail in favor of stylized, simplified forms. The caricature is very popular in creating zany cartoon figures for theatrical short subjects and television com-mercials, and is responsible for the popular stereotype of animated film as a cartoon medium for children. Figures and backgrounds are drawn and distorted in simplified forms—circles, squares, triangles, free forms —that career around the screen with lives of their own, unencumbered by any visual inhibitions except those relating to a sponsor's product—presented with realism.

DECORATIVE FORM

Decorative animation is a style common in Eastern Europe, particu-larly Czechoslovakia, and derives from the techniques used in book illustration. While animated film styles in most nations grew in slavish imitation of the Disney productions, the Czechs adopted his technology but ignored his style. They turned instead to their own folk culture and animated their legends in the charming style of children's book illustrations. Many of their films resemble engravings, water color and wolf pencil drawings, gouache paintings—subjects rendered in the round instead of in a flat pattern—and leave the viewer with the delightful sensation of having seen an answer to his request: "Tell me a story."

Schematics

Schematic interpretation is another step away from realism toward symbolism. Schematic forms usually present a two-dimensional cutaway of a three-dimensional object already known to the viewer. The target audience, at this point, must bring some knowledge of the subject and a degree of film literacy to the viewing in order to properly interpret the schematic forms. Schematic animation is widely used in instructional films and videotapes to reveal hidden layers or the functioning of internal parts.

Symbols

Symbolic animation has a cultural basis in the use of graphic shapes that have a specific meaning to a homogeneous people. The cross, the swastika, the sickle and hammer, carry with them emotional associations that vary according to the cultural values of the viewer. Another step away is the use of graphic symbols having universal meaning—the circle, the arrow, the self-animated (scratch-off) line—used to place emphasis upon various subjects or areas within a scene.

Nonobjective Animation

Nonobjective animation is at the opposite end of the communication spectrum from naturalism. This style is based upon the premise that meaningless forms and colors should themselves be the subjects of art, without relation to recognizable shapes for aesthetic values or identification, and produced without regard to any target audience. Nonobjective animation has often been orchestrated with music in symphonies of the eye and ear to an effect having no counterpart in any other media form.

THE FLINTSTONES. Caricature animation. © *Hanna-Barbera Productions.*

The advent of digital and analogue computers, combined with special effects on the optical printer, now offer new possibilities of creating nonobjective forms in motion.

Animation as Communication

The animated film has enormous potential for teaching purposes in film, television and instructional technology, because it enables the film-maker to present nonrealistic ideas and abstract concepts in their true and understandable relationships. Educational film and television li-

Cartoon style. © *Hanna-Barbera Productions.*

braries are heavily stocked with films about the objective world that reveal a great deal of "what," a certain amount of "how," but very little "why." The "what" and the "how" are, of course, live-action films and videotapes which present facsimiles of things as they are, or visual records of lecturers pointing earnestly to visual aids and talking about things as they are.

The "why" is the educational realm of the animated film; it reveals rather than explains the invisible principles that underlie surface realities. The functions that animation may serve are the *revelation of invisible forces, depiction of processes, simplification of processes, desensitization of subject matter, creation of visual generalizations and projections, re-creation of the past, progressive presentation of related elements, offering of visual cues,* the *animation of visual analogies* and *giving character to ideas.*

REVELATION OF INVISIBLE FORCES

Tangible but invisible forces can be revealed in graphic forms expressive of their true natures: stresses, chemical reactions, light waves, sound waves, gases and such progressive changes as the continental drift.

DEPICTION OF PROCESSES

Animated film can depict processes and abstract relationships which cannot otherwise be portrayed. Mathematical forms and quantitative relationships that exist in a conceptual sense, but have no realistic shapes to render in living form with the motion picture or image orthicon camera, can be graphically presented in animated form, with color codes used to separate parts or emphasize elements. Such unseen biological processes as changing genetic chromosome patterns, the neurological response modes between brain and limbs, the cause and effect relationships between medication and internal organs of the body, and the forms and functions of the DNA molecule can easily be portrayed in animated film. The unseen processes awaiting rendition in animated form may number in the hundreds of thousands in chemistry, physics, electronics, oceanography, medicine, aerospace, mechanical engineering and technological areas almost without end.

SIMPLIFICATION OF PROCESSES

Through animation the filmmaker can simplify processes, ideas, organisms and technical structures so complex in reality as to defy visual presentation by any other means: the essential functions and sub-functions of the digital and analogue computer, with each aspect selected in its turn for a graphic presentation of relationships; the orbital and gravitational relationships between astral bodies; the electrochemical processes of the nervous system; the spread of a primary carcinoma of the lungs to neighboring lymph nodes, and further extension through the body; the effects of pollution on the ecological processes of the sea, or the effects of thermal change on the transmission of sound waves in the ocean; the processes of conception, development and parturition in every form of life; the basic structural relationship of the space rocket. All of these complex processes may be simplified and presented in their essences—one selective phase at a time—through the infinitely variable visual capabilities of the animated film.

DESENSITIZATION OF SUBJECT MATTER

Desensitizing subject matter is a corollary function of animation. Subjects in the nature of menstruation, defecation, sexual conception, menopause and so forth may be offensive and indelicate if presented to a lay audience in terms of living persons. By presenting those processes in animation, the filmmaker may transform them from a specific to a generalized form and give them the breadth of scope and universality they should have, unencumbered by identification with any live individuals portrayed on the screen. A superb example of this was found in *Generation to Generation*; Philip Stapp animated the complete cycle of human sexual reproduction, from conception through parturition, in forms that were clear and to the point, yet acceptably generalized, and given a beauty that stood at the threshold of art.

CREATION OF VISUAL GENERALIZATIONS AND PROJECTIONS

Animation can be used to make visual generalizations and projections from specific examples and broadcast to all those persons who might be interested. A small scientific experiment with limited immediate use, but with incalculable future possibilities, may have its true potential visualized for the lay but influential viewer who may not be a reader of obscure journals. Many a scientific discovery lies fallow for decades, or is forgotten in dusty journals, when it could be utilized for the benefit of mankind if presented to the public in a visual language they can readily understand. Moreover, the once broad public support for research that has shriveled in recent years might be renewed if people could be made to understand the benefits that may ensue from their funding of certain research and development projects, whose favorable consequences were projected in animation. The gap between scientific discovery and implementation is most often a gap in communication between those who make discoveries and those who have the power to implement them—a chasm that may be bridged by the visual generalizations and projections of animation.

RE-CREATION OF THE PAST

Animation may be used to re-create the past as well as project the future. The formation of mountain ranges, the sinking and rising of the ocean floor, the shifting relationships between changing land masses and the migrations of ancient peoples, the religious and cultural rituals of long-dead nations, the evolution of various forms of extinct life over millennia, and the re-creation of paleontological patterns that reach as far back in the genesis of life as lies within the ken of man, may be given graphic contemporary form. The past and the future can be re-created in the present.

PROGRESSIVE PRESENTATION OF RELATED ELEMENTS

A progressive accumulation of related elements is a teaching technique that finds unique application through animation. A base element may be introduced, and other animated elements then added to it. To the presentation of a skeleton, for example, may be progressively added the forms and functions of gross muscle structure, the cardiovascular system, the nervous system, the major glands and their functions and so forth to the final epidermal skin. With each new accumulation of elements, the functional relationship of the new parts to what was presented earlier may be shown in phase-by-phase animation. The teaching principle of starting with a base element and adding new elements to it, through animation, may have vast applications to the physical and biological sciences and to the teaching of such ideographic written languages as Chinese.

Conversely, progressive subtraction of related elements may be used to trace effects to their causes and delve down through succeeding layers to points of origin. The possibilities of subtractive animation are multivarious in engineering and science, from the simple progressive reduction of an engine to its motive crankshaft, to the evolution-in-reverse of a living organism.

Offering Visual Cues

Visual cues may be animated to point out what is important and subdue or eliminate what is unimportant in any phase of the film.

Color changes may draw the attention of the viewer to a selected part, such as the location of the pituitary gland, and through selective animation relate its functions to blood vessel tone, water metabolism and uterine contractions.

Changes of values—shades of light and dark—can shift in and out when introducing each part in relation to the whole, as when describing cell collaboration with the nervous system in adjusting the body to the buffetings of changes in the environment.

Arrows, circles, dotted lines and scratch-off lines (apparently self-animated lines moving across the screen) may appear and act independently to point out important parts and functions, and then relate those elements to other parts and functions within the same scene.

Movements of one part may be presented at normal speed while the movements of all other parts are accelerated, decelerated or held still in limbo, to express precisely those ideas the filmmaker wishes to communicate.

Animation may reveal not only how things work, but what they *mean*. Although concepts such as prejudice, tolerance and freedom are intangible, they can nevertheless be given credible, visible form through animation. In *Boundary Lines*, for example, the invisible lines of racial and religious prejudices that separate man from man were recounted through the infinite variations of a single animated line, rendering itself into recognizable expressions of a nonrealistic concept. Creativity, that most intangible of human capabilities, was explored in the film *Why Man Creates*, expressing each primary circumstance and condition under which man is stimulated to innovative thought. The conditions of idea stimulation were recounted in animation, its expression was rendered in live-action footage, and reception by the lay viewer was expressed in special effects humor—all tangible, cinematic, perceptual expressions of real but nonrealistic ideas.

ANIMATION OF VISUAL ANALOGIES

Animated analogies may be drawn for young viewers to introduce the unfamiliar in terms of the familiar and expand their inventory of understanding. The force of gravity may be explained in terms of the familiar magnet. An infection and its treatment may be portrayed as an invasion by an army of bacteria and its defeat by the body's defensive white blood cells, assisted by administered medication. The principles of atomic energy may be told in terms of a target range. The functions of the human eye may be revealed as an analogy to the lens of a camera. Although analogy may be misleading if improperly used, and is sometimes educationally suspect, it nevertheless permits the placing of accents and emphasis exactly where they should be for maximum teaching effectiveness. Animated analogies have been used with exceptional success to teach abstract ideas to retarded children who could not otherwise understand them.

GIVING CHARACTER TO IDEAS

The animated cartoon figure can give character to ideas in teaching films for children, recounting historical trends and abstract forces in symbolic form and sparking viewer interest in subjects that otherwise lack intrinsic interest for many of them. The animated film can recount the essence and spirit of great events in the shapes of cartoon figures, armies, cities, industries and civilizations, all rendered in the liveliest form of the liveliest art.

Through animation, all the elements of line, form, color, value and movement are at the filmmaker's command to communicate his ideas exactly, uninhibited by the strictures of naturalism.

Combining Live Action with Animation

The differences between live action and animation have been listed at length. What of the possibilities of combining live action with animation?

Live-action stories that include cartoon characters and animated films that include live-action characters have been with us since the great days of the Disney animation studios. *The Three Caballeros* was a Disney film containing both forms in brief charming vignettes, a film

that did so successfully. In most combinations of live action with animation for entertainment purposes, however, there is something jarring
and unnatural about seeing them interacting on the screen at the same
time. All one form or the other does not challenge credibility, but seeing
them together on the screen does. The viewer seems to approach live-
action and animated films with different frames of reference, prepared
to accept either on its own terms. When the two forms are combined,
however, they appear to be dramatically neither fish nor fowl.

In education, on the other hand, combining animation with live-
action footage offers critically important advantages by simultaneously
presenting internal and external views. Live-action footage of a running
athlete may be reduced to slow motion, or held static in a freeze-frame,
while animation is superimposed over the torso to reveal changes in
body metabolism in meeting the exertion. The effects of chemical pollution in the ocean may be portrayed in animation superimposed over live-
action footage of the sea bed. Because the viewer approaches an educational experience expecting to learn rather than be entertained, the
unnatural effect of joining two distinct art forms is unimportant.

The more common educational practice in combining live action
with animation is to have completely animated sequences within a live-
action film. The animated sequences are interspersed periodically to
elucidate in art what has previously been rendered by photographed
reality. More than one-third of all educational films have some form of
animation included in longer live-action films, either as superimposed
images or interjected sequences, to reveal the inner workings of some
external image. From an emotional-identification point-of-view, every
such combination is jarring. From an intellectual-learning point-of-
view, it provides the best of two worlds in relating inner to outer reality.

Related Animation Forms

One chapter can scarcely encompass all the other multivarious
forms taken by the infinitely variable animated film. The following
genres comprise some of those developed to meet specialized needs or
unique aesthetic goals.

ANIMATION OF OBJECTS

Animation of objects is an easy, inexpensive form of animation
frequently used to depict processes in teaching, business and industrial

SHADOWS OF TIME. Animation of objects. *Pyramid Films.*

films, and to sell products in television commercials. The method, stated simplistically, is as follows: First, the filmmaker must decide how long it will take his object, such as a frankfurter, to leap to the embrace of a bun. This time is multiplied by 24 frames per second (sound speed) to determine how many increments the hot dog will have to be moved to reach the object of its passion. Then, the actual distance of its move is marked off in the total number of time increments. Finally, the object is moved one increment for each exposure until it has been moved and photographed for the full distance. When projected on the screen— presto—the hot dog has raced to the arms of the bun. If mustard or relish are to be added to create a *ménage à trois*, they would be animated in the same way.

Animation within objects is a variant in which an object apparently unfolds itself to expose its internal structure. A common use is in television commercials, where products and packages unfold themselves to reveal their delectable contents and tempt the viewer to buy. Another is the use of models and single-frame photography to portray such processes as sedimentation in a river delta. The great advantage of object animation, as communication, is its quality of maximum realism.

Puppet Animation

Puppet animation is more closely related to live-action cinematography in its concepts than it is to animation. Puppets are staged on a lighted set and photographed by a tripod-mounted camera, with varying lenses and scene sizes, mobile camera and shifting lens movements, and other production characteristics more typically found in conventional

Sesame Street. Puppet animation. *Children's Television Workshop.*

cinematography. What places puppet films within the realm of animation is that the subject is always static at the time of photography, and is photographed after each increment of a move. It remains still photography on motion picture film. Puppets may be delightful if they are fanciful caricatures, as is true of the puppet forms of Czechoslovakia, whose filmmakers are the masters of this animation form. Naturalistic puppets, however, invite comparison with reality, and in this comparison may sometimes become macabre. Puppetry properly belongs to the world of unabashed make-believe.

CUTOUT ANIMATION

Cutout animation, or collage animation, is found mostly within art education and the closed coterie of the experimental film. Cutout animation usually takes three forms: the painted cutout with jointed limbs, which is lighted from the top of the animation stand in the conventional way; painted cutouts which are mounted on unphotographed sticks; and the black cutout, with jointed limbs, lighted from beneath to throw the animation into silhouette. The esoteric genre of black cutout animation has been raised to the level of an art form by Lotte Reinegger of Germany; her animated figures are cut from black paper with the delicacy of filigree work, assembled with fine joints and photographed in silhouette to exquisite effect. At the other extreme, the kindergarten level, few things will give an art teacher more pleasure than the delighted reactions of her little charges to the projection of their own cutout animation.

FILMOGRAPH

A filmograph is an animation technique which utilizes still photographs or artwork and infuses them with implied movement by means of optical effects, zooms and pans. If the filmmaker keeps the still photographs in almost continuous motion, the viewer will tend to accept the film as a genre of motion picture. Historical filmographs have been made that had so much of the spirit of life and the illusion of motion as to defy detection as deriving from still illustrations. The filmograph is most widely used in art, documentary and historical films, and as sequences within those live-action films in which the needed representation of events has no other visual form.

VISUAL SQUEEZE

Visual squeeze is a form of filmograph in which related still pictures are presented so rapidly that the viewer can scarcely perceive one image before it is replaced by another. The entire history of the United States was presented in four minutes with hundreds of pictures by the visual squeeze technique, and managed to include most of the major events and dominant figures.

PIXILATION

Pixilation, the technique of photographing live actors with still-frame photography, yields a flickering, tricky effect as the actors move from point to point and pause en route to be photographed a frame at a time. Pixilation began in experimental film and found its way into the humorous television commercial.

ULTRAVIOLET ANIMATION

Ultraviolet animation is a form of object animation in which the animated subjects are coated with a fluorescent surface and everything else is painted a flat black. The subject is lighted with "black light" and moved by an assistant wearing black gloves, to the effect that only the images of the animated model appear on film. This technique is used by institutes of technology for specialized purposes.

PAINTED ANIMATION

Painting animation directly on clear film stock—picture and sound —was developed by Norman McLaren at the National Film Board of Canada. This eye-straining technique involves special magnifying devices and the patience of Job, but yields an experimental effect that is nothing less than sensational.

PINHEAD SHADOW ANIMATION

Pinhead shadow animation is a unique form in which rows of pins pressed in a board are raised and lowered, with strong cross-lighting, and the changes of shadow patterns rendered by stop-motion photography.

PASTEL ANIMATION

Pastel animation substitutes changes in a chalk drawing, between exposures, for changes of cels. This technique spreads the focus point of making a pastel drawing from the end product to the process of making it. A little chalk is added or smeared between each exposure of a frame of film until the pastel drawing is finished. When projected, the film reveals a drawing that draws itself. This technique finds promising use in art education and, to some degree, in the biological sciences.

Restricted Use of Animation

Granted that animation has immense content areas of application to education, why, then, is it not more widely used?

Cost is the first factor. Traditional cel animation requires that 1,440 cels be drawn, inked and painted for each *minute* of screen time, a labor-cost factor that precludes the use of animated film in education in all but the most vitally needed areas. The educational communication society has heretofore been too poor to afford the needed animation capability.

Image is the second factor. Funny cartoons for the kids that go bang-wham-zap, and animated corn flakes that go snap-crackle-pop, have unfortunately created an image that seems incompatible with the goals of education. The mention of animation in education tends to evoke smiles among teachers, and the introduction of animated film in the curriculum evokes academic humor about "our Mickey Mouse course." This image is wearing thin as more and more content experts become aware that the only way they can communicate their ideas is through the medium of animated films, but a degree of stigmatic humor remains.

The shortage of animators with a high enough level of education to visualize abstract ideas is a vital factor. Getting the hard content from the minds of those who know and understand to the mind of an animator who can visualize and communicate is the obstacle. The spreading inclusion of animated film production in the curricula of various schools of communication in colleges and universities may in part remedy this situation.

All of these factors that have tended to make educational film and television producers avoid the use of animated film in teaching may now be nullified or mitigated by a revolutionary new development—the computer-animated film.

The Computer-Animated Film

A revolutionary new technique has been developed which is transforming animated film from the status of being the most difficult, laborious, time-consuming and expensive of the media, to one of the simplest, quickest and least expensive. Through the use of analogue and digital computers, it is now possible to produce animated films in a third of the time and at a tenth of the cost of standard animated films. Had these new techniques been available to Walt Disney, he might have produced *Snow White and the Seven Dwarfs* in a matter of months instead of the years required with standard animation techniques. And the future impact of the computer-animated image upon educational film and television programs can scarcely be exaggerated.

The principle of computer animation is that the subject to be animated is displayed upon a 525-line cathode ray tube for external photography in real time by a 16-mm. or 35-mm. camera or recording on videotape. This display-photography relationship is common to both analogue and digital computer animation.

ANALOGUE COMPUTER ANIMATION

The analogue computer works on the basis of variable levels of electronic voltage, and therefore has a "continuous nature" enabling it to render images quickly, in real time. It has the capacity to receive and translate images from real artwork, prepared especially for this use and viewed by a vidicon camera, onto the surface of a cathode ray tube, and animate them in real time by means of sectioned rasters which are moved by vertical, horizontal and depth oscillators under the direct artistic and technical control of the operator and his art associates.

The analogue computer is quick, infinitely variable, low-cost (because it does not require the programming of tapes or cards) and permits aesthetic decisions to be made on a trial and error basis. The analogue computer is—in a very real sense—a new artistic tool which permits creative endeavor while eliminating the labor of doing "in-betweens" and much of the other drudgery of standard animation. Its limitations are twofold: there is a tendency for the image to "drift"

Analogue computer animated character. *Computer Image Corp.*

over a period of time, which affects precision, and it has a small memory bank.

"Scanimate" is a designation used to define a certain kind of analogue computer film production, created by The Computer Image Corporation, designed to animate actual artwork by scanning-oscillation techniques. The equipment consists of two vidicon cameras to view the artwork, which are connected to two monitors (a television viewing monitor and the cathode ray tube), an oscilloscope, a camera with its lens focused on the cathode ray tube, and an extremely complex set of oscillation and raster controls to animate the artwork and create a set of special effects. The electronic basis of Scanimate involves manipulation of scan lines, sine waves, sinusoidal waves and sectioned control of parts of the cathode ray tube raster, to achieve filmograph and limited animation effects.

CAESAR is an acronym for "Computer-Animated Episodes with Single-Axis Rotation," a system also created by the Computer Image Corporation. The CAESAR technique is a form of analogue computer animation capable of rendering cartoon figures and other subjects, in motion, with a plasticity rivaling hand-drawn animation. Moreover, as

Analogue computer animation. *Computer Image Corp.*

its name indicates, it offers full rotational capability: cartoon characters can perform such realistic motions as walking, running and jumping in any direction, turning at any time to walk toward the viewer or stride away toward the horizon. The result is an animated image in four dimensions: height, width, depth and motion.

The CAESAR system also has a visual storage feature which makes its animation performances available for reviewing on demand. When the animator has completed a sequence, he may store it in a digital memory unit. As each sequence is visually created, it is electronically stored. When all the animation has been created, it can be recalled in whatever order is desired, and the sequence edited electronically to tighten up the dramatic tempo. The digital storage unit offers the further advantage of providing a flurry of sub-routines. Standard animated motions, such as running or walking, can be stored in the memory bank and called up to animate any subject.

Any energy output can be used to modulate the image or any of its components as the animator watches the rendering of his animation on the monitor. He can produce animation by drawing with a joystick or by manipulating knobs, with the first lending itself better to the free-form drawing habits of an artist. As in the Scanimate system, there is a videosonic circuit system by which lip-animation can be done directly through a special circuit, without sound reading or bar sheets, and music can be used to animate the image, in perfect synchrony with a sound track.

DIGITAL COMPUTER ANIMATION

The digital computer is a quantitative system whose principles are based upon a vastly extended capability of following the simple instructions of yes or no, add or subtract, multiply or divide, but with the advantages of reliability, speed, precision, wide range of applications and a large memory bank capacity. The digital computer is ideal for business data processing and reduction of statistical data where a large number of simple calculations are performed and repeated over and over again.

Its disadvantages to film and videotape animation are a high hourly cost because of the need to program large quantities of tapes and cards for each frame of film, inflexibility and the inability of the operator to see what he is doing until it is done. The application of the digital computer to computer-animated films requires a machine language designed to control the image on the cathode tube, programming of immense quantities of information and little flexibility or tolerance of trial and error. Digital computer animation does have the advantage of precision in rendering images, which makes the system of value in some kinds of scientific and technical renderings. The digital computer is not presently capable of rendering images in real time because of the great quantity of data needed to produce an image, nor is the use of oscillators for animation compatible with the digital system.

An electronic microfilm recorder can plot points and draw lines a million times faster, and far more accurately, than a human draftsman. The digital computer–animated film therefore becomes important when precision of rendering becomes important, as in mathematical and scientific treatments. From this simple repertoire, programmed on cards and tapes, it can draw 10,000 to 100,000 points, lines or characters per second.

A special machine language must be designed to be used on any digital computer system and the language is unique to that system. The two main programming languages used are FORTRAN with microfilm commands added, and the mosaic-picture system called BEFLIX.

The system is essentially this: A card deck of instructions is fed to the computer, and a tape is written containing spot-by-spot picture descriptions, later to be read by a microfilm printer. These are intended to activate a 252-by-184 mosaic of spots arrayed in shades of gray, numbered 0 to 7. The computer keeps a complete current map of the picture presented to it, packed in the high-speed memory bank, three bits per spot.

The programmer uses two levels of language. At the first and most detailed level of control he directs scanners to peruse the two-dimensional mosaic array, reading numbers and optionally writing new numbers into these positions. At the second level of control the programmer instructs the system to draw lines, arcs, letters and other curves, using its own scanners for doing most of the work. The operator can also program instructions for copying, shifting, transliterating, zooming, dissolving and filling in areas bounded by previously drawn lines. A still unsolved problem of the digital computer–animated film is that of the "hidden line"—it is not presently possible to put one subject behind another without revealing the full lines of both subjects, a problem already solved in the technique of the analogue computer–animated film.

8

The Concepts of Special Effects

"Special effect" is a catchall term most often used to refer to the combining of the visual elements of two or more scenes into one single scene. The concept refers generally to any visual or optical relationship that cannot be successfully achieved by means of a single sound-speed exposure in the camera: the humble dissolve; superimposures; clear titles over a live-action background; animation combined with live-action footage; live-action subjects photographed in a studio combined with live-action backgrounds photographed at a distant location; incongruous and surrealistic relationships, such as a man shrinking down to so small a size that he can take a fantastic voyage through the veins and arteries of a human being.

All of the indicated optical tricks fall into the nebulous category of special effects. The conceptual and technical means of achieving them run into the hundreds, perhaps thousands—far more than could be treated within the scope of a single chapter. We will present only the basic conceptual means of creating the major forms of special effects most commonly used in the major genres of film and television, with no more presentation of technical details than is necessary to communicate the essential relationships required in the processes.

172

BEDKNOBS AND BROOMSTICKS. Live action and animation. © *Walt Disney Productions.*

Origins

The first cinematic special effects were created in 1900 by a professional magician named Georges Méliès who discovered that more than one image could be photographed on the same length of film. He proceeded to astound viewers by having people appear and disappear before their boggled eyes with the first dissolves. The spirit of magic and the traditions of the experimental filmmaker have ever since provided the impetus for the special effect.

The avant-grade movement in painting—implemented by artists who believed in the artistic validity of nonobjective forms—caught on among the experimental painters of the twenties. Art-for-art's-sake movies were first produced in Germany by two nonobjective artists, Hans Richter and Viking Eggeling, who were struggling to express visual themes on canvas in the way a musical composer might weave a theme into a symphony. They experimented first with the Chinese scroll concept, in which the artwork was unrolled to reveal the visual themes, permitting them to control themes in time as well as in space. The scroll method, however, did not enable them to control pacing and surface area, or to imply the movements found in music, so they turned to motion pictures. In 1921 the two men made the first experimental-animated films; Richter produced *Rhythmus 21*, and Eggeling made *Symphonie Diagonale*, the first applications of special effects for purely aesthetic goals.

In this new experimental form the camera became the artist's brush and was used to create rhythms, tricks and effects that were virtually nonobjective forms in motion. All storytelling in the entertainment sense was discarded. Actors, settings, narratives and dramatic conflicts were done away with, and the intent and content of studio films rejected. Instead, double-exposures, masks and cutouts were used to explore changing visual relationships of shapes devoid of meaningful content moving in space and time. Experiments were tried with lens and prism distortions, the shock effects of unexpected objects, the aesthetic possibilities of kaleidoscopic textures and lights, the excitement of animating inanimate objects—all of these given added cinematic dynamism by the rhythms of editing.

Content-expressive uses of special effects in experimental film were soon to follow: William Ruttmann created fluid impressionistic shapes to give gothic form to terrifying dreams, as in the black hawks montage of Fritz Lang's film, *Kreinhild's Revenge*. Oskar Fischinger followed with animated films to create visual counterparts to orchestral work in a forerunner to *Fantasia*. René Clair created a masterpiece of Dada art in *Entr'Acte*, a surrealistic comedy in which a legless man leaped to his feet and ran, a cadaver sprang to life from his casket, and the repeated low-angle shots of a ballerina's lovely legs were revealed by a slow tilt to be the underpinnings of a heavily bearded gentleman, glowering at the viewer through his pince-nez.

Cubist painters moved into film to exploit the rhythms of common objects in industrial society. Levers, gears, wheels, pots, pans, pendulums and technological mechanisms of every kind were photographed at varying film speeds, superimposed and contrasted, in ways that were at first the utilization of meaningful objects for intrinsically meaningless but aesthetically pleasing effects. Numbers and words were stripped of context and content and intercut with circles, squares and triangles for purely visual excitement.

The rhythmic arabesques of throbbing machines, spinning wheels, plunging pistons, weaving railroad tracks, opening windows and closing shutters, bubbling crucibles and faceless births and deaths were lovely, poetic, exciting things in themselves. Their surface values were delightful, but their substance really had little to say. The experimental film tradition went into limbo with the coming of the Depression, the rise of Hitler and the onslaught of World War II. Art-for-art's-sake seemed somehow frivolous and pretentious in the face of starvation, destitution, war and ruin, and the experimental film movement withered before the clarion call of social change advocated by the documentary film.

The avant-garde filmmakers of the twenties established an optical effects experimental tradition which has reemerged in the present as the "Underground film." As before, the goal is a search for novel effects. Color and sound have been added, along with pubic hair and sexual obsession, but the nonobjective concepts are quite similar to those of five decades ago. Moreover, the special effects developed by the real innovators have been since adopted, and adapted, for meaningful uses in entertainment, educational and documentary film, where they are now commonly used in the functional language of cinema.

Special Effects Techniques

Many of the special effects techniques adopted by the film and television industry were eventually systematized into certain technical procedures, implemented by equipment developed for that purpose. The most commonly used means of creating special effects are the *optical printer, the aerial image unit and the animation stand, the chroma-key unit, the Technimatte system* and *the process screen projector.*

OPTICAL PRINTER

The optical printer is the laboratory machine used to print films and achieve many optical effects. It is essentially a precise camera interlocked with a projector, used for rephotographing a previously exposed scene. The projector of the optical printer moves a length of film frame by frame through its aperture, with a focused beam of light behind the film in the projector's aperture. The camera lens of the optical printer is synchronously focused on each frame of film as it appears in the projector's aperture, thus rephotographing it on the fine-grain film stock in the camera's magazine.

During the process of rephotographing the scene the images of the original footage may be modified within the optical printer: A prism lens may multiply the single image of a subject into dozens of images of that subject within the reprinted scene, all performing the same identical actions. A ripple lens may distort the normal view of a subject into one seen through the warped perceptions of a person drunk or on drugs. Or, colored filters may be used to raise or lower the emotional temperature of a dramatic sequence; during the lovemaking sequence of *A Man and a Woman*, for example, the passionate scenes were printed through an orange filter to connote the intensity of the couple's feelings, while the aftermath of passion was printed with a gray filter to imply ennui and fatigue.

The optical printer is the most commonly used means of combining the visual elements of two or more scenes into one scene. The underlying principle is multiple exposure of the fine-grain film stock in the camera magazine of the optical printer with the scenes placed before it in the projector. The execution of multiple-run effects derives from the same rerun principle used in making the dissolve: the images of one scene are exposed first; then the film is run in reverse with the shutter closed to the starting point of the first scene, and the succeeding scene is photographed. The dissolve thereby executed is a simple optical effect combining the images of two scenes.

Multiple-exposure techniques to combine the visual elements of two or more scenes—with the elements of each occupying distinct and separate areas in the optically printed scene—is a more complex matter. Photographic mattes—opaque black in interdicting areas and transparently clear in print-through areas—must be used in succeeding runs through the projector and camera. The photographic black-and-clear mattes are used to conceal unexposed portions of the fine-grain raw film so those areas may be rephotographed later with the visual elements of the second scene.

Combining live-action footage with animated images in the optical printer is achieved by the photographic matte process just described,

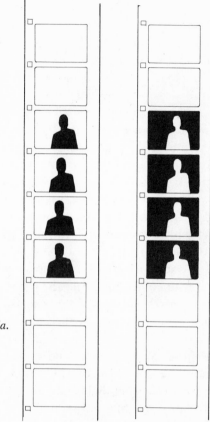

Photographic mattes.
Drawing by Glen Shimada.

with some variations. The first step is to photograph both live-action footage and animation footage to obtain the lengths of film whose visual elements are to be combined. The photographic black-and-clear mattes are then created on the animation stand: each animation cel, with its inked and painted subject, is photographed in silhouette by lighting it from the back and then photographing it from the front with high-contrast film stock. The photographic matte thus obtained has opaque black areas and transparently clear areas. A reverse print is made of this silhouette matte to obtain a negative version, which has a reverse relationship of transparently clear areas and opaque black areas. The two photographic mattes have a male-female relationship, matching each other perfectly, and matching the animation areas and live-action areas of the films to be printed together.

The live-action footage and the animation footage are then run separately through the optical printer, each accompanied by a photographic matte. When live-action A and matte A are run together through the projector of the optical printer, the opaque portion of the matte prevents the exposure of the corresponding area of the raw film stock, while the clear areas of the matte permit the desired images to be printed through to the raw film stock. When animation B and print B are run together through the optical printer, the already exposed areas of the previous run are protected by the black portions of matte B, and the formerly masked areas are now exposed with the images of print B. The desired images of live-action A are thus combined with the images of animation B, uniting live action with animation in print C.

Live-action footage photographed out on a distant location may be combined with live-action footage photographed in the studio by a similar photographic matte process. In this instance, however, the black-and-white mattes are obtained by a twofold camera and background lighting technique: A studio camera is equipped with a double film magazine, one loaded with color film stock, the other with high-contrast black-and-white film. Behind the lens of this camera is a prism which directs the same image simultaneously to the color stock and to the high-contrast film.

The lighting of the subject and its background is the basis for obtaining the photographic mattes: The subjects are lighted in the foreground by conventional lights having a color spectrum which corresponds to that of the film emulsion. The blank background behind the subjects, however, is lighted with lamps having a color from so narrow a segment of the color spectrum in its illumination that it will *not* expose normal color film emulsion—but *will* expose the high-contrast black-and-white film.

When the subjects are staged and photographed before this kind of background, the images pass through the lens to the prism, where they are redirected simultaneously to the color film stock and to the high-contrast film. The color film then records the images of the foreground subjects, but its background emulsion area remains unexposed. The high-contrast stock records the background area, but leaves the subject areas unexposed. As described earlier, a negative version is printed from the photographic black-and-white matte, providing a reverse matte that matches the other perfectly.

In the optical printer the subjects photographed in the studio may be combined with a background photographed anywhere in the world by using the same technique of printing A image to A matte, and B image to B matte, to obtain a C print which unites subjects and backgrounds in the same scene.

Combining images on the optical printer offers many advantages: Either the studio subject or the background scene can be photographed first, depending upon which is more convenient. Once the foreground subjects have been photographed in the studio, the background scene can be changed as many times as desired—and errors corrected—during composite printing without ever having to rephotograph expensive talent in the studio to make a correction. The photographic quality of the studio scene and its background can be produced separately at optimum levels and printed together for the best color balance. If it should be desired to change the sharpness of either the foreground subjects or the background images, or to modify the depth of field, it can easily be done through manipulation of the separate images in the optical printer.

BEDKNOBS AND BROOMSTICKS. Location and studio scenes. © *Walt Disney Productions*.

BEDKNOBS AND BROOMSTICKS.
Combined images. © *Walt
Disney Productions.*

The optical printer is to a creative filmmaker what paint, brushes and a gigantic canvas are to a painter—infinite in its possible rendering of themes, concepts, subjects and interpretations. It provides the filmmaker with a canvas broad enough to encompass any idea he can conceive and photographically render—manipulating the images in any sequence, relationship or time continuity—to the limits of the viewer's comprehension.

The optical printer has disadvantages, too, first among them being cost. The device is itself an expensive item of equipment, and the salaries paid to those who can operate it are high. Even more, the planning time required to plot and implement combined image and multiple-image effects tends to inflate production costs.

Its disadvantages are conceptual. Since the studio subjects and the background scenes are photographed at different times, it is impossible for the filmmaker to view the actors against their backgrounds while they perform, in order to be sure that the composition and perspective elements are correct. The actors, in turn, find it difficult to react to a background they cannot see and which may not yet exist. Panning and tilting movements are virtually precluded because they would require corresponding movements across a background that cannot be seen.

AERIAL IMAGE UNIT AND ANIMATION STAND

The aerial image unit and animation stand is a second technological means of combining several images into one scene. In principle, the unit has a projector and a camera, which is used to project and rephotograph the background scene—plus whatever animation images are placed in the path of the background projection.

A film projector is positioned to the right of the animation stand and electrically interlocked with the animation camera. Each frame of the previously exposed live-action footage is projected to a mirror under the table, where it is then reflected up through condenser lenses onto the raw film emulsion in the camera. Each animation cel is placed in the path of each projected live-action image, and when the exposure is made it comprises both live action and animation.

The aerial image technique is ideal for television because it obviates any need for the high-cost photographic matte technique. Moreover, minor changes may be made at low cost; if a sponsor has changed the label on his product, the label on a television commercial may be changed by the aerial image method without having to redo the entire commercial. The disadvantage, however, is that the live-action background presents a degraded second-generation film image in comparison with the first-generation animation image. While this is hard to perceive on television, because of the 525-line raster of American television receivers, the difference in film grain is instantly perceivable in a projected film.

CHROMA-KEY UNIT

Chroma-key, a video electronic system recently developed in the television industry, offers a third means of combining live action with animation, or live action with live action. Color separation is the basis for combining the visual elements of two different scenes into one. In this respect, its concept is similar to that of the color-key lighting technique described earlier, except that its technology is not chemical but electronic.

Chroma-key is a color matrix system based upon the capability of a color spectrum unit to electronically suppress all luminance information of selected portions of the spectrum. For example: If a live-action subject is photographed against a yellow-screen background—when yellow is the color suppressed by the color-key unit—the background of the subject will remain an undeveloped area, prepared to receive the images of the animation footage and its background. The images of the live-action subject (with yellow-screen background) and the images of the animation or special effects are channeled through the chroma-key unit and the special effects amplifier to a videotape recorder, where the animated images or special effects are electronically imprinted upon the yellow-screen background of the live-action background, thereby becoming an integrated composite on videotape. Editing is done electronically by the filmmaker, while watching each visual element over videotape monitors, and then the composite videotape is ready for broadcast over television.

The chroma-key system has two obvious advantages in its immediacy and low production costs. Its disadvantages are also twofold: First, the lack of an accurate registration system makes it difficult to achieve eye-to-eye relationships between the combined subjects. Second, because the images are combined by electronically "cutting a hole" in the background to receive the subjects in the foreground, the edges between the two are delineated by a hard blue halo, which is easy to see.

TECHNIMATTE SYSTEM

Technimatte is the trade name for a new electronic means of combining separate images on one television monitor for recording on videotape. The Technimatte system, developed by the Vidtronics Division of the Technicolor Corporation, makes it possible to electronically combine foreground subjects that are translucent or transparent with an opaque background—and see through the foreground to the background. Glass, smoke and liquids become realistically translucent. With chroma-key, and all other matting techniques, there is a hard edge separating foreground subjects from the background, and no possibility of creating the effect of seeing through one to the other without great expense and months of effort. With the Technimatte system the effect is achievable in microseconds and the cost is negligible.

A color matrix system is used to electronically suppress all color information of a selected portion of the spectrum, usually blue. In this respect, the technique resembles chroma-key. With Technimatte, however, the system is so selective that it permits the subject to wear blue clothing without apparently disappearing from the neck down, and to have blue eyes without seeming to have two neutral holes in his sockets, as is the effect when using chroma-key.

The Technimatte system uses color suppression to unite the images from two different monitors, one from the foreground and one from the background. Combined with this separation technique, however, is an electronic "additive system" which permits the incorporation of some foreground elements into the background. Thus, a glass of wine poured in the foreground would electronically add its liquid effects to the background. The delicacy of smoke, bubbles and aerosol spray may be realistically combined with any kind of background without the telltale hard edges that reveal a film matte technique, or the blue halo and tearing of edges that so often announce the chroma-key system. Moreover, the colors of the two images are realistically combined; the glass of wine or smoke in the foreground would reveal hues influenced by the colors of the background. The Technimatte additive system is so sensitive and flexible that it is possible to transfer the shadows of a subject in the foreground to the background in the combined image, an effect so difficult in other forms of matting that any revelation of subject shadows is carefully avoided. A foreground subject genuinely appears to be at the location suggested when the foreground and background are combined by the Technimatte process, because the two images are truly fused into one.

With the growing perfection of videotape-to-film transfer systems there seems a great probability that the Technimatte system of combining studio scenes with location backgrounds may supersede all other matting systems in the production of effects for feature films, as well as those videotape productions intended only for television.

Process Screen Projector

Process screen projection is a fifth means of combining studio subjects with unrelated backgrounds photographed at a distant location. The technique consists essentially of having actors stand before a translucent screen on which the slide or motion picture background is projected from the rear, and photographing the subjects and their backgrounds together. Scenes of lovers whispering sweet nothings before Niagara Falls are often photographed this way, as are closeups of "our hero" walking a tightrope over the Grand Canyon or standing alone with one cartridge in a jammed revolver against a herd of thundering buffalo, or the war-whooping braves of an Indian tribe on the warpath. More commonly, rear- and front-screen projection is used in conversations that take place in automobiles to show a city whizzing by outside the car windows.

Screen projection of backgrounds offers some important creative advantages: The filmmaker can see both the actors and their background at the time of studio cinematography, enabling him to compose their visual relationships carefully. The actor can see the background projected and react appropriately to it. And the cinematographer can freely pan, tilt and truck his camera, within the limits of the screen, while the actor performs.

The screen projection system also offers other, broader advantages. Difficult or dangerous scenes can be produced in the studio in comfort and safety; an actor can apparently dangle from a ledge on the fiftieth floor of the Empire State Building, while actually hanging five inches off the studio floor. Background scenes of distant locales may be photographed separately and integrated visually with foreground action staged in a studio. Finally, exterior and interior photography may be executed separately, enabling the filmmaker to pay careful attention to each visual component.

Disadvantages exist, too: There is often a "hot spot" in the center of the screen, from the projector bulb, and a tendency of the projected scene to soften into a vignette around its periphery. There is also a difference in the film grain quality of the subject and his background, because the background image is actually being photographed a second time, and is further diffused in passing through the translucent screen. All subject lighting must be kept off the screen. Rear-screen projection is probably the most practical low-cost means of combining studio actors and scenes of a distant location, particularly when television projection will obscure the degraded grain of the background.

Minor Special Effects

A number of minor special effects have been developed for esoteric purposes, some of which are achieved in cinematography, and some in the printing process. These are *slow motion, time lapse, distortion, the spin, freeze-frame, reverse movements, skip-framing, multiple-image effects* and *multiscreen presentations.*

SLOW MOTION

Slow motion, the portrayal of a dramatic action in a far longer span of time than it would really take to occur, is a cinematography special effect used to connote several meanings, depending upon the circumstances of the story. This effect is achieved by photographing the action at faster than sound speed, and then projecting the film at the slower rate of speed. The use of slow motion to expand the important instant of death, first used by Japanese filmmakers, is now widely adopted in American films. In *They Shoot Horses, Don't They?*, the mercy killing of a horse at the beginning of the film, and the slaying of a woman at its end, were rendered in slow motion as the slain creatures floated rather than fell to the ground. Other uses of the slow-motion technique are to simulate the feelings or viewpoint of someone who is fantasizing, drunk or on drugs.

TIME LAPSE

Time-lapse photography is a means of recording movements in subjects whose changes are so slow as to be imperceptible to the unaided eye. The technique consists essentially of exposing one frame of film at widely separated intervals of time; the professional method is to use a device called the intervalometer, which can be preset to trip the camera shutter at specific intervals of time. A common application of time-lapse photography is the photographic recording of growth in plants. A frame of film exposed at one-minute intervals could render the growth, budding and flowering of a plant which would present, when projected at sound speed, a graphic portrayal of growth patterns. Time-lapse photography is used in a wide range of scientific work and for such aesthetic effects as accelerating the rising and setting of the sun.

DISTORTION

Distortions in the perception of a subject are often used to create subjective connotations that the person is drunk, on drugs or having

New York City; optical distortions. *Pyramid Films/Francis Thompson.*

hallucinations. A distortion may be created with a special lens designed specifically to achieve that effect. An ordinary automobile, for example, can be smeared by a distortion lens until it looks like a caterpillar humping along the road—a visual analogy made realistically plausible only by optical distortion. Other forms of distortion, such as ripple dissolves and ripple effects, can be achieved by lenses designed for that purpose, or by ripple glass inserted between camera and subject, to achieve all kinds of surrealistic effects. Lenses have been created that will render virtually any kind of distortion desired by the film-maker.

THE SPIN

The spin consists of revolving a scene or a title around its own center point. The spinning movement is seldom more than an eye-catcher used to hold the gaze of the viewer until the whirling scene slows down and stops, enabling him to read the name of the commercial product, or whatever is intended to be the center of the viewer's attracted attention. The spin may be executed by a rotating lens on an optical printer or a rotation unit on an animation stand.

THE FREEZE-FRAME

The freeze-frame is a single frame within a motion picture that is held still on the screen for the viewer's perusal, before returning to motion. The freeze-frame is used when the content of a single frame is intrinsically so meaningful or poignant that the filmmaker feels it should not be lost in movement, but drawn to the attention of the viewer. At the point of the freeze-frame the medium changes from moving to a still picture, telling the audience to look carefully.

REVERSE MOVEMENTS

Reverse movements present a subject moving backward instead of forward, seeming to defy normal directions of locomotion, the laws of gravity and the continuity of time. The reverse movement of a subject is achieved by loading the unexposed film stock on the take-up reel of the camera magazine, instead of the supply reel, and then exposing the film in reverse. When the film is processed and projected in the normal forward motion, the subjects will move backward. The same effect may be achieved by printing film in reverse in the optical printer. Reverse movements are most often used for comic effects.

SKIP-FRAMING

Skip-framing is an optical printing technique in which frames of the original scene are periodically omitted in printing. The effect is to introduce a slight jitter in the subject's movements and to apparently speed up the action. The carefree actions of a child playing, or a puppy gamboling, can be emphasized by introducing skip-framing. The effect is achieved by setting the optical printer to skip every fifth or sixth frame, depending on how jittery an effect is desired. The skipping may be done at any preselected interval of frames, but the practical maximum distance of the effect is about every twelve frames, at half-second projection intervals. Beyond the half-second perception time it tends to be interpreted as an error or a jump cut. Skip-framing finds its greatest uses in comic effects and television commercials.

MULTIPLE-IMAGE EFFECTS

The multiple-image effect, in which several events are occurring simultaneously in separate panels within a single scene, is a current vogue giving vigorous exercise to the film literacy of the lay viewer. The separate images are supposed to add up to a third meaning not inherent in any of the events occurring on the screen—the meaning being inferred by the viewer.

In the dramatic film *Grand Prix*, for example, multiple-image panels were used to show each of the racing cars being started, the determined frenzy of the mechanics and the intensity of the drivers. Later, during the most competitive moments of the race, multiple-image panels were presented to show the simultaneous anxiety and excitement of the bystanders and the determined faces of the drivers. And when tragedy struck, the viewer saw the instantaneous reactions of widely separated viewers.

Another dramatic application of the multiple-image concept appeared in *The Andromeda Strain*. A woman scientist began to think about various aspects of a scientific problem, her image filling the screen completely. Her image was then reduced to a small square in one corner of the screen, while her ideas were visualized one at a time in other panels on the screen. The visual sum total of the various aspects of the problem sequentially added up to her solution of the dilemma, leading the viewer visually through her thought process.

Educational films and television programs make use of the multiple-image effect to demonstrate how different aspects of the same process occur at the same time. In the Scripp's Institute production of the film *Deep Sea Drilling* interactions of sonar, drilling, computer analyses readouts, and scenes of scientists manipulating the equipment, were shown simultaneously at each phase of the process at any given point in time.

Moreover, special effects within special effects may be implemented by having some of the multiple images combine live action and animation, while others have wipes, superimposures, freeze-frames, polarized images—each in a separate image panel, each image relating to every other image on the screen in some meaningful or aesthetic way.

Multiple images may be used to present several different subjects having only an implied content relationship, with that relationship to be inferred by the viewer. A scene might contain, for example, separate images of a snowy forest, a mechanized lumbering operation, deer browsing on spruce twigs, children tobogganing down a slope, and a Canada jay scolding a man shoveling his front walk—the sum total meaning revealing the life style in Quebec.

One great advantage of the multiple-image technique is flexibility. Thanks to the optical printer's capacity to place images of any size anywhere on the printing film stock—in separate passes—each image may be printed at any desired size, time and place in any given scene, with a perfect relationship to all other images similarly printed. (Multiple-image effects may also be done with an aerial image unit or a chroma-key unit, but with less flexibility.) Moreover, because the separate images are printed in separate runs through the optical printer, each image may be modified in printing with filters and special lenses, independently of any other image. The multiple-image concept offers promise of rivaling the novel in its potential for offering insights not formerly possible in the cinema, and may be no less than revolutionary when applied to educational films and television programs.

The technique is less suitable for television because of the smallness of the screen, but two or three panels are practicable. One disadvantage of the split-screen image concept is that it begins to lose force when more than five panels are used, because the viewer is forced to keep track of too many centers of interest and fuse them in his mind, with a resultant breakdown in continuity.

MULTISCREEN PRESENTATIONS

Multiscreen presentation—many screens and many projectors operating simultaneously—have been attempted since 1925, when they were first tried in Paris by Abel Gance. The basic intent is to manipulate the relationships between the images on separate screens in order to imply a third meaning not inherent in any of them. Some of the screens may be left black, so the viewer can concentrate on the others, or all may be used at once to kaleidoscopic effect. Different views of the same subject may be presented on all the screens, or all the screens can present views of different subjects having only an implicit relationship.

The multiscreen presentation may also be a multimedia presentation, combining films, slides, filmstrips, television and live performers in the kind of tour de force done so brilliantly by the Czechoslovakian filmmakers. Moreover, screens may be moved, or multiple images presented on a single screen, or a single image fragmented over many screens. The multi-media, multi-screen presentation is often a refreshing change from the usual single screen film and television presentation. It requires a high degree of technical and creative competence, however, to present it successfully. Timing and technology are important: If unrelated images appear simultaneously, or any of the projectors break down, the result will be a kind of chaos unsurpassed since the Dada film, *An Appeal to Reason*.

Electronic Special Effects

Electronic techniques for achieving special effects are being developed rapidly. The Special Effects Recorder, also known as the HS-200 disc system, is a new innovation for achieving many effects resembling those achieved in film, and many more that are original. The Special Effects Recorder works on a principle resembling that of the Random Access Videotape Editor in the sense that all the scenes recorded on films and videotapes are transmitted to magnetic discs. These discs then rotate at high speed and their electronically recorded scenes are scanned by a magnetic head for reproduction. By manipulating the way the head scans the discs, and the rotational speed of the discs, the following effects may be achieved:

The dissolve, a fade-in combined with a fade-out, is achieved electronically by taking scan input A and scan input B and fusing them electronically through a composite mixer (a switch panel system) programmed to combine the two scenes within a specified number of frames. A freeze-frame is created by having the magnetic head repeatedly scan the same frame scan line on the disc. Skip-framing is done by having the magnetic head skip frames as it scans the rotating discs. Flutter-framing, in which a subject seems to flutter back and forth as it moves forward, is done by repeat-scanning of the tail frames of a forward movement. The highly flexible HS-200 Special Effects Recorder also permits the creating of such effects as slow motion, double-speed playback, variable-frame animation, multiple-image effects and single-frame animation.

Electronic special effects are sometimes improvised during the production of a video-film. During the production of 200 *Motels*, a feature film originally produced on videotape, the engineers manipulated the electronic controls and experimented with improvised visual effects and distortions. They played with short circuits, sinex waves, sinecoidal waves and depth oscillation waves, enhancing and dropping out colors, until the director saw a special effect that he liked. Then he asked the engineers to hold that effect while the actors and musicians gave their performance. The sequences were electronically photographed with the distortions as integral parts of the performances. The videotape was subsequently transferred to film, by the Vidtronics tape-to-film transfer system, and the production distributed to theaters as a feature motion picture.

The electronic area of special effects seems destined to be the area of greatest potential for both films and videotapes. The shortcomings of the system at the present state of the art are those that were discussed in the chapter on "Videotape and Film: The New Synthesis." Given the rapid rate of improvements in electronic technology, however, it seems only a matter of time before they will all be resolved, to achieve a true synthesis of the media in special effects for video-film.

The Dramatic Film

9

Dramatic Structure in Cinema-Television

The opening moments of the dramatic film are golden: the viewer sits facing the screen with his heart and mind open, receptive to anything the film may present, willing to yield his consciousness of self to the story told by the film. The average viewer comes to a dramatic film or television program in order to leave behind for a few hours the banality and frustrations of his daily life and live another life on the screen through identification with its characters in conflict. He seeks an emotional catharsis in losing consciousness of self and living vicariously through stories of mystery, intrigue, comedy, history and adventure. He willingly surrenders his being with the first fade-in to experience the destinies of other men, and when he regains awareness of self, after the last fade-out, he awakens, hopefully, refreshed.

Dramatic Appeal

Elemental emotions are the bases of appeal in dramatic films, emotions that lie deeper than culture and cut across all strata of society to touch the viewer's instinctive soul. Love, pity, hate, tenderness, courage and desperation are the timeless emotional truths of drama that run deeper than the topical experiences of daily life. The viewer recognizes these emotional truths from his own experiences, and through this recognition he identifies with the characters on the screen and vicariously projects his own emotions into their conflicts. Any man sitting in the audience who has ever felt passion for a woman may identify with a scene of passion on the screen. Any woman who has ever loved a man may identify with scenes portraying a woman in love. Any boy or girl who has ever felt helpless in the power of adults may feel frightened by a story of kidnapping. The viewer experiences the events on the screen because he vicariously projects the emotions he has known in his own life to the characters experiencing those emotional truths in the dramatic film.

Intellectual ideas are seldom successful as the basis of a dramatic story unless they simultaneously touch emotions common to all men. When "message" films have been successful it has been because the filmmaker has also offered insights into the human soul, and its relationships with others, through the perceptual form of motion pictures. When human relations are staged to serve ideological ends, the characters frequently become pedagogical and preach their messages to the mind, rather than to the emotions, to the effect that the viewer fails to lose consciousness of self and identify with the life on the screen—the film has failed as drama.

There are times of national crisis when the population is keyed up to a *cause sacré* and may identify with message films, but these are the exception. In most cases, when dramatic films have been successfully based upon intellectual messages, the message has been exemplified by a story of people caught up in moving circumstances, and it has been the dramatic excellence of the film, rather than the message, that has assured its success with the viewer. It is worth remembering that the dramatic form exists primarily to provide vicarious emotional fulfillment for the viewer, and that other forms, such as the documentary, exist more suitably to convey intellectual messages.

Conflict

Conflict is fundamental to American dramatic film; the story consists of a series of clashes between adversaries, and the resolution is not revealed until the end. Conflict fascinates the viewer because it is only under stress that the veneers of civilization are peeled back to reveal the basic characteristics of men. Without a sustained struggle to reveal character, unify the story, develop action and provide suspense—all organized and motivated by a plot—it would be difficult to engage the attention of the average viewer for the length of a feature film.

Conflict is generally found in five forms in American drama: the struggles of *man against himself, man against man, man against society, man against the elements* and *society against society*, where the individual finds his destiny within the outcome of a greater struggle.

MAN AGAINST HIMSELF

Man against himself is a theme that deals with otherwise remarkable persons who have unfortunate personality or character traits which militate against and perhaps destroy them. Classic examples of the theme of man against himself are Hamlet, who could not make up his mind, and Macbeth, who destroyed himself through ruthless ambition. For the first fifty years of American dramatic film this theme was largely buried under action-oriented, situation-centered stories, but with the shift of action dramas to television, the theatrical film industry began to make cinematic journeys into the self of character.

Patton was constructed on the theme of man against himself. This feature film made a study of the World War II American general who could not control his temper, keep his mouth shut or show good judgment in anything except his leadership of an army into battle. Because Patton the man was incompatible with Patton the general, his irrational personality traits culminated in the destruction of the brilliant military career that was his life.

A major cinematic problem with the man-against-himself concept is how to visually render what is primarily an internal conflict. A novel may explain a man's emotions, but film must show them. While the intent may be to subordinate plot and action to the revelation of character, it is difficult to reveal character without vision in motion. Without visual action, the only other recourse to the revelation of inner feelings is dialogue, which is essentially uncinematic.

MAN AGAINST MAN

Man against man has been, until recently, the most common form of conflict found in American dramatic film, an interest probably based upon the strong national emphasis upon competition, a fascination with who is the better man in any given conflict. Or, perhaps, the appeal of man against man exists as a universal instinctive pleasure of watching a pair of anything fight for supremacy. The pitting of two men against each other has most frequently been motivated by their common desire for a woman, their clash over land, money or something else of value. If the object of contention relates to the eternal triangle—two men competing for a woman or two women for a man—then the object is the primary consideration. If the object of the struggle is materialistic, it serves only as the occasion for action, a catalyst for the clash between men and the revelation of their characters.

MAN AGAINST SOCIETY

Man against society presents the theme of the underdog struggling to fulfill himself despite the perversity and restraints of the people or the institutions about him. The concept of the "loner" who fights against great odds to achieve a goal is immensely popular with the American people, perhaps because of a national strand of persistent individualism, or perhaps through identification with inner feelings of rebellion against the conformities imposed by an industrialized society. The dramatic structure of the man-against-society theme is characterized by crises and obstacles which are almost impersonal elements of opposition to the protagonist in the film. Sometimes these elements are expressed in the form of callousness by collective man, and sometimes as institutionalized oppression in the form of inexorable pressures by the law.

Lonely Are the Brave told the story of a cowboy trying to live the old free life, without a job or identification or social security, in a modern America criss-crossed by barbed wire, broad highways and law enforcement. In his simple attempt to help a friend in trouble, he managed to cut down fences, get thrown into jail, break out of jail, be hunted through the mountains by law officers and the air force, shoot down a helicopter and escape—only to be killed by a truck filled with privies when he tried to ride his horse across a highway in a rainstorm. This poignant story told what may happen to a free man who stubbornly refuses to be absorbed into a technological world, and the price one may pay to be a man against society.

MAN AGAINST THE ELEMENTS

In the classic Aristotelian sense man against the elements meant man against the gods or against his own destiny. In American film it has most often referred to the struggle of pioneers to tame a wilderness with the opening of the Far West. This is the epic tale of men who match the mountains, harness the rivers and turn the land with one hand on a plow and the other on a gun.

In man against the elements the story is provided by the stubborn resistance of primeval nature to the pioneers, and the possible destruction of their hard-won gains through natural disasters or the actions of hostile natives. The characters are usually portrayed as larger than life, and treated simplistically as Pioneers, Heroic Women, Good Men and Bad. The plot is as formally standardized as the rituals of the Kabuki theater, and the pleasures derived from films about man against the elements are apparently not those of surprise, but the satisfactions of savoring variations on an old but well-loved theme.

Little Big Man presented the opening of the Wild West in all its brawling tumultuous spirit, portraying the changes in the land and its people from the time of bitter hardship and Indian attacks through the days of gunfighters and outlaws to eventual peace and prosperity. All the ingredients were there: the noble red man, pioneers, charlatans, gunfighters, whores and good women who wrung their hands and tried to get their men to put away their guns and go to church. And when the film ended in the era of the tape recorder, the old Westerner was left dreaming of the great days (as were the male viewers) when men really lived the epic tradition of man against the elements.

SOCIETY AGAINST SOCIETY

Society against society presents a struggle greater than the individuals participating within it, with each individual resolving his personal conflicts and realizing his personal destiny through the victory or defeat of his side in the struggle. This format is common in many film genres of the Soviet Union, but exists in American film primarily in movies about war—the only occasion where the society-versus-society concept has seemed dramatically plausible. The dramatic structure of this concept usually exists on three levels: First, a climactic event looms to decide the outcome of a struggle between two great contenders, often in the form of a battle that will decide the fate of everyone. Second, a group of men have a mission to fulfill whose outcome may be the hinge of victory, and this group is directly opposed by a comparable group on the other side. Third, personal animosities and conflicts exist among the men of each group. All three strata of conflict—society against society, group against group, man against man—are resolved in the final climactic struggle.

The Enemy Below told the story of a life-or-death struggle at sea between an American destroyer and a German submarine, with the commanders and crews of both vessels matching their wits, skills and courage in a contest whose outcome meant life for one side and death for the other. Within each vessel the men argued over each decision, struggled to carry out their missions, maneuvered for personal advantage, sweated and cursed straight through to the crunch of steel on steel that was the climax.

Plot

The importance of plot is directly proportional to the length of the film, the degree of character development and the complexity of the story. A short film may present a dramatic vignette which is improvised on location, casually photographed, freely edited and a delight to view on the screen; its artistic and cinematic elements are easy to keep under control. A long film of feature length, on the other hand, usually presents many characters, many conflicts, many locations—all interrelated—and this requires the organization of a plot in order to capture and maintain the interest of the average viewer. A feature-length film without a plot needs the guiding hand of a genius to keep from falling apart. Once a story line has been plotted, however, improvisation of new dramatic sequences may add the refreshing insights of the impromptu to solid dramatic structure and offer the best of two genres to the viewer.

The plot, in American feature-length films, has certain elements used to provide a framework for the telling of the story and the revelation of characters in conflict. These dramatic elements are *theme, pivotal character, joining the conflict, crises* with *reversals of fortune* and *recognition of self-delusion, obligatory scene, climax* and *denouement*. These concepts must be defined before their relationships to characters in conflict may be analyzed.

THEME

The theme of a drama is an emotional truth that the screenwriter wishes to express about the nature of man under a given set of circumstances. Themes may derive from timeless human emotions of love, jealousy, avarice, heroism and so forth, or they may derive from a unique situation having dramatic potentialities needing only a theme to give them meaning and suggest a climax. When the writer fails to establish a theme in his screenplay, the film may drift and lack dramatic impact. Without a clear-cut theme—that says something about the nature of man—the film will tend to bore the average viewer, however slick its production. The emphasis in thematic plot structure should not be upon *how* the dramatic actions occur, but on *why* they occur.

The theme of *High Noon*, a western, evolved from a dramatic situation in which the sheriff of a small town was faced with the return from prison of a convicted murderer who had sworn to kill him for revenge. The sheriff had spent years ridding the town and territory of outlaws and he felt confident that the good men of the community would rally behind him, guns in hand, to face the returned killer and his gang. One by one, however, the townsmen found reasons not to support the sheriff —they hid away or crept away or whined their way out of fighting by his side. The sheriff was urged by everyone, including his new bride, to run away and not face the gunmen. But he was a courageous man; in the end he strapped on his guns, fought alone against the outlaws and won. After the last bullet had been fired the men of the town shuffled shamefacedly out from their hiding places. The sheriff tore off his tin star and threw it on the ground before the cowardly townsmen. The screenwriter's theme: *When serious trouble comes, don't count on anyone but yourself.*

PIVOTAL CHARACTER

The pivotal character is the person whose actions set all the dramatic forces in motion, and whose persistence keeps them in motion to the end of the film. The pivotal character must be someone determined to get what he wants, who will not settle for less, and who sets out to achieve his purposes in a way that sets forces and counterforces in motion—people for and against him. His sustained struggle gradually builds in intensity from the first joining of a conflict to its final resolution in the climax, and he never gives up from beginning to end. If the pivotal character were to give up anywhere along the way, there would be no story, no conflict, no drama. The pivotal character and those who oppose him provide unity of plot for the entire film.

The pivotal character may be the major character, who is the protagonist, or a minor supporting character. In *The Ox Bow Incident* it
was the relentless determination of a minor character, a cowboy, to
avenge the alleged death of his buddy that joined a conflict which led to
the lynching of three innocent men by the major characters portrayed in
the film.

JOINING THE CONFLICT

Joining the conflict means presenting the opposing adversaries in a
drama, be it man against himself, man against man or man against
society. Conflicts are joined within five to ten minutes of the opening in
American dramatic films, and continue with growing intensity throughout the length of the film until resolved in the outcome.

CRISES

Crises, which constitute the main body of the film, are the dramatic
events that create suspense between the first joining of a conflict and
their resolution in the outcome of the story. Crises are created by the
attempts of the pivotal character to achieve his goals again and again, in
each dramatic sequence, and each time he is frustrated. Every dramatic
sequence contains one crisis—in which the pivotal character is frustrated in his attempts—and is followed by another in which the pivotal
character tries again to achieve his goal. This pattern continues with
rising intensity until the drama reaches its peak in the climax.

The crisis pattern of *Midnight Cowboy* was typical: Joe Buck, a
dishwasher from Texas who traveled to New York to become a gigolo,
met with these concatenated crises while attempting to become a paid
lover. He approached a woman out walking her dog on the streets of
New York, went with her to her apartment and made love to her, only
to have her tears persuade him to pay her for the affair. Joe then tried to
force himself into a woman's rooming house, expecting to be welcomed
by a line of lustful women, only to find himself thrown bodily out the
door. Desperate for money, Joe allowed himself to be seduced by a
homosexual boy, but discovered too late that the boy did not have a
dime. Eventually, Joe attended a drug and drink party and found a
woman willing to pay for his sexual services, only to find that hard times
and hard narcotics had made him sexually impotent. Although Joe

Buck eventually succeeded in his copulation for pay, he came to the conclusion that being a stud was the most miserable way in the world to make a living. Each of his attempts to become a gigolo was frustrated, creating a new crisis.

Crises appear on the surface to have two dramatic forces in motion —the drive of the pivotal character to achieve his goals and the counterforce of whoever or whatever opposes him. More deeply, however, each crisis has a triangular relationship. There is always a third force present, seen or felt, which gives the pivotal character another option for action or exists as a potential threat. This third force either impels the pivotal character to go on with what he is trying to achieve or provides him with an alternative. The importance of the third point in the triangle lies in its creation of suspense by giving the pivotal character two stresses in every crisis.

The eternal triangle of a woman forced to choose between two men provides a graphic example: In *Ryan's Daughter*, a tale of adultery set in Ireland, Rosie found herself in a triangular dilemma in every crisis leading up to the climax. The pervading triangle was, of course, the dilemma of fidelity to a good husband or fulfillment with a good lover, and whenever she was faced by her husband or lover the other existed as an alternative. Rosie was always *faced with a choice*. In some crises the triangle was formed by Rosie, her lover and the villagers; in others it was Rosie, the priest and her husband. Rosie, as the pivotal character seeking sexual fulfillment, was the constant point in the triangle, the other characters taking turns at the points of the triangle to provide crises as she sought fulfillment.

The triangle of crisis does not receive equal emphasis on all points; there are always two dominant points and one subordinate point, with the importance of any given point rising or falling from one crisis to the next according to the changing motivations and circumstances of the characters involved. The triangle is a dramatic device which may be used under as many circumstances as there are characters in conflict. The only true constant in the changing triangular relationships is the point of the pivotal character. The concept of triangular crisis structure as it relates to the motivation of characters will be treated at length in the following chapter, "Cinematic Development of Characters."

Crisis structure is a means to the end of revealing characters in conflict, their *reversals of fortune* and their *recognition of self-delusion*. Reversals of fortune are the high points of each crisis, and the climax.

Each time the pivotal character or protagonist tries to achieve his goals —and seems about to achieve them—something unexpected occurs to reverse his fortunes at that point in the story, leaving him with no alternative but to try another alternative. This in turn leads to fresh obstacles and new forms of opposition in each succeeding crisis until the final reversal of fortune in the climax. The constant reversals of fortune to which the character is subjected have a cumulative effect upon his attitudes, values and aspirations, and in the ultimate reversal of fortune —the climax—a change traditionally occurs within the character by which he either accepts the permanent reversal of fortune or faces death. For Rosie, the permanent reversal of fortune came with the death of her lover and the recognition that she would no longer live for sexual fulfillment. Her change of character, recognition of self-delusion, was revealed when she gently kissed the ugly face of the village idiot, a visage that had so revulsed her at the outset of the film that she had not allowed him to touch her.

OBLIGATORY SCENE

The obligatory scene is the dramatic event the viewer is led to believe will be the "climax," and if the viewer is not presented with an obligatory scene, in addition to the climax, he may leave the film dissatisfied. These two climactic events are closely related at the conclusion of the film, and the usual order is first obligatory scene and then climax.

In *Midnight Cowboy* Joe Buck, the would-be stud and pivotal character, set out for New York City to become a hired lover for the jaded ladies of that city, and it was *obligatory* that at some time in the story his virility pay off in bed. The secondary story line, interwoven with the primary, related to Joe's crippled friend, Ratso, who desperately wished to cure his growing cough and regain his health by going to Florida, and it was *obligatory* that Ratso reach Florida. Both men fulfilled their obligatory scenes, with Joe being paid for making love and then financing Ratso's sojourn to Florida, as the viewer expected they would. But then the climax came in the form of death to Ratso, and the transformation of Joe Buck from a smirking punk trying to make an easy dollar to a mature man willing to do honest work. The viewers received the fulfillment of the expected obligatory scene, and then the fulfillment of a surprise climax which realized the screenwriter's theme in a dramatic action.

CLIMAX

The climax of a dramatic film is that point in the story in which the protagonist and pivotal character gets what he wants or is defeated, all conflicts are resolved one way or the other, and the theme of the screenwriter is *realized in action*. It may be worth stressing that a theme is not realized in dialogue, but in a *dramatic action* carried out by the major characters.

DENOUEMENT

The denouement consists of an explanation by one of the characters, after the climax and the obligatory scene, of all the loose ends in the plot which the screenwriter was unable to resolve in these two dramatic high points. Ideally, there should be no denouement at all—the film should end immediately after the climax and leave the viewer with a theme expressed in action. In films of a genre that emphasize mystery and suspense, however, it is sometimes necessary for the detective to explain, while settling back with his pipe before the fireplace, what hidden clues led him to his elementary conclusion. In *Perry Mason*, a defunct television lawyer series, it was a program practice to have the screenwriter leave out those clues that might enable the viewer to anticipate the climax, in order to provide for a denouement in which the great private eye would explain at complex and dubious length how he solved the crime. The denouement is a crutch for weak dramatic writers; as a rule, the lazier the screenwriter, the longer the denouement.

The Point of Dramatic Attack

To this point dramatic structure has been presented as something rigid rather than organic. But while basic dramatic structure demands that certain elements be present, it is an infinitely plastic and flexible in its forms and applications as the human beings who live their roles for a few hours on the screen or the viewers who sit and watch them. Dramatic structure exists to assure that conflicts will occur in a logical, cohesive, interesting order that will reveal the characters of men in action and hold the interest of the viewer. Plot is a way of eliminating the superfluous; without it, drama would be as banal as the daily lives of most of those who come to drama for emotional catharsis and escape.

Plot is a means of dropping a series of psychological (or physical) bombs to which each character in the story responds according to his nature, enabling each to discover the truth about himself and, concomitantly, revealing to the viewer some aspect of the truth about himself.

Having defined the basic parts of plot structure, it seems appropriate to discuss when and where these elements are used, and to describe their organic relationships. The first five to ten minutes of a dramatic film are packed with exposition. The point of dramatic attack presents, within that brief period of time, *the context of the conflict and the pivotal character, the background to the conflict, the event that triggers the conflict and the joining of the conflict*, and plants clues to the *obligatory scene, the climax* and *the denouement*. All these dramatic elements should occur within the first ten minutes of a feature-length film, and all were found as follows in David Lean's film *Ryan's Daughter*.

The Context and Pivotal Character

The context of the conflict and the pivotal character were presented immediately in *Ryan's Daughter*. Rosie, the pivotal character and protagonist, was introduced as she read a racy romantic novel on a rugged cliff overlooking the tumultuous Irish sea, dressed in fancier clothes and parasol than any of the other town girls could afford—a fact pointed out by the village priest who then appeared. Rosie's precious attitude about herself was further revealed by her revulsion against being touched by the ugly village idiot who accompanied the priest. The second major setting was then established in Ryan's tavern in a small Irish village; the conversation around the bar concerned the British Army fighting the Germans in World War I, the people's sympathies for the Germans and the help given by the Germans to the Irish revolutionaries then fighting for their independence. The intrusion of two British soldiers, coming in for a dram, revealed that the town was occupied by a British garrison. Within ten minutes of the first fade-in, the pivotal character and protagonist, Rosie, was introduced, as well as the time, place, location, physical topography and emotional setting of *Ryan's Daughter*.

The Background

The background to the joining of the conflict lay in the indulgence of Rosie's every wish by her father, Ryan, an informer for the British, who used his money to pamper his "princess." Rosie married a middle-aged schoolteacher to satisfy her yearnings for romance and sexual fulfillment, and when he failed on both counts, she was for the first time frustrated in the attainment of her wishes. Rosie was thereby psychologically prepared to seek fulfillment through the passion of another man, because Ryan's daughter had always had what she wanted and would not settle for less than complete sexual gratification.

THE TRIGGERING EVENT

The event that triggered the conflict was the arrival of a young and handsome English major, wounded in body and spirit, a Byronic hero who exemplified all the romance, passion and sexual fulfillment Rosie had been seeking. And when she achieved fulfillment, she set herself against the forces of her own conscience, the will of the village priest, the feelings of her husband and the wrath of the Irish villagers, who were doubly outraged by her flagrant adultery and consort with an enemy officer.

JOINING OF THE CONFLICT

The joining of the conflict must reveal the nature of the conflict, and the opening sequences of this film revealed four levels of conflict relating to Rosie's adultery with the English major: Rosie against her own desires of the flesh; Rosie against her husband; Rosie against the Irish villagers and the priest; and Ireland against Britain in a war for independence, in which the German enemies of the British were supplying guns to the Irish revolutionary movement.

CLUES TO OBLIGATORY SCENE, CLIMAX AND DENOUEMENT

The *obligatory scene* was Rosie's punishment by mob violence at the hands of the Irish villagers for the sin of adultery, a punishment whose seeds were planted near the beginning of the film in the mob's abuse of Michael, the village idiot. Michael had brought a lobster into the village, and the villagers began to taunt and humiliate him for sport, throwing his lobster back and forth until it was torn to shreds and trampled underfoot, and he was reduced to crawling on his knees before them. This clue to the villagers' capacity for mass cruelty, just for the fun of it, made credible their viciousness in stripping Rosie and shearing her long hair in the obligatory scene.

RYAN'S DAUGHTER. Background to the conflict. *Metro-Goldwyn-Mayer,* © 1970.

RYAN'S DAUGHTER. Joining the conflict. *Metro-Goldwyn-Mayer,* © 1970.

RYAN'S DAUGHTER. Obligatory scene. *Metro-Goldwyn-Mayer,* © *1970.*

RYAN'S DAUGHTER. Climax. *Metro-Goldwyn-Mayer,* © *1970.*

The *climax* came with the suicide of the English major who was the passionate fulfillment of Rosie's young life. In Western culture suicide is considered a coward's way out of a dilemma, and his essential cowardice was established almost immediately upon his arrival in the Irish village. Flashbacks seen through his mind's eye revealed that he had not really been a hero in the fighting, despite his Victoria Cross, but a coward who had crawled into a hole during the attack, covered his head with his hands and lain there trembling and cringing. It was further established when a minor character, a captain departing for the battles in France, confessed that he was not afraid of death, but only of being a coward—and the major's reactions revealed his cowardice, which was explicitly realized in the climax. After the stripping and shearing of Rosie in the obligatory scene, the major's affair with her had clearly ended, and with it went his courage to go on living. When Michael led the major to a box of dynamite that had washed up on the beach during the storm, the major took the coward's way out by committing suicide, in the climax.

The *denouement* to *Ryan's Daughter* came with Rosie's expulsion from the village, where she had never really belonged, her forgiveness by the priest she had opposed and the husband she had wronged, and the change of character in Rosie brought about as a consequence of her searing experiences. These resolutions, too, were planted early in the film. The priest had begged her not to indulge her hopes for love when dissatisfied in marriage, and had forgiven Rosie and the villagers their shortcomings from the beginning. Her husband's capacity for forgiveness and understanding were revealed in his repeated kindnesses to his students, his quickness to rationalize the rude behavior of the villagers, and in Rosie's snappish comment—"Do you always believe the best of everyone?" Rosie's change of character, as a result of her experiences, was signalled by her bestowal of a farewell kiss on the ugly face of the village idiot, Michael. Even hope for Rosie and her husband was offered to the viewer, as part of the denouement, when the priest admonished him: "Don't leave Rosie!"

Dramatic Unity

The most intimate relationship exists between the foregoing elements at the outset of the film and the obligatory scene and climax at the outcome. And all of the crises in between these two derive from the first and lead to the second. The unity of a dramatic film is maintained by relating all conflicts, crises and character actions to either the obligatory scene or the climax, and this unity of the whole begins at the first joining of the conflict: the seeds that make the outcome of the story plausible and probable should be planted in the earliest moments of the drama.

The relationship between the obligatory scene and the climax is one of interwoven deception. The clues to the obligatory scene lie on the surface, revealed clearly to the viewer in every crisis, because the entire story centers about the attempts of the pivotal character or protagonist to achieve his goals, realized in success or failure in the obligatory scene. Periodically, however, clues to the climax must be quietly planted, preferably in every crisis leading to the obligatory scene, so that when the climax comes it will appear plausible. The Irish villagers' resentment of Rosie and her superior aspirations and attitudes was intimated in every crisis scene, as well as their indignation at her adultery with an officer of the English enemy, and when her shearing and stripping came in the obligatory scene, it was plausible. The English major's cowardice was revealed in conversations with the captain about to leave for the western front, and the montages which revealed that he had been a coward in the fighting; and when he committed suicide in the climax, that, too, was credible. Both elements were planted at the beginning and cultivated in almost every crisis throughout the length of the film.

Coincidence is unacceptable as a solution to crises, climax or obligatory scene, because dramatic events must be constructed with a cause and effect relationship in order to seem credible to the viewer. In real life, as we all know, coincidence and random circumstances play an important role in the destinies of men and nations. But dramatic film is an art, a medium intended to create order out of the chaos of life and give it meaningful form. Art makes use of the stuff of life in its forms, but art is not life, and coincidence is unacceptable at all points in a drama except one—the beginning. In the first joining of a conflict almost any fortuitous circumstance is acceptable, because at that point the viewer has not yet established a frame of reference. Thereafter, however, to the end of the film, the crises in all their ramifications, and the reactions of all characters to every crisis, must have a cause and effect relationship in order to be credible to the viewer.

Suspense

Suspense that rises unabated to the climax is indispensable in holding the attention of the viewer. Suspense as a structural plot device exists at five levels: *developing complications, the race against time, the chase, increasing intensity of crises* and *unexpected deception.*

DEVELOPING COMPLICATIONS

Developing complications are an outgrowth of the first joining of the conflict, when several threads of conflict are established in terms of character, exposition, plot, theme and setting that may weave in and out through each succeeding crisis.

The dominant pattern of complication, of course, centers about the pivotal character, who wants something very much and will settle for nothing less, and his stimulus of major characters in opposition who provide surface reversals of fortune. At a second level, the pivotal character may have inadvertently made a friend or enemy of a minor or major character, and that character may credibly reappear late in the story, motivated to assist or frustrate the pivotal character or protagonist. At a third level, his actions may be an offense to customs, public opinion or law and order, and hence provoke a perfectly credible reaction by the forces of society. And at a fourth level, there may be independent and unrelated forces occurring at the same time as the main story and its sub-plots—wars, famines, monsoons—that may plausibly be drawn upon to provide unexpected developments of complication.

THE RACE AGAINST TIME

The race against time is a common plot device for creating suspense, dramatized by establishing an inevitable terminating event that will forcibly change the circumstances of the characters according to how they act before it occurs. In *High Noon* the story revolved around the drama of a sheriff trying to enlist the armed support of the men in his community before the arrival of three outlaws on the noon train. The clock was seen, felt and heard throughout the film, even to the extent of editing the scenes to the beat of a metronome. Other race-against-time devices may include the hoary due date of a mortgage payment, or an impending attack, death or disaster. Any inevitable event that will forcibly change the relationship of the characters in conflict may be used.

THE CHASE

The chase is another suspense device, often used in conjunction with a race against time. A chase seems inherently exciting, perhaps because it appeals to some atavistic hunting instinct, perhaps because the viewer has been conditioned to expect that the outcome of a story will be found in the outcome of a hunter-hunted pursuit. The climax of the story and the realization of the theme is frequently exemplified in a story which is a protracted chase, as in the conclusion of *The French Connection*.

INCREASING INTENSITY OF CRISES

Suspense is also created through increasing the intensity of the crises. Each obstacle is made more difficult than the one before, forcing the pivotal character to try ever more strenuously to surmount it. With each crisis of progressively increasing intensity, there is a corresponding increase in suspense on the part of the viewer until the outcome of the story is revealed. Building suspense is in large degree a matter of gradually raising the height of the flaming hoops through which the pivotal character must leap to achieve his goal, so that the cumulative effect on the viewer is an increasing sense of suspense.

UNEXPECTED DECEPTION

Unexpected deception is the ultimate key to suspense, and it lies within the triangular structure of the crisis. Whatever the pivotal character tries to do in a given dramatic sequence, the audience must identify with him and believe he will do it, and be as surprised as he is when his attempt is foiled. The expectation of the audience must always be cheated from crisis to crisis in order to create suspense. But the cheating of expectation must be plausible in the sense that the event could genuinely occur under the circumstances. When Joe Buck forced his way into the women's boarding house, expecting to find the ladies lined up with stud fees in hand, neither he nor the audience expected him to be bounced out unceremoniously. But he was, and it was plausible under the circumstances. It was also delightfully funny, and pathetic, because of the self-deception of Joe and his friend Ratso and the deception of the expectations of the viewer. The principle of dramatic delight in crisis structure is to promise one thing to the viewer and give him something else, but *plausibly.*

Time Span and Story Scope

Time span and story scope are important factors in creating dramatic impact. Compression is a salient characteristic of cinema, one that lends itself to the depiction of stories occurring within a relatively brief period of time. The portrayal of long periods of time often weakens the film's continuity and lessens the intensity of its crises. The flow of continuity breaks down a little with each transition of years to a new time segment, and each time segment tends to become a self-contained vignette, a short story within an anthology, bound to the other vignettes by cinematic conventions rather than emotional ties. Cinematic techniques such as the dissolve and the fade-out/fade-in are conventions now clearly understood as representing the passage of time, but they do exact the price of loss of dramatic force.

A film with a long span of time tends to become narrative rather than dramatic, telling the viewer what is happening rather than carrying him along with the life on the screen through identification. Dramatic force is sacrificed because crises seldom seem progressively intense when years elapse between them. And crises so weakened rarely build emotionally to the climax, although they may relate logically to the outcome of the story in the obligatory scene.

Historical and biographical films have achieved great popular success, *Gone With the Wind* and *Little Big Man* being typical examples. But these, too, have tended to suffer from the string-of-beads weakness in their plots, with themes and conflicts never quite resolved in the obligatory scenes and the climax. Both films had an extended time span and story scope and comprised a series of self-contained dramatic episodes, each of which had a separate story and internal dramatic structure that might have permitted it to stand alone as a short dramatic film. Both lacked an overall unity and a sense of rising suspense, but compensated with interesting characters and colorful historical events.

Comic Relief

Comic relief is a moment of levity used in a long film to relieve tension in the viewer. If the film is a very heavy drama, fraught with wringing human emotions and turgid dramatic actions, the viewer must be given an opportunity to relax from time to time or he may begin to laugh during a love scene or some other climactic event. The author once saw an audience laugh hilariously during the climax of a film in which a character died impaled on a steel spike, because the film had earlier failed to provide any form of comic relief.

The Improvised Plot

Dramatic structure in most American films is designed to tell a story logically, reveal insight into characters by means of tightly plotted conflicts of progressively increasing intensity, realize a theme in the climax and fulfill a story in the obligatory scene. From Europe has come another form of cinematic dramatic structure in which characters in conflict are interpreted differently—the improvised plot.

The improvised plot presents a series of sequences which symbolically reveal character, theme or circumstance. These sequences are not necessarily crises caused by the pivotal character attempting to achieve a goal, for in the improvised plot events "just happen" by fortuitous circumstance, as they do in real life, often bearing little logical relationship to what has gone before or what comes after, except in a symbolic sense. The improvised plot presents a cinematic approximation of the relationships of life itself. Such stories seldom have a strongly defined joining of a conflict, climax and obligatory scenes, to which all the characters in conflict and their crises are related. Instead, each sequence is staged and photographed as a dramatic vignette, as the director spontaneously thinks of them, and strung end to end in the manner of a string of beads.

The improvised dramatic film often has moments of exquisite beauty, insight and realism in forms characterized by experimentation and frequently a high order of originality. The improvised form is vulnerable, however, to such weaknesses as illogical continuity, inconsistent and often meaningless crises, flaccid character development and relationships, and a conclusion without a climax. The classic concept of a story having a beginning, a middle and an end does not necessarily apply to the improvised plot, and if it does, those elements may not always occur in that order. The elements may occur as a middle, an end and a beginning, or as an end, a beginning and a middle. The frequent absence of a pivotal character as a dramatic force tends to render improvised films unreal, or so subjectively symbolic as to seem abstract to the lay viewer. The themes presented most often derive from nagging interpersonal irritations, dressed up to pose as eternal verities, and tend to exemplify Sartre's thesis: "Hell is other people."

Symbolism

Symbolism in lieu of plot is another recent trend of European origin. Continental directors are often more concerned with expressing a subjective statement about some aspect of life than with telling a good story, and they frequently ignore the disciplines of dramatic structure in favor of amorphous symbols. In Bergman and Fellini films, for example, staged symbols of death and futility follow each other furiously from first fade-in to last fade-out with scarcely a breather in between. Instead of dramatic suspense, there are filmed essays on the nature and destiny of man, and what it all means in the grand scheme of the Cosmos, with little concern that the viewer identify with the life on the screen and experience an emotional catharsis. Symbolic films are aimed at the intellect, rather than at the emotions, and are intended for an elite audience.

Television Dramatic Structure

Television dramatic structure differs in certain respects from the theatrical form, the differences deriving from the circumstances under which each is viewed. The theatrical film viewer has paid money to see a feature film and is prepared to sit through its entirety; therefore, the conflict may be joined gradually and the crisis intensify progressively from the beginning to the end of the film, with all dramatic elements given proportionate form to develop character and tell the story. The television viewer, on the other hand, pays nothing to watch any of the programs offered simultaneously over several channels, and therefore he will unhesitatingly turn to another channel between programs and during commercials if he is bored for even a moment.

Television dramas therefore begin with furious intensity, to deter the viewer from switching channels or turning off the set. So intense is the competition for the viewer's attention at the beginning of the hour that the conflict is often joined and the story is well under way even before the appearance of the program's title.

Crises are also treated differently in theatrical and television dramatic forms. In theatrical film the crises are derived from an emotional truth as it relates to a character trying to achieve his goals while being opposed by an antagonist at a given point in the drama, with the length of the dramatic sequence and the intensity of the crisis dependent upon their relationship to the climax and the obligatory scenes. In television drama each crisis may be given more emphasis than it deserves because of its proximity to a sales commercial, in order to hold the viewer's interest through the commercial until the story resumes once more. Thus a crisis is often given strident emphasis regardless of its real importance to the obligatory scenes and the climax (although, to be sure, screenplays for television are often carefully written to make such crisis-commercial relationships appear natural).

Recapitulation is another characteristic of television drama deriving from the interruption of television commercials. After each commercial one character usually makes a one-line statement of dialogue describing what occurred in the crisis just before the commercial. This refreshes the memory of the viewer and fills in the story for those who have tuned in late. On those television dramas that run as long as an hour it is common practice to recapitulate the story at some length after the half-hour break so that a viewer who tunes in at that time may follow the story to the end.

Recapitulation is seldom done in theatrical dramas unless the film is so long that it is broken into two segments, separated by an intermission. Theatrical films are conceived and executed as one uninterrupted flow of drama from beginning to end, while television dramas are specifically conceived as segments to be inserted between sales commercials.

Cinematic renderings of drama also differ according to whether they are intended for theatrical or television release. Theatrical films are now projected onto immense screens which may fill the viewer's entire scope of vision, to the effect that sweeping vistas and monumental actions will enhance the realism and impact of the film, while closeups must be used with discretion or they may become grotesque. Television films, to the contrary, have small viewing screens which correspondingly reduce the size of the images presented on them, to the effect that closeups and medium shots predominate, while broad views and vast actions must be used sparingly. Great movements are reduced to a minuscule creep and lose their impact on the little television screen.

10

Cinematic Development of Characters

Film viewers are people-watchers. The cleverest plot will not long hold the interest of the viewer unless he is made to care about what happens to the people in the story. Believable screen characters arouse the emotions of the viewer through identification, and give life, conflict and meaning to the plot. They must appear cinematically as flesh and blood human beings who are interesting to watch as they act and react to the turmoils of conflict in the story. Dramatic film appeals primarily to this voyeur instinct in the viewer, to his fascination for seeing what people do when their social facades are skinned off by the knife of necessity, to his profound curiosity about the only inexhaustible subject—man.

Cinematic development of characters involves concepts and techniques that may be taught and learned by any intelligent person, but can be really comprehended and applied to film only by those having a native intuitive understanding of what motivates human beings. The dramatic filmmaker must have an innate ability to put himself in the other man's shoes and understand why, given that man's mentality, background and circumstances, he embezzled money, beat a child, committed a brutal murder, threw himself over a grenade to save the lives of his comrades. It demands the ability to view the actions of other men with suspended moral judgment in order to ask the question "Why did he do it?"—and then understand the infinitely variable answers well enough to present them in a dramatic film. For a truly moving cinematic development of character, the filmmaker must become that person and view his actions from within.

Characterization in Cinema

Characters are developed differently in film and television dramas than they are in novels or on the stage. In film many emotions that are revealed in other forms by dialogue and exposition are rendered by the lens of the camera, by photographed movements expressing inner thoughts (the flicker of an eyelid may often say more than words) and by editing scenes together into a sequence whose sum total meaning conveys a message different from that of the individual scenes.

Because the credibility and acceptability of a screen character is related to the experience viewers have had in judging people in real life, a given character is expected to look like the kind of person he is attempting to portray. And given the closeup capability of the motion picture camera, a premium is placed upon such factors as facial mobility, facial types and stereotypes, general impressions or attractiveness of appearance, and physique and posture in relation to role, height and weight as compared to other characters. The motivation of screen characters, however, derives from the same Aristotelean dramatic principles found in other dramatic and narrative forms—inner nature expressed through overt action—modified by the angles from which the subjects are photographed, the lighting given the subjects, the movements of the subjects, the tempo of the editing and the length of time a scene may be held on the screen.

Plot and Character Relationships

The comparative importance of character and plot is largely a matter of geography. For example: The West Europeans tend to feel that a cinematic revelation of character through symbols and dialogue, and a filmed essay on the state of man, are more important than a good story. The Communist position is that both plot and character development are subordinate to the communication of ideological concepts. The American cinematic tradition has been strongly plot-oriented, with a subordination of character development and little ideological content

TRUE GRIT. Casting to type: Western. *Paramount Pictures Corp.*, © *1969*.

except in wartime. The American tradition is changing rapidly and there is now a marked trend away from simplistic situation-oriented plots toward a strong development of character, with the inclusion of some ideological content.

Characterization and plot, ideally, should be intimately interrelated, with each aspect of one mutually dependent upon and closely related to the other. Without a good story there are few interesting ways to reveal the nature of a character through action. Without interesting characters, the viewer would not identify with the life on the screen, and the most ingenious story would soon begin to pall.

The creative reality of dramatic filmmaking is that the amorphous blob of an idea, as it coalesces in the mind of the filmmaker, usually takes the form of a generalized dramatic situation in which characters gradually appear to implement the screenwriter's theme. Sometimes the characters grow out of a dramatic situation, sometimes the situation out of a dramatic character, depending upon the circumstances and the orientation of the filmmaker. There are no iron-clad rules for developing the relationship between plot and screen character, and the final film is usually conceived in pain and born in agony after innumerable revisions of both. Character and plot are warp and woof of the same cloth and must be considered as one.

Screen Personality and Character

Personality and character are two dimensions of a person in dramatic film that are used as contradictory foils in a major character, and complementary elements in minor characters.

Personality is what lies on the surface, the face we prepare to meet other faces, the smiles or surliness, the amiability or irascibility, the grace or grouchiness borne of life experiences and the need to get along with other people, one way or another. A pleasant personality, cultivated or ingenuous, is a collation of agreeable traits—friendliness, courtesy, goodwill—difficult to define, but, like true love, we know it when we see it. An unpleasant personality is simply the reverse, a collation of such disagreeable traits as hostility, rudeness, ill will and so forth.

Character lies deeper than personality and is usually revealed only in conflict. Character refers to the inner essential qualities of the man: honesty, duplicity, courage, cowardice, things that can be known only when he is subjected to an ordeal with something vital at stake. A primary basis of dramatic appeal is the interest viewers have in seeing what people do when their personalities are seared away by an ordeal and their true inner selves stand revealed. Two men may have similar qualities of character, such as the trait of courage, and yet one may be quiet and retiring, the other outgoing and gregarious; on the surface they may seem a chasm apart, and yet when it comes to the purgation of conflict—character revealed in action—each would probably be brave in similar ways, even though their personalities are different, because both have the steel spine of courage. Conversely, two men may appear to be very much alike on the surface, with personality traits of geniality, courtesy and apparent goodwill toward all, but when faced with adversity or temptation, one may reveal his inner self as that of a prince among men, the other, a prize rat.

Consistency of Character

Probability and necessity are terms which refer to the consistency and credibility of a screen character's responses to the crises of a story, which in turn derive from his personality and character. The screen character must at all times react in a manner which is "probable," given his collation of personality and character traits, and "necessary," given the pressures of a conflict. In real life the average citizen is a walking bundle of internal contradictions; he may be kind to children and dogs, pick the wings off flies, give generously to charities, and cheat his colleagues—without any apparent awareness of his contradictory behavior. Such inconsistency of personality and character traits is unacceptable in a screen character. The same viewer who would accept inconsistencies in his fellow man with a shrug of the shoulder would insist upon consistency in a screen character and scoff at contradictions as being unrealistic.

PATTON. Casting for character. *20th Century-Fox.*

In *The Ox Bow Incident*, a story of the lynching of three innocent men, a kindly, intelligent old man opposed the formation of the illegal posse and its every action through the final deaths of the three victims at the ends of their ropes. Had the gentle man then said, "What the hell— win a few, lose a few," he would have acted in a manner inconsistent with his personality and character, contrary to this probability and necessity.

Character Development

The selection of personality and character traits to be included in a story is contingent upon their relevance to the story. Realistic screen characters are created by selecting only those traits for revelation that somehow relate to the joining of the conflict, the crises, the climax and the obligatory scene, and deleting all others. One does not create a believable character by literally transposing every trait of a living person to the screen anymore than a landscape painter would render every twig on a tree. Such an interpretation would be true in fact but false in spirit. Film aims not at the transcription of life, but at its *dramatization* and only that which is meaningful should be selected for inclusion in a drama. The fact that a murderer may be good to his mother, or that a romantic lead may leave a ring around the bathtub, is dramatically irrelevant if it does not contribute to the story. In his selection and highlighting of relevant traits and his suppression and elimination of others the filmmaker creates characters that seem real in the context of the story.

A cinematic character should be developed *specifically* in terms of his age, sex, physical characteristics, education, occupation, religion and political-social-economic milieu, because the viewer can see and judge his every action; if the screen character strikes a false note in any aspect, it may break the viewer's absorption in the life on the screen and evoke derision. A believable screen character should be developed in three dimensions—*physical, environmental* and *psychological*.

PHYSICAL TRAITS

The development of a character in terms of his physical aspects means, on the surface level, presenting an actor who physically resem-

JOE. Typecast: blue-collar couple. *Cannon Films*.

bles the kind of person he is intended to represent. And these surface aspects in turn are modified by the cinematic interpretation of the char-. acter's facial expressions, walk and gesture, and manner of speech and dialogue. In a sense, casting for appearance means taking cognizance of the fact that the viewer carries to the film certain stereotypes (valid and invalid), born of personal experiences and prejudices, reading books and magazines, and watching other films, that may affect his acceptance of the screen character.

However much the practice of typecasting may misrepresent life itself, however unfair it may be in its exclusion of fine actors from roles for which they do not look the part, it remains one of the tyrannies of dramatic film. In *Airport*, for example, the chief mechanic was a burly, ham-handed, cigar-chewing man of action who was so aggressively masculine that when he unhesitatingly risked the destruction of an expensive airliner in order to save it, this bold action seemed in character with his appearance. Had the mechanic been a tall, slender, reedy-voiced man smoking a cigarette in an engraved holder, he would have appeared out of character, or his action would have had a comically incongruous effect.

Typecasting is more important for a minor than for a major character, because it enables the viewer to recognize who and what the character represents without recourse to extensive dialogue and expository actions.

Beyond typecasting, however, the physical appearance of a person relates importantly to his basic attitudes, aspirations and probability of response to any given situation. An individual who has been attractive from infancy probably received pampering from friends and relatives, became the teacher's favorite, was sought out by members of the opposite sex and received preferred treatment in the world of work. Robert Frost wrote, "The beautiful shall be choosers," and this unfair truism tends to shape the lucky individual into a person of serene self-confidence, or a spoiled brat, who faces many of life's crises with the conviction that the world and its inhabitants exist primarily to provide the anointed one with the best of every good thing. Rosie of *Ryan's Daughter* was a case in point; she had been spoiled and pampered throughout her young attractive life, and when her marriage proved a sexual disappointment, probably the first frustration of her life, she unhesitatingly sought fulfillment with a lover.

At the other extreme, a person who has been unattractive from infancy may have learned of it quickly through the indifference of playmates, relatives, teachers, members of the opposite sex, and later, lost opportunities in the workaday world. In the process of maturation, this unattractive individual may have acquired a full complement of inhibiting complexes that would affect his response to a crisis.

In between these simplistic extremes are physical eccentricities that may engender personality quirks: A short man may develop the aggressiveness of a bantam rooster to compensate for his stature. A woman with gross ears may become so sensitive about them that she may wear an unbecoming hair style to cover them up, and avoid any kind of athletic activity that would expose her ears. Moreover, people may change from one kind of person to another as a consequence of physical changes. A brave man may degenerate into cowardice with age, infirmity or crippling. A woman once serene in her beauty may become wildly neurotic with the disfigurement of a scar.

Every adult viewer knows instinctively that physical traits are important in shaping the outlook of a human being, and the cinematic portrayal of a screen character should be consistent with his or her physical appearance to be credible. To present a stunningly beautiful woman who lacks social confidence with men would be, under most circumstances, out of character. To present a male lead who had been crippled without any effect on his morale would again be out of character. The English major of *Ryan's Daughter* was a typical case in point; he had lost a leg in battle, and with it, full confidence in his manhood. When convulsions of fear shot through the major, Rosie took his hand, and he turned to her for the needed love and reassurance.

Physiology is another physical factor contributing to an individual's outlook on life. A chronically sour stomach may contribute to a chronically sour outlook. A high or low hormone level may explain why a man is dynamic or lazy, friendly or irritable, arrogant or humble, confident or diffident. Nobody escapes his burden of flesh and the ills to which it is heir, and in a dramatic film any property of a screen character that the viewer can perceive should be compatible with the role he plays in the story.

ENVIRONMENTAL TRAITS

Environment is a second shaping influence in the development of a screen character. A person with a given set of physical and intellectual characteristics may grow up into as many different kinds of human being as there are circumstances in which to be reared. A girl who grows up in a dirty city tenement, surrounded by crumbling walls, cockroaches and diseased people, will react differently to a given crisis than she would if reared in the antiseptic environment of a clean suburb, surrounded by leafy trees, singing birds and buoyant people.

The development of a person's character is most influenced by his early life at home: Were the parents living or dead, together or divorced, loving or hostile, dutiful or negligent? Did the father make a good living, barely eke out subsistence or desert the family? Were the parents' life habits a ritual of church attendance and good works, a round of cocktail parties and bridge games, a flabby vacillation between watching television and doing nothing, or an all-out commitment to climbing the socioeconomic ladder? By the time a child is ten years old the matrix of his family life will be indelibly stamped on his soul, and evidences of its influences on his attitudes will not be expunged if he lives to be a hundred. And when a dramatic character appears on the screen, it should be clear to the viewer exactly what kind of family life he was reared in by his reactions to crises in the story.

Other environmental factors that may influence a person's reactions to a crisis include his racial and ethnic heritage, his religious upbringing or lack of it, his educational background—aptitudes, good subjects and bad, how easily he learned and what marks he received for his work. And ultimately, his occupation—what kind of work he does, how long his hours are, how remunerative the job is, how suited he is to his work.

All of these physical and environmental factors will be immediately

JOE. Slum environment. *Cannon Films.*

apparent in a person's facial expressions, style of dress, manner of speech, walk and gestures, and attitudes toward other people. The average adult need see another person in action for only a brief period of time to assess where he came from and the major influences in his life—a skill that he brings to the viewing of a film. Ratso of *Midnight Cowboy* had not appeared on the screen for more than a minute before he had revealed by his mannerisms that he had grown up crippled and neglected in an impoverished home, and had survived his physical disabilities and miserable environment by developing the kind of cunning for which he had received his nickname. Ratso's physical and environmental background had fused to create the third dimension of individual development that is of greatest interest to the filmmaker and the viewer—his psychological reactions to crises.

PSYCHOLOGICAL TRAITS

The psychology of the individual provides the real interest in drama; what draws the viewer to dramatic film is a fascination with how people behave under stress when they think no one is looking. By offering the viewer insight into human motivations on the screen, the filmmaker offers the viewer insight into himself.

The psychology of an individual comprises his physical and environmental influences, but constitutes more than the sum of these parts. To these measurable elements must be added the infinitely variable and intangible elements of personal premise: What does he live for—power, money, security, prestige, God? Does he want to make a contribution to his country and his times, be the salesman with the highest commissions in his corporation, the panderer with the biggest stable of prostitutes in the city, an artist demanding the right to creative fulfillment, or an intellectual with a clamant need to communicate a new idea. An individual's personal premise and amibition may have grown from an inner need demanding expression, or it may have been formulated for him by his peers, but it is often the strongest single element of human motivation. The degree to which a person's basic attitude is aggressive or resigned, militant or defeatist, and his temperament is optimistic or pessimistic, irascible or easygoing, depends in large measure on whether his inner gyroscope has successfully steered a life's course compatible with his personal premise. And the degree to which this personal premise has been fulfilled or frustrated will affect a screen character's every act and reaction from the first joining of a conflict through the final denouement.

Other aspects of psychology in a person may include his love life, satisfying or unsatisfying; talents and intellectual potential, developed or latent; his social expertise, poised or gauche. Amusements are another important indice of character. Does a man in his leisure hours read books, play bridge, go hunting, bet on horse races, chase women, or watch television for hours on end? A man reveals himself in his pastimes, and these, too, may be used in the development of a screen character.

What is "probable and necessary" in the response of any screen character to any crisis in the story is born of the sum total of his physical, environmental and psychological characteristics, all of which should be lucidly drawn for the understanding of the viewer. The screen characters must react under most circumstances to cause and effect relationships that are clear at the time they occur, or are made clear before the conclusion of the film. Loose ends have a way of irritating the viewer. The principle of three-dimensional characters developed in terms of their physical, environmental and psychological aspects provides the filmmaker with an almost unlimited scope in the development of believable and interesting screen characters, because the manipulation of any component of these elements will create a different kind of person who will react differently to a given crisis, according to what is probable and necessary in his nature.

Interrelationship of Characters

MAJOR AND MINOR CHARACTERS

Major and minor screen characters differ in the degree to which they are given three-dimensional development, with every step away from the major roles resulting in more simplification. Major characters, about whom the story revolves, often have an essential character quite different from the personalities they display in the film, and in the climax their true characters stand revealed, and transformed, as the outcome of their experiences. Minor characters, on the other hand, do not as a rule change; they are presented with consistent characters and personalities throughout the story, because it would tend to dilute the viewer's interest in the major characters if the minor characters were also developed in the round. Almost everyone has seen a film in which a minor character has stolen the show, evidence of weak writing or directing, or possibly an incompetent performance by an actor playing a major character.

The protagonist, whose passion sends the spindrift flying, and the antagonist, whose determination resists with equal dramatic force, must be developed into living, breathing human beings with whom the viewer can identify, with their physical, environmental and psychological natures made evident in all responses. Minor characters should also be created with these basic traits in mind, but rendered in a flatter, more stereotyped manner. The low profile of a minor character holds true even at those times when he may be the pivotal character. The principle of subordination in the presentation of minor characters is important because they exist primarily as foils to the majors and as plot and expositional devices. Any minor character not serving these functions, however charming he may be, should be deleted. The development of a minor character relates proportionately to his importance to the major characters and the story.

ORCHESTRATION OF CHARACTERS

Orchestration of characters refers to the inclusion of individuals in the story who range the spectrum of personality and character types and have inherent conflicts of interest. If an artist, a businessman, a scientist, a playboy, a politician and a drug pusher were sequestered together, there would soon be friction among them because of their disparate characters and personalities. Put these mismatched human beings into circumstances in which one of them wants something the others do not wish him to have, and there will be dramatic conflict. Each of the persons involved in the struggle will react to every crisis according to what is probable and necessary in the light of his own physical, environmental and psychological background. Each will consider his own actions fully justified in terms of his own value system. And each will, by the sum total differences of his personality and character, have a different way of opposing the pivotal character.

The orchestration of characters in a story, to include those kinds of human beings who would be in conflict under any circumstances, adds to the options of the filmmaker in providing third points in the triangle

JOE. Mr. Compton meets the boys. *Cannon Films.*

of crisis structure (discussed in the previous chapter) and enables him to introduce a wide variety of unexpected crises based upon the differing natures of the screen characters.

Change in the Protagonist

Change is the only constant we may be sure of; nothing is immutable, all things are in motion, people change. Place an individual in conflict with another force and he will soon act against the disturbing element to bring it into harmony with his own wishes; but, unwittingly, he himself will change while trying to effect a change. You can't go home again.

Realization that life and people change constantly is a form of unspoken knowledge the viewer brings to dramatic film. The viewer expects the major characters of a drama to change as a result of their experiences in the story, as he himself has changed as a consequence of his battles through life. If the major characters do not change during the course of the dramatic film, the viewer will leave the film dissatisfied, and rightly so. Only in bad drama do the major characters fail to change in some way. Bad drama is bad (for one reason) because it is not true to the one eternal verity of life—change.

Change in the broadest sense should occur within the major characters as a result of the climax, when they confront the truth about themselves and are transformed in some way from the persons they were to someone new, or die from inability to change. The transformations of their inner natures should crystallize after the climax, and be reflected by changes in the emotional color of the film:

Joe begins in intolerance and ends in tragedy.

The Graduate begins in apathy and ends in commitment.

Ryan's Daughter begins in passion and self-indulgence and ends in mature restraint and selflessness.

Midnight Cowboy begins in vanity, self-delusion and selfishness, and ends in humility, understanding and friendship.

In each of these films a fundamental change or death came to the major characters as a result of their actions, and the emotional tenor of the film at the end was different from that with which it began.

Just as there ought to be an overall transfiguration of the emotional tenor of the film, there must also be a progressive change in the nature of the pivotal character, or the final transformation may appear too abrupt to be credible. Rosie's progressive changes as she sought sexual fulfillment in *Ryan's Daughter* were as follows:

Yearning to passion for the schoolmaster.
Passion to disillusionment in her marriage to the teacher.
Disillusionment to frustration as she remained unfulfilled.
Frustration to passion upon meeting the English major.
Passion to sexual fulfillment through adultery with the major.
Fulfillment to fear of the consequences of adultery.
Fear to humiliation as she was stripped and shorn by the villagers.

Humiliation to anguish at the suicide of her lover.
Anguish to mature resignation to her husband, the teacher.

The transformation of Rosie was most conspicuous in the obligatory scene and the climax—her stripping by the Irish villagers and the suicide of her lover—but the change was progressive throughout the crises of the film.

Self-sufficiency in a screen character makes for poor dramatic material. A man who seems genuinely able to go it alone, neither demanding nor dependent, needing nor wanting, can seldom be used as a screen character, because it is unfulfilled desire, and the will to act on the desire, that leads to conflict. Drama means interrelationships between people.

Emotional changes should take place within each crisis sequence as well as progressively over the length of the film. A crisis should begin on one emotional note and end on another as the pivotal character tries and fails to attain his goals. When Joe Buck of *Midnight Cowboy* forced his way into a women's rooming house to sell his sexual services, he and his friend Ratso dreamed wild fantasies of running through the surf on the sun-soaked beaches of Florida with the bed-earned money. But Joe was thrown out bodily, and their dreams were dashed with him to the sidewalk. The emotional color of the crisis changed from soaring hope to grinding despair, modifying in process the outlook of Joe and Ratso.

Dramatic Dialectics

Dramatic dialectics is a process of effecting changes in screen characters through a resolution of their internal contradictions. Dialectics, a three-step method used in pursuit of philosophical truth, consists of first stating a premise, called *thesis*. Then a force arises in opposition to the thesis, called *antithesis*. The original thesis, after open conflict with its antithesis, reformulates itself by incorporating elements of the antithesis into a new concept called *synthesis*.

Dialectics when applied to character development means that people change in the direction of their opposing forces, becoming more like the people against them. They synthesize the thesis of their own original natures with the antithesis of the forces that oppose them into a fundamental change within themselves. Most human beings are filled with internal contradictions in a constant state of resolution through thesis, antithesis, synthesis, and out of each synthesis emerges a new person, who then submits a new thesis . . .

The dramatic application of dialectics may be stated in this way: The pivotal character suffers the internal contradiction of wanting something he does not have. He strikes out to attain what he wants in a dramatic thesis. The pivotal character's desire is intolerable to the antagonist, who opposes him in antithesis. The conflict is joined and maximum effort is fought with maximum resistance. When the pivotal character realizes that he cannot have what he wants on his original terms, he combines his original thesis with something of value learned from his adversary in a synthesis of change within himself, or he dies.

The potential for change must lie within the characters from the outset; the seeds of change are planted in their physical and emotional makeup, their temperament and backgrounds, and especially, in their desires for change. The pivotal character, by the nature of his striking out for something he wants that he does not yet have, expresses in his desires and actions that he has within him the potential for change. To a lesser degree, so do those forces that actively oppose him. The dialectics of change often work both ways in the better thematic concepts—right versus right—with both protagonist and antagonist emerging from their conflict fundamentally changed.

Minor characters seldom have within them the same potential for change as do the major characters because they are not developed in terms of full motivations, serving as they do the role of foils, and changes in their attitudes tend to come as a surprise. A minor character, however, need not be a shallow character, and if clearly though briefly drawn, may be shown as emotionally affected by the outcome of the major contest. A story in which all the major and minor characters play their proportionate roles in the conflicts, and all are proportionately and believably transformed by the climax, reflects a high order of dramatic ability in the filmmaker, and may be deeply refreshing to the viewer.

Conflict

PROTRACTED CONFLICT

Strength of will is required in the two major adversaries for them to carry on a protracted conflict for the length of a dramatic film. Obviously, if either side were willing to shake hands halfway through the struggle and forget about the issue, the drama would be over immediately without fulfillment. No conflict, no drama. The pivotal character or protagonist may start weakly and gain strength with each surmounted crisis, or he may start strongly and weaken with each obstacle, but he must have the stamina to carry on the struggle to the climax. The same holds true of the opposition. Whether the antagonist starts weakly and grows in strength, or begins strongly and declines with each crisis, he must have the pertinacity to struggle through to the climax. This strength of will on both sides provides the framework of unity for the whole film, and is therefore called the "unity of opposites."

Weak characters are those who cannot take a stand or make a move despite the provocations of the story. A weak human being, however, may be considered a strong screen character if he has the tenacity to endure in his weakness no matter how he is abused—his stamina is a form of strength. A weak screen character is one who cannot make up his mind; he vacillates with each dramatic wind, never acting, never resisting, never committing himself. A weak character may serve in a minor role as a foil or stimulus to a pivotal character or his antagonist, but he usually lacks the will or tenacity to be a major screen character.

The antagonists should be evenly matched in order to arouse interest and suspense about the outcome. Few viewers would take pleasure in watching a one-sided battle in which David fought Goliath with his bare knuckles instead of with a sling. The issue should be in doubt. The adversaries must lock in a contest of wills whose intensity grows steadily as the pivotal character strikes out for what he wants and the antagonist resists him. Each must know what he wants from the struggle, because there can be no direction or purpose in a screen character who does not know what he wants.

Attack and counterattack are the bases of all forms of conflict, however complex the struggle, and these give the dramatic film movement and life. The cleverest dialogue and slickest production techniques will not sustain the viewer's interest if they do not further the conflict between adversaries. Only the sustained and rising attack of a pivotal character trying to attain his ends, and the counterattack of determined antagonists, can generate the kind of suspense that may hold the attention of the average viewer.

THEMATIC CONFLICT

Right versus right in character motivation offers a more interesting form of conflict than right versus wrong. The viewer may become more emotionally involved in the struggle when he understands that both the pivotal character and the antagonist have something right and something wrong in their points-of-view, which in turn provides a basis for dialectical change in those characters. For example: In *Lonely Are the Brave* the cowboy had broken into jail to free a friend, and then broken out of jail to free himself. Most viewers would respect his altruism in wanting to free a friend, and sympathize with his desire to free himself when it transpired that his friend did not want help. No criminal intent was involved. On the other hand, the cowboy had slugged one police officer, insulted a second, beat a third unconscious with a rifle butt, sawed through the bars of a jail and shot down an air force helicopter. Society could scarcely take this lying down. Any reasonable viewer would understand that this trail of mayhem, however nobly motivated, violated a volume of laws and had to arouse the pursuit of police officers who were also in the right. The police had the right to capture an escaped prisoner who had the right to freedom.

The dullest of dramas are those in which one side is simon pure and the other is completely culpable. Dramatic excitement is better served by right versus right.

PSYCHOLOGICAL CONFLICT

Internal psychological conflicts are difficult to render in a motion picture because cinema is a perceptual medium that lends itself primarily to dramatic actions that may be photographed. Several solutions have been attempted in both the pictorial and the sound dimensions to express inner turmoil in a screen character.

One cinematic solution has been to render a stream-of-consciousness visual montage, scenes linked by dissolves, superimposed over a closeup of the person thinking those thoughts. Such was the case in *Midnight Cowboy* when Joe Buck remembered his love affair with a young woman while being seduced by a homosexual boy. Another form is the traditional closeup, used primarily to render a simple reaction or imply thought without specific articulation.

Evocative sound effects and voice-over snatches of dialogue have been used to express inner emotional conflicts with varying degrees of success. The sound montage, a collation of key words and graphic effects, was used effectively in *The Best Years of Our Lives*, when the young pilot sat in the abandoned hulk of his World War II bomber and relived, in his mind, his battles in the air. A weaker form is the soliloquy spoken over a silent closeup of the screen character, thinking to himself. As a rule, dialogue is the least cinematic of film elements.

Commentative music is a ballad in which the singer gives voice to the inner thoughts of the screen character, a highly effective technique when the ballad is appropriate to the subject. In *I Walk the Line* the dilemma of a middle-aged sheriff of a mountain community, bored by his dowdy wife and tempted by the second chance in life represented by a nubile young woman, is articulated in a ballad sung while the character simply stares ahead while driving his car, giving exposition of a unique kind. Commentative singing is essentially narrative, but since it is not self-conscious like the device of having a character speak his own thoughts out loud, it seems to blend in more acceptably and may be the better solution for the revelation of inner conflicts in many kinds of films.

THE OBJECT OF CONTENTION

What is at stake in a serious conflict must be something of value to the viewer as well as to the pivotal character and his antagonist. In *Lonely Are the Brave* the issue at stake was "freedom." In *Ryan's Daughter* the goal was "fulfillment in love." What is at stake should be something elemental the viewer would himself fight for, given the circumstances of the story, in order to arouse his emotions of identification. In real life, as we all know, men often fight over trivial matters. No tribe of African cannibals ever pursued a vendetta more viciously than a clique of college professors avenging an academic slur, or a coterie of artists trying to stamp out a differing mode of artistic expression. But these same people will demand that something of elemental importance be at stake in their dramatic films—life, death, love, freedom.

The Point of Dramatic Attack

The point of dramatic attack, as character relates to plot, should come at a time when the pivotal character's emotions are boiling over, when *he is prepared to act*. A man may endure the proverbial slings and arrows of outrageous fortune for many years, but until he is prepared to do something about it, he is of no dramatic interest. If, however, after many years of hoping for the best, he has had enough, he becomes of interest as a pivotal character. Almost daily we read in the newspapers about some apparently mild-mannered individual, respected and law-abiding, who suddenly goes berserk and slays several of his associates at work. Temporary insanity? Possibly. More likely, however, his colleagues have been playing political games in which others have taken credit for his efforts, or he thinks they have, and he has been repeatedly passed over for a rightful promotion. One day, perhaps because of a trivial occurrence, he has had enough and lashes out, thereby becoming a pivotal character.

There are four classic points of dramatic attack, having one denominator in common—*necessity*:

An important or traumatic event, such as the death of someone important, a declaration of war or a flood, may release interpersonal conflicts and set events in motion. In *I Never Sang for My Father* the conflict between father and son was joined by the death of the mother who had formerly been the arbiter of peace between them.

A pending event, such as a mission to fulfill, a river to cross, a beachhead to assault, may ignite and give direction to dramatic fires. In *The Bridge on the River Kwai* the need to construct a wooden bridge over a tropical river by a given date drew men and nations into battle.

A vital object of contention means something worth fighting for: a woman desired by two men, an important job, land for the taking, money, may arouse a fight between those who want whatever is at stake. *The Treasure of the Sierra Madre* told the story of the effects of greed on three impoverished prospectors who found their gold mine in the mountains.

A turning point in the life of the pivotal character could occur when his life style or environment has changed so much that his life could no longer go on as it had before. This may be a force of inner need or outer necessity. In *Ryan's Daughter* the ripening inner passion of youth compelled Rosie to seek sexual fulfillment. In *The Grapes of Wrath* the outer forces of destitution, born of drouth, drove Tom Joad and his family off their land on a trek to California—they could no longer survive on the farm they had occupied for generations.

In each of these points of dramatic attack, *irresistible necessity* compelled the pivotal character to act, and with that action began the story.

Sex in Cinema

Sex in cinema is nothing new, but recent trends would indicate that many theatrical films are being produced to appeal primarily to the prurient interest. Pornography, once a simple matter of photographing sexual activity, is now being dignified with the subterfuge of a story having dramatic structure in order to sneak the film through the courts by offering specious socially redeeming values. A school of screenwriters has sprung up, called "tweeny writers," to create windy dialogue about freedom, truth and the destiny of man for the pimps, whores and studs to mouth between bouts of sexual intercourse, fellatio, cunnilingus and other bedroom gynmastics. The writing is a ruse, of course, to camouflage the salacious intent of the films.

Sexual activity, however, is a vital element in human relations, and as such falls within the legitimate scope of the artist. Sexual activity in motion pictures, even if graphically portrayed, may serve such dramatic functions as motivation, the joining of a conflict, a crisis, a turning point, an obligatory scene or a climax. And if it is tastefully executed, it may be dramatically acceptable. In *The Killing of Sister George*, for example, the change of allegiance between lesbians was revealed by a scene of breast fondling, an action so integral to the story and the development of character at that point that it scarcely drew attention to itself as sex per se. It is worth pointing out, however, that implied sexual activity may be just as clearly understood as graphic sexual activity, and less carnal.

Formats in Dramatic Film and Television

Theatrical films and television serial films require certain differences in their concepts and techniques of characterization. In theatrical drama there is a need for an emotional transformation in the outlook of the protagonist as a consequence of his experiences in the story, a factor that holds true as well in those feature films produced only for television release. In a television series, however, with its continuing cast of characters from one episode to the next, the characters cannot change fundamentally in each program and maintain a consistent role throughout the season. The problem of the need for change is circumvented by introducing a new "guest protagonist" in each new episode, who becomes the pivotal character who undergoes an emotional change in the climax, or dies. The main characters, meanwhile, continue unchanged from episode to episode and season to season, the ratings willing.

Depth of characterization is another factor. Theatrical films may last as long as four hours, sometimes longer, time enough to explore subtle ramifications of motivation and the relationships between characters, all within a smoothly flowing story having a steadily rising pitch of intensity. Television serial dramas, on the other hand, are usually subject to half-hour and one-hour draconian time slots, further segmented by commercials and station breaks. The time slot is itself too brief to permit sensitive development of characters and their relationships, and the interruptions to the flow of the story tend to distort the characters' actions because of the need to present a cliff-hanger before each commercial. The effect on the television dramatic form is to emphasize vigorous action to the subordination of character development, the exact reverse of the trend in theatrical film.

Acting for Films and Television

Acting for films and television requires specialized techniques on the part of the performer, based upon the proximity of the lens and camera and the scene size being photographed. As a rule, the nearer the camera and focus of the lens, the closer the scene size, and the lower and more restrained must be the performance of the actor. A woman saying "Please wait" to her lover, would say it quite differently in a closeup than she would in an establishing shot. In the closeup her voice would be lowered, her facial expressions muted, her bodily gestures restrained. In an establishing shot her voice would be raised, her facial expressions more graphic, her body gestures more theatrical. If these two interpretations were reversed in the same scene sizes, she would appear ludicrous in the closeup and noncommunicative in the establishing shot. The scene size is the primary determinant of the actor's interpretation. This is one of the primary reasons for the authority of the director in cinema; he understands the degree of emphasis required in a given performance for a given scene size, and the relationship of that scene to the edited film.

Master scene cinematography requires that dramatic scenes be photographed out of the chronological sequences into which they will be edited in the finished film (see "The Grammar of Cinematography"). Scenes and sequences occurring at a given location are all photographed at the same time, regardless of where they will appear in the edited film, to reduce production costs.

This out-of-context requirement necessitates not only that the actor adapt his performance to the demands of the lens and its scene size, but also that he interpret his role without any sense of continuity, and often without any interaction with other actors. He may be asked in one day to perform a death scene for the end of the film, a love scene for the middle and a library perusal for the beginning—one after the other— simply because these events occur at a given location and have certain lighting requirements. To give a convincing performance under such scrambled conditions the actor must understand his role so deeply that he becomes that character under all dramatic circumstances and knows intuitively how that character would react to any given crisis. Only thus can the actor "turn it on" for a brief roll of the camera.

The film editor provides the third dimension of screen acting, because he makes the decision of what scene to use and what scene to discard in editing the film. The same performance may be photographed in a full shot, a medium and a closeup; and it is the film editor who decides what scenes will be used in the film and what scenes will end up on the cutting room floor. At critical points, of course, he does this in consultation with the director.

In making his decisions the editor is influenced in large part by the performances of the actor in the various scenes, but also by the exigencies of cinematic technique in editing—logical continuity, intercharacter motivations, suspense, cutting on movements, cutaways, inserts, expanded and contracted cinematic time and distance, and cross-cutting between parallel dramatic sequences. The film editor can very nearly make or break a screen actor's performance by his selection of scenes and the way he interrelates them in the edited film. Scenes of objects may replace what an actor considers his finest lines of dialogue, if dramatically justified, or his reaction shots and gestures may be used in ways entirely different from the original intent of the performance in master scene cinematography. If the actor's performance is inconsistent from scene to scene (photographed out of context), he may find himself replaced by a cutaway to a scene back at the ranch.

The final performance in the edited film is all that matters, and it may appear better or worse than the performer's actual portrayal of the character at the time of cinematography. An actress may, for example, deliver dialogue so woodenly that her lines are chopped out of the film and her scenes played primarily on the reaction shots, to the effect that she receives critical praise for her "quiet, sensitive performance." The personal feelings of any actor or actress are subordinate (in theory) to the goal of creating a character so convincing and believable that the viewer loses all consciousness of self and vicariously lives that life on the screen.

11

Adaptation: Novels and Stage Plays into Cinema-Television

The Play

The photographed stage play was among the earliest events rendered in motion picture form at the turn of the century. The first screen stories were stage stories, and the first screen actors were stage actors. The first technique of cinematography consisted of setting the camera up in a fixed position to photograph the entire stage, and then having the actors go through their gestures and movements until the camera ran out of film. The actors would stop in mid-action until the camera was reloaded, and then resume their roles until the camera was empty again, and so forth. At first it was considered unthinkable to photograph less than the whole stage and all of the actor, because it was thought the viewer would not pay to see half a stage, let alone half an actor. When the Divine Sarah Bernhardt swooned before the camera she insisted upon being the full-size center of interest in every frame of film.

But it soon became apparent to everyone that a photographed stage play was different from the original play in aspects other than the absence of sound, and the difference was detrimental. And worse, the Great Unwashed would not pay to watch the photographed stage play because it was boring. With D. W. Griffith's development of the unique language of film and the use of stories appropriate to the new medium, the stage play and the screenplay went their separate ways, both having dramatic structure in common, yet each unique in its modes of expres-

244

sion. What they do have in common, however, plus the publicity value of a successful play, will always tempt someone to turn a profit by adapting a play for the screen.

Stage plays are frequently thought to lend themselves to film adaptations more readily than novels because the two forms have conceptual and physical properties in common. Both have similar dramatic structures; both utilize actors carrying forth dramatic actions; both make use of spoken dialogue. But adaptations of superb and popular stage plays to film have frequently been a great disappointment because there are perceptual differences between the two forms. The flow of drama across the boards that seemed so sweeping when the lights were dimmed looks closed in and cramped on film. The gestures of actors that seemed so dynamic from the balcony appear overblown on the screen. The dialogue that seemed so rich and fraught with meaning when it came trippingly from the tongues of fine actors has become so much numbing chatter from people, who, it seems, will never stop talking so we can relax and watch the film.

The resemblance between theater and cinema is superficial and deceptive; and the nature of the resemblance is such as to make the adaptation of a stage play to film far more difficult, in many ways, than the adaptation of a novel. The difficulty lies in the irreconcilable natures of the concepts and physical properties that at first glance make them appear alike.

Any successful adaptation of a stage play to film will require that the filmmaker understand what common elements of these two deceptively similar art forms will lend themselves to a change of medium, what elements will require a change in the mode of expression, and what will need to be eliminated. The elements the film adaptor must be concerned with are *dramatic structure, characterizations, physical media differences, real time and cinematic time, dialogue exposition, actors and acting techniques* and *the spirit of the original play.*

DRAMATIC STRUCTURE

Dramatic structure is the first common denominator. Both forms join a conflict immediately, presenting the origins and circumstances of the conflict, the time, the place and the setting, with clues to the climax and the obligatory scenes. Both present their points of dramatic attack as deriving from a traumatic event, a pending event, an object of contention or the duress of having to change a life style. Both employ a pivotal character who wants something and strikes out for it, and an antagonist who sets forces in opposition, forces which are either changed by the protagonist or cause his death. And both ascend through a series of crises to an obligatory scene, a climax and a denouement.

The internal crisis structure of the stage play and the screenplay are different, however, because of the differences between stage continuity and screen continuity. The modern stage play has been cast in the stylistic structure of the one-act, two-act and three-act play, with a curtain fall between the acts of the longer forms. This segmentation of the dramatic action exists for practical reasons: to permit a change of sets and costumes, to allow a passage of dramatic time and to give a respite to actors and audience alike. While the stage concept of the "act" is an artistic convention sanctified by centuries of use, the segmentation disrupts the flow of the story—the antithesis of cinema.

Cinematic continuity is best served by an *uninterrupted* flow of story and action from the first fade-in to the last fade-out, without any respites along the way, except in the case of those very long films, such as *Gone With the Wind*, in which viewer discomfort may be a factor. The act format of the stage play must be expunged and the dramatic structure revised to provide an unbroken flow of cinematic continuity. This often requires reduced emphasis in the high-crisis structure near the end of an act to one of progressive build. Failure to make this modification in the crisis structure will tend to segment the film; although the story may continue without a break in its physical continuity, the viewer may sense the lumbering down of the unseen curtain.

CHARACTERIZATION

Characterization is the second common denominator. In both the stage play and the dramatic film the major characters are rendered in the round, presenting such fully considered traits as their physical and physiological characteristics, their environmental factors of upbringing, education, occupation and life style, and such psychological factors as intelligence, attitudes, quirks and personal premises. Both art forms present minor characters in perspective to the major, using them as foils and expositional devices, and both orchestrate their characters to enhance the dramatic conflict. The realism of character portrayal in stage and screen are different, however, because of the differing media in which they are rendered.

The stage character is a *universal type*, containing in one individual most of the elements found in a class of human beings. Because of the distance from which a stage character is viewed, the audience is never permitted to look closely into his eyes during his moments of individual triumph and tragedy. The viewer never feels the emotion of an individual, but sees on the broad canvas of stage characterization the common exaltation and anguish of humanity. Because of the universality of his characteristics and the slightly detached quality of his projection, the stage character tends to appear larger than life-size.

The screen character, on the other hand, is an *individual*, because of the intimacy with which he may be viewed in closeup. The character's problems in the story may be those conflicts common to the rest of us in human bondage, but the outcome of the story concerns his individual solution to the problem. The stage play *I Never Sang for My Father* presented a universal story of the inability of father and son to communicate in any meaningful way. But when it was adapted to film, the story became that of individuals who had to solve their problem in a unique way, a solution not necessarily having universal implications. This change was not so much a consequence of adaptation, but of the differing media techniques used to present the characters.

Physical Media Differences

The physical differences of the media are a major stumbling block in adapting the stage play to film. The play is usually presented within the confines of a single proscenium stage, with only a few changes of background. Although the technique of limbo-lighting two or three settings within a given background has offered it some of the flexibility of film, the dramatic action occurs within a narrow physical scope. Within the world of the theater, with its warm, breathing humanity and actor-to-audience rapport, this narrow physical scope seems more than adequate.

But when a play is photographed within a setting as strictured as the original stage, the resulting film takes on a cramped, closed-in quality. The viewer suddenly feels confined when he watches a small action spread out on a large screen and deprived of mobility. The viewer who comes to see a film expects to see a mobile medium that moves with alacrity from person to person and setting to setting. A photographed stage play merely provides the narrowness of action of the live theater without its life, the worst of two worlds. If the film adaptor is so in awe of the original stage play that he is afraid to cut it with the knife of cinematic need, he will be recording only the facts, thereby violating the spirit that had made the play significant.

The relative control over the playgoer's gaze and that of the viewer is another fundamental difference. A playgoer is free to look where he will. If an ensemble scene is presented on the stage, a person sitting in the audience has the options of looking at the actor who is speaking, watching the actors who are listening or admiring the decorations on the proscenium arch. To some degree the stage director may control the playgoer's areas of interest by lighting and blocking action, but in the final analysis the playgoer's gaze is free to wander.

In a motion picture the converse is true—the film determines what the viewer will see at any point in time by presenting him with only one image to look at. The filmmaker decides whether the viewer's attention should be drawn to an action, a reaction or an objective detail. The viewer's gaze is completely subject to the centers of interest, movements and tempos created for him by the filmmaker.

Opening up the closed-in stage play is important in any adaptation to film. One ploy is to place the opening sequences out of doors, before the drama actually begins indoors, leaving the viewer with a residual impression of openness to the extent that a great deal of interior dramatic action may be subsequently presented before the audience becomes aware of the cloistered context. In *The Boys in the Band,* for example, the opening scenes under the titles presented a montage of the homosexuals who would participate in the drama, portraying their life roles in a wide variety of activities—being executives, teachers, delivery boys—to compensate in part for the fact that the entire succeeding drama would take place in two small sets. Eventually the closed-in quality of the drama became obvious, but the nature of the story was such that the transition progressively enhanced the rising tension of the conflict, and seemed to present a dramatic progression that started with the broad establishing scenes out of doors and ended with a tight little conflict indoors.

Exposition should be combed to find legitimate reasons, inherent to the story, for providing cinematic excitement in the adaptation to film.

This exposition is usually embedded in the dialogue of one character to excuse the absence of another. If the original stage play contains dialogue indicating that another character has gone to the airport to pick up a third character, that exposition may become an excuse to take the camera outside and relieve the cramped quality of the original setting to show sweeping airfields, cavernous terminals, the hubbub of passing crowds and the ruthless alacrity of conveyor belts banging up expensive luggage.

A "ride in the park" is another common subterfuge for getting outside. If two characters are engaged in a conversation or a quarrel in which one location is as good as any other, the two may talk in an automobile as well as in a living room, thereby adding movement as the world goes whizzing by outside. The walk in the garden is another ruse for adding blue sky as a relief from uninterrupted walls. In *I Never Sang for My Father* the son's confrontations with his father were interspersed with automobile drives taken to visit him, talks in the garden with his sister and arrivals at airports and railroad stations, cinematic perforations that succeeded to some extent in providing exterior relief for an interior story.

The mobile camera, however, is the most commonly used solution for leavening a cramped set, a technique used with conspicuous success in *I Never Sang for My Father*. Crane-mounted cameras prowled through the sets and among the characters during establishing scenes, transitional shots and times of confrontation; the lenses smoothly glided after those characters moving from one part of the room to the other or one room to the next, providing variety in camera angles for editing.

Dramatic compositions that exaggerate the depth from object to subject, or subject to subject, are other camera techniques used to telescope the set. Another is the slip-focus shot, which shifts the viewer's attention from foreground to background or background to foreground, providing movement in depth when the characters are static. Pans and tilts add horizontal and vertical movement to a physically static relationship when cuts might otherwise be preferable. Movements by the subject directly forward toward the camera and directly away also build the impression that there is more room for activity than really exists on the set. And, of course, there are subjective camera shots as the characters advance, or turn to look out a window at a sweeping panorama of landscape or watch the approach of another character.

Lighting techniques can be used to contribute depth. Splashes of light may be thrown on a set wall that diminish in illumination level as they recede in the distance. Radical changes in the lighting levels and the mood from one dramatic sequence to the next offer variety. Distance may be implied by letting a character emerge from the shadows or recede through darkened doors, and by staging one scene in halftone and the next in a full flood of light.

The editing techniques used in film adaptations of stage plays are somewhat different from those used in stories having naturally cinematic material. Sequences that would be edited rather simply in other stories are cut very rapidly in adaptations in the hope that frequent changes of camera angle and scene within a brief period of time will compensate for the lack of change in the setting. An accelerated editing tempo at every crisis and opportunity is typical of the filmed adaptation.

Real Time and Cinematic Time

Real time and cinematic time are two fundamental differences between the stage play and the film. Real time requires that living people walk across a solid stage in whatever time it takes to physically transport themselves from one place to the other. The time portrayed in the play usually corresponds to the length of the play itself, with a long passage of time (frequently) implied by a curtain fall, and a note in the program to the effect that the next act takes place "two weeks later." During the course of the dramatic action the actors are as earthbound and timebound as the playgoers watching them. Real time as a stage concept is reinforced by the dialogue that carries the bulk of the exposition and character development. There is no way to expedite dialogue —the time needed to speak the words is rooted to the tyranny of the clock—except to eliminate it.

Cinematic time is created by the elimination of all superfluous and intervening actions; a three-minute climb up a stage staircase might be reduced to seconds in a film by a dissolve, with the intervening ascent deleted unless it had dramatic significance. The motion picture is free of the bondage of the real time needed to execute a physical act and can imply transitions of time and location without being forced to reveal them. Any adaptation from stage play to film, then, would require the deletion of many of the real-time dramatic actions of the play.

DIALOGUE EXPOSITION

Dialogue exposition is possibly the biggest of the stumbling blocks in the transmutation of a stage play to film. Drama on the boards is essentially spoken drama in which plot, character development, crises and offscreen actions are rendered in dialogue. The exposition is embedded primarily in *words* (the antithesis of cinema) and secondarily in gestures. Although some motion picture techniques have been adapted to the stage, such as limbo-lighting of separate contemporaneous actions (part of a continuing cross-pollination of the arts), the substantive exposition of a stage play continues to be locked into words.

Exposition on film is locked into *images*. Film requires that the story and character development be revealed primarily through cinematography and editing, not through dialogue; exposition is photographed, not described. The most earthbound, least cinematic moments in most films come when the characters talk to each other and the story is frozen in real time. The magnificent passages of a fine soliloquy, so moving when presented on the stage, become redundant and superfluous in film. If stage play exposition is inseparable from words and cinematic exposition is visual—the antithesis of words—how, then, does one proceed? By ruthlessly cutting out those splendid, glowing descriptive passages from the dialogue and rendering them photographically, cries of outrage from the playwright notwithstanding. The verbal description of something being presented visually cannot be retained because it will have an obvious labeling effect, creating a patronizing impression that is at best annoying, at worst laughable.

Shakespearean plays and other classics present the film adaptor with a real dilemma, because their greatness, to a large extent, lies in their literary qualities. If the play is being filmed with the original dialogue, the filmmaker should select only those lines that work cinematically, render exposition visually, and be prepared to take the critical consequences.

Stage dialogue transferred to the screen needs to be subdued, with high-blown phraseology and pretentious lines deleted. The adaptor must, in particular, watch out for such lines as, "Mary, you are looking at me with distrust and disdain in your eyes." This kind of stage dialogue is intended to compensate for the inability of the playgoer to see the expression in Mary's eyes. In cinema, of course, the viewer is presented with a closeup enabling him to see the expression in her eyes, and if the speaker then makes that kind of remark, the audience will be rolling in the aisles (or walking up them).

ACTORS AND ACTING TECHNIQUES

Actors and acting techniques, too, are different in the stage play and the film. Performing on the boards offers the actor an opportunity to fully live his role for the length of the play, virtually without interruption. Performers from the theater frequently detest acting for the cinema (while enjoying the income) because they are unable to render a complete performance and revel in the plaudits of the audience, and feel artistic satisfaction.

Acting for the camera means acting only in brief snips and scenes under the iron hand of a director who will later supervise the editing of the scenes into a complete performance. The filmmaker is in command, not the actor. It is quite possible for an actor to give a sterling film performance with only the foggiest idea of what the story is all about— if he can follow directions before the camera—something virtually impossible to do on the stage, where the actor must be cognizant of all the ramifications of his performance. Many film producers who adapt Broadway successes to motion picture form refuse to use the cast of the original production because stage actors frequently resent the different modes of expression in film, and because stage actors often persist in projecting themselves to the third balcony while being photographed in closeup.

THE SPIRIT OF THE ORIGINAL PLAY

The spirit of the original play includes the rapport between the actors and the audience. This is an intangible and sometimes magical atmosphere that varies from performance to performance, depending upon the quality and disposition of the cast, the characters and attitudes of the audience, and the traffic the latter has had to contend with to attend the performance. The excitement of an evening at the theater, the festive air, affects the performance and pacing of the actors, and the interplay between the playgoers and the performers can make the play a living thing. This sense of human presence and rapport is a quality missed by those who have first seen the play and then watched the screen adaptation. The critics are often the first to decry the discrepancy because they often do not clearly understand the essentially different natures of the two art forms. When they object to the different dramatic impact, they are insisting that an apple should taste like a pear because both are fruits grown in the same soil.

Interaction between a completed motion picture and the viewer simply does not exist. A finished film presentation remains the same whether it plays to a full house or an empty one, and the reaction of the viewers and critics, one way or the other, will not modify the presentation. The spirit of the living play is one fundamental characteristic that cannot be adapted to the screen.

The best that may be hoped for in an adaptation from stage to screen is to recreate in cinematic form the playwright's premise, joining of the conflict, major crises, obligatory scene and climax, and the essential development of the major characters involved in the story. All stage techniques must be scrapped in favor of cinematic techniques used to express the same ideas. Stage dialogue exposition should be discarded and, whenever possible, plot, exposition and characterization should be translated into moving pictures. The dialogue itself should not have the solidity of the stage, but the weightlessness of the cinema, and should be used only when visual expression is impossible and it is necessary to give verbal information, reveal verbal character or offer verbal humor.

The filmmaker who intends to make a motion picture true to the spirit, story and characteristics of the original play must, paradoxically, be prepared to ruthlessly cut apart its stage characteristics and reassemble its fundamental elements into true cinematic form. He must be prepared to resist the rage of the playwright, ignore the howls of the star and the supporting actors, and burn the reviews of the critics.

The Novel

The premiere of a film adaptation of a novel is usually followed by a chorus of complaints from the author, the critics and the reader-viewers alike that the film version has butchered the novel. Sometimes this is true. More often, however, the complaints are based on the assumption that the characters, events and spirit of the novel are freely interchangeable with the characters, events and spirit of the dramatic film, a premise which in turn implies that the novel provides the standard and the norm from which the film adaptation deviates at its peril. This assumption fails to recognize that the novel and the motion picture represent different artistic genera, as different from each other as music and sculpture. Those who object strenuously that their film-viewing experience was different from their novel-reading experience are sometimes unaware that fundamental elements of an intrinsic nature preclude the direct transfer of a novel's conceptual form into a dramatic film.

Differences intrinsic to the novel and the film determine many of the changes required in any adaptation from one medium to the other, but the pattern of changes tends to be consistent, subject to variations in the story content of the novels themselves. When transmuting novel into film the adaptor is concerned with such elements as *media differences, suitability of a novel for adaptation, condensation of the novel, continuity revisions, viewpoint relationships, equivalence, leading characters, action sequences, settings, dialogue, love, sex, and violence, matters of taste* and *universal issues.*

Media Differences

Differences in the media require changes in the means and modes of expressing a given idea. Most fundamental of these changes is the transmutation of *verbal content* into *visual content*.

The novel is deaf and blind. The sounds of voice and music, the rustle of leaves, the din of battle, the whimper of a child and the whispers of love, all are heard through symbols which are echoed in the sound chamber of the mind's ear. The sight of leaves turning crimson after a frost, the first snow in a pine forest, the swath of death cut by a cannonball, the sudden blush of a lovely woman, can be seen by the reader only through the stimuli of words which project their images on the screen of the mind's eye. Because every reader varies in his literacy level, each will ascribe his own interpretations to the words, creating his own sights and sounds.

The motion picture, to the contrary, is a perceptual art form which presents all viewers with the same identical sights and sounds. All viewers see the identical images of Dr. Zhivago riding across the snow-covered taiga to a rendezvous with Lara, the Scots' cavalry hurling themselves in waves against the cannons of Napoleon at Waterloo, and the supple bodies of a Man and a Woman making love. All hear the same sounds of hoof beats on packed snow, the cries of wounded and dying men as they fall and the whispers of love. While it is true that each viewer tends to look for those things that are familiar and significant to him, the motion picture nevertheless offers a common experience far less vulnerable to variations in interpretation than the arbitrary word.

The novel, moreover, makes use of such literary devices as tropes, which have no counterpart in the experience of film. Expressions like "the slings and arrows of outrageous fortune" and "she flung the javelin of her will" cannot, for obvious reasons, be transmuted to motion pictures. Similes and metaphors may enrich the pages of the novel, to the great pleasure of the reader, and be, moreover, a salient characteristic of the author's style; yet they cannot be practicably rendered on film without becoming laughable. The broad spectrum of colors and flavors unique to the printed word cannot be transmuted to the motion picture.

The cinema, on the other hand, has its unique modes of expression. The closeup and extreme closeup yield an emotional impact different in kind and quality from a written expression or an exclamation point, and may be used in ways having no counterpart in the novel. Furthermore, seeing a subject tells more about him in an instant, more explicitly, than pages of exposition. The motion picture medium not only expresses similar concepts by means fundamentally different from those of the novel, but it may express ideas and emotions that are outside the ken of the printed word.

SUITABILITY FOR ADAPTATION

The suitability of a novel for adaptation depends upon whether the author's style is introspective or descriptive.

The introspective novel tends to probe into the psyches of its characters to reveal what they think, how they feel, their fears, fantasies and phobias, sometimes with little overt action on the part of the characters. This kind of novel is difficult to adapt to cinematic form because its elements do not have the objective forms in real life needed for cinematography. A life lived inside the skull of a character cannot be transmuted to the screen without contriving some form of cinematic action that did not exist in the novel, an act which often desecrates the original concept of the novel. The film adapted from the introspective novel, however successful and popular the novel may be, almost invariably disappoints those reader-viewers who have looked forward to enjoying a cinematic portrayal of their reading pleasure.

The descriptive novel tends to tell the story in overt dramatic action, physical actions, with the development of characters revealed in outward movements and dialogue. The descriptive novel lends itself best to adaptation because it resembles the classic form of the screenplay, with introductory exposition to establish the setting, followed by straight dialogue and dramatic actions. Although this kind of book may be a denatured novel, in the sense that it avoids getting into the minds of its characters, it is the kind that lends itself best to a film version with the least amount of mutilation to the original concepts.

CONDENSATION

Condensation is frequently necessary because the scope of the book more often than not exceeds the potential scope of a single motion picture. The novel may encompass a time span of years, even millennia, moving easily between the past, present and future within a paragraph, without disrupting the continuity or for an instant losing the reader. Novels cast in the epic mold of James Michener's *Hawaii*, which encompass the lifetimes of generations of characters, cannot be filmed with anything like the scope of the original book. The best that can be done is to take one brief segment, select a few out of the many hundreds of characters, and adapt that story to the screen.

Serialized versions of novels adapted for television, such as *The Possessed* or the *Forsyte Saga*, are less demanding in this regard. The need for condensation, however, is almost universal, and the criteria used in the selection of content should not be literary but cinematic.

CONTINUITY REVISIONS

In order to change the narrative story line of the novel into the dramatic structure of a film it is frequently necessary to make continuity revisions. In the course of making such revisions some events and characters may be moved up to the first joining of the conflict, while other sub-plots, events and minor characters may be moved back or eliminated. Chronological sequence is more often the rule in the film than in the novel; when events must be presented out of a chronological time sequence they are presented in a flashback, in flutter-cut scenes, through cross-cutting or in a stream-of-consciousness montage.

VIEWPOINT RELATIONSHIPS

A different viewpoint relationship exists between the characters of many descriptive novels and the reader than that between the characters of a film and the viewer. In many descriptive novels, particularly mystery novels the characters know the answers to the story and its conflicts, and the reader must complete the novel to discover what at least one of the characters knows ("Elementary, my dear Watson...").

In most films, on the other hand, the characters are groping toward or against each other in the film, trying to find out what the viewer already knows. The viewer can watch the separate actions of the pivotal character and his adversaries, through parallel editing and cutaways, while the screen characters struggle blindly against each other. In *Lonely Are the Brave*, for example, the viewer could watch the attempts of the vagrant cowboy to escape from the law, while also being presented with the attempts of the sheriff, the posse and the air force—through cross-cutting and cutaways—to run him down. When the cowboy was about to run the gantlet of a police ambush, the viewer could watch its preparation and execution from the points-of-view of all sides, while none of the screen adversaries knew for sure what the others were doing.

The film version will most often be told from a third-person point-of-view—the omniscient viewpoint—regardless of the narrative viewpoint of the novelist. Almost ninety percent of the novels adapted to film have been rendered from the omniscient viewpoint characteristic of cinema, and those film versions that took the first-person viewpoint often reverted to the third-person viewpoint in order to present events that would be outside the scope of a first-person narrative.

When the film uses the first-person viewpoint, it is usually handled in two ways: through the use of the subjective camera, in which the viewer sees through the eyes of the subject and thereby experiences his perceptions; and through the use of a voice-over narrator, in which the subject speaks directly to the viewer. Both of these techniques were used in Norman Corwin's classic adaptation, *Lust for Life*. The visual viewpoint alternated between subjective camera techniques and the third-person point-of-view in order to reveal Van Gogh's view of the world and the world's view of him. In the sound track of the same film Corwin allowed the artist to speak directly to the viewer, over scenes of Van Gogh's subjects and paintings, to express his inner feelings about art in a way that could not be revealed in dramatic action.

EQUIVALENCE

Equivalence is an important concern in most film versions of the novel, the author's complaints notwithstanding. In the majority of adaptations the film versions retain the main characters, story line and dramatic actions of the original novel; and, within the limits of cinema, attempts are made to find film equivalents for many of the literary devices of the book. The title of the novel is almost invariably retained for its publicity value.

The dramatic film's need for a broader audience carries with it, rightly or wrongly, the assumption that viewer comprehension is on the whole lower than reader comprehension, with a concomitant need for simplification of content. In the course of adaptation dialogue is shortened, modernized, given a conversational rather than a literary tone, and words not readily understood by anyone over fourteen years of age are deleted. The names of characters are changed when they are difficult to pronounce, resemble the names of other characters or carry inappropriate connotations to the contemporary viewer. Ideas and complex forms of knowledge are simplified and, if dated, given modern form by relating them to topical events. The explicitness of film, which renders subtleties directly into graphic perceptual images, contributes to this simplification.

LEADING CHARACTERS

The leading characters in films adapted from novels usually follow the general characterizations of those persons found in the book. Certain dramatic actions may have to be transferred or omitted because of cinematic exigencies, but, for the most part, the screen portrayal of character essentially conforms to the novelist's portrayal of character.

Actors and actresses are usually chosen and act their roles with a serious attempt at following the novelist's conception of the characters. But modifications in the interpretation of a character are sometimes prompted by the need to expand a screen character's role in order to

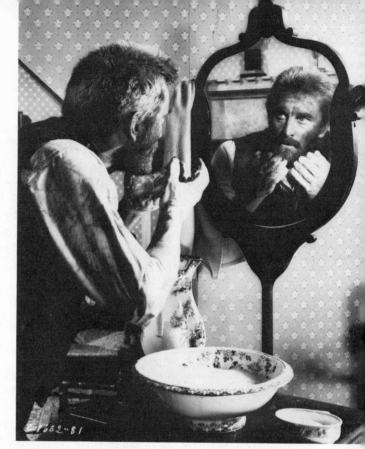

LUST FOR LIFE. Equivalence of character. *Metro-Goldwyn-Mayer*, © *1956*.

meet the demands of a star performer; this is simply a factor of the film industry. New actions may be added to exploit the actor's abilities that were not in the novel; actions in which he dominates may be retained, while actions dominated by others are eliminated; actions implemented by other characters in the novel may be transferred in the film to the star performer; and dramatic sequences in which the star is acting may be strategically relocated in order to emphasize his performance. The last scene of a dramatic film seldom fades out on a minor character.

ACTION SEQUENCES

The parts of a novel most frequently selected for adaptation to the screen are action sequences. To exploit the cinema's ability to dramatize actions and movements, the film adaptation tends to emphasize plot rather than character development. Passive passages in the novel are rewritten whenever possible to be revealed in action and dialogue. Static passages, such as the author's insights, implications and philosophical commentary, may simply have to be deleted unless they can be given cinematic form.

New action sequences having no counterpart in the book are inserted in more than half the novels adapted to flesh out the cinematic qualities of the film. Sometimes these action sequences are created to exploit the motion picture's unique modes of expression, yet they enhance the thematic or dramatic qualities of the story. Other action sequences are inserted for their alleged enhancement of audience appeal, such as scenes of sexual activity and violence, sequences that are frequently antithetical to the concept of the novel.

SETTINGS

Settings play an important role in both the novel and the film because they provide the physical and emotional context for the story and its revelations of character. Settings that require pages of exposition in a novel may be shown in seconds on the screen. Visual rendition may easily communicate settings that the viewer may grasp in an instant, without effort, and without awareness of so doing. Because of most filmmakers' concern for transmuting as many elements of the original novel as possible, the settings of the film version are often the very essence of their description in the novel. To avoid the monotony of repetition, the screen version usually supplies a variety of settings not always found in the original book. Those settings found in the novel that do not lend themselves to cinematography are usually deleted.

DIALOGUE

Dialogue written for the eye is different from that written for the ear. In the novel a character may deliver a declamation that runs on for pages, and in fact, be making a speech. In the novel *Lust for Life*, for example, there were sentences half a page long, extensive enough to exhaust the lungs of a filibustering Senator. Moreover, they were written as grammatically correct statements, complete with commas and semicolons, and replete with a wide range of expressions having poetic, literary merit. Such forms of written dialogue usually pass unchallenged by the reader because they do not invite direct comparison with reality, and because they are conceded as literary license in permitting the author to express his views.

Dialogue written for the ear, however, invites comparison with the tongues of reality, the speech of daily life. Unfortunately, the average viewer does not always respond kindly to speeches loaded with poetic and literary allusions that try to pass as normal conversation. The viewer may laugh aloud at the same dialogue spoken in a dramatic film that he read without cavil in the novel.

When dialogue is adapted from a novel to dramatic film, the following changes are recommended: Only that original dialogue should be used that is required to develop character and give exposition in the film—*as film*—regardless of its importance in the novel. The dialogue selected for use may need shortening so it can be said in one breath, and revision so it is easy to articulate by the actors. Literary allusions may also need to be pruned to make the lines palatable to a mass audience.

LUST FOR LIFE. Equivalence of setting. *Metro-Goldwyn-Mayer,* © *1956.*

The author's views, so often rendered as dialogue in the novel, should find expression in action in the climax of the dramatic film.

LOVE, SEX AND VIOLENCE

Love, sex and violence are often strongly emphasized in the theatrical film to lure the viewer away from his television set.

The love interest of a novel is often inflated in the film version. The exaltation of romance in the dramatic film sometimes eclipses everything else adapted from the novel, even though it may have been only a minor thread in the original story. The adaptation is usually written to create hero and heroine roles in which their love relationship determines the inclusion or omission of other characters, subplot and events from the novel. The American film and television industry has as one of its cherished beliefs the canard that the average viewer wants most of all to see a love story; as long as this belief prevails, matters of the heart will be preeminent in most film adaptations, even though the novel may have emphasized other things.

Once upon a time the sexual aspects of a novel's love story were gently glossed over in the film adaptation. Today, the dramatic film version is likely to graphically portray more than one kind of climax on the screen, complete with grunts and groans and a sea of perspiring flesh. The emphasis on sexual activity is now apt to be exaggerated in order to present the adult viewer with the kind of visual experience he is unlikely to witness on his television set. Brutality, violence and sadism are part of the same trend, tending to be used more lavishly and graphically in the film than in the original book. Violence was once treated circumspectly or eliminated; now many film adaptors cull the text for violence to be vividly exploited on the screen, regardless of its importance to the story and the development of characters. Profanities, obscenities and vulgarities—once omitted or played down in deference to public taste—are now frequently emphasized, flaunted and dignified by the name of "realistic adult entertainment."

TASTE

Matters of taste, however, still tend to impose some limitations upon what may be adapted from the novel to the screen. Many serious novels conclude on a note of futility, despair, frustration or indecision. This kind of emotional note is often unacceptable to the average American viewer, but is acceptable to European and Asian audiences. The film version is therefore sometimes made with two endings to accommodate domestic and foreign tastes. For an American audience, the films have traditionally concluded on a note of hope and affirmation; for the others, on a note of futility. *The Key* concluded with a man racing down a railroad platform to catch a departing train on which the woman he loved was riding out of his life. In the American version he caught the train and implicitly regained the woman. In the foreign version the train outraced him and he lost her forever. There has been a recent trend away from the happy ending in American films, toward tragic or nihilist conclusions typical of the foreign film.

Universal Issues

The universal issues presented in a novel are often changed in their implications to offer a personal solution. Seldom does the film adaptation retain the catholic character of the original novel. Instead, the practice has been to particularize all personalities to such a degree as to eliminate universal meanings. The outcome of the story has been most often presented in terms of the consequences to an individual character, and thus drained of broader implications.

Good and evil also tend to be personified. In the novel evil exists in institutions and social forces, and the villain is generally made the instrument through which evil works. The novel carries the implication that as long as evil social forces exist, evil persons will exist to do their dirty work. This relationship is reversed in the film adaptation of the novel: all the properties of evil are invested in a specific individual, whose evil apparently exists without context, and whose destruction provides the solution to the conflict and an end to evil. The polarized philosophy that mankind is divided into two groups, good and bad, and that a slaying of evil will leave only good, is commonly found in films other than screen adaptations, but recent trends in contemporary cinema are away from such simplistic interpretations of life.

Social criticism is sometimes modified or deleted when it is thought to be offensive to sizable segments of the American viewing public. Religious and political institutions are seldom subject to the criticism, derision and ridicule found in the original novel. Whenever such an attack is central to the theme of the novel, the film versions tend to shift the blame to an individual who is an exception, not a representative of his group, or to eliminate the attack altogether. The same holds true in attacks on corporate practices, medical abuses and other economic interests. Even attacks on criminal organizations are soft-pedaled when they carry an implicit attack on a large ethnic minority, as was the case in *The Godfather*.

12

The Action Film and the Psychodrama

Action films and psychodramas are probably the most Aristotelean form of cinema in the sense that they tell the story and reveal character essentially by action. Sophisticated dialogue and subtle character inter-relationships are subordinated to a tightly organized, fast-moving plot in which vigorous action and visual excitement are often enhanced by highly dramatic settings. Although it may be difficult to define exactly what constitutes an action film, since any subject may be treated pri-marily in action, there are certain genres that consistently emphasize story line to the subordination of other dramatic elements. These genres are the *western*, the *war film*, the *gangster film*, the *spy film*, the *psycho-drama* and the *horror film*. These traditional forms are often highly stylized and the viewer knows from the outset how the films will end, but takes his pleasure from savoring variations on old and well-loved classic forms.

The Western

The first western was also the first motion picture to tell a story in a truly cinematic way. *The Great Train Robbery* (1903) was a sensa-tional pioneering effort that simultaneously created a film genre and established the cinema in America as a source of mass entertainment.

The eager patrons who queued up before the nickelodeons liked their westerns so much that at first it was difficult to tell whether they were seeing the horse operas because they were movies, or movies because they were westerns. When television came along and films began to dominate prime time programming, the lowly western soon galloped to the fore in popularity ratings.

THE ARCHETYPAL WESTERN

The Westerner is the last "man of honor" and his cinematic genre one of the few film forms in which the concept of personal integrity retains its credibility. His archaic code of conduct would make him appear ridiculous by contemporary standards if it were not for the fact that he is potentially willing to kill or be killed rather than to compromise his integrity. He is self-defined, self-contained, and demands that all others accept him on his own terms. He judges himself by a rigid standard of deportment—courage regardless of the odds. The Westerner is as psychologically alone on a crowded street as he is on the sweeping plains. His loneliness is the price of honor; it is not imposed upon him by outer circumstances.

The Westerner seems a man of independent means, appearing unemployed even when wearing a star or working a ranch. He is never trying to rise in the world, even if the story recounts a struggle for land or cattle, because he has already arrived in every important sense: he can ride a mustang skillfully, face a sworn enemy without flinching, and shoot a pistol with quick and deadly aim. He is seldom conspicuously rich or poor, and money appears in his hand only when he slaps a silver dollar down on the bar to pay for his whiskey. He often seems to own only his revolver, his horse and one dusty suit of clothes. If the adventure happens to be a television series, like *Gunsmoke*, he may wear the same clothes for eighteen years without ever changing his shirt. Whether he runs a ranch or a saloon, or operates out of the town jail as the marshal, these places never really exist as possessions, but only as settings, and sometimes as occasions for action.

Love may be offered to him and he may accept it, but love seems at best peripheral to the dramatic action of men, guns and horses. The Westerner is constantly in dangerous situations where love must play third fiddle to death and honor. The women in his love life tend to fall into two simplistic categories: the woman from the East and the woman of the West, each endowed with a galaxy of stereotyped values.

The woman from the East, whom he loves, seems unable to understand his motives. She is morally opposed to violence for any reason and cannot grasp the code of honor that compels him to shoot it out with a deadly enemy instead of filing a complaint with the local sheriff or hiding in the basement until the bad man goes away. She tends to embody purity, gentility, education and civilization, and provides the occasion for a clash of cultures between the settled East and the wild West. The woman from the East represents a kind of refined wisdom in a world of crude men that will eventually be changed by her gentle hand.

The woman of the West, who loves him, is a prostitute camouflaged as a barroom entertainer. She lacks the winning graces and refinements of her rival from the East, but she shares the Westerner's understanding of life on the frontier and his need to act on what he sees is the honorable thing to do. The prostitute often loves the Westerner in a deep if practical way, but understands that he cannot marry her because of her unsavory trade. Nor does she need to lean on anyone for love or protection. Although caked with rouge, she is stridently independent and as tough at heart as the men she services. She is owned by no one, accountable to no one, and pays for this independence by ending up alone. And when the Westerner abandons her for a woman from the East, he is symbolically forsaking the frontier life of the old West.

Other women of the West, settlers' wives and cattlemen's sisters, tend to be portrayed in two extremes: if they live out in the wilderness with their families, they tend to be flinty and self-reliant, as tough as the frontier. If they live in town, they tend to be rendered as church-going, psalm-singing pillars of the community, wringing their hands with righteousness. Women of Spanish-speaking descent are portrayed, for some reason, with exceptional deference and gallantry.

The story usually figures as a struggle over land, cattle, water or gold, but these are not really the objects of contention, only the occasion for action. Nobody cares about the gold—only about the men pitted against each other. The plot usually follows the Aristotelean format in which a pivotal character strikes out for what he wants and is resisted by another force with maximum effort; the characters of each are revealed and the story told in action sequences portraying desperate physical efforts. Inasmuch as the men involved represent moral values to be resolved, the plot of a western usually ends in some form of duel to the death and the ritual slaying of evil.

Melancholy underlies the western because of the constant threat of violence, the nearness of death. Guns are the uniform expression of the code of honor and constitute the symbolic moral center of the drama. Always the pistol is waiting on the Westerner's hip, in his hand, hung on the wall behind him, or on the persons of his adversaries. It is only a matter of time before a confrontation results in the killing of the Westerner or his enemy.

In *Butch Cassidy and the Sundance Kid* two middle-aged robbers were confronted with the spread of law and order in the Old West, a place in which they no longer had the right to exist. Banks were bolted impregnably, lawmen were everywhere, and the railroads, so often robbed, began to employ gunmen the equal of the two outlaws and trackers who could follow paths over solid rock—hounding them to the brink of death. Barely escaping with their lives, they fled from America to relive the wild old days in Bolivia. But time soon ran out in South America. They were hunted down and trapped by hundreds of soldiers of the Bolivian army and faced with the choice of surrender or death. Common sense would suggest that they throw out their revolvers to save their lives. Honor dictated that they die fighting. Butch and Sundance came out with their guns roaring defiance and paid the death price that gives life to the concept of honor in the western.

Horses and the open land are the sphere of action and represent the ultimate freedom that appeals to so many urban viewers—an escape from the cement linings of their strictured lives. The sun may stare down fervidly on scenes of shabby prairie towns, on lonely and dirty people, on material bareness so far below the poverty line as to justify massive welfare expenditures, yet the viewer sees only the swirls of freedom on horseback and the expansionism of a romanticized frontier life.

The time-theme of the western is usually the three-decade period of 1870–1898, a transitional phase of dramatic turmoil when the Indians were making their last desperate stands, the cattlemen were building their lariat empires, *pistoleros* swaggered up and down the land, nesters were beginning to squat around waterholes and the United States Cavalry was thundering across the plains in endless skirmishes with the red man. Always the time-theme seems to hinge upon the fading of the frontier, when the rough-handed men who subdued the wilderness were forced to yield to the pale-handed encroachments of a civilized life style in which issues and justice are resolved in courts of law. The time-theme of *Butch Cassidy and the Sundance Kid* was typical. Butch and Sundance had enjoyed twenty years of happy robbery and did not know quite what to make of it when they, the hunters, became the hunted. Quite simply, they had outlived their time. Nearly run to earth by lawmen in the United States, they fled to Bolivia in a repetition of the "end of the frontier" time-theme that contributes much to the melancholy of the western.

CONTEMPORARY TWISTS

There has been a recent reversal in the interpretations of former heroes in "adult" or psychological westerns. The new version often presents the former hero as a coward or a sadist at heart, the cattleman as a concerned ecologist, the cavalry officer as a power-mad psychotic, the Indian as a Noble Red Man and the coming of civilization as the advent of corruption. This reversed relationship has been extended to stories about the morality of being a professional gunfighter or bounty hunter, the triangular struggles between the Indians, cavalry and settlers, the range wars between the cattlemen on one side and the nesters or sheepmen on the other, the corruption of Indian agents, the racist extremists in white and Indian camps, the fights for law and order in the face of timorous townspeople and the dying of the frontier. Contemporary issues are commonly injected into stories set in the Old West in which they historically had no real relevance. The new cynicism is often as far removed from reality as the old romanticism.

THE TELEVISION WESTERN

Television requires certain changes for the genre to be suitable for serial broadcasts. Obviously, the drama of kill or be killed cannot be played out to the death of the key figure or the series would end immediately. Instead, there is a guest pivotal character—the stranger who drifts into town seeking revenge, money, power or interference in the life of one of the continuing characters—and the drama is played out to *his* death. Usually, he represents evil in some form, or is a warped personality, who is killed by the western hero in the ritual duel to the death at the end.

BUTCH CASSIDY AND THE SUNDANCE KID. Honor in the Western. *20th Century-Fox.*

Other modifications for television include a further simplification of stereotypes, more interplay of family life in the town and increased emphasis on clean, folksy virtues. Women throw themselves at the westerner hero with greater frequency in the television form; but if he has ever been married, his wife has died and left him with a platoon of lusty sons.

APPEAL

The universal appeal of the western to the modern viewer (predominantly to males) has been analyzed time and again, because the genre certainly offers no solutions to the problems of contemporary life. The consensus opinion of many who have studied the phenomenon is that the genre is so gratifying because it portrays a life style offering personal freedom, clarity of issues and certainty of purpose. Its decisiveness seems refreshing to the average urban viewer, who finds himself dangling impotently amid social and economic forces largely outside his control. The viewer sees the western hero unencumbered by a wife and dependents, free from the banality of a dreary job needed to pay his monthly bills, unfettered by the rules and restraints needed to fit into some bureaucratic niche. The western hero is never dominated by a boss. Baffled by competing moral standards, bewildered by impersonal and often exploitative relationships, the viewer seems to watch westerns to vicariously experience control over personal destiny.

The War Film

War seems made to order for rendition in film, and the motion picture ideal for the depiction of war. Battle scenes are full of cinegenic

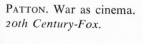

PATTON. War as cinema.
20th Century-Fox.

actions of men fighting, bombs exploding, planes streaking across the sky and other powerful pictorial movements that lend themselves to rendition by motion pictures. Moreover, film, with its capacity for showing faces in closeup, can present the fascinating spectacle of how conflict peels away the veneer of formalized social behavior and throws the characters of men into stark relief. Under fire, men often become leaders, cowards, heroes, sadists, egomaniacs, and sometimes, psychotic degenerates, and the gradual change of each man under stress can be portrayed exquisitely on film and television.

THE CONVENTIONS OF THE GENRE

The hero of a war film is usually a leader or volunteer for a dangerous mission, or a maverick misfit in the armed forces who is transformed by a crisis into a leader or a volunteer. The basis of action is occasionally the psychological eccentricities of a leader, such as in *Patton*. The coming battle or mission that most often provides the story framework is interpreted as a dirty job that needs to be done by the key figure. The concept of the "war hero" who risks his life for idealistic goals is out of style in American films. The soldier's motivations are practical ones—orders from higher up, cannons menacing the straits of a sea passage, comrades trapped by the enemy. There is sometimes a thematic denial of the pretentiously heroic—get the job done and stay alive. War films tend to invest violence with legitimacy and the hero with the (reluctant) responsibility for executing it.

The war film resembles the western in its emphasis upon bravery—courage to fight is the measure of the man. In the preparations for battle that usually constitute the elements of a war story, men may reveal themselves to be rats of varying dimensions and degrees, but if they prove themselves courageous under fire, all is forgiven. If they prove cowardly under fire, it matters little what other good qualities they may have.

As in the western, the concept of honor permeates the action and evolves into a "Brotherhood of Arms" that transcends the conflicts of individuals within it. A special kind of friendship and camaraderie springs up among men who risk their lives in combat together, and if they survive, their relationship often lasts for years after the war. One need only watch filmed television interviews with young soldiers who speak fiercely of never leaving a wounded buddy behind to realize that this loyalty between comrades in arms exists almost as an atavistic warrior instinct, a theme of the brotherhood of arms which strikes a chord in many male viewers.

There seems to be an instinct in the human race to admire courage, and the sight of brave men fighting almost compels male viewers to identify, while not necessarily approving at a conscious level. The motion picture can reveal as no other medium can the final result of all that bullets and bombs can do to ravage mortal flesh; the current trend toward antiwar war films demonstrates with unflinching realism that there are no "nice deaths." Yet the sight of courageous fighting compels identification with the men in action, even when the consequences are horrible. *Patton* made the viewer want to be a tank commander. *The Great Escape*, a prisoner of war. *Paisan*, a guerrilla. *Tora, Tora, Tora*, a sailor scrambling for the nearest machine gun to stave off the Japanese attack on Pearl Harbor. The strong modes of identification inherent in the dramatic form add further ties of absorption in the combat on the screen. War films have been popular primarily because they provide vicarious adventure, comradeship, a cause to embrace, discipline to simplify ambiguities and resolve weaknesses, and an escape from banality, monotony and monogamy.

Simplistic personification of character traits is common in war films. The nature of combat reduces men to their elemental natures, which are rendered on film in the form of two-dimensional stereotypes: the power-mad officers who willingly trade the lives of their subordinates for victory; the brave but foul-mouthed sergeant who tries to fight the war while protecting the lives of his men; the coward who tries to hide in a farmhouse that becomes the command post of the enemy and who dies under shellfire; the nice guy who insists he is frightened but proves himself a hero; the scrounger who will buy or sell anything, is too clever to get involved in combat, yet in the end volunteers for the dangerous mission. In war films the men are reduced to symbols of character traits in human beings, easily recognizable, yet not quite three-dimensional in the sense demanded by viewers in other genres of film. Since men live at a nervous animal pitch in war, such simplistic renditions of character development tend to seem credible. The greater the number of screen characters, the more simplistically the soldiers are rendered as leaders, cowards, heroes, weaklings and so forth.

The personification of social, economic and military classes in conflict is a plot device used in war films. The armed forces provide a great

TORA! TORA! TORA! Identification in war films. *20th Century-Fox.*

mixing bag into which men are dumped indiscriminately during wartime, many of them drafted and most of them from widely disparate
strata of society. The rich, the poor, the ignorant, the educated, the
farm boy, the guttersnipe, the redneck—all may be comrades in the
same platoon. Put men together who bring such widely differing social,
economic and political values, and their rough and unfitting edges tend
to generate personal sparks before they face battle as a unit. Class
quarrels and hostilities are inevitable, which lend themselves to the orchestration of characters in a war film. Class conflicts are most often
used to create tension within a given combat unit of one side or the
other as the men prepare for the great battle that will resolve all issues.
In some European films, such as those of the Soviet Union, class warfare is a major fabric of the dramatic conflict, and individuals find their

destiny only within the outcome of the greater class struggle. In American films, however, class consciousness is used primarily to provide tensions between members of the same combat unit.

Traditionally, wartime war films trick the viewer into accepting a double standard of morality; a ruthless attack is glorious if done by our side and heinous if done by the other side. This double standard permeates the war films of all war-making nations, because the intent is to increase the wartime commitment of soldiers and civilians alike.

THEMES

The themes running through the wartime war films of most nations are similar to these: The personal courage and total commitment of the individual soldier makes victory possible. Teamwork wins battles and individual differences must be subordinated to the efficiency of the combat team. We hate war and its incalculable cost, but war has been forced upon us by the enemy and we must crush him to teach him a lesson he will never forget. We are up against a vicious, unscrupulous foe who will stoop to any tactic to win; therefore we are justified in using a few vicious, unscrupulous tactics of our own. We have complete confidence in the quality of our leadership and the integrity and fighting ability of our allies. Our ultimate military victory will be worth any sacrifice, because on it rests the future of mankind.

Postwar war films are another matter. Cynicism and disenchantment become the dominant themes. Cowardice becomes clever (*The Americanization of Emily*), malingering smart (*Catch-22*) and heroism the self-delusion of a fool (*The Young Lions*). Victory came because the enemy was even more corrupt, venal and stupid than our side. The corruption and atrocities that were buried in the interests of commitment to the war effort are dug up and dramatized in all their seaminess. Sometimes cynicism becomes so extreme that historical facts are reversed in dramatic films in order to make an antiwar statement. In *Bridge at Remagen*, for example, psycho American officers were shown forcing hapless G.I.'s to charge into withering German gunfire to take the last bridge left standing over the Rhine River. In historical fact, the Germans, fleeing in haste, had forgotten to detonate the charges they had set under the bridge—a disastrous oversight—and the American soldiers simply walked across the bridge and took it with no resistance whatever.

War without glory is now the most universal theme. The current interpretation of the second oldest profession is to examine the cost of war in terms of its human consequences without taking sides on the issues of the war or the causes of the conflict. This theme has been with us since *What Price Glory?* of the silent-film days, but never so heavily emphasized as now. Current war films clearly portray the ruthless discipline of training for military life, the corruption that follows armies into battle, and the confusion and pain as bewildered boys clash with the enemy amid scenes of overpowering violence and brutality, followed by a tide of screaming faces, smeared with blood and mud. In the contemporary war film the viewer is less likely to see waving flags than oozing entrails. And when the soldier has killed an enemy, he is often filled with remorse and respect for the fallen foe. The viewer is made to realize that war gives nothing and may take away everything.

THE TELEVISION WAR FILM

War films for television require certain adaptations to be suitable for serial broadcast to an audience of millions. As in the western, there is a guest protagonist—a new man in the combat unit, a traitor in the ranks, a spy among the civilians, a new commander among the enemy —who becomes the pivotal character until all issues are resolved in the climactic battle. The platoon leader obviously cannot be killed off in any combat episode of World War II (completely refought on television), and the new man has to provide the dramatic conflict within the story and at the climax.

Personification of character traits is carried to its ultimate in the war television series. The stoic hero lives again, as does the blue-eyed boy in his first battle, the super-tough sergeant and the ramrod-straight and monocled Nazi officer. Personification of class or race conflicts, however, is played down, in deference to the mass mixed audience that watches television, potential buyers of the sponsor's product. The issues of war simply do not exist in the television war film, and the issues of conflict are largely personified into good guys versus bad guys. Idealism and cynicism alike are diluted or eliminated, and the final viewing product is a pablum of innocuous action.

War films have often been transformed into situation comedies for television. The famous stage play *Stalag 17* found its echo in *Hogan's Heroes*, a television comedy in which "The Crud" became a swell guy who used his genius for fast dealing for the good of his comrades and country and the frustration of the buffoons who represented the German guards. The war film as situation comedy will be treated in the chapter on "The Comedy and the Musical."

The Gangster Film

AN AMERICAN GENRE

The gangster film, like the western, is a uniquely American form, and the stories of both genres have taken on an allegorical and ritualistic quality. Similarly, the gangster genre resembles a Homeric legend in which criminal heroes prove their courage by passing through ordeals of (gun) fire. In a sense, the gangster concept is a morality film concerned with contemporary affairs, much as the western is concerned with the past.

The gangster genre had a serious purpose from the outset in the sense that it was used to explore the urban conditions that made the mobster possible. The idea of the slums as a breeding ground for criminals, prostitutes and drug addicts has been treated from *Little Caesar* (1930) and *The Public Enemy* (1931) to the present. The tale of the bought politician and the corrupt policeman has been revealed in all its aberrations as symptomatic of a sickness we have not yet learned how to cure. The genre embodies the American tendency to personify complex social problems and to find dramatic solutions in the shooting or jailing of a representative offender.

The cinematic interpretation of the gangster's origins has occurred at three general levels: First there is the victim of the slums theory, in which a basically good if wild boy went wrong because of bad companions, his desperation born of poverty or a sense of tragic injustice to himself or someone he loved—a circumstance in which he was as much sinned against as sinning. The second interpretation is that he is an emotionally warped and psychologically unbalanced human being who is driven by neuroses beyond his own control. The third view is that the contemporary gangster is neither a psychological cripple nor a product of the slums, but a cool and intelligent man who freely chooses the business of crime simply to make money the easiest, quickest way.

The gangster was originally portrayed cinematically as vulgar and without a trace of the civilizing graces, except that he was good to his mother. A city animal, his vocation was unceasing activity in the pursuit of money and power, his pastime was unrestrained indulgence in "booze and broads." The gangster had an aura of loneliness and melancholy because his actions had put him in the position where everyone itched to see him over the sights of a gun, and sooner or later someone did. Crude and brutal, noisy and ambitious, nervous and loveless, he nevertheless knew what he wanted—to be the Big Boss.

Speed, sharpness and vigor typified the cinematography, editing and dialogue of the early gangster film. The dialogue came right out of the gutter: "We was double-crossed. He squealed on us—the dirty stool pigeon." Based on facts born of the headline, and rendered with the crispest realism, the gangster film excited audiences of the thirties and became an overnight box office sensation.

The life style of the gangster is cinematic. Guns, girls, combat and fast cars are its visual elements. The plots are filled with rousing action and triangular conflicts between rival gangsters and the police. Little mystery, but lots of excitement over who will win.

THE THEME AND SETTING

The essential theme of the gangster genre is: Grab the money and run, and kill whoever tries to stop you. In the course of grabbing the money and running, the gangster characteristically shoots men in the back, beats women, takes baseball bats to the arms and legs of those who do not pay off, and places the feet of squealers in cement for a walk on the bottom of the East River.

The concept of honor plays a role in the gangster genre as it does in the western—but in reverse. Where it is a point of pride for the western hero to draw second and shoot first, the gangster shoots first at every opportunity, keeps on shooting first, and does so when the other man is disarmed, looking the other way or buying flowers for Mother's Day. Where the interest in the western hero derives in part from his unflappable self-control, the fascination with the gangster lies in his lack of self-discipline—he is unpredictable, and will start shooting on the most trivial pretext.

The setting of the gangster film may be any of five cities in the United States. New York is popular for its squalid slums and sensational skyline, but Chicago retains its machine-gun reputation as the birthplace of the gangster and the Queen City of Corruption in the Twenties. Los Angeles, San Francisco or New Orleans will do if certain kinds of local color are required. But the settings are simple and stylized: cement canyons filled with teeming streets of people and automobiles, a context of busy activity so anonymous and impersonal that stark stories and characters can be presented in bold relief.

EVALUATION OF A FORMULA

The gangster story formula is usually simpler than those of the western or war film—a simple recounting of the rise and fall of a mobster. The urban circumstances that drove or lead him to a life of crime are rationalized with a logic that usually creates a degree of sociological emphathy. In a bucolic version of the gangster genre, *Bonnie and Clyde*, the criminal phases that began with adolescent thrill-seeking progressed gradually through increasingly vicious criminal actions until the two met death at the hands of vengeful police; with unusual success, the film sympathetically revealed that those two merciless killers were really lovable at heart.

The gangster film has reached the stage of evolution where it is no longer a socially conscious derivative of the daily headlines, but represents instead a sub-culture of oily businessmen with feet planted on both sides of the law, who resort to the gun when that is the most effective way to do business. Morality scarcely exists in either the gangster or his police antagonist. It is a true cinematic underworld, self-contained and autonomous, with its own disciplines and regulations, having only a peripheral relationship to the crude realities of the original gangster film.

APPEAL

The appeal of the gangster as a folk hero is difficult to understand. Perhaps many viewers would like to beat up a bettor who cannot pay off, brutalize a woman, kill or humiliate a policeman or plant a bomb in City Hall, and the gangster film provides them with vicarious fulfillment. Or perhaps there is a mistaken carry-over of the Robin Hood appeal, in which an outlaw (criminal) operates outside the law to right injustices protected by loopholes in the law. It strains credulity, however, to portray a gangster as robbing the rich and giving to the poor. In reality, the loot goes no farther than his own pockets, to be spent on his own pleasures.

At the bottom of the gangster's appeal may lie the average American's sneaking admiration for the individual fighting for himself against the powerful forces of the establishment. It is the perverse appeal of the loner thumbing his nose at the world and backing his defiance with a "gat" or a machine gun. This urban *pistolero* is exciting because he is dangerous in his protest against oppressive urbanism, his determination to beat the system. Moreover, he enjoys membership in a secret society of conspiracy that permits its members to lash out at contemporary life as many viewers might like to do.

THE TELEVISION FORM

In its television form the cops-and-robbers genre shifts in emphasis from the gangster to the side of law enforcement, and focuses on the efforts of one or two police officers to capture a gangster or break up a syndicate. Almost every American police agency has been glorified in television form: *Dragnet* recounted the adventures of Sergeant Friday, a municipal detective in Los Angeles. *O'Hara of the Treasury* presented the sleuthing of an Internal Revenue Agent. Other television series have been based upon the Federal Bureau of Investigation, Interpol, the Secret Service and the United States Border Patrol.

The television form tends to be highly factual, with dramas based upon cases drawn from police files. Many of them are rendered in semi-documentary fashion, with voice-over narration used to add facts and sound official, and dialogue written to sound terse and realistic. There is little glorification of the criminal on television, in contrast to the theatrical form of the gangster genre, and certainly no Robin Hood characters. The stories do not recount the rise and fall of a mobster, giving sociological background, but the solution of a single criminal case by an officer of the law, with the criminal eventually being captured and penalized.

The Spy Film

Blood brother to the movie gangster is the spy—another urban man with a gun. Spies have been with us almost from the beginning of movies—men with blond crew cuts, monacles and mid-European accents determined to obtain the plans of a new weapon to assure victory for the Fatherland. The modern spy, however, was born after World War II and sprang from the rib of 007, James Bond. This glamour boy exists in a fantasy world bordering on science fiction. He is equipped with a pistol having a foot-long silencer, backup guns in his tie clip and shoelaces, knockout gas in his cigarette lighter, automobiles that can do anything an engineer can imagine, including fire rockets that will take the occupants safely over bridgeless rivers.

His adversary has a comparable array of gadgets and commands a platoon of karate experts. Our hero's love life would exhaust anyone but this urban superman—he has mistresses galore and a woman adversary with a gun turret installed in each brassiere cup. For the viewer who likes a wild yarn laced with improbable sex and adventure, there is no further escape from reality than the James Bond form of the spy film.

The Television Form

The television form of this genre is very much like its theatrical counterpart, except that the heavy-handed sexuality is eliminated and the more brutal forms of mayhem are modified. The spy film has been adapted frequently into the ubiquitous television situation comedy, to be discussed in the next chapter. The shifting plot structure, changes of character identity and number of "double-crosses" found in a spy film take us to the threshold of the psychodrama.

The Psychodrama

Themes and the Central Figure

The psychodrama is based upon human corruptibility and mental aberrations, with dramatic emphasis upon tightening screws of suspense. The unexpected is the essence of this genre, with characters, plot and cinematic techniques manipulated to cheat the expectation of the audience.

In the psychodrama the characters change their identity kaleidoscopically as the story is told, in contrast to other action films, in which the viewer gets better acquainted with the characters as the film progresses. The key character with whom the audience identifies finds himself in a morass of shifting relationships with the other characters—with good and evil inseparably interwoven—until the audience becomes tense trying to keep track of who is who and what is what. Every sequence thematically reveals the impurity of human motives, the evil abnormality that may fester under surface normality, the unreality of what seems real, the sickening assumption that "we are all guilty," and the grim realization that human relationships are an eternal quagmire of anguish and misunderstanding.

The central figure is usually alone and vulnerable, even within the city, and is portrayed as the hunter-hunted. The story strikes at the atavistic fear of being helplessly trapped by maniacal forces, and usually figures irrational panic. The motivations of the protagonist are often instinctive, based upon trust or suspicion, and many dramatic actions

PSYCHO. Settings for psychodrama. *Universal Studios.*

are begun by a hunch. The concepts of honor found in many action films scarcely exist in this genre, or in the related forms of mystery, spy, murder, "gothic" and horror films—only degrees of venality and corruption.

The setting of the psychodrama is an important factor in enshrouding the key figure in an ominous atmosphere: forbidding regions of sullen cliffs and eerie mists; impersonal scientific chambers with mysterious flashing lights and noises; lonely houses set in wilderness areas, far from the nearest help; airplanes seized in mid-flight by a maniac, or flying out of control; skyscrapers abandoned for the weekend; cellar passages that terminate in a soundproof cul-de-sac room; sewers that wind endlessly through labyrinthine passages under a city. Any setting that isolates the central figure and cuts off the possibility of assistance may heighten the mood of latent menace.

SUSPENSE TECHNIQUES

Certain plot devices are used to create suspense: joining the conflict at the beginning with a deadly predicament that belongs chronologically to the end, and to which the audience is led in flashback; elaborate preparations by the villain for an act of violence; repeated postponement of inevitable violence by unexpected and trivial interruptions, such as a telephone call; the sudden transformation of a trusted friend into an unexpected enemy—a betrayal. The cheating of expectation in any human relationship within the story may be used to enhance suspense.

Camera techniques do much in the psychodrama to heighten the emotions of the subject and the horrors of the dramatic action. In Hitchcock's *Psycho*, when Norman Bates carried the body of his mother out of the bedroom and down the seemingly endless stairs, a crane-mounted camera with a wide-angle lens was used to follow him, conveying the impression that he was sinking into fathomless depths. At the climax of the film a wide-angle lens encompassed the basement room for a long, long time, until the mother's chair was turned around. Then a swift zoom-in to the shriveled, eyeless face of the mummy made the audience scream in terror.

Editing is important in creating suspense. A shocking scene is usually preceded by a series of repetitive static scenes, held a long time on the screen, to lull the viewer's senses. Most often the lulling scenes are wide-angle, full or establishing shots, because these sizes tend to carry the implications of passivity. When the shocker comes, it is usually in the form of a swift zoom-in or a cut to a closeup. In *Play Misty for Me* the key figure was groping through a night-shrouded house overlooking a cliff, searching for an insane woman whose love for him, having been rejected, had been transformed into hatred. Every move he made through the velvety darkness was a static wide-angle scene, until she lunged at him with a knife—a smashing zoom-in to a closeup— followed by a wide-angle exterior shot as he hurled her through a window to be killed on the cliff below.

Unpredictable surprise and richness of detail are the essence of the psychodrama, with every cinematic technique used to arouse anxiety in the viewer: arbitrary changes of viewpoint; subjective camera techniques at points of pending violence; extreme camera mobility to create the sense of being helplessly "carried away"; high-angle shots to emphasize helplessness, a sense of vertigo, a bottomless pit, a sinking into quagmires of uncertainty; zooms for orientation shock effect, to create the sense of being trapped and to transform relief into fear; tensions created by pans and tilts so abnormally long that they cry out for a cut; editing to create suspense by alerting the audience to a danger that the victim knows nothing about, then cross-cutting for the peril-and-rescue sequence, and then progressively shortening the length of scenes to heighten excitement as the story nears its climax. Every cinematic technique is used to restrict the viewer to sharing the experiences, the single consciousness of the person in danger.

Other anxiety-inducing factors may be created by sound effects: jumbles of conversation in which one key word stands out; footsteps in the fog; the creak of an opening door; the cry of a loon over a mist-shrouded lake; long, long silences which are then punctuated by a significant sound; mysterious dragging noises; the metallic click of a cartridge being chambered in a weapon. All of these sound effects may exploit fear of the unknown.

Bizarre death, or the threat of it, is an integral part of the psychodrama. In *North by Northwest* the key figure ran desperately across a flat prairie to escape from the propeller blades of an airplane. In *The Pit and the Pendulum* the victim awaited the slow-ticking descent of a swinging pendulum-ax, while rats danced on his face. In *The Virgin Spring* the father of a raped and murdered girl prepared for his revenge on the killers by a ritual of purification that ended with his knifing of an innocent boy.

The appeal of the psychodrama seems to lie in the viewer's fascination with an apparently normal person, like himself, who sinks into neurosis or insanity, or tries to retain his sanity when he finds himself in a desperately insane situation. It seems to derive from the viewer's voyeuristic desire to peer into a personality torn between outer order and inner chaos, and his morbid curiosity—sometimes sexual in nature —about the secret life of another person. The appeal of this genre is based, in part, upon the realization that it is impossible to understand another human being in the profoundest sense.

The television version of the psychodrama usually deals with essentially the same themes and stories found in the theatrical versions, with some modifications. Scenes depicting suicide or violence in the extreme are toned down or eliminated in favor of implications rendered in the sound track or shown in reaction shots. Scenes that might terrify children, such as those of kidnapping, sadism, and masochism, are eliminated in the television versions. And the sexual connotations of the psychodrama, if any, are usually cut out in deference to the family viewing context of television. If the program is part of a continuing television series, with the same cast of continuing characters, the person suffering mental aberrations is usually a guest protagonist, whose discontent with the real world is expressed in crises intercut with the commercials.

The Horror Film

THE GENRE

The dramatic horror film is the farthest extremity of the action film and the psychodrama. Through the magic of special effects almost any fantastic monster or abnormal relationship can be visualized with credibility. The very term "horror film" evokes images of the Golem and Frankenstein monsters, resurrected mummies, It from the Ooze and so forth, turned loose on the living. The characters and their stories are nearly divorced from reality and horror itself is the purpose of the film: monsters from other planets or unnatural worlds, so immense in their powers that nobody can cope with them; mad scientists pouring fuming liquids from beaker to beaker to concoct a bomb that can blow up the world; ghost stories about the dead who lust for the living, or cannot rest until they avenge themselves on those responsible for their demise.

The evil goals in these horror films are usually the sexual lust of the dead for the living, bestiality, sadism, necrophilia, masochism, a conspiracy to conquer the world or a taste for mankind as livestock. "Horror film" evokes images of altars and coffins flickering with candles, demented scientists, blood-sucking vampires and innocent victims gibbering with fear.

The dramatic horror film is often gruesome and semi-pornographic, and occurs in a setting remote in time and place. A major problem in this genre is maintaining a balance between horror and absurdity. There is a tendency to present one incredible event after another until the viewer becomes shockproof, desensitized and incredulous. To be effective, the shocks must be injected gradually, with progressive intensity, in order to maintain suspense in a story which remains credible. Horror is most effective if implied rather than shown through most of the film. The event that is most overpowering should be saved for the end of the film, or all that comes after it may seem anticlimactic. If any event within the body of the film goes beyond the limits of taste or credibility the viewer may become disgusted, dissolve into laughter or walk out on the film. High in the art of making a horror film is a sense of proportion.

HORROR IN OTHER FILM GENRES

Horror has specialized uses in other kinds of films, and can serve as a crisis point within other forms of serious drama.

Horror may even serve a useful purpose in documentary and educational films. In *Night and Fog*, the French documentary film about the attempted genocide of European Jews by the Nazis, ghastly scenes revealed massive ditches being filled with the naked bodies of people who had starved to death, piles of gold-filled teeth, mountains of hair taken from human beings, lampshades made of skin flayed from women and children, and closeups of the faces of once pretty girls who were about to be dumped into a mass grave. The message of this horror—never again!

A functional use of horror in the educational film is similarly found in those driver training films that show hideous closeups of bloody bodies to reveal what may happen to a careless driver or his victim. This kind of horror, used in documentary and educational films, must be treated with discretion. Such scenes may be traumatic to the young or the emotionally unstable. Moreover, they should be of brief duration. A film that piles horror on horror for too long a period of time may produce either of two reactions in the viewer. He may become accustomed to the horror and thereby desensitized. Or, he may set up a defensive-avoidance reaction and mentally tune out for the rest of the film.

There are some dramatic-documentary subjects in which the horror is inherent in the subject and the power of the closeup only brings it to the viewer's attention. In *The Hellstrom Chronicle*, for example, the power of insects to survive atomic explosions and disasters of incredible magnitude was depicted with horrifying reality. The tiny spiders, ants, bees and mayflies that we take so casually were enlarged to juggernaut proportions on the screen and presented as the rivals of the human race for hegemony over the earth. The film recounted in intimate closeup the savage battles for survival among the insects, with casualties in the uncounted trillions, and no price in the loss of life too high to pay for the supremacy of their kind. The horror of this natural contest left the lay viewer shaken and wondering if he were only a guest of the insect on earth—with the invertebrates programmed for victory.

Some dramatic situations in serious psychodramas have within them elements of horror: In *Psycho* an attractive young woman stayed for the night in a motel, and was savagely stabbed to death in the shower by a complete stranger—without apparent motive. In *The Nanny* there was a macabre scene in which Nanny watched a woman die of a heart attack and refused to give her the needed medicine—while taunting her. In *Soldier Blue* the cavalry was shown chopping the arms and heads off helpless Indians in a surprise attack on a peaceful village—an orgy of sadism. The sense of horror is evoked in such situations by their senseless, callous inhumanity.

Nightmares, dreams and hallucinations may also infuse horror into serious films. In *Rosemary's Baby* the copulation of Rosemary and Satan, during a black mass, was rendered in a distorted stream-of-consciousness montage, as if it were only a nightmare induced by a drug, a vision that yielded at parturition the son of Satan.

The next step away from reality leads us to the horror that could become true in the tomorrowland of science fiction: *The Andromeda*

Strain recounted the holocaust of death and horror that took place when a space vehicle returned to earth bearing a virus that could annihilate the human race. The *Village of the Damned* told of cold-blooded zombie-like children conditioned to survive atomic warfare. *Alphaville* portrayed a mankind subjugated by the computer. And *The Incredible Shrinking Man* revealed the possible grotesqueries of scientific experimentation conducted without regard to its effects upon living organisms. These films do not require a suspension of disbelief, but remain fully credible, and therein lies their horror.

The television derivatives of the horror film are also affected by the family viewing context. Films containing scenes of sadism, bestiality, and strong sexual connotations are either presented at a very late hour, when the children have traditionally gone to sleep, or they have the offensive scenes deleted for television broadcast. Monster movies, on the other hand, are shown on Saturday morning and afternoons—kiddie prime time—on the apparent assumption that the portrayed violence is so extravagant that watching it could not affect anyone.

The appeal of the horror film, in the science fiction version so popular on television, may be attributed in part to novelty. The special effects experts have worked overtime to show the world splitting down the middle, colliding with other worlds, or exploding with a loud cinematic bang. Monsters and robots have lurched up from the bowels of the earth, out of radioactive explosions, and down the gangplanks of spaceships, accompanied by flashing lights, electronic pings and clangs, and all the whirring gadgetry attendant to computer data processing. The moog synthesizer and electronic filters have assured that the music and the monster's speaking voices have sounded suitably other-worldly. Television horror film apparently appeals to a certain kind of viewer by presenting a hysterical view of the world allegedly to come.

13

The Comedy
and the
Musical

The Comedy

Laughter has been prized by people everywhere, and used for diversion, subversion, joy and hostility. Even the Teuton warrior saw the battle value of a good laugh to leaven hard times. General Ludendorff, impressed by the fighting morale of the British soldiers during World War I, sent out his spies to find the cause. The gist of their report was: "A sense of humor." To which the good general replied: "Was ist humor?" After hearing the lengthy explanation, General Ludendorff decided that this secret weapon should also serve the Fatherland. He directed the publication and distribution of a handbook on humor, explaining what it was, where to find it, how to enjoy it, and describing its salutary effects—and he ordered the German Army to study the book and develop a sense of humor. A sense of humor, however, is not born of study, knowledge or understanding, but of perception—it is a way of looking at things. Laughter comes spontaneously or not at all.

Film comedy began with a sneeze. *Sneeze*, produced in 1894, showed a man sneezing. The film was no longer than it took to sneeze, and revealed how hilarious it is for someone else to have a cold. Two years later, in 1896, the Lumière brothers demonstrated the delights of giving someone else a cold: a gardener was sprinkling the yard with a hose. A child stepped on the hose, stopping the flow of water. When the gardener, puzzled, stared into the nozzle, the child stepped off the hose.

The film comedy was then expanded into a genre primarily by one man, Mack Sennett. In 1911 he wandered onto a film set where D. W. Griffith, creator of the language of cinema, was shooting a film. He returned to watch every day thereafter and applied what he learned to film comedy. Sennett created a zany film world in which nothing was sacred and corruption abounded: lawyers were crooks, policemen were stupid, churchgoers were hypocrites, honest men were fools, the villain got the girl and all social problems could be solved with a good kick in the rump. Sennett's stable of comedians included Charlie Chaplin, W. C. Fields, Harold Lloyd, Buster Keaton—a veritable Who's Who in the creation of film comedy. Mack Sennett's sight gags were a caricature of life in which events that would ordinarily be disastrous and tragic had no more effect than a custard pie in the face, and so wildly improbable that even the police laughed at the Keystone Cops. Sennett's sight gags and satires were so delightful that he never received a single complaint from any special interest group.

The advent of sound was the first blow to the great era of the pantomime slapstick comedian. The second blow was dealt by Mickey Mouse and Donald Duck, whose animated pratfalls were wilder and more extreme than anything mortal flesh could endure. First to fall under the dual blows were the innocent comedians who could not tell a joke, or whose style of humor was blunted by words—deadpan comics like Ben Turpin and Buster Keaton. Laurel and Hardy, however, succeeded in making the transition to sound, as did W. C. Fields and the Marx Brothers. The new style in film comedy became the team of one comic and one straight man, one to tell the jokes and the other to take the pratfalls, a tradition that came straight from vaudeville and still persists on television. Laurel and Hardy were followed by Abbot and Costello, who were followed by Dean Martin and Jerry Lewis, who were succeeded by Desi Arnaz and Lucille Ball of television. In between those mentioned were dozens of other fine comedians. Many comedians, like Bob Hope and Red Skelton, came to film comedy from radio, and later returned to broadcasting with the advent of television. With the evolution to television, the progression from the visual to the verbal basis of evoking laughter accelerated.

When comedy came to television, it soon evolved into the situation comedy, with a set of characters in familiar weekly situations of buffoonery. The comic forms of television (as is true of other television

I Love Lucy. Television situation comedy. *CBS Television Network.*

genres) are primarily verbal. There is a great use of puns, jokes and plays on words, with situation smart alecks and stand-up comedians providing the humor. The pratfalls and zany visual jokes developed by earlier film comedians are combined with verbal humor on the better television situation comedies, such as the classic *I Love Lucy* and *The Honeymooners.*

COMEDY AND HUMOR

Comedy and humor are terms often used interchangeably, but each has a unique meaning and application:

Comedy is essentially based upon human foibles, self-delusions and weaknesses. Comedy pokes fun at duplicity, hypocrisy and vanity, a parody of the little man pretending to be more than he really is. It is the tale of a confident approach to a situation, an unexpected fall, a realization of what has happened and a sense of humiliation. Comedy is essentially timeless and the silent-film pratfalls are often as funny today as they were a half century ago.

Humor is based upon content and is therefore topical and transient. The humorist gleefully hurls satirical barbs at politics, politicians and such movements as Women's Liberation, pricking the balloon of difference between form and substance. Humor, like comedy, is based upon the unexpected weakness and has as its goal the humiliation of the subject. Humor changes quickly with the times and soon becomes dated. *Alice in Wonderland*, a masterpiece of satirical humor, has survived because of its literary qualities, but with the passage of time and the burial of its original targets, the work became almost meaningless. The Disney animated film *Alice in Wonderland* was a virtuoso cinematic abstraction whose meaning was virtually lost on the modern audience.

THE COMIC SPIRIT

What's funny? The question is difficult to answer because laughter lies in the viewer, rather than the event, and one man's buffo is another man's boredom. Almost every man prides himself on having a sense of humor; only slightly less insulting than a slur on the beauty of a man's wife is the implication that he lacks a sense of humor. And laughter there is for almost everyone according to his likes and tastes, a ladder of laughter that begins with the grossest jokes about genitalia and excrement and ascends to the subtlest visual-verbal satire in the world of ideas. Not all things are funny—laughter is unique to a given event and its perception by the viewer.

Tradition holds that the world is a comedy for those who think and a tragedy for those who feel. Actually, laughter is evoked by situations having the elements of both comedy and tragedy, and as often as not the world is a comedy for those who feel and a tragedy for those who think. This paradox was exemplified in the films of Charlie Chaplin. The essence of his cinematic comedy lay in the pathos that tripped into absurdity, the laughter that died into tragedy, the recognition that comic elements are present in life's profoundest moments.

Attempts to explain what is funny have usually failed because the explainer takes himself seriously, and laughter seriously, in relating fun

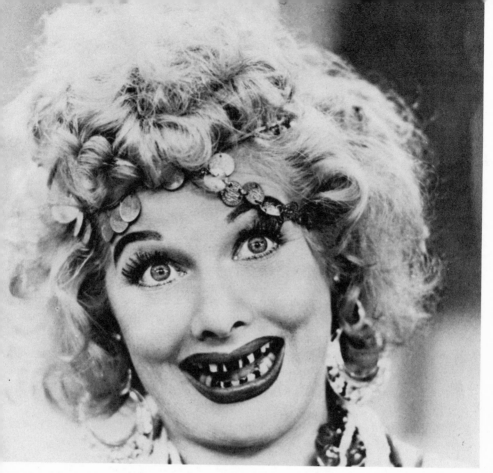

I Love Lucy. A sight gag. *CBS Television Network.*

to serious life. Being funny means playing around, abandoning the
sober dictum that life is grim, life is earnest. At the heart of evoking
laughter is the importance of not being earnest. Even animals sense the
mood of play and will romp through mock battles that are understood
not to be taken seriously. A dog may be flung this way and that, and
will react with loud snarls, barks and mock ferocity, but his tail will be
laughing out loud.

SIGHT GAGS AND VERBAL GAGS

What is the comic element? Aristotle defined it as something ugly or
distorted, but not painful. Kant defined it as an expectation which suddenly comes to nothing. Within these two definitions lie the skeletons of
the sight gag and the verbal gag.

Sight gags and verbal gags are the two major kinds of film and television jokes, with variations in the way they are handled in counterpoint dependent upon whether they are intended for theatrical or television release.

A *sight gag* is a visual joke, an extension of the unexpected banana-peel routine in which the payoff makes the subject look ludicrous. The heyday of the sight gag was the era of the silent film, when a joke had to be visual or it was no joke at all. Pantomime, not wisecracks, is the basis of the sight gag, with all the surprises the comedian can incorporate and all the situations he can concoct. The ultimate form of the sight gag may be found in the animated cartoon, because there are no limits to the pratfalls to which the characters can be subjected: characters ricochet off walls and each other, are dismembered and reassembled, metamorphose with the explosion of each stick of dynamite, and generally indulge in acrobatics that defy the laws of man and nature.

Verbal gags are a practical joke on the mind. They lead the listener down a logical corridor of expectation toward an unexpected banana-peel waiting in the dark, and then drop him flat. For example:

"Daddy, can I go out and play?"
"Shut up and deal."

This gag is purely verbal and is contingent upon the absence of vision for its unexpected twist. Purely verbal jokes are usable in film and television primarily by the stand-up comedian telling an anecdote. But our concern is with humor and comedy that relate to and support the living image: the sight gag that requires verbal wit to make its point; the verbal joke that is meaningless without its visual point.

A delightful example of a sight gag linked to verbal wit was found in *Some Like It Hot*. Jack Lemmon played the part of a seedy musician from Chicago who had to impersonate a female and flee to Florida to escape from being the machine-gun victim of a gangster. In Florida the quasi-female caught the lascivious eye of a dirty old millionaire, who pursued him-her with less than honorable intentions, a ludicrous and incongruous relationship. The absurdity of his courtship grew in hilarity as the millionaire became more and more persuasive, to the point where the quasi-female forgot he was not a female and began to listen seriously to the millionaire's propositions and proposals. When the millionaire offered to marry him and make her an honest woman, she forgot himself and consented.

The millionaire and his confused bride-to-be departed on a motorboat to begin a honeymoon on his yacht. On the way, the female impersonator remembered he was not a female and exclaimed: "Hey—I'm not a woman!" And the millionaire answered: "Nobody's perfect." The visual absurdity of their relationship and the impossibility of their marriage—a sight gag—was capped by delicious verbal wit, each of which was laughable only in context with the other.

The sight gag is played down in television in deference to the verbal gag. This is due in part to the medium's origins in radio, and in part to the small television screen. Comedians are so small on the television screen in any scene size large enough to show a sight gag that many of their pantomime actions are lost to the viewer, and with them the laughter. Hence, the vaudeville joke teller and the situation comedy are the primary sources of laughter on television.

THE VIEWER'S MOTIVATION

What is it in a comic situation that releases inner tension in the film and television viewer and dispels it into outer laughter? Malice. Relief. Feelings of superiority. It is that sudden tremendous sense of satisfaction and glee that comes with the realization that humiliation has come to a proxy victim and not to the viewer. A dirty word blurted in a polite social setting, a pratfall leading to a loss of dignity, a faux pas in a tense social situation, a prank at someone else's expense, these are the crimes without punishment—except for the humiliation of being laughed at—that delight the average viewer. The viewer sees a hapless character in a situation with which he can identify, doing something he has done or might have done, and when that person is humiliated, the viewer laughs.

In *M.A.S.H.*, a film comedy about the doctors and nurses serving in the Korean War, there was a beautiful blonde nurse who served as a proxy victim. She was superficially prudish, correct and very Regular Army, and her arrogance rubbed all the civilian doctors the wrong way. Also in the medical unit was a Regular Army doctor, who agreed with this nurse that the slovenly civilian surgeons were a disgrace to the service, and he, too, antagonized the civilian doctors with his superior attitude.

One night, in her tent, the two became lovers. They were talking in a way that was clearly leading toward lovemaking, when they happened to be overheard by a civilian doctor passing by outside. The civilian obtained a microphone and slipped it under the edge of their tent, near the bed, and connected the plug to the camp's public address system. Immediately their passionate words and kisses, grunts and groans, squeaks and squeals, were broadcast to the thousands of personnel in the camp. When the two lovers began to hear the vibrating echoes of their own words, they searched for and were horrified to find the hidden microphone. The audience laughed uproariously at their humiliation.

Laughter's friend is cruelty and its enemy is compassion. Jesus, Moses and Mohammed are never known to have joked; they took serious pity on persons in distress, and they were therefore humorless. Their compassion was as boundless as their souls. There has to be a slight streak of sadism in a person to take pleasure in the sights and sounds of anguish in others. There are a few aristocrats who can genuinely laugh at a humiliating joke on themselves, but not many. There is no shortage of those who take delight in the other man's humiliation.

Malevolence underlies most forms of comedy and humor, with one qualification: We laugh only when the malevolent situation is not really true. A slapstick comedy in which the comedian is knocked cross-eyed when hit in the head by a thrown brick may evoke a gust of laughter—the viewer knows it is only play-acting. A documentary film showing a man knocked senseless by a maliciously thrown brick will arouse indignation in the average viewer—the injury is real, and it is not funny. This distinction is important; humor may have a sadistic substratum, but real physical injuries to people and animals are not funny to the average viewer.

There is comedy and humor for every level of intelligence and every class in society. There are jokes related to age, sex, level of education, political, social and economic milieus. There are jokes understood and appreciated only in hippie communes, college faculty meetings and obstetrician conventions, and lost on those who are not members of the select group. More often than otherwise, the jokes are at the expense of others to whom that group is somehow related. Hippies throw barbs at the "straights," professors poke fun at the students (and the reverse), and obstetricians have their parturition puns. The joke is on the outsider, but listeners must be on the inside to appreciate the humor. A cartoon once showed two doctors leaving a patient's room; one doctor said to the other: "He's a terminal case—he's run out of money." This cartoon would be bitterly funny to an ex-patient, but not funny at all to the average doctor.

THE COMIC ELEMENTS

What's funny about a given comic figure or a situation? Three elements in either tend to make people laugh. These are the *ludicrous*, the *incongruous* and the *unexpected*.

Anything *ludicrous* is out of proportion, it is exaggerated. A ludicrous trait in a comedian means that something is the matter with him, something is out of normal proportions. It may be a physical exaggeration: a comic figure may be too fat, too thin, drunk, dumb, big-nosed, big-eared, big-mouthed or big-footed, or speak with a funny accent. Or, it may be a personality or character trait that is disproportionate. He may have prejudices that are commonly known but never discussed, and exaggerated to the point of being ludicrous. Archie Bunker of the television series *All in the Family* is a caricature of exaggerated prejudice against every conceivable minority in the United States, a quivering bundle of bigotry toward all who are different, regardless of race, creed or place of national origin. Because his traits are recognizable and identifiable, he is a credible character. Because those traits are exaggerated to the point of being ludicrous, he seems funny to the average viewer.

A ludicrous situation is one that has elements of normality, or begins normally, but has been exaggerated out of proportion. When Stan Laurel of Laurel and Hardy attended a formal dinner, he found himself unable to scoop up a maraschino cherry that had fallen off the top of his dessert. A relatively normal minor mishap. But when Laurel pursued the cherry in dead earnest around the rim of his dish about ten times, the situation became amusing. When the cherry fell off his plate and he pursued it in front of the gentleman seated beside him, the situation became absurd. And when he spooned his way furiously around the edge of the formal dinner table, climbing over the laps and working around the heads of dowagers and tycoons—to get a maraschino cherry —it became utterly ludicrous. And funny.

Laughter can come from a ludicrous way of looking at ordinary actions: W. C. Fields played a sequence on the golf course in which he spent eighteen minutes preparing to hit the ball, and then retired without ever swinging the club.

Proportion and timing are indispensable elements in keeping a comic action plausibly ludicrous. Had W. C. Fields dragged out his eighteen-minute warmup to twenty minutes, the comic effect might have mired down into ennui and died with a yawn. There are no guiding principles of proportion and timing for ludicrous effect; comedians are born rather than made, and the individual either has or has not the instinctive knack for the ludicrous.

The incongruous in comedy and humor means discovering mismatched characters in a normal setting, or normal characters in a mismatched setting. The important consideration is that the relationship always be visually or verbally a square peg in a round hole. Laurel and Hardy were funny on sight because they were physically incongruous together: Laurel was small and skinny, Hardy big and fat. The relationship of a character to his situation can be equally incongruous: W. C. Fields was filmed in a scene in which he accidentally fell out of an airplane to what was apparently to be his death. On his way down he decided to enjoy one last cigarette, but could not decide whether to smoke a regular or a king-size cigarette before ending in a puff. His entire descent was given over to a sober, rational discussion of the relative merits of regular and king-size cigarettes—an incongruous and funny situation.

Incongruity within a character refers to the discovery of a weakness, foible or inconsistency in a character who, on the surface, appears to be other than what he really is. If a heavyweight boxing champion were shown rubbing a tattered remnant of his baby blanket between rounds of a title fight, it would be funny because of the incongruity of a professional fighter needing this kind of reassurance. If preacher Billy Graham were photographed at a secret Black Mass, it would probably be hilarious to many viewers because it would be so outrageously incongruous.

Incongruity is the heart of television situation comedy and hinges upon the orchestration of mismatched characters in a difficult setting. *All in the Family* provided a television example of comic incongruity. Living in one house were the following characters: Archie Bunker, a hatemonger who considered himself a thumb in the dike against a rising tide of "kikes," "niggers" and "wops"; his wife Edith, a sweet but silly old cow who might as well have worked in penal servitude as slave away in Archie's house; their daughter Gloria, a charming intellectual flyweight who giggled, wept and wiggled as the young blond newly-wed with nothing upstairs but good will and temperament; and the son-in-law Mike, a pretentious freeloader and perpetual sociology student, who gave himself a sense of personal worth by mouthing liberal slogans as silly and ineffectual as Archie's bigoted ranting. Under one roof were found a generation gap, a personality conflict, a political clash, a socio-economic conflict, the battle of the sexes and the eternal struggle between the ignorant solid citizen and the pseudo-intellectual sponge—classic incongruities for a situation comedy.

The *unexpected* is the third dimension of laughter. It may take two forms. The unexpected may be something unforeseen that the viewer does not anticipate, but the comedian does, as is true of verbal gags. Or, it may be something the viewer expects, but the proxy victim does not, as is often true of sight gags.

In *M.A.S.H.* the discovery that the beautiful nurse had a lover stimulated a spirited discussion over the weighty issue of whether she was a natural blonde or a bleached blonde. Bets were taken among the civilian doctors and a project implemented to ascertain whether Hotlips, as she was now called, was blonde all over. The only way to find out for sure was to catch her in the nude, and the only reasonable place to do this was the women's shower. The doctors rigged the shower's outer curtain to an overhead pulley, weighted the other end of the pulley rope and then lined up on chairs to await the coming of Hotlips. She arrived in due course and entered the shower, stripped to the skin and began to bathe. A signal sent the shower curtain roaring up and revealed Hotlips in the raw. Before she could double up and hide, all leaned forward to confirm that Hotlips was indeed a natural blonde.

This incident had all of the comic elements: it was ludicrous, incongruous and unexpected to the humiliated but honest blonde.

One additional trait is needed for program longevity in a television situation comedy: the viewer must like the cast of continuing characters. *I Love Lucy* was probably the most successful comedy series of all time because Lucy's pranks were warm-hearted and well-intentioned, and Desi portrayed a hard-working Cuban trying to make a living. Lucy was always trying to get her way like a mischievous little girl, and Desi was always blowing his top in defense of reason and common sense, but there was never any meanness between them. When Lucy tried to get a singing part in Desi's show by holding a bunch of carrots and bursting into an aria, she was lovable. Even the jokes about Desi's heavy Cuban accent were done with pointed affection. Their neighbors, dowdy Ethel

M.A.S.H. Ludicrous,
incongruous, and unexpected.
20th Century-Fox.

and cheapskate Fred, were at heart likable human beings. And when these four made fools of themselves in situations that were ludicrous, incongruous and unexpected, the viewer laughed with them as well as at them. The validity of this approach is corroborated by the latest ratings: twenty years after the production of *I Love Lucy*, the reruns have higher ratings than most of the latest television situation comedies.

LEVELS OF LAUGHTER

Certain patterns of visual and verbal humor have shown themselves to be consistently funny to great numbers of people watching film and television programs. They have in common the elements of the ludicrous, incongruous and unexpected discussed earlier, aimed for the most part at the humiliation of a proxy victim. The patterns ascend in degrees from the visual to the verbal, the physical to the abstract, the denotative to the connotative. This ladder of laughter includes *obscenity, physical mishaps, plot devices, verbal wit, high comedy* and *satire.* It should be noted that each step up in the ladder may include elements from the rungs below—they are cumulative.

Obscenity in film humor features sexual comedy of every conceivable kind, heterosexual, homosexual and bestial. We are not concerned here with the legal ramifications of obscenity in film, but how it functions as the lowest rung in the ladder of laughter. Obscenity is a crude form of male comedy based upon female sex organs.

A film entitled *Hollywood Blue* contained sexual humor in content and editing. One animated film segment, within a live-action film, portrayed a man about to have sexual intercourse with a woman. When his penis entered her vagina, it bumped into an alarm clock, an anvil, assorted tools and bric-a-brac, and finally a crab—which clamped its claws on the tip. His penis, recoiling in pain, disengaged itself from the groin and ran away from the mutually frustrated man and woman. This was supposed to be funny.

Another sequence in the same film emphasized editing as a technique for sexual humor. Scenes of a man and woman having sexual intercourse, performing fellatio and cunnilingus, were intercut with completely unrelated scenes of former actor Ronald Reagan at the speaker's platform of a banquet. Each scene of a sexual act was followed by a cut to newsreel footage of Mr. Reagan saying, in effect, "I wouldn't miss this for anything," and "Let's do this more often" and so forth. The cross-cutting between unrelated scenes was funny in large measure because it was humiliating to the image of a man who had become the governor of California. Editing plays an important role in obscene humor because incongruous and completely unrelated scenes may be intercut for a comic effect not inherent in any of the scenes.

Physical mishaps is the second level of humor. In the silent-film days comedians were expected to be half stunt man, half imbecile, as they floundered through pratfalls, drove off cliffs, sat on detonated bombs and fell down open elevator shafts. Comedians were clobbered by custard pies, knocked into wet cement, brained by rocks and swinging beams, chased by hornets, dogs, husbands and policemen, and blasted into low orbit by the ubiquitous banana peel.

Another form of the physical mishap is the slow-building sight gag which progressively becomes more insane; each event is plausible in terms of what preceded it, and logical in terms of what follows, but the climax is so wildly improbable as to be hilarious. The story usually takes the form of an average person innocently getting involved in some situation with slightly embarrassing overtones, and in his efforts to extricate himself the situations become wilder and wilder. In *Safety Last* Harold Lloyd was portrayed as a man-in-the-street inveigled into substituting for a stunt man in climbing up the outside of a skyscraper. The higher he climbed, the more awful became his physical mishaps. Popcorn showered on him from the floor above and a swarm of pigeons flocked to him as they would to a feed trough. A mouse ran up his trouser leg and he danced a jig on a flagpole, to the wild applause of the crowd below. Each new floor he ascended provided him with a more ludicrous physical mishap than the last, raising to a new high the crescendo of laughter from the audience.

The *plot device* is a third level of humor common to all film comedies, and to most television situation comedies of a half-hour or longer. It consists of planting visual or verbal clues that seem to have no point until they culminate near the end with a humiliating sight gag. The dramatic value of the plot device is that it progressively builds a tense social situation which prepares the viewer to laugh at the ultimate humiliation.

In a film comedy called *A Shot in the Dark* Inspector Cluzot was shown from the beginning to be developing his judo skills and reflexes in order to be able to fight off surprise attacks. In obedience to Cluzot's orders his assistant pounced at him at unexpected times and unusual places, and launched savage judo attacks which Cluzot tried to fight off, invariably without success. Later in the film Inspector Cluzot found himself the lucky subject of a beautiful woman's passion; she drew him down to bed with the tenderest of words and the gentlest of embraces. As Cluzot knelt amorously over her, feeling himself the luckiest man in the world, his assistant launched a wild judo attack and dragged him off the woman—a humiliating sight gag which paid off the earlier visual clues.

Verbal wit, puns and plays on words are the next rung up, and they, too, emphasize the ludicrous, incongruous and unexpected. In an episode of *I Love Lucy* called "Job Switching" the man of the house came stomping home in a rage after discovering that Lucy was overdrawing their checking account. Their dialogue confrontation revealed a typical pun:

HE HOLDS UP A CHECK

RICKY
Your check to the beauty parlor.

LUCY
Well, I write a check to the beauty parlor every month.

RICKY
Yes, but it doesn't always have a note like this on the back.
HE TURNS IT OVER AND READS
Dear Teller: Be a lamb and don't put this through till next month!—Well, what have you to say?

LUCY
I'll never trust a teller again.

RICKY
Lu-cy.

LUCY
No wonder they call them tellers—they go around blabbing everything they know.

High Comedy, the fifth rung in the ladder of laughter, is based upon human foibles in cultural stress situations known to a given national or ethnic audience. The television situation comedy has become the essence of this form; it is a cultural comedy that pokes fun at problems recognized by a broadly based segment of the public, and gives people a chance to laugh at themselves through identifiable proxy victims placed in ludicrous and incongruous situations.

Identification is important in cultural comedies; the audience must see itself in the themes. Therefore, each new television season brings forth a fresh crop of time-tested situations. Family life is universal in America and ubiquitous on television, as evidenced in annual variations on the breakfast table situations developed in *I Love Lucy, The Dick Van Dyke Show, The Mothers-In-Law, Father Knows Best* and *All in the Family*. Other recurrent themes are based on the situation of coming of age in the metropolis, such as the beautiful young bachelorette aswing in the city, charming her way to the top, or the handsome young executive with girls by the dozen, making it at both levels.

A high-comedy program may be universally popular in its originating nation, yet die in another country. *Father Knows Best*, an American television situation comedy which portrayed the man of the house as a bungling boob and his wife as all-wise, all-knowing and all-powerful, proved highly offensive to audiences in as widely separated nations as Italy, Mexico and Japan. In those nations *machismo*, male dominance, still holds sway, and the degrading image of the husband portrayed in that series sent hackles rising on their masculine backs. To them the series was simply not funny.

The culture-bound nature of high comedy works both ways. One Japanese film recounted the story of a man so hen-pecked by his wife, mother and mistress that he sought true friendship and understanding in the companionship of a cat. The Japanese viewers sitting in the audience laughed until tears streamed down their cheeks. The American viewers, reading the subtitles as they watched, sat stony-eyed at the lines that drew the greatest laughter from the others. The comedy was so bound to cultural factors recognizable only to the Japanese that it was entirely lost on the Americans.

Although physical mishaps and plot devices are used in television situation comedies, the television form tends to be radio with pictures, emphasizing verbal wit, jokes, puns and plays on words. In many of the

I Love Lucy. Identification in cultural comedy. *CBS Television Network.*

television comedies the picture can be turned off and the jokes enjoyed without missing anything but the color. The jokes stand alone.

The better high comedies use both verbal and visual plot devices. The classic television comedy series *I Love Lucy* followed the practice of building a tense social situation by using Lucy for the pratfalls and Desi Arnaz's Cuban accent for the verbal puns. In one episode the conflict was joined when Lucy (an incorrigible spendthrift) bought one expensive hat too many, and her husband Desi (a Cuban hothead) lost his temper once too often. Each accused the other of irresponsibility and they made a one-month bet that she would not be able to resist buying another hat before he next lost his temper.

Lucy weakened first and secretly bought a new hat, making it imperative that she force Desi to lose his temper before the hat was delivered. To this end she dumped crackers in his bed, poured tomato juice on his white dinner jacket and goaded him in the most infuriating ways she could think of. When he muttered quiet Cuban epithets through gritted teeth and a painted smile, she mocked his foreign accent and his mannerisms—to no avail. In the meanwhile, Desi discovered that in learning to control his temper he was able to drive down the asking price of a performer he wanted to hire, and he made a sizable profit. Desi felt so good and so generous at discovering the value of a cool head that he offered to call off the bet and to buy whatever hat she wanted with the extra profit.

Lucy pretended to telephone the boutique and ask to have the hat delivered, and it was—two seconds after she hung up. Desi realized that she had secretly bought the hat while the bet was still on, and had subjected him to a purgatory of frustration in order to make him lose his temper and the bet. As the payoff, Desi's temper exploded and he turned Lucy over his knee to spank her—a humiliating sight gag.

Satire is a world of ideas—a humorous lampoon flung at the pretensions of society, puncturing the cushion between what pretends to be and what really is.

Satire must be audacious to be funny. The court jester was the only man who could launch barbs at the king with impunity, so long as he speared only his vanity and not his vital organs. This is the basis of delight in satire directed at important persons—their pretensions are punctured and they seem cut down to size. Yet the barbs are funny only when they do not cut to the marrow. Satire must be aimed at the differences between the target as he is and as he pretends to be. There is a matter of taste involved in the selection of a subject fit for satire. A satire on law enforcement in the cities may be in order, but a satire on the murder of a policeman killed in the line of duty is unacceptable.

The Apartment hurled a barrage of barbs at the Great American Dream of individual initiative, hard work, free enterprise and personal integrity as the means of achieving success in a modern corporation. This saga recounted the rise of an insurance clerk to a high post in his firm by turning his only capital, an apartment, to profit by exploiting the interest of his superiors in illicit sex. The clerk loaned the key to his apartment to his superiors, who, in turn, wrote glowing reports about his work, and promotion followed promotion as he left his integrity in a file drawer with his night school diploma and rose to the top through the reversal of every Horatio Alger virtue. And what was his reward in the room at the top? His keys to the executive toilet.

The Apartment did more than tell a comic story about a pandering relationship; it knifed our urban way of life without mercy until the American Dream lay bleeding from laughter—but always with the light touch of revealing the incongruity between facade and reality. Almost every scene had its humorous counterpoint. When the young man on the make asked the fair young maiden how many men had seduced her, she answered, "Three," but unwittingly raised four fingers.

Satire must not be too bitter or it becomes hot and heavy scorn. Once the light thrust of the rapier is exchanged for the heavy chop of the saber, the playfulness that makes satire funny disappears into sober contemplation of the facts. The rapier of satire punctures the skin of pretension, the saber of drama slashes through to the bone and muscle of reality. The saber may be justified under some dramatic circumstances, but it cuts at the price of laughter. The satirist is most effective if he clearly remembers the phrase "make fun of." Charlie Chaplin made a cinematic spoof of Adolf Hitler's personal quirks and foibles that was hilarious in many sequences of *The Great Dictator*. As long as the film dealt lightly with the pretensions of those carrying the banner of the double-cross, the lampoon was amusing to most viewers. When the film changed character, however, and got to the flesh and bones of the true meaning of the Nazi and Facist movements, it became self-consciously melodramatic, embarrassing to watch, and undid much that had been said in moments of levity.

Reformers have often tried to use laughter as a means of attack against corrupt institutions and officials. For the most part, however, such attempts have only made their audiences uncomfortable. Reformers tend to be in dead earnest, and humor is incompatible with a crusading attitude. Satire works best against petty sinners, the petty sins of the great or the pretensions of the highly placed. Satire seldom pierces the substance of corruption, only its camouflage. The reformer satirist can achieve some of his goals by flaying his victim of all the features that might inspire sympathy in the viewer (being good to his mother, petting a puppy), and by avoiding emotional involvement—but not by being in earnest.

Great men can make themselves vulnerable or invulnerable to satire by their personal pretensions. President Truman was vain about the singing ability of his daughter Margaret, who had aspirations to a concert career. The critics did not share the President's high regard for Margaret's singing and said so in their critical reviews. Mr. Truman reacted indignantly and vehemently to bad reviews of her performances —setting himself up as a juicy target for every comedian and cartoonist in the nation. His paterfamilias pride had nothing whatever to do with the Marshall Plan and his other undertakings at the national and international level, but it revealed a personal foible that invited a personal attack. President Eisenhower, on the other hand, was devoid of pretensions about himself and his family, and thus nearly invulnerable to satirical attack.

Comic relief is important in serious feature-length dramas, especially in psychodramas. If the tension created by heavy dramatic actions is not relieved from time to time by a touch of humor, the viewer may burst into laughter during a love scene, a murder or just as the pathological vampire sinks his teeth into the throat of the young heroine. Comic relief may appear at interludes between major crises, and may be no more than an unexpected kitten chasing a fallen ball of yarn, or the reappearance of the same panhandler whining the same appeal to the same key figure with progressively increasing humor. Comic relief may also be used just before a tragic climax to make it seem all the more poignant: In *Midnight Cowboy* Joe and his dying friend Ratso were at last seated on the bus to Florida, when Ratso lost control of his bladder and urinated—to his intense humiliation. Joe chuckled and said: "You've just made an unscheduled rest stop," and the two men, and the viewer, enjoyed an instant of comic relief that sharpened the pain of Ratso's subsequent death.

The Musical

The musical is difficult to describe without music, because melodies sung and danced are themselves the heart of the film, and all other elements are window dressing.

The first talking picture, *The Jazz Singer* (1927), was also the first singing picture, with Al Jolson down on his knees crooning "Mammy." Warner Brothers followed this sensational first by expanding the sound track to the mathematically ludicrous proportions of "100% singing, 100% talking, 100% dancing" in *On With the Show* (1929). The film with music and the musical film have been with us ever since, and the genre now fills much of the prime-time programming on network television.

The musical is a paradox in its cycles of popularity. The genre is a frivolous, artificial, lighthearted form that flowers most beautifully in the gravel of hard times. It was born in the Depression, flourished brightly during World War II, enjoyed a renaissance during the Korean War, and became immensely popular on television during the sickest days of racial discord and the sourest phases of the Vietnam War. Conversely, with every rise in our national fortunes the musical has seemed to decline in popularity. Although escapism can be used to justify anything, the thin stories and minuscule messages of the average musical make it clear that the only reason it thrives during days of ordeal is that it offers the national audience collective pleasure, relaxation and escapism. Film and television musicals really find their social value, if they need one, in giving the viewer something to sing about and in providing a respite from continual confrontation with The Problems.

Film and television musicals are the American counterpart of the operettas found in other parts of the world. The cinematic musical has proliferated into a tremendous variety of variants: the comic farce with music, such as *Thoroughly Modern Millie*; the operetta, as found in *Naughty Marietta* and the other Nelson Eddy–Jeannette Macdonald films; the cartoon musical ranging from the jolly *Snow White and the Seven Dwarfs* to the dignified *Fantasia*; the serious dramas, with moments of singing and dancing at emotional high points, such as *The Sound of Music*; the dance films, from the toe-tapping of Fred Astaire and the chorus girl abstractions of Busby Berkeley, to the ballerina twirls found in *The Red Shoes* and *Tales of Hoffman*. Every one of these forms has been cross-pollinated at times with one or more of the other forms to yield a lively cinematic hybrid. And now, scarcely an evening of television passes without a program given over to song and dance routines, rendered on videotape in dazzling color.

STORIES AND THEMES

The stories and themes of the film musical are often unabashed fantasies, folk art and romantic escapism. Their plots and social messages seem diaphanously thin because the musical is seldom intended to be more than diversion. Although the genre is potentially as capable of presenting ideas as opera or ballet, the plot and theme structures of the film and television musical have been used primarily as vehicles for presenting delightful songs and dances. Through songs, emotions may be expressed and longings given voice that would be laughed at if presented seriously. Through songs, values may be declared that the viewer would still like to believe, but has laid aside with his lost saints.

The stories are usually variations on the theme of love. *Gigi* recounted the pangs of adolescence and first love, culminating in wholesome marriage. *Camelot* told of a love triangle in the legendary court of King Arthur. *Oklahoma* affirmed the joys of love rivalry and life on the high plains in an exhuberant world of towering corn. *West Side Story* linked love to ethnic warfare on the streets of New York. *The Sound of Music* sang joyously of love and family loyalty in the tragedy of Hitler's Anschluss with Austria. The real crises of most these stories are those of the heart and the soul in finding fulfillment on the rocky road to true love. A new wrinkle may be found in *Woodstock*, a documentary musical which was reflective of a hippie way of life and set of values, but a film essentially without the framework of a dramatic structure.

Cabaret added another dimension to the musical genre. The film portrayed the decadence of Germany during the early days of the Nazi movement, as revealed through the songs and life of a nightclub thrush. The drama was essentially serious, with elements of humor as well as brutality, and the songs she sang served as commentary on her own fantasies as well as on the decadent values of the declining Weimar Republic.

Songs and dances do not constitute all or even the largest portion of most musicals, even though they are the reason for the film's existence. Ninety minutes of solid singing and sensational choreography would soon pall on even the most devoted aficionado. Instead, the musical numbers are presented periodically in the story. The points chosen are either natural pauses in the story, when the situation is appropriate for the expression of an emotion, or emotional crescendos, when nothing less than a full-blown song can give vent to the character's feelings. In *Thoroughly Modern Millie* a young lady who went adventuring in New York to seek her fortune and true love met an incredibly handsome young man who was to be her new boss. After meeting him, there was a brief pause in the story and, of course, this was the occasion for the singing star to express her joy in song.

CHARACTERS

The characters in a musical are highly stylized. They have to be; in real life a person who went about singing and dancing would be taken gently but firmly to the Happy House. When the singers and dancers are acting, there is a stereotyped quality to the roles they play, as if they were representative of a certain kind of human being, rather than a believable individual. There is a sense of posing to their performances, with self-conscious mannerisms and movements that are not intended to hold the mirror to reality, but to serve as appetizers between the main courses of singing and dancing. Some stories may have elements of tragedy, such as *West Side Story*, but even at the moments of greatest poignancy, when defeat and death hold the screen, the dramatic confrontations between the characters are not realistically believable, because the apogee of each emotional conflict is then resolved in song. Realism is the outsider in rendering character in the make-believe world of film and television musicals.

THE DANCE MUSICAL

The dance musical is a kind of fertility rite on the screen. If there is a dancing team, a duet, the routines often have overtones of deep sexuality in a modern dance format. Long gliding movements, with intimate contact between the couple, are followed by bursts of separation and circling. Pauses are held in positions of dramatic contrast and symbolic attitude, with much bending back of the female and leaning forward by the male. If the musical film involves dance routines by large numbers of persons, there are usually plenty of leggy and attractive girls writhing about the stage, with one or two men grinning and dancing. The hundred-men-and-a-girl routine has seldom been popular in the film musical, although in the television version it is sometimes used with a female star.

The sets used in a film musical are often stupendous, opulent affairs, baroque and overwhelming. The richness of color and design very often dominate the singers and dancers performing before them. The sugary sweetness of the sets is an attempt to overcome some of the editing lethargy inherent in song and dance routines, particularly in those productions that have been adapted from Broadway spectaculars. The rich design gives an ethereal quality to the set, and thereby compensates for the earthbound quality of the routines performed before it. The appeal of many such musicals is primarily scenic and choreographic.

Cinematography in the dance musical follows a distinct pattern. Fluidity and long, sustained scenes, probably photographed from a mobile crane, are by far the most common cinematic technique. There are many high-angle tracking shots. The scene sizes tend to be all of the wide-angle variety, ranging from large establishing shots and infinite variations on the full shot, to an occasional tight two-shot in the clinches. Because movements of a broad nature predominate in the dance sequences, closeups are seldom used. Trick photography and special effects enhance the fantasy effect of dancing in dreamland. When a film musical is adapted from a stage play, such as *West Side Story*, the dance numbers are usually photographed in large master scenes, because the original concept cannot be changed too much in cinematography without violating what made the production a Broadway hit.

EDITING THE MUSICAL

The importance of editing tends to be secondary in the filmed or videotaped musical. The emphasis in this genre has been placed overwhelmingly upon fluid cinematography, rich colors, visual special effects and stupendous sets. The editor's role is generally limited to eliminating bad takes and splicing together those long beautiful scenes. Videotape has really come into its own with the television musical, and has largely superceded the use of film per se. Whenever dynamic editing is unimportant, and the medium exists primarily to record the talent before the camera, the palm goes to videotape for its convenience and immediacy. Given the emphasis upon juicy interior colors for television musicals and the negligible value of editing, the viewer can be

MARY POPPINS. The cinematic musical. © *Walt Disney Productions.*

certain that those long, slow pans, tilts and zooms over the singers and dancers are being rendered on videotape.

The generalization that musicals tend to be slow or static in editing does not necessarily hold true if the musical is originally conceived as a film, and if the producer has complete control over the talent and the final form of the musical. In *Mary Poppins*, for example, film was used as cinema and not just a recording device, with editing for timing, for tempo, for counterpoint and for scene-to-scene associated images. The singing and dancing of Julie Andrews and Dick Van Dyke were delightfully integrated into a fast-moving story rendered in the purest cinema. The producer's control over the final film product, coupled with untrammeled imagination and the gamut of special effects, yielded a delightful soufflé of whimsy.

The egocentricism of a singing star sometimes bogs down the mobility of cinematography and the dynamism of editing. Too frequently the performer insists, "Just turn the cameras on me singing and the film will be great." This generalization holds true primarily with female singers who do not dance. The singer sometimes understands, rather nervously, that the camera has to move a little to show all sides of her and provide a little visual variety, but seldom thinks of editing as being more than splicing two pieces of film or videotape together. A cut in the middle of her song would disrupt her big moment, and a cutaway would be an upstaging insult. As a consequence, when an egocentric singer is pouring out her soul under limbo lighting, the cinematographer or videotape cameraman usually records long, slow scenes with soft, oozy camera movements, while the editor is reduced to simply splicing the scene into the film or television program.

Comedy is often interwoven with the musical. In *Thoroughly Modern Millie*, the young lady attempted to "modernize" her torso by buying a brassiere that would flatten her bosom in accordance with the fashions of the twenties. She no sooner walked out of the store onto the streets of New York, however, than the brassiere strap broke, and her twin breasts rose airily like a pair of surfacing whales, much to the astonishment of the passersby and the chagrin of Millie. A film musical is often combined with film comedy to include sight gags and verbal gags, and to embrace almost every rung in the ladder of laughter.

Documentary and Persuasive Forms

14

The Classic Documentary Film

The Documentary Concept

"Documentary film" is a term which has expanded in meaning with the years and has proliferated with sub-forms to the point where it is now applied to almost any kind of nontheatrical film, and seems to mean all things to all people. All the sub forms, however, have certain elements in common. The elusive documentary concept has been defined in various ways by distinguished men and organizations:

John Grierson, founder of the documentary movement, called the genre "a creative treatment of actuality."

Forsyth Hardy called it "a selective dramatization of fact in terms of their human consequences."

Willard Van Dyke was more expansive: "A film, usually non-fiction, in which the elements of dramatic conflict are provided by ideas and political or economic forces."

The Academy of Motion Picture Arts and Sciences went further: "Documentary films are defined as those that deal with historical, social, scientific, or economic subjects, either photographed in actual occurrence or re-enacted, and where the emphasis is more on factual content than on entertainment."

Jean Benoit-Levy gave this definition: "Documentary films are those which reproduce life in all of its manifestations—the life of man, of animals, of nature—without the assistance of professional actors or studios and on condition that the film represents a free artistic creation. We are led to name this genre *films of life*."

From these definitions a pattern of characteristics common to the documentary-film genre emerges.

In *subject matter* the documentary film is concerned with the factual aspects of the lives of men, animals and other living creatures, unleavened by fictional concepts or techniques.

In *concept* the documentary is a drama of ideas whose thrust is toward social change, not aesthetic satisfaction, entertainment or even education as it is usually defined.

In *purpose* the documentary is intended to alert the viewer to some aspect of reality that should be his legitimate concern, or serious interest, and to illuminate a social problem. The purpose of this genre is best defined in terms of its classic goals: to crystallize public sentiments on an issue, to inspire initiative, to develop a sense of will to act decisively in the public interest and to establish standards of civilized behavior. It is an attempt to persuade the viewer to act on the solution of today's problems today, with the intention that any given film be discarded when it has achieved its intended behavioral goal of an improvement in some aspect of a nation's life.

In *theme* the classic documentary is concerned with what happens to people—it is an emotional statement of the facts in terms of their human consequences.

In *technique* the documentary film is a motion picture record of real people living real events, photographed and edited to present the closest possible approximation of their true relationships.

History of the Genre

The documentary film evolved in five major strands in the following nations: the United States, Great Britain, the Soviet Union, France and Germany, beginning with the end of World War I. Each strand was reflective of its national origin and the conditions in which it was born, and each continues in some form down to the present time. The five major strands are as follows:

THE NATURALIST DOCUMENTARY

The naturalist documentary was the first documentary film, and had its origin in a film about life among the Eskimos entitled *Nanook of the North*, produced in 1922 by an American named Robert Flaherty. This was the first film to treat the true-life realities of a people. Photographed on location, it tended to interpret the subject with an epic man-against-the-sky approach which emphasized the heroic, exciting, human and humorous aspects of the Eskimos' lives. Flaherty and his romantic-naturalist followers down to the present have tended to dwell upon the beauties of primitive man and primeval nature, while ignoring the urban ills of the modern world. This romantic strand continues today in such examples as Walt Disney's *Peoples of the World*, and such television specials as the *National Geographic* presentations.

THE SOCIAL ACTION DOCUMENTARY

The social action documentary is a British genre, created in 1929 with the film *Drifters*, produced by John Grierson. This polemic form has since tended to become generic with the term "documentary film." Grierson insisted that the people in documentary films should be representative of classes and social problems, not actors playing out a story, and that life itself should be the sole source of ideas, research and cinematography. The British social action documentary was adopted by American filmmakers during the Depression of the 1930s to promote New Deal programs, and it has since become a major strand in American documentary film.

THE NEWSREEL DOCUMENTARY

The newsreel and the propaganda film are the two documentary forms that sprang from the tormented soul of the Soviet Union during the first decade of the Communist state.

The newsreel documentary was created by Dziga Vertov and his co-workers of the Kino-Eye, who not only reported the cataclysmic events of the Revolution and its aftermath of civil war between Reds and Whites, from 1918 to 1923, but also recorded the daily lives of the common people in order to provide their posterity with a cinematic document of all aspects of that transitional period in Russian history.

NANOOK OF THE NORTH. The first documentary film. *Contemporary Films/ McGraw-Hill.*

SEAFARERS OF THE NORTH. The romantic documentary. *National Geographic Society/Wolper Productions.*

The newsreel concept was quickly picked up in the United States, presented as a short subject in theaters between features, and is vitally alive today on American television news broadcasts.

THE PROPAGANDA FILM

The propaganda film—the highly structured, emotionally appealing, conclusion-forming film that seems to defy intellectual processes— was the second Russian innovation in documentary film. Lenin decreed that all art should serve the policies of the state, and declared that the cinema was chosen to become the dominant art form of the Soviet Union because of its propaganda potential. The goal of Soviet documentary films, then and now, is to persuade their own people to support the ideals, practices and policies of the government in achieving their vision of a Communist state. Sustained propaganda programs are possible and persuasive in the Soviet Union because of that government's control over all sources of information.

THE REALISTIC DOCUMENTARY

The realistic documentary was conceived in France with Cavalcanti's *Rien Que Les Heures*, in 1926, and in Germany with Ruttmann's *Berlin*, in 1927.

The realistic documentary is essentially a slice-of-life concept which attempts to portray the sum total of all events occurring within a brief period of time, such as one day, without necessarily dwelling upon a representative type or even rendering a subjective interpretation of those events. This form turns away in purpose from the sentimental idylls of America, the searching polemics of Britain and the shrill propaganda of the Soviet Union to present—without comment—the patterns and rhythms of various aspects of daily life. To avoid making a documentary film which may be as dull as daily life, however, the filmmaker frequently transcends earthbound realism by utilizing cinematography and editing techniques which exploit the natural tempos and movements of the subject to create cinematic symphonies. Paradoxically, the techniques used to create an exciting realistic documentary film sometimes become so self-consciously arty as to slide the films out of the documentary genre and into the "art film" category. The realistic documentary is found today in *cinéma vérité* camera techniques, and in

THE EXILES. The realistic documentary. *Contemporary Films/McGraw-Hill.*

a television documentary form now called the *Slice-of-Life Documentary*.

The social action film will be considered for the remainder of this chapter as generic with the term "documentary film." The other forms have evolved unique characteristics that will be considered in succeeding chapters treating "The Television Documentary," "Historical, Ethnographic and Natural History Film" and "The Propaganda Film." The documentary is here defined as an honest persuasion film, objective in content and candid in cinematic technique, yet espousing a point of view which attempts to enlist the active support of the viewer for some kind of political, social or economic change. This documentary form is concerned with behavioral change in the viewer, and is therefore also concerned with basic kinds of responses in the viewer and basic kinds of content structure in the film to assure persuasive appeal.

Basic Viewer Responses and Persuasive Appeal

The basic kinds of responses in the viewer are usually variants of one of the following five categories: *Indifference* is caused primarily by the failure of the filmmaker to relate the subject and its interpretation to the age, sex, level of formal education, socioeconomic-political milieu and life space of the viewer. *Conversion*, the active change of a viewer's allegiance and actions, comes at a time when the march of events has shaken his belief in the answer of the past, and he is susceptible to a skillfully made persuasion film which presents new ideas and solutions. *Precipitation* means the viewer's mind is already aware of and receptive to new ideas and alternatives currently being discussed for the solution of a problem, and needs only a stimulus trigger to arouse his active support. *Confirmation* entails reinforcing what the viewer already believes and knows, and corroborating the correctness of his thoughts and actions. And in the *Boomerang effect* an existing bias of the viewer is reinforced because the film or television program has inadvertently launched a frontal attack on some aspect of his ego and value systems and made him angry.

For persuasive films to be effective the viewer must be prepared to act, or persuaded to act, to achieve the behavioral purposes of the film or television program. In the case of the viewer being already prepared to act—such as voting in an election—it is a matter of structuring information in such a way as to channel his actions toward the desired goal of the filmmaker or his sponsor. Persuading the viewer to act when *he is not predisposed to act* is another matter. The contented viewer is much like a contented cow until an urge is born within him that stirs him to action. Before the comfortable viewer can be persuaded to act he must be made a little uncomfortable, made to want something, by means of motivational situations built into the persuasive film.

To live in harmony with one's environment, called "homeostasis," is a state sought by all living organisms, and once attained, is preserved, if possible, against the intrusion of discordant elements. As long as that environment is secure, satisfactory and consistent in its internal relationships, there will be very little inclination by the individual to change anything. Introduce a discordant element that threatens the stability of that environment, however, and the viewer may act immediately to bring the new discordant element into harmony with the old so that he may sink back once more into contentment. There are four basic conceptual approaches intended to motivate the viewer to act: *the altruistic appeal, the threat approach, the promissory appeal* and *the assurance of continued satisfaction.*

The Altruistic Appeal

The altruistic appeal is based upon identification with life space. The viewer sees a problem situation in which the people in the film are very much like himself, by virtue of similar backgrounds, needs and aspirations, and he is urged to act on their behalf. The appeal may be as narrowly targeted as the members of a religious denomination, with emphasis upon those rituals, music and dogma the subject and the viewer have in common. Or the approach may be broadly directed to the population at large, and base its appeal on such universal elements as children in need, indigent families and so forth. The altruistic appeal should establish the closest possible correlation between the contents of the film and the characteristics of the target audience.

The Threat Approach

The threat approach to the viewer may arouse him to action by evoking feelings of fear, anger and hate. In this situation the viewer is presented with events in which those like himself, or living very near him, are suffering dangers and damages to which he himself may eventually be subjected unless he acts as directed by the film. This appeal to fear is widely used in wartime to flog the population into greater efforts and sacrifices, and in totalitarian states to unify the people in support of the regime against the threat of allegedly hostile nations. In peacetime the scare approach is usually more difficult to use in an open society unless the threat is credible, but it has worked successfully. The movement to give black Americans their just civil rights and economic opportunities may have been expedited by television documentaries using the threat approach implicit in presenting the acts of mob violence which have occurred during riots and demonstrations. If the threat approach is overdone, however, it may produce such intense anxiety that it evokes a defensive-avoidance reaction in which the viewer resists having to cope with the problem, perhaps becoming inattentive to extremely disturbing aspects of the film or even becoming belligerent toward the film's content in a boomerang effect.

THE PROMISSORY APPROACH

Usually an appeal to pleasurable emotions of joy and self-indulgence, or to an anticipated satisfaction of the viewer's needs, the promissory approach is based upon the premise that there are wants latent within the viewer that may be exploited by those who would promise fulfillment. The promissory appeal is widely used in the advertising industry to sell products that will grant the viewer his heart's desire, if only he will buy a given product. The approach is also used negatively in political campaigns to appeal to voter resentments; one need look no further for an example than the perennial promise of the political candidate to reduce taxes if elected to office.

THE ASSURANCE OF CONTINUED SATISFACTION

The assurance of continued satisfaction approach is intended to reinforce the status quo and have the viewer continue to do whatever he is doing, rather than to stir him to a new and different activity. In the political arena the incumbent candidate proudly presents his record of achievements to the voters and assures them of their continued satisfaction if they reelect him to office. In advertising it is used as reinforcement to retain the product loyalty of users and, in addition, to encourage others to switch brands by showing the deep satisfaction enjoyed by regular users of the advertised product. In totalitarian states the people are frequently subjected to a stream of propaganda films assuring them that they are living under the best of all possible systems, and more of the same is guaranteed if they continue their unstinting support of the regime.

Human feelings are important factors of identification in a documentary film when they present the attitudes and opinions of a victim with whom the viewer can identify: How does it feel to find a burning cross on the front lawn or be threatened with a bomb? What emotional traumas does the wife of a prisoner of war undergo when a malicious crank calls her on the telephone, pretending to represent the Department of Defense, to inform her that her husband is dead? With what bitterness does an educated man work as a cab driver because the government has cut off funds for research in that area to which he has committed his professional life? Such mishaps and tragedies may touch the life space of any adult; and because the viewers may identify with persons trapped in such circumstances, those feelings on film have become persuasive documentary facts.

Documentary Formats

The pristine documentary film has three basic formats: *pure, mixed* and *dramatized*.

THE PURE DOCUMENTARY

The pure documentary consists essentially of film footage taken on natural locations, unmodified in any way, of people and other living things going about their business as if they were not being viewed by a lens, and events occurring as if there were no cameramen about to record them on film.

Pure documentaries usually derive from events in which the people involved are so preoccupied with what they are doing that they have no time to be self-conscious about their images on film, for example, in war and natural catastrophe. *The Battle of San Pietro*, a World War II film report to Congress that became a classic antiwar documentary, presented brave soldiers launching suicidal attacks ordered by implicitly incompetent commanders; a suddenly orphaned child wandering pathetically and stunned around the ruins of his home, a husband weeping in unspeakable anguish as the body of his wife was unearthed from the rubble of a bomb-blasted building. Such subjects are the stuff of the pure documentary, but they may also be obtained in peacetime through the use of the hidden camera.

THE MIXED DOCUMENTARY

The mixed documentary, consisting in part of authentic on-location footage and in part of scenes acted or staged, derives from the intrinsic problem of getting meaningful events to occur when a cameraman is there to photograph them. As often as not the action occurs when a cameraman is nowhere around. If a filmmaker wants to produce a documentary film about a problem deriving from an event at which he was not present, and for which there may be no stock shots or still photographs available, he may have no recourse but to recreate the event in order to present the truth.

Restaging, or more accurately re-creating, an event that actually occurred or is representative of the truth may be justifiable in order to present a balanced, objective interpretation of the event, but such re-creations if detected, tend to arouse skepticism in the viewer about the validity of the whole film.

THE DRAMATIZED DOCUMENTARY

The "dramatized documentary" is an attempt to re-create an event as it actually occurred, or to state the facts in a way representative of the truth, in a film that will pass for being a documentary film. This is not easy to do because when dialogue is written to be spoken by professional actors the end product too easily slides over into the genre of drama, thereby losing its credibility as a documentary film. The old *March of Time* series presented in-depth current affairs documentaries between 1935 and 1951 which had completely dramatized sequences presented as documentary truths. The reenactments may have been valid and justified, but the use of actors speaking written dialogue was so obvious as to arouse the viewer's skepticism.

A more credible form of dramatized documentary is the kind in which ordinary people are asked to perform the normal acts of their daily lives in ways that can be photographed, but without being asked to speak written dialogue. Very few laymen can speak words written for them without sounding stilted and self-conscious. The more successful documentaries, such as *The Quiet One*, have a story line based upon a representative truth, and the persons seen in the film are those who would live the part in reality, but all words are spoken in voice-over narration. The use of professional actors as substitutes, even in voice-over films, tends to be a poor choice because the Stanislavsky method shows through and the mannerisms of acting are glaringly obvious in realistic settings. Moreover, actors seldom have the familiar skills of a person doing a job he was trained to do; in a documentary film about garage mechanics no one can handle a grease gun like a genuine garage mechanic.

THE DRAMATIC FILM CUM DOCUMENTARY TECHNIQUES

At the farthest end of the documentary spectrum is the dramatic film that has moved from the studio to the street and concerned itself with social purpose rather than amusement, using real people in their natural settings to tell a story based upon a social dilemma. Strong thematic statements are characteristic of such dramatic films. *The Battle of Algiers*, for example, took the theme of "valor" in its presentation of a starkly realistic reenactment of events as they essentially occurred in the revolution against the French regime in the capital of Algeria, the valor of a people fighting for the right to choose their own destiny and govern themselves badly.

The differences between the dramatized documentary and the dramatic film which is based upon social realities relate to the uses of artistic conventions; that is, they relate to the differences between a story and a plot, between a person and a character.

THE QUIET ONE. The dramatized documentary. *Contemporary Films/ McGraw-Hill.*

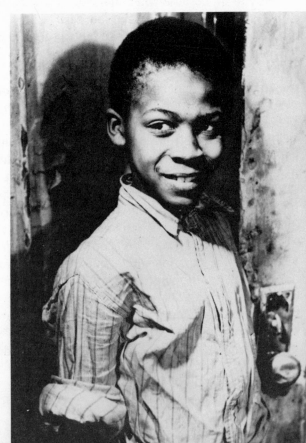

A *story* is a portrayal of a series of events, having a basis in fact, which may or may not have a formal outcome. A *plot* is an artificial dramatic structure involving such conventions as a defined conflict between protagonist and antagonist, a pivotal character, crises, climax and denouement—very few of which elements are found in the Persian carpet patterns of real life. A *person* in a documentary story is someone portraying himself, but as a representative of a breed of men that participated in an event. A *character*, on the other hand, is an artificial creation from the mind of a screenwriter who exists to play a role in a carefully designed plot intended to provide the viewer with amusement or escape from reality.

Documentary Truth

Documentary truth means using representative types which have in themselves characteristics common to them all. The representative type must always be sought out because the documentary film is concerned less with the fate of individuals than it is with the fate of a group or class of human beings. In selecting graphic elements to represent a given group of human beings or locations, the documentary filmmaker is, in fact, creating stereotypes that will enable the viewer to recognize such persons and their problems elsewhere, and to act upon them.

For a subject to be true in a documentary sense he must be a representative epitome of all such subjects. The subject of a film about motorcycle gangs would exemplify in one person those things typically found in the others: long dirty hair; black leather jackets with silver conchos on the front pockets and the club affiliation splashed across the back; huge black motorcycles spangled with reflectors and skull heads; and the inevitable "sheep," his female counterpart, riding behind the seat with her long greasy hair fluttering in the wind. These are the characteristics, endemic to all motorcycle gangs, that would enable the viewer of a documentary film to recognize the subject immediately and feel "I know you."

The same documentary truth applies to selecting representative locations—they must be the quintessence of all such locations. The street of a tenement should contain those graphic elements that epitomize all tenement districts: weary walls and chalk graffiti; rickety stairs and tired windows; a mixed bag of loitering children and aimless adults.

UPTOWN. The representative location. *Contemporary Films/McGraw-Hill.*

These are the memorable graphic elements that say to the viewer, "This is what it is like to live on the street of a tenement district."

Sometimes not all of the elements typical of a group of persons or a representative location may be found in a single individual or specific setting. And occasionally there are graphic elements present which are not typical and may be misleading if included in the film. Under such circumstances it may be necessary to risk a little "staging." The content values of a scene perhaps ought to be heightened by adding items that are typical under most such circumstances, but happen not to be present in a specific scene; or it may be necessary to remove those that may be misleading, atypical or out of character: a Cadillac parked in the driveway of a slum dwelling will do little to arouse the sympathy of the viewer for the tenant, and it is not a documentary truth.

All forms of documentary film have one characteristic in common—they were taken on the spot. This gives the film a certitude and authenticity that only cinematography on location with the real subjects can give. Authenticity is never sacrificed for cinematic fireworks; a fruit picker may be asked to pluck a tangerine at a certain time of day, when the light is right for color cinematography, but he should never be asked to do it in a special way for a fancy effect or under artificial conditions. It is up to the documentary filmmaker to select those aspects of the subject's natural activities for photography that will lend themselves to a film which is an emotional presentation of the facts, but he should never impose an artifice upon the subject.

Producing the Documentary

The documentary film is usually produced by a very small team of filmmakers—writer, director, cameraman and editor. Sometimes one of these persons will perform more than one function, such as a writer-editor, or one will serve as the producer for the whole operation. In contrast to the compartmentalization typical of dramatic film production, with a specialist as master for each phase of its development, the work of all filmmakers on a documentary team is interrelated from the first brainstorming session to the final viewing of a release print. Each person's experience and viewpoint contributes to the shape of the film as it takes persuasive form, its cinematic elements become dynamic, and at last a documentary film reaches out hopefully to awaken the viewer to a clamant human need.

A documentary film idea is most frequently born from the gut reaction of a filmmaker that something he sees—some human condition—needs to be changed. Rambling and browsing is the next phase of development, because the documentarist is seeking a familiarity with the problem that will enable him to select those aspects of it that will graphically bring the issue into sharp focus. Immersion in the subject at its source is essential because no amount of library research (important as it may be) and preliminary discussions will get to the heart of the matter as will a complete personal experience on location. If the filmmaker is producing a film about the poor whites from Appalachia who have drifted to Chicago seeking work, he should join a family at their dinner of fatback and grits, stand in line for food stamps, walk the streets with them in their search for work and find out why they were refused, sleep in their ratty beds, join in their pastime of pitching pennies at a crack in the sidewalk, and stand with the men gathered around the guitar-strummer as they sing plaintively, "I want to go home."

DOCUMENTARY FACTS

From experiences on location, the documentary facts will reveal themselves. Documentary facts are visual facts that exemplify the problems, while arousing at the same time the empathy of the viewer: the rat-nibbled mattress; the hypodermic needle lying in a dirty dish; the silent empty house in the hills with ragweed growing up through the porch; the old migrant laborer, past the age of earning his keep, who slouches on an orange crate as he stares vacantly and twitches his gnarled empty hands. Documentary facts are those which exist in a *specific visual form*, rather than as verbal description or statistical abstraction, because life is itself specific and visual. But the filmmaker will also study stock shots, still photographs, tape recordings, newspaper and magazine clips and books; and he will interview victims of the problem, perpetrators of the problem, authorities on the problem—he will prowl down any alley or byway that may give him some form of insight that he can communicate to the viewer.

THEME

A theme will emerge from whatever subject is undertaken that forms the intellectual framework of the documentary film, a central concept that can usually be expressed in a single sentence: "Pollution is so huge a problem that we can't afford to clean it up, and can't afford to ignore it." Or, "Some fanatics are reducing our freedoms by abusing theirs." These thematic statements should come from the subjects themselves, not from an official spokesman giving out a public relations statement, or even from the filmmakers themselves. Most often, the theme will be spoken with unpretentious eloquence by some individual affected by the problem: a farmer, an unemployed engineer, a research assistant or informed social worker. By listening carefully, the documentary filmmaker will hear his subject say something that will provide the film with an intellectual framework and thematic summing up.

STORY LINE

Story line in documentary film tends to derive from a natural sequence of events, or a logical cause and effect relationship between events, that lends itself cinematically to becoming a drama of ideas. To a large extent the story line and its cinematic rendering are dictated by the nature of the subject.

If the purpose of the documentary film is to gain support for a flood control or reforestation project, the filmed sequences would probably show the chronological progression of events that brought about the need for remedial action in the same essential sequence in which the events actually occurred: excessive lumbering; overgrazing by livestock; wasteful agricultural usages; dumping of corrosive acids into the river; growing erosion and lack of water controls. And then the inevitable results—the river is swollen by excessive water runoff and nature exacts vengeance by flooding the homes and industries of its human exploiters. The conclusion of the film would show what needs to be done to rectify the damage and tell the viewer what he can do to stimulate remedial action.

Graphic materials of all kinds may be included in the film if it helps to communicate the idea—newsreel footage, candid camera film, stock shots, still photographs given movement on an animation stand, animated films and special effects, are all acceptable if they give the viewer information and perspective. The viewer of a documentary film, by his selective exposure to that film, is indicating his willingness, to some degree, to be affected by the film's content, and therefore tends to watch with suspended judgment and look for anything that will help him to understand. The viewer comes to a documentary film with a different frame of reference than he would bring to a dramatic film; he tends to be seeking reality, not avoiding it, and he is less critical of production finesse. Where the documentary genre is concerned, anything goes in terms of what content may be included, and cinematic style and production slickness are subordinate to the graphic communication of the idea.

CINEMATOGRAPHY

Cinematography for a documentary film should occur, ideally, when people are unaware of the camera's presence, for only then do they really behave in a manner which is completely normal and relaxed.

Disconcerting realism is the goal of documentary film, the recording of those strange human moments when people are really tired or really busy, those times of stress and anguish, temptation and revelation, when the social veneers peel back and the lens may record real people being themselves instead of behaving as they want to be perceived.

The hidden camera may sometimes be used under specialized circumstances, and at other times, when the subjects are so preoccupied with their tasks that they are unaware or heedless of being photographed, the camera will function as if it were hidden.

More often, however, the documentary filmmakers must move into people's lives, homes and places of employment in order to make the film. They must set up cameras and lights and reflectors and engage in all kinds of activities which, if they are not actually disruptive of the subject's normal activities, are at the least distracting.

Disruption of the subjects' lives and environment should be kept to a minimum for three primary reasons: First, it may change or distort the subjects' normal patterns of behavior and activities and thereby distort the facts being presented in the documentary film. Second, the physical rearrangement of objects to suit the exigencies of film production may kill the spontaneity of a place where people live and work. Third, there may be a temptation to arrange subjects and objects before the camera in a way that is too satisfying aesthetically and a betrayal of the truth—to transform poverty and dirt into artistic tonal arrangements that please the eye and distract the mind from unpleasant realities. In documentary film production dissonance of content is sometimes important in order to persuade the viewer to support the filmmaker's proposed solution to the problem.

Multicamera setups are frequently advisable when retakes would lower the spontaneity of the subject, in order to capture sensitive human expressions for cinematic interpretations. And the multicamera technique is useful for obtaining overlapped, matching action for good editing technique; the need for establishing shots, medium shots and closeups is nearly as important in the documentary genre as in dramatic film, because jump cuts are a distraction from the communication of ideas.

Multicamera setups, useful though the technique may be, come at the price of consistency and quality in the lighting of the scenes. What may be an ideally lighted scene from one camera angle may mean low-key lighting from the second camera position and high-key lighting from the third, yielding inconsistencies of tonality that may seem glaring when the scenes are intercut in editing. But if the end result is the capture of evanescent human impressions on film footage, which may then be sensitively edited to reveal insight into human consequences, it is well worth the price of inconsistent lighting.

Single-camera setups are inadvisable because they frequently require that a subject repeat his actions in order to obtain matching-action footage, a kind of skill that few nonactors can manage. Retakes of scenes should be kept to a minimum because they tire the subject and wither his spontaneity. The surest way to avoid such repetitions is to know, understand and anticipate the real movements of the subject, and then capture the flow of his natural actions with multiple-camera setups.

Before taking down the lights for any given sequence the documentary filmmaker should make sure that he has photographed the beginnings and endings of the action—the times and places where the subject normally pauses—and a cutaway or two to take the curse off a jump cut should there be any aspect he has overlooked.

DIRECTING THE NONACTOR

Directing the nonactor for cinematography, while avoiding any influence on his natural actions or making him feel self-conscious, involves psychological problems that may reduce all others to trivial proportions.

Casting the subjects to suit a representative type is, of course, a first consideration; the appearance and mannerisms of the individual should be representative of the many. The visual impression of the subject is important, as is his familiarity with the actions he is to carry out before the camera.

Casting frequently offers interpersonal problems, as when presenting several members of a family or a professional team working together in a film. Such groups tend to have internal pecking orders, and sometimes they harbor aggressions among themselves that do not become apparent until production is well under way. A father and son may work well enough when photographed separately, but not at all well when they are together, and the differences in attitude and personality may become apparent when the scenes are intercut. Directives to nonactors who are being photographed together should be given separately, if possible, so that direct rapport and understanding may be established between the filmmaker and each subject, outside the influence of a third party. Giving separate directives to nonactors who will be playing in scenes together also tends to enhance the spontaneity and naturalness of their actions. The filmmaker should enter such documentary productions with an awareness that a sense of tact may be needed, and be alert to delicate situations.

Self-consciousness before the camera is the greatest single problem in dealing with the nonactor. If a relaxed atmosphere can be maintained during cinematography it will contribute a great deal to reducing his tenseness and self-consciousness, and no opportunity for levity and good humor should pass unused. The nonactor must never be allowed to feel that a calamity has occurred if he happens to spoil a take by dropping a tool, but be reassured that the mishap is of no consequence. With time and a few intelligent explanations about film technique, the subject may acquire a sense of what is expected of him, relax and become more adaptable.

Natural movements before the camera are important. Rehearsals and retakes have a deadening effect upon nonactors, and it is preferable to keep them to a minimum. If necessary, some time should be allowed to pass between rehearsals and cinematography, using other persons as stand-ins for lighting and blocking action, to keep the nonactor from becoming self-conscious.

Asking a nonactor to act and speak written lines is inadvisable; he may stiffen up and become a walking fence post mouthing wooden dialogue. Instead, he should receive an explanation of what has to be done, and be allowed to carry out the actions with his normal behavioral patterns while making whatever remarks he deems appropriate at the time. If a given emotional reaction of some kind will be needed at certain points in the edited film, it may be necessary to resort to tricks to evoke that response, but nothing should be done that will embarrass him, and such actions must be left until last, after everything else has been photographed. The subject may not like surprises, even if sprung on him in order to obtain necessary film footage, and his resentment may spoil future sequences.

A nonactor tends to be sensitive about the quality of his performances and needs to be reassured. He may suspect that those long inaudible conversations between the director and the cameramen are about his delivery during the last scene, and he is probably right. It is usually advisable to work out a code system in advance between the cameraman and the director. If the cameraman says "That's great," it can mean "That's terrible, let's try it some other way." These innocent duplicities harm no one and may spare the feelings of the nonactor for a better performance later, and ultimately result in a more credible documentary film. For the same reason it is inadvisable to show the nonactor the unedited rushes of his scenes; usually he cannot anticipate how he will appear when the scenes are edited into a film, and he may become discouraged after viewing several flawed takes of the same scene.

The pride of an individual often reveals something important about the documentary subject and may be used as a means of identification with the viewer. With men, pride is apt to be related to their work or profession—a skill or special kind of ability—and a nonactor should be given the opportunity to display his proficiency before the cameras: first, because it will bolster his confidence in performing for other scenes to know he has been photographed at his best; second, because his skill will demonstrate to the viewer that the subject is a person of integrity and achievement who has been trapped by circumstances and deserves aid. But a filmmaker should never trifle with a man's professional pride by asking him to do something that seems professionally foolish for cinematic effect, such as asking a farmer to milk a dry cow. Such requests will annoy the nonactor and the cow and lower the respect of both for the film in progress.

Nonactors usually know little about professional film production and seldom understand why it takes so long to light a room and compose a scene, or why multiple takes are necessary for matching action in editing. (What's taking so long? Why are you fooling around with the lights? Why didn't you get it right the first time?) Their experiences in making films, if any, have been confined to home movies, and they often fail to understand why it is not as simple as setting up the camera and photographing the scene.

The solution to chinking the interstices of time between takes and retakes lies in having the writer converse with the subject about other aspects of his life and problems, continuing research for hidden themes and concepts while at the same time humoring him. Sometimes the most telling and poignant insights into a problem will emerge inadvertently during a shooting break while having a casual cup of coffee.

Editing the Documentary

Editing the documentary film, combining the picture track with narration, music and sound effects, follows the classic pattern of film production, but with some variations. Typically, the work print is edited to the rough-cut stage; then the commentary is written and the continuity tightened to a fine cut; and finally, the music and effects are timed, synchronized and integrated to the length of each sequence. When the essential pictorial statement has been made, the writer enters the cutting room and threads up the work print in the Moviola, takes out the continuity script and begins to write the narration. He watches the images pass through the picture head, times the length of each sequence, writes his narration and reads it aloud to the moving images, revising his words again and again until picture and sound fuse into a single message. The intent is to have neither picture nor sound apparently dominate the other, but to give the viewer one indivisible impression.

Narration in a documentary film may be used to add verbal information, to relate scenes on the screen to preceding scenes, to add color, mood and feeling, to point out an important detail, to increase or hold back the tempo and to tell the viewer what action to take as the consequence of having seen the documentary film. Narration should never precede or dominate the editing of the visual track. Some producers are guilty of writing the narration first and cutting the film to fit the words, a method calculated to turn out a profusely illustrated lecture, not a persuasive documentary film. Narration should be written to support the visual statement, not the other way around.

Narration need not be continuous; in fact, if it is continuous, the viewer will mentally tune out. It is usually advisable to space out the narration, leaving room to include music and sound effects for the emotional energy and realism that these important elements may add to the effectiveness of the film.

If *music* rather than narration is dominant in the sound track, the working relationship varies somewhat. The work print is first edited to nearly a fine-cut stage. Then the music is composed, orchestrated and recorded, and the music track is returned to the editor. Finally the filmmaker returns to his editing Moviola to find inspiration in the musical detail, and he may recut portions of the picture track to exploit the expressive powers of the music. If original music is composed for the film (a rare luxury in the usually tight budget of a documentary film) each passage should be timed to match the length of the sequence it accompanies and every point of emphasis made to complement the visuals.

Thematic music may be used to enhance the dramatic and expressive powers of the documentary film, either as a complement to the visuals or as counterpoint, but the music should reflect the subjects themselves unless the intent is satirical. In the classic documentary film *The River* scenes of eroded land and ruined farms are accompanied by plaintive bars from the early American folk tune, "Go Tell Aunt Rhody the Old Gray Goose Is Dead."

Sound effects in documentary film are most often used in either of two ways: to provide realistic sounds to accompany the events on the screen, or to present sound as commentary which interprets the scenes on the screen. Sequences portraying refugees fleeing a clash of armies, for example, may be accompanied by the sounds of tank treads, marching jackboots and machine gun fire, to create, through counterpoint, a sum total impression of pursuers and pursued.

Validity

The validity of a documentary film must be compared again and again with reality as the film develops. The filmmakers must repeatedly ask themselves three questions: Is it true? Is the message visual and cinematic? Does the documentary film have those factors of identification and appeal that may influence the target audience to act in support of a solution to the problem?

The truthfulness of the message may be tested by submitting a fine cut of the visual and sound tracks to the criticism of the subjects of the film and to experts in the field. The cinematic quality is best assessed by film-producing colleagues. The effectiveness of the documentary film on its intended target audience—the reason for the film's existence—should be tried on a sample cross-section of the target audience before proceeding with a first answer print. It is a rare documentary film that can pass through these three flaming hoops without needing modification.

Ideally, the finished documentary film should not only add to the viewer's understanding of a people and their problems, but should also, in the broadest sense, add to his understanding of human life and its relationship to all other forms of life. The authentic documentary film offers a window on life through which the viewer sees the truth about the world, but a truth sharpened and shaped to direct him toward a course of action to better that world.

15

The Television Documentary Film

Television pumps into the American collective mind an unending torrent of information, moral concepts, aesthetic values and opinions in the forms of entertainment, advertising, news and documentary films. Television is so pervasive that we are immersed in its effects like fish in the sea.

The three commercial national networks—CBS, NBC and ABC—now play the roles of friend, parent, teacher, counselor, representative of government, creator of ideals and aspirations and eye on the world for millions of people for whom television is the dominant cultural influence. Given the vastness of this distribution system for communications, anyone having something to say can present his point of view on television with an impact on greater numbers of people than by any other means. Some individual television documentaries, such as *The Real West* or *Biography of a Bookie Joint*, may have been seen by dozens of millions of viewers, possibly by an audience more vast than that reached by all the documentary films ever produced before the advent of television.

Origins

But the television documentary had its genesis in radio, not motion pictures, and therein lies the basis of fundamental differences between the classic documentary film and the television documentary. The first radio station was built in 1926, to be followed by a rapid proliferation of other stations across the United States. Radio was essentially an entertainment and advertising medium, with news reporting thrown in as an extra. Advertisers and advertising agencies virtually ran the networks and they were extremely sensitive about the inclusion of controversial subjects on programs advertising their clients' products, a sensitivity that extended to reporting of the news. News reporting then consisted of no more than having a reporter on location to describe an event as it occurred. The newscasts of the 1920s and 1930s contained little analysis, criticism or personal opinion; they were bland in interpretation and tended to avoid controversy or attempts to effect social, political or economic changes. This neutrality was the antithesis of what was taking place in the concurrent development of the classic documentary film.

This avoidance of probing into sensitive subjects or taking a stand on a public issue was reinforced by the United States government. A series of congressional acts evolved into what has since become known as the Fairness Doctrine. The Government Radio Act of 1927 authorized radio stations to editorialize, but urged them to permit other points of view to be expressed. With passage of the Communication Act of 1934 and the establishment of the watchdog Federal Communications Commission, the impetus to assure the presentation of opposing points of view became stronger. In 1949 it was promulgated as formal doctrine that opposing points of view should be given equal broadcast time, and in 1959 Congress enacted an amendment to the Communication Act of 1934 which gave the equal-time provision the force of law.

The Fairness Doctrine assures broadcasters freedom of speech in the sense that they are allowed to exercise their own editorial judgment, but, paradoxically, inhibits free speech in the sense that an exercise of editorial prerogative carries with it an obligation to give equal time on the air for the expression of opposing viewpoints. Therefore, controversiality had two potentially expensive consequences: it could alienate listeners and sponsors alike, and it could cost money in terms of air time given over to the opposition. The classic goals of the documentary concept became impracticable under the economic and regulatory system of the American broadcast industry.

The advent of television at the end of World War II did little, initially, to change the innocuous nature of news reporting; advertisers were still shy of controversy, the Fairness Doctrine continued in effect, the television audience was small and few people had receivers, and the much higher cost of presenting a visual program discouraged innovation. The first news and documentary productions were plodding affairs that consisted essentially of radio-with-pictures, produced live as if motion pictures did not exist. All of the dramatic productions in the earliest days were also live performances. Only the wildly erratic variations in rehearsal and show-time performances, with some programs having to be chopped off at the end as time ran out and others left with several minutes of blank screen as the production finished too soon, forced television producers to turn to motion pictures for flexibility of control.

The advantages of film were immediately apparent to television journalists, but the networks did not want to become involved with the motion picture unions. Instead they sub-contracted for the production of newsreel footage with firms then producing such footage for theatrical short subjects, and this was the entrée of documentary film to television. The now traditional television news format of having a commentator read the news and then introduce a film sequence emerged during that period.

The television documentary as we know it was born in 1951 with the CBS series *See It Now*, produced by Edward R. Murrow and Fred Friendly, as a natural evolution from an earlier documentary radio series, *Hear It Now*, also produced by Murrow and Friendly. Their first television broadcast consisted of badly composed and out-of-focus views of the Atlantic and Pacific coastlines presented simultaneously, accompanied by much gee-whiz commentary about the importance of the occasion and the majesty of the event. But Murrow and Friendly soon felt at home with their vast audience and undertook more important presentations, aided by the new financial sponsorship of Alcoa, the Aluminum Company of America. They signed a contract with the Hearst–MGM News of the Day for cameramen and editors on a cost-plus basis, and for the first two years *See It Now* examined many of the current events of the day, introduced by Murrow and produced by Friendly in the documentary film format. Soon thereafter, the other formats developed in the classic documentary film also moved to television.

But the old strictures still persisted in the new television form; in

Edward R. Murrow.
CBS News.

Fred Friendly's own words, the early *See It Now* films lacked "conviction, controversy, and a point of view." And they ignored a very unsavory trend of that time: For years the cruel tactics of Senator Joseph Mc-Carthy, while investigating alleged Communist infiltration of the federal government, had ruined the careers and reputations of innocent men. Murrow and Friendly at last decided that fear had gone far enough, turned their documentary guns on Senator McCarthy, and presented a *See It Now* report on the inquisitor using film kinesic techniques of his own image to expose the character of that Senator. They then gave him equal time to respond, passed him the sword, as it were, knowing full well he could not use it as skillfully. The thrall of fear was broken by that *See It Now* broadcast, and Senator McCarthy was subsequently censured for his investigative tactics by the United States Senate.

The effects of *See It Now* were threefold: It created a current-event matrix for the content of television documentary film. It triggered the beginning of ambitious documentary film projects by the other two networks and the proliferation of new purviews of content. And it gave network documentary film producers a degree of latitude in undertaking controversial subjects in the public interest which, in a sense, have redefined the documentary concept.

Comparative Forms

The classic documentary film and the television documentary are alike in certain respects: Both forms are concerned, in subject matter, with the factual aspects of the lives of men and other living things, unalloyed by fictional artistic conventions. Both are concerned, in cinematic technique, with presenting a motion picture record which portrays real people living real events, edited to state their truest possible relationship. And both the classic documentary and the television documentary are concerned with such forms of content as urban man and primitive nature, the reporting of news events, the portrayal of history and the presentation of reality. But there the similarity ends.

The classic documentary film in theme, concept and purpose is deliberately constructed as a persuasive instrument of social action and is often ideological in nature, which means it presents a distinct point of view on a subject and tries to enlist the support of the viewer for a specified *course of action*. The social action documentary is a clarion call for the reform of some contemporary institution, and the film is created as a single production. The classic documentary filmmaker often pays out of pocket to put his ideas on film and more or less expects to be bloodied for his attacks on vested interests.

Television documentary films, antithetically, are seldom permitted to raise the banner of a Cause. Far to the contrary, producers are specifically enjoined not to take sides, even if the facts would seem to warrant it, and if they express a point of view they must give equal time to the opposition. Television documentaries are planned and produced in large numbers, in series, by a staff of filmmakers and reporters retained by the networks for that purpose. Because of the vast audience reached by television, the sensitivity of sponsors to controversy and the equal-time provision of the Fairness Doctrine, the basic content considerations are taboos: Will the film offend any sponsors, any vested interest groups, any lobby in Washington, the Federal Communications Commission or any sizable segment of the viewing audience with a letterhead and the power to retaliate in an organized way? The classic definition of the documentary film as an ideological instrument for deliberately implementing social change is therefore difficult to apply to the television documentary film.

The Functions of the Television Documentary

If the television documentary filmmakers may not, as a rule, set out to reform the nation, what, then, may they permissibly do?

The functions of television documentary are threefold: *to sensitize the viewer's perceptions, to provide a stimulus* and *to provide a record of our time.*

SENSITIZING THE VIEWER'S PERCEPTIONS

To sensitize the viewer's perceptions to a new subject, or to reveal some previously unknown aspect of an old subject, is the primary function of the television documentary. By bringing news and commentary to the viewer the filmmaker is alerting the viewer's perceptions to a subject he may never have known about or thought about, because it had never previously impinged upon his life space. The television documentary therein achieves three purposes: It has made the first presenta-

A REAL CASE OF MURDER. Sensitizing perceptions. *CBS News.*

tion on a new issue, thereby forming an opinion about that new subject which the viewer will subsequently tend to protect by selective exposure, perception and retention. It has broadened the viewer's awareness levels and apperception and he will thereafter be alert to further information on the same subject. And it may, if the nature of the subject relates to the vital interest and life space of the viewer, motivate the viewer to take a course of action implicit in the presentation without the filmmaker having to violate the strictures of the Fairness Doctrine.

The television documentary serves an invaluable function in sensitizing the perceptions and apperceptions of the viewer to the existence of an event, trend, movement or problem, publicizes it and overtly presents the viewer with those plain pertinent facts that will enable him to make up his own mind. Covertly, however, there are many conceptual and cinematic ways in which television documentarists may interpret their subjects to influence the viewer's interpretation of the subject, equal time notwithstanding.

PROVIDING A STIMULUS

To provide a stimulus to the viewer is a second use of the television documentary, and one which serves a cultural apperceptive role. If the viewer watches a film about political activity at the local level, such as *Campaign, American Style*, and is stimulated to participate in the activities of his own party at the local level, then that documentary has served a political stimulus function. If the viewer watches a television documentary about an artist and his work, such as *Vincent Van Gogh: A Self-Portrait*, and as a consequence begins to attend art exhibitions, then that documentary has served a cultural stimulus function. If the viewer watches any of the many television documentaries now being produced on the topical subject of ecology, and actively participates in the work of the Sierra Club or some other conservation group, he is again reacting to the stimulus function of the television documentary film.

PROVIDING A RECORD OF OUR TIME

To provide a record of our time is a third function of the television documentary, and one which, perhaps, exceeds the other two in lasting importance. The television documentaries produced by the three major networks have explored the history of the recent past and probed deeply into many of the major trends, problems and personalities of our time, presenting them in a cogent motion picture form to the public. The subjects of juvenile delinquency, racial discrimination, drug abuse, police corruption, urban blight and other contemporary trends have been examined in depth, with authorities on the subjects retained to assure the documentary's authenticity. The international political events of our time, such as the origins and development of the war in Vietnam, the Arab-Israeli dispute, the problems of the emerging nations, the rise of the European Common Market, the complexities of the Sino-Soviet geopolitical rivalry, have been presented in historical perspective. The list of influential personages who have expounded their insights for the edification of the public reads like a Who's Who of the global power elite. And the history of the distant past has been given comprehensive and moving form through the use of old paintings and photographs and the still-in-motion techniques of the animation stand.

These television documentaries are in some cases the only formal studies made of important issues, trends and processes, and even more frequently the only studies made in a form interesting to the general public—motion pictures. After nationwide broadcast, these films find their way into educational film libraries and educational television stations, to be used in high schools, colleges and universities, semester after semester, year after year, for the continuing education of the young. The television documentary film is not a one-shot presentation but a continuing contribution to the enlightenment of the American nation.

Television Documentary Formats

The time slot is the fundamental peculiarity of television. Every production that reaches the screen must conform to the basic segmentation of half-hour/full-hour time allocations, whether or not these are appropriate for presenting a subject. Pictures, words and ideas must be tailored to time and footage, and the stopwatch often severs the subjects into two sizes—too large and too small. If the subject is too vast or complex to fit into its allotted time, the producer must perform a lobotomy and leave out vital material. If the subject lacks enough substance to fill out the necessary time, he must review what was presented earlier or flesh out the time with cinematic flab.

Three formats tend to dominate television documentary film: a mini-documentary introduced by a visible reporter, who then proceeds to narrate the commentary in the voice-over technique, as in the daily evening newscasts; the classic documentary format, in which the narrator is off-screen at all times, but tells the audience about the subject in a manner that is all-seeing, all-knowing; and the subjective first-person narrative, in which the participant in an event or the victim of a problem tells his own story, in lip-synchronous dialogue, and presents an interpretation as seen through his own eyes. Of the three approaches, the techniques of presenting a commentator and his mini-documentary and the subject telling his own story are unique to television. The subject-narrative approach has an emotional force, and occasional moments of revelation, that even skillfully written third-person narration seldom equals.

The *television documentary form* has proliferated so numerously into sub-forms that the term should be redefined according to its specific uses and characteristics. With a concern that the label on the can reveal its contents, we submit the following television documentary forms: *live, news, exposé, in-depth, slice-of-life, interview, biographical, information, digest, dramatized, historical compilation, ethnographic* and *natural history film.*

THE LIVE DOCUMENTARY

The live documentary is one in which an event is telecast live as it occurs, and the viewers who watch their television screens are seeing the event almost instantaneously, as if they were present on location. The live documentary is the original broadcast documentary; it offers a sense of immediacy, of being there on location, and the excitement of the unexpected. Many Americans were watching their television sets when President Kennedy was assassinated in Dallas; even more were watching when the alleged assassin, Lee Harvey Oswald, was himself murdered while accompanied by two Texas policemen; and virtually all Americans attended the funeral of John Fitzgerald Kennedy by means of the live television documentary.

If the events of a live documentary prove uninteresting, however, then the viewer may become bored and commit the cardinal sin of turning to another channel. It is because the television networks want to maintain a high interest level in their documentaries that they prefer to record events on film or videotape, and then edit the resulting footage in order to select only those images that are meaningful and dramatic and

THE JOURNEY OF ROBERT F. KENNEDY. The live documentary.
Wolper Productions.

discard all those that are irrelevant and dull. The conditioning of the viewer to the language of film requires that documentary films offer cinematic excitement. Therefore, the networks now produce live documentaries only for such intrinsically interesting events as a presidential inauguration or an Apollo moon mission.

THE NEWS DOCUMENTARY

The news documentary presents an event that a reporter believes should be brought to the attention of the public. The event may be something concerned with the public interest, a bizarre or brutal happening, or an occurrence having a broad common denominator of human-interest appeal. Sometimes a continuing situation that had escaped attention becomes "news" when it is discovered, as in the case of mercury contamination of edible fish.

News is some kind of *interesting change* that has been seen by an (ideally) impartial observer, an outsider to the event, who tries to relate what he has seen to other outsiders—the television viewing audience—without implying his approval or disapproval. The documentary filmmaker does this by photographing those scenes that are the most representative of what actually happened in the news event, and then editing them into a logical film sequence which portrays the substance and flavor of the event.

The news documentary takes two basic forms. The first is that of the *mini-documentary* used on daily newscasts, film or videotape sequences seldom exceeding five minutes in length and ranging in sophistication from a plain film clip to a fully edited sequence. The mini-documentary is a standard inclusion in the daily newscast format; the commentator first discusses the news event and then presents a mini-documentary to give the viewer a glimpse of the event. These journalistic clips consist for the most part of newsreel footage photographed by film units, combat cameramen and stringers, footage that has been edited into brief but self-contained visual vignettes.

Limitations of time are the primary considerations in the mini-documentary, because each sequence constitutes only a small part of the newscast. Compression and placement are critical and must suggest whole areas of information and emotion at a stroke. Music is seldom used in daily newscasts, because of the exigencies of time, but when used it is concerned with essences and atmosphere that is felt, not heard, pushing the viewer toward an emotional experience compatible with the edited (information) footage of the mini-documentary.

The mini-documentary is often the product of careful research, and its revelations in the news have effected dramatic social changes. Two mini-documentaries produced by Jay McMullen for inclusion in Walter Cronkite newscasts over CBS revealed the improper sales and distribution of amphetamines and barbiturates by (mail order) pharmaceutical houses, and the failure of certain mail order laboratories to make accurate diagnoses of dangerous bacilli. These mini-documentaries led to congressional enactment of the Drug Control Act Amendment of 1965 and the Clinical Laboratories Improvement Act of 1967.

The second form of the news documentary is the *special*, often presented on the heels of some dramatic event as a form of instant documentary. The news documentary special may range anywhere from a half-hour to three hours in length. The news special is often a hasty assemblage of available film clips and mini-documentaries, presented in conjunction with a panel of correspondents and authorities on the subject who discuss the implications and importance of the news event.

The news documentary has immeasurably expanded the awareness of people to the world around them and enabled them not only *to see*, but *to experience* the Russian invasion of Czechoslovakia, the famine in Biafra, the morass of Vietnam, the incursion into Cambodia, as well as such domestic matters as turmoil on the college campuses, racial disorders and the human consequences of pollution and poverty. People are so sensitized by television to the current issues of our time that they frequently criticize the networks for inadequate exposure of these events when they would not have known about many of them in the first place had they not been presented in television news documentaries. Sometimes these news programs have been so convincing in communicating the substance and emotional quality of an event, such as a riot on a college campus, that the program itself has become the target of public outrage—as if the news documentary reporting it had perpetrated the riot.

The Exposé Documentary

The exposé documentary is a direct outgrowth of the news-gathering function, but one requiring investigatory reporting more closely resembling police detective work than journalism. The exposé documentary is most frequently concerned with revealing some kind of corruption or criminal activity that affects the public interest, rather than with exposure of private peccadilloes. Its purpose is to lay bare the corruption for public inspection and, hopefully, to stimulate civic action to rectify the abuses.

Biography of a Bookie Joint was a classic exposé documentary concerned with revealing the extent of illicit gambling and police complicity in the city of Boston. Secret cameras were set up in an upstairs apartment across the street from a key shop that served as a front for the bookie joint, and other cameras were carried into the shop itself, hidden in lunchboxes and attaché cases, to photograph gamblers and policemen as they entered to lay wagers or to pick up their payoffs. Then interviews were held with officials at the state, local and national levels who had public and private knowledge of the gambling operation and police connivance. The resulting footage was edited into an exposé documentary which revealed the form and function of the whole corrupt system.

Biography of a Bookie Joint was broadcast to viewers all over the United States—except in the city of Boston, where it was blacked out. After the ensuing uproar throughout Massachusetts, which caused the police administrative structure of the state and of the city of Boston to be reformed, bookies prosecuted and derelict officers punished, this exposé documentary, with additional clips reporting the reforms, was again broadcast to the nation—this time including the grateful city of Boston.

THE IN-DEPTH DOCUMENTARY

The in-depth documentary is often a departure from the immediate news emphasis that tends to dominate the television documentary film. In the case of most current events, the correspondent gathers the salient facts, obtains suitable film footage, writes appropriate commentary, presents it to the public and goes on to the next assignment. Many contemporary problems, however, do not reveal themselves clearly on the surface and may have many more ramifications than first meet the eye. A suspicious thread sticking out in New York may, if pulled and followed, unravel through unexpected patterns of corruption and lead to other nations on the far side of the world. The in-depth filmmaker is one who, after the general facts about a surface event have been established, continues to search for the hidden relationships.

The in-depth documentary often takes the conceptual framework of an educational film in order to communicate its concepts clearly: A problem is posed, evidence is produced and events explained in a logical way, and the conclusion presented in terms of its human consequences. The purpose is to explain a process to the viewer in a cogent way; therefore, this form of television documentary utilizes nearly every kind of film footage, still photograph, tape recording, object, graphic aid and animated film in order to make the viewer understand the subject.

The Business of Heroin introduced the problems of heroin addiction and trafficking on the streets of New York, and then followed the path of the poppy from the sun-drenched fields of Turkey through its chemical processings, smuggling, marketing and final injection into an American artery. The writer-producer interviewed officials, policemen and smugglers in Turkey, where it is grown; in Syria, through which it is smuggled; in Lebanon, where it is processed into a morphine base; in France, where it is converted into heroin; in Italy, from whence it is smuggled into the United States. Then he followed the white powdery heroin from its first cutting by a wholesaler, to its second cutting by the "ounce-man," to the street-pusher, to the addict. Every step of the pernicious process was clearly explained with motion pictures, animated maps, graphics, still photographs and interviews; no adult viewer could fail to understand the filthy business of heroin—in depth.

THE BUSINESS OF HEROIN. In-depth documentary. *CBS News.*

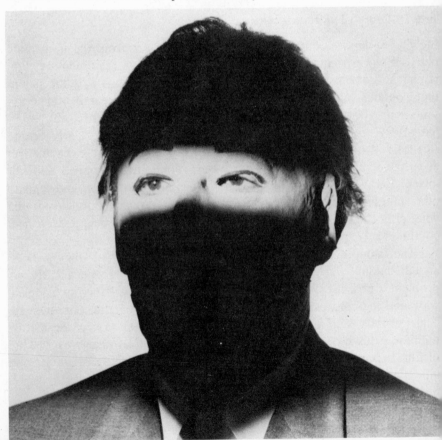

THE SLICE-OF-LIFE DOCUMENTARY

The slice-of-life documentary attempts to present all the meaningful aspects of the life space of representative individuals, who often exemplify problems, within a relatively short period of time. The salient characteristic of this television documentary form is its intimacy. Instead of having a narrator give the facts about the subject and his activities, the slice-of-life documentary permits the subject to speak for himself in interviews given extemporaneously within his own environment, and presents all the factors of the environment that impinge upon the subject within a given time slot, usually one day. The filmmaker does research in advance to determine what kinds of activities are significant to the subject within the allotted time and sees to it that his production crew is in a position to photograph these activities with a minimum disturbance of the naturalness and spontaneity essential to the slice-of-life documentary.

The Tenement was a classic example of this documentary approach. This CBS film permitted the black tenants of a condemned slum dwelling to express their feelings about their hopes, their fears, their lot in life, with the time element created by the coming of the wrecker's ball that would drive them all out of their homes. Each individual spoke in terms of his personal problems, as if he were unique, yet each was a representative sample of a cross-section which exemplified the broad problems of the impoverished black American: large matriarchal families, with husbands dead or deserted; fathers who brought their families to the city with ballooning hopes for a better life, only to have them popped by the needle of poverty; dreams of education and a better chance for the children; street gangs formed by boys for self-defense and identification; the promiscuity of lonely girls; abandoned hopes; despair. All this and more was expressed in the words of these representative individuals in their homes as they awaited the smashing of their building.

THE INTERVIEW DOCUMENTARY

The interview documentary exploits the fascination of the public with the lives of the great, the important, the glamourous. The CBS series *Person to Person* began the television form of the formal interview, which has since continued in a variety of frivolous and serious

forms, for example, the peeping-Tom kind of interview in which the curious viewer is shown various aspects of the subject's heretofore hidden private life—family, hobbies, quirks and foibles—and given a peek behind the curtain of his privacy.

A more serious application of the interview documentary involves discussions on matters of state policy, such as those conducted with the President of the United States in such contexts as panel discussions and the presidential news conference. A further extension of this form is the comparative interview, in which the spokesmen for two sides of an issue, such as the Arab-Israeli dispute, are given equal time to present their facts and points-of-view within the same program. And there is the continuing interview show, such as the weekly *Face the Nation* program, in which expert correspondents grill a series of interesting and controversial persons about various aspects of their stated policies and opinions. The interview documentary presents a point-of-view to be reckoned with in an individual of power or influence, who is of intrinsic rather than representative importance.

THE BIOGRAPHICAL DOCUMENTARY

The biographical documentary is another form originating with television. Usually released shortly after the death of a statesman or some other prominent person, the biographical documentary presents the chronological and meaningful events of his life to the extent that they may be revealed by archives and newsreel film footage, still photographs and memorabilia, videotaped personal interviews, his own recorded and written words, and excerpts from statements written and spoken about him by other persons. The biographical documentary is essentially a kind of historical compilation film about a person whose life has had an influence upon his times. This form is often hastily assembled into an instant documentary upon the demise of the great man, although in those instances in which his death was anticipated (Churchill, Eisenhower, De Gaulle), the film is well under way at the time of his passing. The biographical documentary frequently finds its way into schools for use in history and social studies classes.

THE INFORMATION DOCUMENTARY

Information documentaries are essentially educational films presenting information about a subject of intrinsic interest to the general public, but one having some value in creating an informed citizenry. Films such as *Biography of a Missile* present the progressive design and development of a missile, usable as an instrument of war or to send men to the moon, portrayed in an analytical, detached way. In some information documentaries the stock television format is used, in which a narrator appears to introduce film sequences and reappears to conclude and summarize the presentation. More often the voice-over technique is used and the viewer simply hears a narrator explain the visuals and point out what to observe. The information documentary tends to be an illustrated lecture, laying out objective information intended to leave the viewer with solid knowledge about a subject, but not intended to move him in any experiential or emotional sense. Information documentary films, once broadcast, are among the first to be adopted for use in high schools and universities.

THE DIGEST DOCUMENTARY

The digest documentary is a series concept which presents a collation of important current events, arcane but interesting trivia, and humorous insights into local events and human nature. It is a kind of magazine of the air, presenting a little bit of this and a little bit of that, intended in part to inform and in part to amuse. The digest documentary is topical and transitory, seldom intended for later use in schools, and is frequently done with tongue-in-cheek humor or satire to heighten its entertainment value. A typical program may include news from a distant war, clips of the latest space launching, a demand for union status by the chicken-pluckers of America, a hog-calling contest in Arkansas and a housewife presenting her new recipe for martini marmalade. The digest documentary evolved from the CBS series *See It Now*, and continues in such monthly forms as *Sixty Minutes* and *First Tuesday*.

OTHER FORMS

Four other forms of television documentary films are also presented in the form of special broadcasts: the *dramatized documentary*, essentially the same form as that treated in the chapter on "The Classic Documentary Film"; the *historical compilation film*, which attempts to re-create not only the events of the past, but its spiritual and emotional qualities as well; the *ethnographic documentary*, which presents the culture of another race, nation or ethnic entity in terms of its life style, religion, political organization and social mores; and the *natural history film*, in which the life cycles and environment of various species of birds, fish and animals, and sometimes their ecological problems, are explored cinematically for the general interest of the viewer. These last three forms (treated in the following chapter) are also produced outside the television field and have content characteristics which set them apart from the binding cement of the television documentary—current events.

So regenerating has been the effect of television upon the nearly defunct documentary film that some persons who identify with the broadcast industry have asserted that the concept originated with television, and that nothing existed before but darkness and chaos. To expunge the documentary heritage, they have created such names as "telementary," "docudrama," "dramamentary" and other intestinal-sounding terms, but the name that sticks, with good reason, is "documentary film." While it is true that the broadcasting industry has done more for documentary film since 1951 than the motion picture industry had done in five decades, it is also true that most television documentaries are lineal descendents of motion picture forms dating back to World War I. There is no shame in acknowledging the patrimony of a father, but there is an element of sham in pretending to immaculate conception.

News Division Administrative Structure

The news division of the television networks provides the aegis of the television documentary film and, as mentioned earlier, most subjects

Surrender at Appomattox. The dramatized documentary. *Wolper Productions.*

are news-related. The news value of a subject is based upon such factors as its importance to the domestic public, significance to the greatest numbers of persons, dramatic quality and general audience interest as eventually measured by the program's "ratings." A program's rating is based upon a sampling of television sets, keeping a record of the stations tuned in at any given time, in a representative cross-section of the American viewing public. If a newscast program's rating drops, the newscasters and documentarists may change their tack of news selection and cinematic interpretation, but this is about as close as the television news system comes to tailoring its presentation to the characteristics of a target audience.

Most of the characteristics of the individual viewer that are of great concern in other forms of filmmaking—age, sex, level of formal education, socioeconomic and political milieu and life space—tend to be only of marginal consideration in the selection and presentation of news-oriented television documentaries. The journalist's first concern is to get a good story reflecting all significant aspects of an issue and its human consequences. The concept of "the viewer" per se seldom affects the reporter's news judgment, except through an occasional sampling, the ratings, an uproar created by a controversial item and a common-sense prudence about not trampling on the national values of the American viewer. The news and documentary filmmakers present their material as if the viewers were exactly like themselves; although millions of people may be watching the program, the subject is conceived, produced and presented almost as if nobody is watching.

Television documentary filmmakers have taken as their specialty the broad canvas of contemporary affairs all over the world and filled it by sustained film production on a serial, continuing basis. Each of the networks has produced hundreds of one-hour documentaries and news specials, in addition to the nightly half-hour newscasts with a commentator and his mini-documentary films. Current coverage is both immediate and deep, combining topicality with considered, knowledgable commentary. Its themes and content areas are those most directly concerned with the continuing issues of our time, our nation, our world.

The news and documentary division is part of a vast corporate, conglomerate, network structure, and as such is subject to an administrative chain of command which determines policies and their implementation. This chain is linked as follows, using CBS as a representative example:

There is a president of the CBS News Division, and two vice presidents, one in charge of straight news reporting and one in charge of documentary film and public affairs programming. These three men constitute the heart of an "Editorial Board," which sometimes includes concerned executive producers and producers, that approves or vetoes all proposed and completed projects and lays down policies for news operations and television documentary film productions. Each individual project must be defended by its producer, in premise, in evidence and in cinematic interpretation.

The vice president in charge of each strand is concerned with establishing network policy with regard to such matters as how controversial to become in the selection and interpretation of subjects, and to some degree with levels of taste, but generally neither becomes involved with the specific details of production. The vice presidents are also concerned with the network's relationship to the government and its watching eye, the Federal Communications Commission. Theirs is the final policy authority for news, scripts and cinematic interpretations, subject to veto only by the Editorial Board. There are, in fact, informal concentric rings of judgment through which any given production must pass.

There are three or four executive producers, who translate the policies of the vice presidents into action in terms of the subjects selected, the items presented, how much time and money will be committed to a given project, who will implement it, and each supervises a series of projects implemented by producers and sets up target dates for the completion of each individual program. Their function is essentially supervisory, and when the time comes for a program produced under their eyes to be presented before the Editorial Board, they appear with the producer.

The producer of the documentary film, who is frequently the writer and director as well, is responsible for getting the job done. To him falls the day-to-day decision-making, the personal supervision of editing film footage, with the added responsibility of dispatching cameramen and reporters to the scene of an event and seeing to it that film footage for the projected show comes in and is edited on time. The CBS television documentary team has a dozen producers, and at their disposal are associate producers, a production manager, a half-dozen each of cameramen, film editors and sound technicians, and the use of a dozen reporters sometimes assigned individually to a given production. In addition there are "stringers" in cities around the world who are often on location to obtain motion picture footage at the time an unexpected event occurs.

The reporter is an important decision-maker in the sense that he controls the selection of images that actually appear on film, in association with a cameraman, and he is sometimes a field producer of documentary films.

The news editor is responsible for the details of the news, and he works closely with the associate producer to handle news reports, edit film and make a decision about how many feet of the day's filmed violence, and which gory details, should be broadcast over nationwide television.

The writer translates the guidelines of the executive producer into narrative commentary, to be read by the newscaster or spoken in voice-over narration to accompany the mini-documentary. Although writers are not decision-makers, they often affect the interpretation of a subject by the flavor they give the commentary.

The newscaster, or commentator, is the man who appears with the news to the viewer watching his home television receiver. The "star" usually has little responsibility for the formation of the material he is ostensibly reporting, but most of them participate in the formation of policy in daily discussions, and many of them write or rewrite certain segments of their presentations. Commentators sometimes interpret the material they present by kinesics, that is, they convey their opinions to the viewer by changes in facial expression, a technique known in the news trade as "editorial eyebrows."

Television Documentary Production System

The television documentary is a matter of continuing production, with films conceived in series and groups of filmmakers working concurrently on ten or twelve subjects at any given time. In addition, dozens of other possible subjects are under continuous consideration.

The scope and ambitiousness of the documentary program depends to a large degree upon economic and public relations factors. The television documentary may be regarded as an ancillary extra, subordinate to the sales function of network television. If the current income of the network is low, the first place the purse strings will tighten is around the throat of the television documentary, an economy limited only by the power of the Federal Communications Commission. If the income from sponsorship and advertising is high, then the luxury of producing informative television documentaries is indulged. An important factor in the production of television documentaries is the public image of the networks at the moment: it was the nationwide scandal of "fixed" quiz programs in the 1950s that launched the Golden Age of the television documentary film, as the networks tried to polish their tarnished image with many ambitious works in the public interest.

Once the Editorial Board has approved a subject for production, allocated money and personnel to produce it, and set a target date for broadcasting the television documentary, a great deal of independence and discretionary power is granted to the documentary filmmaker. The filmmakers may then disappear for months at a time to live and work with their subjects until they are ready to submit their rough-cut documentary film to the purgatory of evaluation by an Editorial Board. If the interpretation is deemed too biased, the film may either be recut to delete the offending material or the project may be permanently shelved. In the case of the latter, the documentary producer must have an extremely good track record or he will then be looking for a new position.

The actual production team assigned to produce a given documentary film is better equipped and financed but is seldom much larger than the group that produced the classic documentary film. The writer, director, editor and cameraman are still the heart of the team, with the addition of a sound technician because of the television technique of letting subjects speak for themselves. Usually, one of them serves as the executive producer of the documentary.

Basic production techniques on location are essentially those of the classic documentary. Research, filming and sound recording are done, and ideas and cinematic concepts are developed, on location in order to obtain the documentary facts, find a theme to tie the film together, render a story line based upon real events, photograph documentary subjects in their own settings and obtain authentic music and sound effects for thematic and commentative value. Directing the nonactor involves similar problems in dealing with self-consciousness before the camera, professional pride, intrasubject rivalries and frictions and the preservation of spontaneity in the presentation of the subject's natural habits and patterns of movement. The television documentary, like the classic documentary, is truly a team effort in the sharing of ideas and responsibilities, but differs in the sense that the dominant voice in the final form of the film is not that of the director, but the writer-producer.

Two production techniques are commonly used in the television documentary, and one of them is unique to television. The *cinéma vérité* technique of the hand-held camera is used to subjectively convey the experiences of the subject to the viewer. By placing the viewer in the point-of-view of the subject, the filmmaker theoretically obtains emotional identification of viewer with subject. This fine theory, however, has a shortcoming: As we walk we are not aware of tilting horizon lines and buildings bobbing up and down and people wobbling and swaying, as is the effect when viewing film photographed with the hand-held camera. The strange rationale that this is "realistic" or "artistic" seems to grip many documentary cameramen and directors. The hand-held camera may serve a valuable function when the subject is supposed to be drunk or on drugs or frightened, or if the subject can be photographed in no other way—as in a battle situation or over rough terrain (something on film is better than nothing on film)—but for the most part film from the hand-held camera is neither realistic nor artistic, merely distracting.

Cross-cutting of interview scenes is an editing technique that originated with television and is used to make one person issue a comparative statement to another, to make a subject contradict himself with his own words, and to evoke pathos by permitting subjects to exemplify problems by stating them in their own words. The editing technique consists of lifting a scene out of context and splicing it to another in such a way that the second subject makes a rebuttal to the first. In *Harvest of Shame*, for example, a farmer was asked how well he thought the migrant laborers liked their stoop labor in the fields, and he answered: "They love it. They really wouldn't do anything else." This scene was spliced to another in which a woman laborer was asked how well she liked working in the fields and she answered, in effect: "I hate it. I would do anything to get out of working in the fields."

Cross-cutting is one of the more effective documentary forms in arousing pathos and understanding of the subject. In *The Tenement*, a film intended to explore the human consequences of the black dilemma in America, the cross-cut technique was used to let the tenants speak for themselves. Their imminent eviction to make way for an urban renewal project served as an opening gambit for interviews in which they were encouraged to discuss other aspects of their troubled lives. In this way the viewer saw and felt the problem in terms of human feelings.

The Television News Documentary and the Public Interest

Television has become the new political forum of American democracy. What a Senator has to say about an issue for the television cameras may have far more influence than what he says in the Senate; and indeed, if his televised statement evokes a strong public response, it may affect the outcome of a vote on such issues as a law, a treaty or an appropriation. Proposed legislation may be made or broken by its interpretation over television. Matters of national and foreign policy may be affected by the way an important political figure answers or evades difficult questions.

Moreover, the vast public exposure of the television system may shape or even create the events that appear before the camera. It is common knowledge that demonstrators tend to appear and riots explode wherever and whenever it is known in advance that the eye of television will be present to watch, and there is almost invariably a spokesman on the spot prepared to give reporters articulate reasons why the "spontaneous" outburst occurred. Moreover, two "spontaneous" demonstrations seldom take place in the same city at the same time for the simple reason that television crews cannot simultaneously give full coverage to two events. This raises the inevitable question: How many events are staged for the publicity value offered by the television cameras that would not otherwise occur?

Modification of behavior for the benefit of television is another and perhaps more insidious factor. A head of state may speak quite differently when conversing off-the-record with an informal group of correspondents than when addressing a televised press conference. Rioters may riot more violently when viewed by the television cameras, and may concentrate their fury within the scope and depth of focus of a 12-to-120 zoom lens. And even the armed forces may time their military sorties to suit the comfort and convenience of television crews, even though inappropriate for the tactical exigencies of battle, in order to enhance their public image; indeed, the armed forces have been known to stage military actions for the benefit of the cameras in advance of combat so that there would be appropriate documentary film footage to report in the news when the anabasis actually took place. The makers of news and documentary events—politicians, rioters and policemen alike—may change the nature of their actions to accommo-

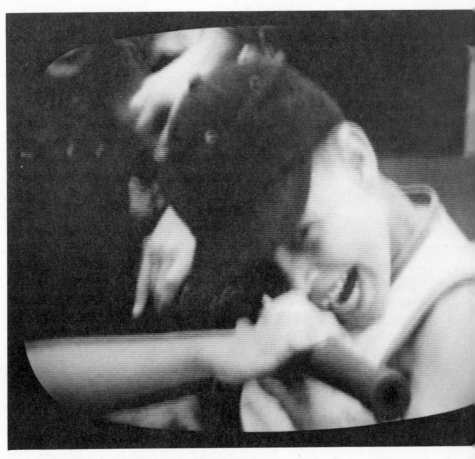

THE SELLING OF THE PENTAGON. *CBS News.*

date the nature of a camera which, in theory, is only there to record the event.

And yet, as measured by any criterion, Americans today are better informed citizens than they have ever been at any time in the history of the Republic, with a broader understanding of current world affairs, a more specific grasp of domestic problems and a greater fund of factual knowledge about friend and foe alike than ever before. This growing awareness is due in large measure to the efforts of the news departments and the documentary filmmakers of CBS, NBC and ABC, who do their dedicated best to present all pertinent facts about an issue over television for the enlightenment of the American people. In this endeavor they have, as a whole, been supported by the policy-making executives of the networks—when it does not gore the interests of a sponsor—and the networks' financial support of news and television documentary film-making has contributed immeasurably to the public interest.

When one considers the long track record of a single television documentary film, beginning with its sensitizing of the perceptions of millions of viewers to important events in the world, its stimulus function in the cultural life of the nation, its exposure of corruption and legal reforms and its repeated services in teaching the young in the schools of America, it seems appropriate to submit that no other film or television form achieves more lasting measurable good than does the television documentary film.

16

Historical, Ethnographic, and Natural History Film

A number of related documentary forms have evolved which have distinctive characteristics and requirements. These forms include the *historical compilation documentary*, the *ethnographic documentary* and the *natural history film*. They are produced for many· purposes, ranging from the entertainment-with-information appeal for a general television audience of millions, to schoolroom instruction for classes numbering in the hundreds of thousands, to research data for scholars counted by the dozens.

The Historical Compilation Documentary

PURPOSES, ORIGINS AND DEVELOPMENT

The historical compilation film is an attempt to re-create the great events of the past so that the viewer may not only see what happened, but also vicariously feel the emotions, experience the drama and capture the flavor of the past through the perceptual forms of motion pictures and television.

The historical film stands apart from other documentary forms in several ways. In purpose, it is theoretically not concerned with persuasion, but with an authentic re-creation and documentation of historical events. In content, it is limited and defined by the events that actually occurred and the men who actually participated. In cinematic substance, it is limited to the visual material the filmmaker can obtain in the forms of archives motion picture footage, videotapes, old photographs and paintings, records and audiotapes, artifacts, buildings and monuments. The filmmaker must work with remnants; what is past is past, and the historical compilation producer cannot go on location to photograph the people and events of bygone days.

Because film compels belief with an authority that compares only with reality itself, historical compilation documentaries are sometimes made by those who wish to use the past to serve the interests of the present by interpreting history to serve their immediate purposes. Such films and television programs are often produced to gain public support for hard-to-understand national policies, to raise money for foundations and other institutions or to inculcate hatred or contempt for another nation or creed. In television, where the genre has reached its zenith, the historical compilation documentary is used primarily to make sentimental journeys into the past, to create inspiring epics of recent history and to educate the public about the origins of contemporary dilemmas and problems.

The historical compilation film may also be used to create an awareness of one's heritage, a personal feeling of continuity and place within the ongoing mainstream of a culture. The CBS film series *Of Black America* recounted the contributions of black Americans to the development of their nation. This historical series revised the simplistic "slave and slum" image of the Negro to one of distinction and pride, providing a stimulus to further achievements by the black American viewer. The historical film may be used to instill patriotism, in the best sense, by revealing the struggles and achievements of national heroes placed in the perspective of history and in context with the mistakes that may have been made along the way.

The historical compilation form was born in the turmoil of the Russian Civil War, after 1918, when Dziga Vertov was inspired to compile the photographed events of that traumatic time and edit the scenes into statements of history, ideology and spirit for the posterity of his nation. The concept of compiling footage photographed at random into definitive statements of time and place then evolved into the realistic documentary of the twenties, with Ruttmann's *Berlin* and Cavalcanti's *Rien Que Les Heures*. During the thirties the film footage photographed in the past began to serve the political exigencies of the present, veering sharply to the political Left and Right, in such films as *The Spanish Earth* and *Triumph of the Will*.

The American historical compilation film has its roots in the Depression *March of Time* series, a journalistic effort which attempted to put the world news of the day in perspective in a way that would enable the viewer to understand its significance. Although some sequences in the series were staged—transparently so—most of the footage was compiled from authentic newsreel footage. With Pearl Harbor and the coming of World War II, a series of films was needed to explain to the American people why the nation found itself with guns in hand, and Frank Capra was assigned to supervise the production of the *Why We Fight* series. These wartime documentaries followed the earlier format of combining newsreel footage with staged scenes and were persuasive at the time (though not many have stood the test of time—styles of acting change). The worldwide conflict was photographically documented on a comprehensive scale, yielding footage for such classics as *The Battle of San Pietro* and *The True Glory*, and later providing the raw material for television's historical compilation series.

The advent of television soon led to the production of great numbers of historical compilation documentaries treating a broad spectrum of topics, under such titles as *The Jazz Age* and *The Thirties*. The single television "special" quickly proved too small a format, however, to undertake the presentation of the complex events of contemporary history. A serialized format was needed to present a comprehensive episode-related history of the great events of the twentieth century.

The serialized historical compilation film was launched by four television series: *Victory at Sea*, created by the National Broadcasting Corporation; *The Valiant Years*, produced by the American Broadcasting Association; *War in the Air*, recounted by the British Broadcasting Corporation; and *The Great War of 1914–18*, presented by the Columbia Broadcasting Corporation. These popular histories were handled very loosely in terms of the real chronology of events, but their relationships were logical and their cinematic interpretations artistic.

Possibly the most magnificent of these historical compilation series was found in the twenty-six-week NBC chronicle of World War II, *Victory at Sea*, launched in 1952. This enormous undertaking first required that the producers, Henry Salomon and Isaac Kleinerman, scan sixty million feet of combat footage—twelve hundred miles long—photographed during the war by combat cameramen from the United States, Britain, France, Japan, Germany and Italy. After a year of marathon viewing, about sixty thousand feet were selected for editing into twenty-six episodes. With completion of the editing phase, the films were ready for their orchestration of image, narration, music and sound effects.

The narration, written by Salomon and Richard Hauser, was terse, low key and contained not one more word than was needed to clarify the living images. A monumental musical score composed by Richard Rodgers for each episode of the saga was perfectly synchronized with the edited film and the narration; the growl of airplane engines was integrated into the musical score and bomb bursts and machine-gun fire were used as percussion. The music was an extraordinary achievement which ranged the gamut of emotional appeals, now martial, now tender, now melodious, now orchestral, but always complementing the edited images: brave men and burning planes; the body of a dead soldier rocking gently in the surf of a beachhead; the near-miss of a kamikaze pilot; the marine holding his helmet over the face of a wounded buddy to keep off the rain. This orchestration of picture and sound created the closest thing to exaltation with carnage as anyone has yet managed to say in film about war.

HISTORICAL SOURCES

Sources of visual material for the historical compilation filmmaker fall into six general categories: *archives film footage, still photographs* and *artwork, monuments* and *artifacts* and *interviews*.

Making do with the *archives film footage* available for compilation raises certain questions and temptations: First, does the archives footage document those events that were of genuine historical importance? Second, since the events that were photographed are likely to have been sensational in nature rather than representative of the times, will a historical film made from such footage place the events in false perspective? A film structured around available footage may be an easy way out for the filmmaker, but it comes at the price of rewriting history for the viewer. Many a "historical compilation film" which has been broadcast over television or produced for educational film libraries has distorted its subject or was flatly erroneous because the filmmaker took the easy way out and produced a film based solely on the available film archives footage.

The supply of unused historical footage is not inexhaustible. Television filmmakers have scoured the archives for untapped reservoirs of newsreel footage to produce such compilation series as *The Twentieth Century* and the Wolper Biographies of great men. Theoretically, there is a bottom to the barrel, and the bottom is being scraped to the extent that the same scenes are being used to represent different events, in different films, produced by different filmmakers. One scene showing Nationalist Chinese soldiers advancing behind a tank has been used repeatedly in films portraying the Sino-Japanese War of the thirties and the Nationalist-Communist Civil War of the forties, apparently on the theory that when you have seen one Chinese soldier walking behind a tank you have seen them all.

Still photographs and *artwork* may be added to historical compilation films to flesh out those events in the past that were not chronicled by cinematography. Filmograph techniques on the animation stand, such as pans and compound moves over static images, may be used to infuse the pictures with movement. Dissolves provide a smooth transition from one still to the next, the yielding quality of the optical effect itself implying movement.

A stunning example of the incorporation of stills with motion picture footage was found in the film *City of Gold*. The film began with contemporary live-action footage of Dawson City in the Yukon, as the producer reminisced over his boyhood days in the weathered remnants of what was once a gold-mining boom town. The motion picture sequence then held a scene in which the subjects were immobile, and a long dissolve began the transition to the filmograph sequences of still photographs in so subtle a way that the viewer was scarcely aware of the transformation. The central portion of the film then recounted the great events of the gold rush over the Chilkoot Pass at the turn of the century rendered in filmograph. In conclusion the film returned once again to live-action footage of Dawson City today, completing the sojourn from film to filmograph and back again to film.

The filmmaker can also turn to extant *monuments* and *artifacts* still available for cinematography: ancient houses, fortifications and castles; rifles, rapiers and cannons; household utensils and furniture; costumes, uniforms and armour; gliders, airplanes and rockets; models, reconstructions and dioramas. And always there are the locations where pivotal events took place, such as Gettysburg, Valley Forge and Independence Hall, Philadelphia, still redolent with the ghosts of great men, great events, great times, waiting to be photographed for mood and atmosphere. To render the scenes he needs on film or videotape, the filmmaker may take his cameras to the ancient objects, or bring the ancient objects to the studio.

Interviews with eyewitnesses or participants in great events may add insight, flavor, richness and a living touch to historical compilation films. Winning generals may relive their victories and sagacious statesmen may relate the essence of their life experiences for the benefit of posterity. When *CBS Reports* filmed then-General Eisenhower on the battle-scarred Normandy beachhead, his descriptions of what happened there during the battle added authenticity and feeling to a living image of a historical turning point. In programs dealing with the distant past scholars may be interviewed in the shadow of artifacts and architecture to offer their expertise on the circumstances surrounding great events in the crucible of history. Sir Kenneth Clark's brilliant BBC television series *Civilisation* was such an example, and history was enlivened by his vital personality.

Western statesmen and public figures now have a tradition of submitting to interviews by reporters to explain their actions and policies, interviews which are recorded on film or videotape. Moreover, the friends, colleagues and associates of the powerful and the famous are also interviewed for permanent record in the media. These comprehensive statements will provide a deep reservoir of narrative material for producers of historical compilation films in the future. So vast has been the commitment of interviews to the media since World War II that merely reviewing material to find a specific item resembles the search for the needle in the haystack. And yet, it is better to have it all than not to have it. The value of these interviews to contemporary historians and historical filmmakers, and to future generations, is incalculable.

The dialogue from an interview may be utilized later as voice-over narration in conjunction with scenes rendering visually what the lecturer or interviewee is discussing. This was the case in *The Valiant Years*, the ABC production of the life of Winston Churchill. Going a step further, the recorded voices of various persons who were participants in great events, or friends and associates of participants, may reveal insights and observations that can later be edited, in subjective microphone technique, to provide a narration track for appropriate visual sequences. Sometimes a phrase spoken casually during an interview may provide a title or theme for the historical compilation film or television program.

These elements, then, are the raw materials from which the historical compilation documentary is made. But the collation of archives film footage, still photographs and artwork, monuments and artifacts, and interviews is only a prelude to the real problems of production.

PRODUCTION

Producing a compilation film means creating an intelligible story with scenes that were photographed at widely separated times and places, without any thought that they would be assembled in this historical documentary relationship. This jumble of random scenes creates serious problems of continuity and consistency, and staggering problems for cinematic excellence. Such niceties as controlling the centers of interest and consistency of film grains from one scene to the next are often impossible; sometimes even fundamentals, such as control of screen directions, are out of the question. The production of a historical compilation film is a matter of utilizing whatever is available from the film archives, adding to it footage taken of artwork and old photographs, plus whatever can be made of artifacts and ruins, and editing them into a reasonably meaningful order. The editor is the dominant creative filmmaker in the production of a historical compilation film.

The writer is second but equal to the editor in importance, and the two are an inseparable team. The writer may enhance the sense of continuity through his narrative pattern of logic and description and create the impression that these scenes, in this order, are exactly the scenes the filmmakers had wanted all along. In some cases, when the visual relationship between scenes is tenuous or nonexistent, the writer may create the only binding continuity that exists.

When certain historical events went unrecorded by any visual means, the writer can make the best of a bad bargain by describing them in voice-over narration and risk having them forgotten by the viewer. An additional shortcoming to presenting unrelated picture and sound tracks is that it tends to split the viewer's attention, so that he mentally flicks back and forth between picture and sound and misses some of each.

The producers of *Czechoslovakia, 1968* found themselves faced with most of the problems inherent in producing a historical compilation film. The filmmakers were given the assignment of recounting the brief independent life of that unlucky nation from its creation after World War I through its crushing under tank treads in 1968, at a time when the mood of the occupiers was one of total control, total censorship, total noncooperation. The filmmakers' cinematic solutions provide a classic example of resourcefulness in obtaining the visual means to make the film, beginning with the most recent events and working back to the earliest.

The filmmakers' first move was to obtain film footage photographed at the time of the foreign invasion. Some of it came from news photographers, some was photographed from television screens at the time and some came from the 8 mm. and Super 8 cameras of Western tourists who were in Prague when the Russians marched in. From these varied sources came footage of the Russian tanks rolling in with a phalanx of marching Soviet troops, and the images of young Czech people carrying their nation's flag dipped in the blood of the slain.

The producers' second move was a search through the film archives to find World War II footage of the earlier invasion of Czechoslovakia by Nazi Germany. The archives yielded scenes of the Munich Pact with Hitler, which sold out Czechoslovakia's independence, Nazi troops sweeping into the Sudetenland, gaunt, cadaverous Jews being herded into pens for the slaughter, and the arrival of the Russian tanks that drove out the defeated Germans.

The filmmakers then searched still farther back in time for scenes of Czechoslovakia's life between the two World Wars and found only a few snippits of folk dancing, a marriage and religious ceremonies. This was not enough, so they ferreted around for old illustrations and slides, and photographed them on the animation stand using filmograph techniques. The filmmakers now had scenes of the contemporary intervention, scenes of World War II and filmograph footage of pastoral prewar Czechoslovakia—the raw material for a historical compilation film.

Visual inconsistency was the next problem. The footage portraying contemporary Czechoslovakia was photographed in black and white as well as in color, in 16 mm., Super-8 and 8 mm. formats. When the smaller formats were enlarged to 16 mm. the inconsistency of the differing film grains became glaring. The World War II footage had been photographed in black and white on old-fashioned coarse-grained film

CZECHOSLOVAKIA, 1968. *Denis Sanders and Robert Fresco.*

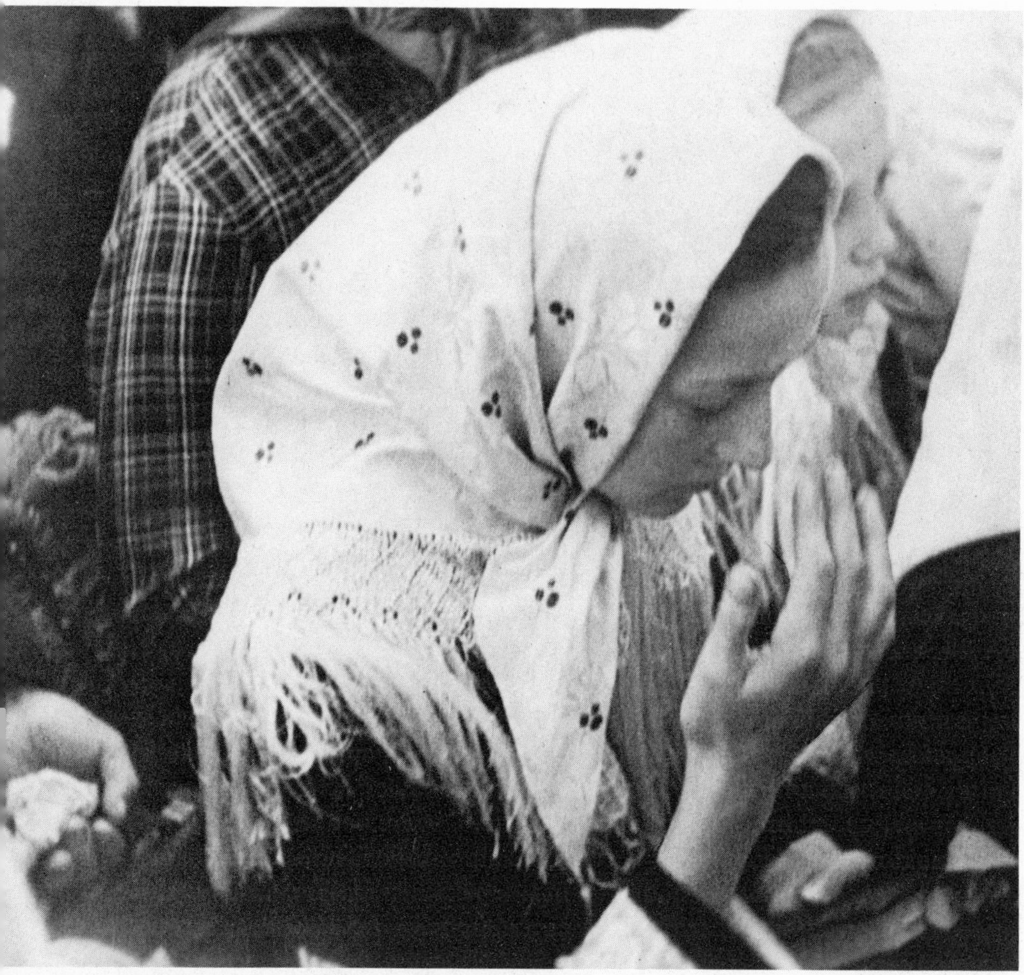

CZECHOSLOVAKIA, 1968. *Denis Sanders and Robert Fresco.*

CZECHOSLOVAKIA, 1968. *Denis Sanders and Robert Fresco.*

CZECHOSLOVAKIA, 1968. *Denis Sanders and Robert Fresco.*

CZECHOSLOVAKIA, 1968. *Denis Sanders and Robert Fresco.*

CZECHOSLOVAKIA, 1968. *Denis Sanders and Robert Fresco.*

CZECHOSLOVAKIA, 1968. *Denis Sanders and Robert Fresco.*

stock, with widely differing exposures. The still older silent-film stock had been photographed at a slower projection speed, and the stills and slides had been taken from faded photographs that varied widely in quality. When the work-print sequences were viewed for editing, they revealed the most glaring inconsistencies from one scene to the next. The filmmakers decided not to apologize for the variations but to exploit them cinematically.

They decided to use a color code to connote different qualities of life in the brief history of Czechoslovakia: black and white for times of grief and anguish, such as the deaths of children and the incarceration of the Jews; amber for reminiscences of early Czechoslovakian history and folkways, and for hard work in relative peace; crimson for the times of war and conquest; and full color for the days of freedom during the Prague Spring.

Still slides and photographs were incorporated in a clever way in *Czechoslovakia, 1968.* The film began with the introduction of a carousel projector and the ostensible projection of slides showing the quality of life in that nation during the early years of its existence after 1917. The stills were photographed on the animation stand with a slight flash of in-out movement, as if being projected and edited into the film with this slight movement. The sparse motion picture archives films of that period, all photographed at silent-film speed, were intercut with the stills in scenes so brief that the slower projection speed was undetectable.

As the years progressed to the sound-film era of World War II (the passage of years noted by closeups of numbers on the slide projector: 41-42-43-44-45, etc.), the transition from stills to silent-film to sound-film speed became virtually complete. For the sake of consistency throughout the film, however, and for dramatic emphasis, the motif of the still was preserved in the periodic use of freeze-frames. A freeze-frame number "68" was the last scene in the tragedy before returning to the image of the carousel projector, as if the entire film had been a slide presentation. Then the light faded out in the projection lamp to end *Czechoslovakia, 1968.*

Narration is sometimes extremely important in compilation films, because the images do not always present a recognizable pattern of events without some explanation. When the visual presentation is extremely disjointed, there may be no alternative but a lengthy explanation. An effective way to link image and sound into one fused impression is to find a quotation, a bit of information or a vivid sentence that will illuminate the images that follow without further explanation. As usual, the fewer statements the better; narration should be concerned with essences, not details, and simultaneously express thought, atmosphere and theme. Compression is vital, timing imperative.

The relationship between the spoken word and the living image should be complementary in a precise and subtle way. *Czechoslovakia, 1968* had only one word of narration—"Svoboda." "Svoboda" was cried out in desperation after the foreign tanks had rolled in to put an end to the Prague Spring, the instant before the Czechoslovakian people took to the streets to resist the invaders. The total absence of narration to that point, coupled with exquisite sensitivity in placing it at the most poignant moment in the film, gave "svoboda" immense emotional impact. Moreover, the context of the word made its meaning so clear that viewers invariably surmise correctly what "svoboda" means—freedom.

Music is another important means of binding unrelated historical scenes together in a semblance of continuity with an overall emotional flavor. A mishmash of random subjects may become a mosaic of subtle relationships through the cohesive quality and character of a song. The days of freedom in *Czechoslovakia, 1968*, for example, were rendered visually by such disparate scenes as a pretty girl eating a fruit, a man applauding a speech, a couple drinking beer, a group of men kidding each other, a car coming off the assembly line and Premier Dubcek smiling at an inside joke with a friend—all unified by the voice of a man singing a Czechoslovakian love song.

The Ethnographic Documentary

Origins

The first ethnographic film was also the first documentary film: *Nanook of the North*, produced in 1922 by Robert Flaherty, told the story of life among the Eskimos through the eyes of one who respected and admired those courageous people. This first report on a dying culture presented scenes of Eskimos fishing, building igloos, feeding sled dogs, harpooning walrus and seal, plus a few novelty stunts, such as having Nanook listen to a phonograph record for the first time. Although the purist filmmaker in ethnography or anthropology might wrinkle his nose today at some of the heroics and obvious faking of events for the benefit of the camera, the ethnographic film began with *Nanook of the North*.

Today, many museums and universities, concerned that ancient cultures may vanish without a trace, have sent film units into the field to record the ways of primitive peoples before they are gone forever. The National Geographic Society has sent teams to the far reaches of the earth to record the social structure, behavioral patterns and relationships, physical types, mores and beliefs, arts, architecture and artifacts of moribund societies, in such films as *Polynesian Adventure*, and *Ethiopia: The Hidden Empire*.

FORMS

Motion pictures and videotape are used in the formal study of ethnology and anthropology primarily as an aid to memory. Few professionals in those fields would any longer rely on taking notes, making sketches and trying to remember the specific details of a culture they were studying. Few would lay aside the camera and the tape recorder and other technological devices that have transformed their professions from "the study of oddments by eccentrics" to respected sciences. The motion picture or videotape camera can recall everything that lends itself to cinematography in explicit detail, "drawing" the living image with far greater exactitude than the artist could in a fraction of the time. The tape recorder can render songs and the subtleties of language more explicitly than the most complex system of notation. The media exist in this field as the most precise system yet devised for one man to present data to another in a language of universal recognition.

Subject matter has been the traditional basis for classifying ethnographic research films. The broad classifications have been *primitive, tribal* and *ethnic subject matter*.

The applications of film and videotape to the study of cultures tend to fall into specific purviews of emphasis: *artifacts*, their production and uses; *ecology*, the relationship of the people under study to their environment; *ritual*, the traditional ceremonies and songs dealing with coming of age, marriage, birth, death, religion and ascension to office; *social structure*, the personal and intragroup behavior and activities that affect the actions and prestige of the individual in his relations with others of the community; *power structure*, the nature and constitution of authority, and the bases for selecting leaders, arbitrating disputes and settling issues of war and peace. These are the basic research areas of the ethnographic or anthropological filmmaker.

Within each category the task of the filmmaker is to collect audio-visual data which he or others will later be able to analyze. This data is modified by three factors: the exhibition of the phenomenon under study; the selective perception of that phenomenon by the filmmaker, who is usually outside the culture of the peoples under study; and the nature of the film, tape and videotape recording technology. In other words, what the viewer will see on the screen is not necessarily pure data, but is modified by what the subject peoples are willing to have photographed, the selective perception of the filmmaker and the forms of activity that fall within the capacity of the media to record. The intent of the filmmaker should be to keep to a minimum the transformation involved between phenomenon and data and the modification inherent in using the data in a film or television program. Every step away from the phenomenon usually leads to some transformation because of the effect of the filmmaker's own tastes and skills on his selective perception while photographing and editing the scenes.

Visual data should be photographed as explicitly as possible, presenting all the points of view necessary to offer a valid understanding of the subject to the viewer from another culture. The visual data of color, motion and interaction must be the closest possible approximation of reality.

The *visual data* are, however, only one of the research tools used in ethnographic and anthropological research, and they are used in conjunction with *written data, material data* and *auditory data. Written data* deal with the time, place, size, shape and temperature of the observed phenomena, noted in the forms of measurements, diagrams and quantified or verbalized information. *Material data* are the collected material, such as soils, plants, foods and such forms of material culture as may lend themselves to subsequent analysis. And finally there are *auditory data,* such as music, language and folklore. All four forms of data, considered together, constitute basic research material for the ethnographer and anthropologist, and elements of these data may subsequently be selected for inclusion in a film or television program.

Finished ethnographic and anthropology films generally fall into three cinematic forms, depending on how they are edited: The *research film* is a collation of visual data spliced together in chronological order, without cinematic or editorial embellishment. The *documentary* form attempts to unite as many cultural elements as is practical to present an overview of the ethnic, tribal or primitive culture, using editing tempo

POLYNESIAN ADVENTURE. Production of artifacts. *National Geographic Society.*

CIRCLE OF THE SUN. Cultural stress. *National Film Board of Canada.*

and other cinematic techniques to capture the flavor and excitement of life among the peoples under study. The *art film* or entertainment film utilizes only those visual elements of the film or videotape footage whose shapes, forms, colors and movements lend themselves to an appeal to the viewer's aesthetic sensibilities.

Films that attempt to treat such abstract and difficult relationships as the Indians' attempts to adjust to the white man, while trying to retain remnants of their old order for their children, are almost forced to take the documentary rather than the research form. In *Circle of the Sun*, for example, it was shown how Indian parents tried to raise their children in the traditions of feathered regalia and ritual dances, while sending them to school to learn white culture and to town to get jobs. The emotional disturbances that accompanied this cultural schizophrenia were revealed in closeups of the faces of distressed Indians and in descriptive insights related by the narrator.

VIEWPOINTS

Objective and subjective viewpoints have a special connotation in films dealing with sociological and ecological relationships, each viewpoint serving a different end purpose.

The *objective viewpoint* is the ethnographic filmmaker's viewpoint, in which he speaks as an omniscient observer, pointing out things for the viewer to observe, explaining the significance of songs, dances, gestures and the pecking order of the society being studied. The objective viewpoint enables him, for example, to relate the Eskimo to the climate of his homeland, the ecology of his terrain, the effects of wildlife migrations on his life style and the influences of white culture, in a way that is meaningful to the lay viewer, in a form that may transcend the Eskimo's own understanding of his culture. Important cultural elements within the scenes can be pointed out that might otherwise slide by unobserved. The objective viewpoint has the disadvantage, however, of imposing the intellectual and cultural framework of an outsider on a film presenting an alien culture.

The *subjective viewpoint* in ethnographic film lets the subject explain how he feels about himself and his work. The subjective viewpoint often reveals feelings, values, attitudes and concerns that lie beyond the conscious control of an alien filmmaker or ethnographer. Ideally, a native Eskimo would make the subjective film about Eskimos. The Eskimo would relate how *he* feels about his songs, dances and sociological structures, how *he* views the land, the climate, the wildlife and the influences of the white man, with *his* value system imposed upon the description of all these relationships. This use of the subjective viewpoint may provide basic data to the ethnographer on the subject culture. A research film of this kind, however, if presented to a lay audience without interpretation, could result in several elements of ethnographic importance passing unnoticed by the viewer. The subjective-film approach tends to discard many cinematic conventions in order to represent the modes of perception and value system of the people under study. The folk labels of the culture are given to the visual data, together with their relationships, with the viewer having to follow it all as best he can.

Both objective and subjective viewpoints attempt to determine and reveal the values of the people under study. Both attempt to explain the motivations and compulsions governing individual and group behavior in a culture. The decision of which to use lies in the intent of the person making the film. If the filmmaker is trying to obtain basic data from which to draw inferences, then the subjective viewpoint is best. If he is trying to explain the culture of one people to the viewers of another, then the objective viewpoint is preferred. In films of fairly long duration, such as a one-hour television special, it may be possible to include both viewpoints alternately: the objective viewpoint may be used to alert the viewer to what he is about to see and hear, then the subjective viewpoint can be presented as the subject speaks for himself, and then the objective viewpoint may be offered once again as the ethnographer explains and clarifies what the viewer has just seen.

MOTION ANALYSIS

New trends of ethnographic analysis utilizing visual data are based upon studies of movements and relationships. Among these are *ethnopediatrics*, which deals with a growing child's relationships with his parents and other members of his society, and the upbringing that socializes him to become a member of the cultural system. *Kinesics* is the study of the connotative meanings of individual gestures. And *nonverbal communication* defines how personal gestures are integrated into personal interaction within the cultural complex. Each of these areas requires the use of cinematic editing techniques of action and reaction to make valid presentations, although they may appear to purists to be a deviation from the essential research film.

When the movements and interactions of the people are themselves the subjects of study, such as what occurs during a dance, cinematography may be faster than sound speed to obtain a slow-motion effect for careful analysis in playback. Other activities that involve long periods of waiting for each change may be recorded at 12 frames per second, or at time-lapse intervals, to obtain the needed visual data while conserving expensive film and videotape. The reasons for selecting the kind of equipment used to record a given social activity should be written down, as well as notations on the limitations encountered in recording the visual data, so the validity of the data could be more accurately assessed.

BIAS

Bias in the subjects' attitudes may be an important factor among the people under study, with societies and individuals reacting in a variety of ways. There are some primitive cultures whose people believe the camera lens represents "the evil eye," and a photograph a "stolen spirit." In other societies the people may have been exposed to the media and have notions about how they should appear on film or television, and thus continuously pose before the lens. In still other societies, such as certain American Indian tribes, the ethnographic film-maker may have to negotiate contracts requiring a payment of earnest money, royalties and residual rights in perpetuity before he can photograph a frame of film. There are a few places in the world where the people have never been exposed to media, such as certain islands of Polynesia and the hinterlands of Ethiopia, and there the subjects may be unconcerned with cinematography. Even in those ideal situations, however, bias remains a factor in recording attitudes because individuals in those cultures are always interacting on a personal basis with the ethnographic filmmakers.

Hostility toward the stranger is not unique to primitive cultures. Taboos against outsiders in general, and outside filmmakers and television producers in particular, are common among those religious groups whose premise is that all manifestations of the modern world are evil. Their policy is often to rigorously exclude all the temptations and corruptions of urbanized life from their society and live in the patterns of the past. Under such circumstances the ethnographic filmmaker may at first find himself facing a solidly closed door. When producers from the National Film Board of Canada first undertook the production of *The Hutterites* the initial response of that group was a flat refusal. The resolution of the problem of gaining entry to the Hutterite colonies, persuading them to temporarily suspend the prohibition against cinematography and converting their attitude from resistance to cooperation deserves study and emulation.

The producers first sought out a liaison who was respected by the Hutterites, sympathetic to their values, but at the same time worldly in the sense of understanding the working relationships between that sect and the public at large. They found their intermediary in the legal counsel to the Hutterites, a former member of Alberta's Parliament, who had assisted the colony with its tax and land title problems. The producers explained the purpose of their projected documentary film— to reveal the true nature of the Hutterite way of life from their own point of view—and thereby to dispel unfounded public prejudices against that community.

THE HUTTERITES. Dispelling prejudice. *National Film Board of Canada.*

The attorney agreed that such a film would serve the Hutterites' own best interests. He wrote a letter to the colony's leaders urging them to consider cooperating in the production of such a film, and asked for a consensus. The letter was read and discussed in the religious community, and a meeting was then convened with the filmmakers. At this meeting all who wished to express their moral opposition to the project were permitted to make resounding statements of Hutterite principle, exalting subservience to God and professing that the example set by the Hutterite communal life served as the true pattern for mankind. This moral pattern, they avowed, did not include watching or appearing in motion pictures or television. In response, the producer pointed out that this production was a government-sponsored, nonprofit venture that would not be shown in commercial theaters, but would be used only in civic showings to engender sympathy and understanding for the Hutterite beliefs and way of life. After the importance of the film to the Hutterites' own best interests was made clear, the community agreed to cooperate fully and the film was successfully produced.

The interview is often the only means of offering insight into the problems of a culture that would not otherwise be revealed to the camera. In *The Hutterites* an interview with a preacher of that faith included some pointed questions about Hutterite beliefs and problems —family factions, colony frictions, dissenters—which partly resolved the ethnographic dilemma of revealing the invisible thorns in that community's side.

The cinematic biases of the filmmaker are important because everything that appears on the screen is the result of his selective perception. If the ethnographer or anthropologist knows how to run a camera, he will probably obtain the kinds of visual data useful for research. The resulting footage may be difficult to make into a literate film or television program, however, because the content expert is often unconcerned with such editing factors as continuity, screen directions, transitions and so forth, and feels that making a good film is just a matter of "splicing the stuff together."

The other side of the bias coin occurs when a filmmaker is sent on assignment into an ethnographic or anthropological context without any content knowledge of the culture, but with high aspirations toward creating a cinematic work of art. He frequently becomes preoccupied with aesthetic factors and slights the job of garnering visual data. Ideally, the ethnographic scientist should learn how to make a film, as well as how to run a camera, to best serve the interests of basic research and ethnographic filmmaking. More pragmatically, since it takes years to become an expert filmmaker, the matter of bias will most often be resolved with a scientist standing at the shoulder of the filmmaker, the two resolving their differences as best they can.

Bias may also creep into the filmmaker's strategy of filming the subjects, depending upon the nature of their activity. Most rituals already have patterns of movement established by long custom which are relatively unaffected by the presence of the ethnographic filmmaker. The subjects simply perform their ceremonies as they always have while the cameras record their movements. Unstructured activity, on the other hand, whether subject-initiated or filmmaker-directed, tends to create the problem of "posing for the camera," with attendant losses of spontaneity and sometimes authenticity. At times the only solution to recording unstructured activity is to follow the subject's natural actions with a shoulder-mounted camera, paying close attention to cultural cues and movements as they reveal themselves. Videotape is often preferable to motion pictures for following unstructured activity, because it can be erased and reused if the recorded activity is not worth keeping, while film, once exposed, is consumed. The best of the videotaped actions can be transferred to film for incorporation in a finished film for projection. Or, conversely, the best of the film footage may be mixed with videotape on a television system for incorporation in a finished videotape for broadcast.

A degree of bias in the interpretation of a culture is also inherent in the technical limitations of equipment. A given locale of extremely rough terrain, narrow paths and heavy vegetation may restrict the film-maker's choice of equipment to what is light and portable, which may in turn prevent him from recording important cultural activities. Weather, time of day, ground conditions and availability of light also affect the interpretation of cultures, because adverse cinematography conditions may preclude making any visual record of an important social activity. Lighting facilities sometimes cause serious reaction problems among those subjects who are unaccustomed to portable artificial lighting. Flashbulbs for still photography, in particular, tend to startle primitive peoples. The ethnographic filmmaker will attempt to record the maximum visual data possible commensurate with the equipment he can take in, and he may supplement motion pictures and videotapes with still photographs which can later be given the illusion of movement on the animation stand.

MUSIC

Music is important in ethnographic films. Songs and chants evoke the very spirit of a society in a way that creates an emotional bridge between cultures. A viewer cannot hear another people's songs of love, birth and death without empathizing with that people and understanding something of their culture. Moreover, music adds authenticity to the visual statement.

While seemingly an abstruse area of filmmaking, the ethnographic and anthropological documentary is an extremely dynamic area in which concerned social scientists, anthropologists and ethnographers are making extensive and determined efforts to document aboriginal cultures before they are expunged by white civilization. These cinematic forms are unique within the documentary genre; the facts themselves create the concepts of the films, rather than facts being selected to put over an idea or to achieve a behavioral goal. Thanks to ethnographic filmmakers, the living images of past and present cultures will live for the future.

The Natural History Film

ORIGINS

The origins of the nature film antedates film itself. As early as 1887 Edweard Muybridge had photographed some 34 animals and birds in 123 kinds of motion by rigging a series of cameras along their routes of movement, with shutters that were tripped by strings stretched across the creatures' paths and broken by their passing. These stills-in-motion probably constituted the first natural history "research" film. Dating back a little farther, about three hundred centuries, one can see the fascination wildlife held for mankind revealed in paintings rendered on the cave walls of Lascaux and Altamira, a fascination that can be traced through the arts of every civilization in the history of the world to the present. And now we see this atavistic love of the wild expressed in the twin major arts of our time: film and television. Like the ethnographic documentary, the natural history film takes three basic forms: *research, documentary* and *art or entertainment.*

FORMS

The first natural history films produced in America were research films. Educational film catalogues, published around 1910, were filled with short studies of flowers blooming, bees pollinating flowers, birds nesting, elk migrating, buffalo giving birth to their young and so forth. These brief educational films, some of them only a minute or two in length, soon evolved into more ambitious forms that attempted to relate the migration patterns of wild ducks and geese, combining animation with maps with live-action sequences of geese in flight, and to make serious attempts at documenting the true ecological life of other wild species. Their quick adoption in the curricula of schools soon led to a continuing trickle of natural history documentaries that had expanded to a small stream by the 1940s.

Eventually, virtually all life sciences courses in American schools at the elementary, secondary and university levels began to make intensive use of natural history films, primarily in research film formats, to expand and enrich the content of their curricula. Like the ethnographic and anthropology documentaries, these research films are concerned with cycles of birth, courtship, mating, migration and death, and the relationship of a given species to other birds and animals and to the general ecology of its life space. Recent trends in nature films have been toward the study of animal instincts and behavior—dominance, the need for affection, territorial imperatives—for their implications for mankind. The impact of industrial pollution on fish, birds and other animals has now become headline news and the subject of countless documentaries, based upon formal research and intended for general public viewing over film and television programming.

The Disney *True Life Nature* series produced for theaters in the 1940s and 1950s transformed the nature documentary from an obscure

GRIZZLY! Television nature studies. *National Geographic Society.*

form studied in the classroom, or enjoyed by a few sportsmen and con-
servationists, to a full-blown entertainment genre. Cameramen were
sent into the American wilderness to chronicle the life cycles of a
Noah's Ark of wildlife, ranging from the love life of the lowly scorpion
to the mating duels of the magnificent grizzly.

In some of the Disney films an ecological approach was used; in
Nature's Half Acre and *The Living Desert* the relationship of creature to creature, hunter to hunted, was presented as comprehensively as
was consonant with entertainment values. In others the life cycle of a
species was treated on a birth-to-death basis or season-to-season cycle,
as in *Bear Country* and *The Olympic Elk*. In still others the animals
were individualized and personified, as in *Perri the Squirrel* and *The
Legend of Lobo*. It was the tendency to humanize wildlife that most
offended critics and many wildlife experts; they felt that anthropo-
morphizing the animals violated the integrity of their relationships in
nature. Moreover, it was apparent to the sharp-eyed observer that
scenes of dozens of different animals were used to portray what was
ostensibly the same animal.

The musical scores of the Disney *True Life Nature* series have often
aroused the delight of the general public and the disdain of critics by
their unabashed humor. In *The Vanishing Prairie* two desert bighorn
sheep rams fought a mating duel to the accompaniment of the "Anvil
Chorus," with the head-to-head collisions edited to the beat of the music
—scarcely a realistic rendition of wildlife in the rutting season. In *The
Living Desert* two scorpions performed their mating rituals to the do-se-
do rhythms of Western square dance music, complete with a caller
chanting "Three legs up and three legs down, swing that scorpion round
and round."

The best of the television nature documentaries have probably been
such National Geographic specials as *The Mystery of Animal Behavior*
and *Grizzly!*—serious studies of creatures in the wild that have proved
immensely popular with the general public. Millions of viewers watched
the struggles for dominance within a troop of baboons; and they saw
how a stuffed leopard, animated by a car's windshield-wiper motor,
aroused a screaming signal by the dominant male for all the males in the
troop to attack. They watched the otter, clown of the sea, break the
shell of a clam by banging it on a stone borne on its chest, and then,
floating elegantly, use its stomach as a dining room table. And they
followed the shuffling lope of the polar bear across his domain of ice, an

animal so fearless that to hunt him is to be hunted by him—a man is just another meal.

PRODUCTION

The patience of Job is required to photograph wildlife for a nature documentary. Some filmmakers have had to spend a year in the field in order to get enough wildlife footage to make even one short film. A cinematographer may see a bear's territorial claw marks on the bark of a tree, set up his camera in a blind, and wait days or weeks for the bear to return. He may find some alligator eggs and wait six weeks for them to hatch. Or, he may need a scene of a heron catching fish and watch the birds for a month before a heron goes fishing within camera range.

Telephoto lenses are all-important in wildlife cinematography, as are automatic cameras, strobe lights and shutter speeds as high as 1/100,000 second. Scenes of insects, their wars and their parasites, require extremely high-powered lenses and infinite pains to get footage that would make sense cinematically. The blind at the waterhole, in which the filmmaker can hide with his camera, is standard equipment. Some birds and animals have bourgeois habits and reappear at the same times and the same places at the same times of day, and the filmmaker can sit in his hiding place and await the appointed hours. Or, if the animal is too wary, a camera may be set up with its lens focused at a given area and the shutter lever connected to a trip wire; to be sure the animal comes to the desired area, it is often necessary to put out bait. Film footage of shy animals, such as the grizzly bear, are often taken over such bait as a carcass; when the bear comes to dinner, he breaks the tripware and photographs scenes of himself.

Scientific methodology has itself become a form of entertainment in other National Geographic Society television specials. Brother naturalists John and Frank Craighead set out to tag individuals of the grizzly species, armed with rifles that shoot hypodermic darts filled with an immobilizing drug. The entire process of selecting individual bears for tagging, shooting them with the drug, examining them for unique and representative characteristics and being chased wildly by grizzlies that recovered too soon was followed by tens of millions of viewers. The natural history documentary has become one form of programming that seems to cut across all strata of society—it is watched avidly by children and adults, laborers and scholars, Republicans and Democrats.

17

The Propaganda Film

Documentary and propaganda films are two ends of the spectrum of cinematic integrity. Honest persuasion films, such as the documentary film or the fairly presented television commercial, tend to be truthful in content and candid in cinematic technique, although admittedly expressing a given point of view; such films are usually watched receptively by the viewer and their objectives given serious consideration. But if the viewer has the faintest suspicion that he is watching a film which makes use of cinematic tricks to deceive him—a propaganda film—he may reject the entire communication and leave the presentation with a hostile attitude toward the objectives of the film.

"Propaganda" is a term that has gradually changed connotation in the past few years in the film and television field. It once meant propagation of a creed or dogma, the interpretation of a subject or event from a doctrinaire point of view. Today, propaganda in television and film has come to connote spurious modes of persuasion in which media duplicity and manipulated facts are used to deceive the viewer, to make him believe or do something he would not believe or do were he presented with the truth in context. For the purposes of this book, the term "propaganda" will be used to mean an attempt to lie or distort the facts on film and television with intent to mislead the viewer.

Propaganda films, like their more honest documentary counterparts, are an attempt to control human behavior by presenting a media message designed to influence the viewer's beliefs in ways desired by the filmmaker or his sponsor. The assumption is that a film or television program may persuade the viewer to react in a predetermined way—a direct cause and effect relationship in which he responds to specific media stimuli.

In a sense all commercially distributed films are intended to be persuasive because they are produced to evoke some behavioral response in the target audience. A television drama exists as an inducement to the viewer to watch the commercial, which in turn exists to persuade the viewer to buy the advertised product. A documentary film exists to persuade the viewer to act on behalf of some social, political or economic goal, or to provide information and insight into a dilemma which aids in the decision-making process. An educational film or television program attempts to persuade students to learn the presented skills and concepts, as measured by such behavioral activities as examinations, laboratory activities and so forth. Virtually all commercial film and television programs, then, are concerned in some respect with persuasion.

What we are concerned with here, however, are those intrinsic elements of propaganda filmmaking that are used to shape the attitudes, opinions, perceptions, emotions and actions of a given target audience to the purposes of the filmmaker—elements of thematic concept and cinematic technique which may find application in every context in which film and television programming is used to change or reinforce the viewer's beliefs.

A fundamental characteristic of propaganda film is its appeal to the emotions, rather than to the intellect, by pairing the topic in question with another having known emotional associations, thereby effecting a transfer of emotions to the new topic in the mind of the viewer. This chapter will explore those factors of emotional transfer and cinematic technique that relate to the propaganda effectiveness of motion pictures and television: *source credibility factors, anxiety levels in the viewer, film techniques of persuasion and propaganda, the sound track, other propaganda devices, the dramatic form in persuasion and wartime propaganda themes.*

Source Credibility Factors

Source credibility is important in any form of persuasive communication because it may make or break viewer acceptability of the message. In television and film source credibility refers to the degree to which the persons responsible for the film's message, or those appearing within it to endorse that message, are considered worthy of belief by the viewer.

In a closed totalitarian society, such as Communist China, source credibility is maintained by state control of all the sources of information and by intersource consistency in the information communicated. If the information about a subject received from all sources by the citizen of a closed society is in agreement, and if the experiences of his daily life provide no evidence to the contrary, he may have little reason to doubt the credibility of his information sources.

Source credibility in open societies, such as Japan or the United States or the nations of Western Europe, is quite another matter. Here different sources compete openly for public support, with different information and points-of-view on the same subject; each source is eager to present information supporting its own point-of-view and expose any sham on the part of the other sources. The viewer is relatively free to see, compare and draw his own conclusions. "Seeing is believing" the saying goes, and the viewer who is presented with a film purportedly documenting an event may well believe this facsimile of reality. On the other hand, the adult viewer in an open society is not automatically receptive. He has seen and heard enough conflicting claims to respond to his films with a certain degree of skepticism. Those viewers accustomed to watching film and television programs have probably acquired a high degree of film literacy, and many are quite aware that film images may be manipulated through cinematography, editing and special effects to create a meaning not inherent in the original film footage. Always there lurks the subcutaneous suspicion that what one is seeing may not be the way it really is—unless it comes from a source one can trust.

Source credibility may derive from the prestige of high office, professional prestige or a consistent level of performance in the past. The "halo effect" refers to the power of some high-status sources to endorse almost anything and thereby transfer their own prestige to the new subject, an example being the effect of statements made by the Pope upon many devout Catholics. Those persons who have distinguished themselves in their professions also have the power, by virtue of the knowledge and skill implicit in their success, to endorse a product or policy and have their endorsement constitute sufficient "proof" of its merit in the mind of the viewer. But proof based upon source credibility is a specialized matter, affected by the whole spectrum of age, sex, level of formal education, socioeconomic-political milieu and life space of the viewer.

To be influenced by a prestigious person the target audience must be interested in the field in which the prestigious person has distinguished himself. The endorsement of a new foreign policy or domestic program by a distinguished intellectual—a Walter Lippmann—may influence those who follow public affairs, but those who take no interest in such matters will remain uninfluenced, except through the mediation of opinion leaders they know and respect. The endorsement of a shaving cream by the football Rookie of the Year may influence football fans, but not those who take no interest in the sport. And the appearance of a recording star in a new skirt length may send many women viewers streaming out to boutiques, credit cards in hand, but most men will remain unimpressed until they receive the bill. If he is to use proof by prestige to influence a given target audience, the filmmaker must first be sure that the chosen spokesman has the kind of prestige that will be considered proof by that audience.

Past performance is another basis on which many viewers learn to trust their sources of information. The viewer gains or loses confidence in a source, such as a television news commentator and his film clips, according to his consistency and predictability in the past. If the news commentator is consistent in presenting his interpretation of events he will come to be trusted by those who follow and endorse his point-of-view; if he never surprises the viewer by a sudden shift, his source credibility will steadily increase. If he becomes mercurial and inconsistent, his source credibility will decline. Moreover, if the commentator gives verbal information that can largely be verified, the visual information within the same program may be accepted at face value, and therein lies the opportunity for the source to slip in some propaganda in its most credible form—film. If whatever is said *verbally* can be subject to immediate challenge and verification, what is said *visually* may slide by acceptably at almost a subliminal level.

Source credibility depends to some degree on whether the source is orginating the film and interpreting the subject, or whether he is being asked only for his tacit approval or disapproval of the film's objective. The producer of a persuasion film is nearly always subject to the viewer's suspicion that he himself may have something to gain or lose by persuading the viewer that something is in the viewer's best interests. A disinterested third party enjoying high status with the target audience, on the other hand, who expresses a favorable opinion with nothing personal to gain may exert a great deal of influence. This third-party transfer of prestige to the film's objectives is modified by the viewer's attitudes toward him, such as affection and admiration, perception of his expertise, trust and confidence in his intelligence and integrity, awe and fear of his power, and the probability of reward or punishment based upon past consequences of his recommendations. It may be worth noting that viewers seldom remember exactly what the high-prestige source had to say about the objectives of the film or television program, only whether he approved or disapproved.

Source credibility is most important in terms of immediate if temporary changes in the viewer's attitudes, opinions, perceptions and actions; and of lasting effect only if the high-prestige source *asks the viewer to do something* that will reinforce the change—write to a Congressman, speak in the defense of the new position, buy the new product. An active commitment on the part of the viewer is imperative to achieve any kind of lasting change, otherwise the effect of the film or television program may fade away almost as if it had never existed.

The lasting effects of high versus low source credibility appear to be negligible. The viewer tends to remember the film's visual contents, while its association with a high or a low credibility source may be forgotten. If the substance of a film or television program has validity, and its contents are corroborated from other sources, the viewer may, with time, divorce content from source and accept the film's message— even if it comes from a low credibility source—while discounting the source.

Method of Presentation

Propaganda content may be presented in two basic ways to skirt the prejudices of the viewer. The *progressive method* is used when the means to an end are acceptable, but the end itself is not. The *single-point method* is used when the goal is acceptable, but the means of achieving it are not.

THE PROGRESSIVE METHOD

In the progressive method those ideas should be presented first of which the viewer can only approve. The trick is to get the viewer to nod approval of point after point while leading up to a dubious end purpose. For example, if an industry plans to build a factory having a waste disposal problem in a community where the inhabitants might object to the pollution, it might release a public relations film having the following content progression: The film would introduce the number of new jobs that would become available, apprise the business sector of the new customers it could anticipate, predict lower taxes because of the broader industrial base and point out the probability of improved roads as the state met its transportation responsibilities in the area. And finally, in the narration near the end of the film, there might be a passing admission of a possible waste disposal problem, but "nothing that cannot be resolved by reasonable men."

THE SINGLE-POINT METHOD

In the single-point propaganda technique the tactics are exactly the reverse. The more unsavory the means, the more glorified the end must be to justify ruthless tactics. In wartime the most savage atrocities are committed in the name of "peace." One old Bolshevik wrote of Communist goals in the Russian Civil War: "For peace, justice, and the brotherhood of man, we killed and killed and killed."

Anxiety

The anxiety level of the viewer may affect his degree of susceptibility to propaganda film and television programming. Viewers who are part of a stable society in which they have found a secure and satisfactory place tend to be resistant to media influences whose messages run counter to the experiences of their daily lives. As discussed in Chapter I "Cinema-Television and the Viewer," the soldiers of a winning army tend to laugh at the enemy's propaganda; only when their own forces crumble and their anxiety levels rise do they listen to the blandishments of the enemy, or to other sources of influence, and consider the possibility of surrender.

Anxiety in a viewer, resulting from the sudden instability of the old order of his society or as a consequence of finding himself in a strange situation in which his past behavioral patterns and beliefs do not apply, may engender any of three kinds of behavioral change: First, he may tend to watch and listen indiscriminately to all media influences in his search for solutions to his dilemma. Second, he may lose the capacity to judge between high- and low-credibility sources, giving nearly equal credence to all information sources; and he is as likely, while experiencing high levels of anxiety, to be influenced by a dishonest propaganda film as by an honest documentary. Third, he may reduce his anxiety over finding a satisfactory society in which to function by accepting the message of what appears to be a plausible solution to his problem, if it offers something to which he can make a commitment and act upon.

The value of viewer anxiety in planning propaganda films should not be underestimated, because it finds application to many other forms of film. In advertising, if a high-prestige source is seen using a product not used by the viewer, an inward cognitive dissonance is set up which may be resolved either by the viewer switching to the new product or by revising his opinion of the high-status source. In teaching, an incorrect answer to a problem may yield an unpleasant result—a low grade—and stimulate efforts in the student to achieve a more harmonious result—a high grade. Discordant elements should not, however, be overdone, for if the average viewer's sense of well-being is extremely disturbed, the end result may be that he will turn off the program.

Film Techniques of Propaganda

For a persuasive film to be effective it must first be understood; therefore, those scenes selected for inclusion in the film must be meaningful to the viewer as well as carriers of the filmmaker's message. The same holds true of the way the scenes are edited and the vocabulary level of the narration used in the sound track. Acceptance by the viewer of the message in the film, and his emotional and active enlistment in support of the goals of the film, are purposes to which all the techniques of film must be slanted. The visual techniques we are most concerned with are *visual communication, emotional transfer,* the *either-or fallacy, cinematography techniques, kinesics, emotionally loaded pictures and words, film scenes selected out of context, juxtaposition of scenes to convey a meaning not inherent in the scenes, misrepresentation, use of the confident manner* and *proof by repeated assertion.*

VISUAL COMMUNICATION

Visual communication is even more important in propaganda film than in other film genres, because we make emotional decisions based upon what we see at so low an awareness level that we are frequently unaware of coming to a decision until it has been made. Verbal communication, on the other hand, tends to be received with skepticism: "Don't tell me, show me." A filmmaker may say almost anything with pictures, and if it is plausible, it may pass without question. But if the same content statement is put into words, it is subject to immediate challenge. It has been estimated that in personal face-to-face relationships, about thirty-five percent of the meaning of a statement is carried in the spoken words, while the other sixty-five percent is conveyed by the manner in which the words are said. For effective propaganda films, in which the visuals are highly organized to communicate ideas from a biased point of view, the content and message of the film should be more than ninety percent visual.

A presentation of the human consequences of a problem is the most persuasive means of enlisting the support of the viewer, whatever the nature of the content. Mercury poisoning and its effect upon the brain may seem mildly alarming when described in written or spoken words, but when presented visually in a scene depicting a twelve-year-old boy gone stark, screaming mad—strapped down by all four limbs to a hospital bed—it is likely to arouse the viewer to action, if only out of fear of eventual consequences to himself.

Long statistical presentations are of dubious value in a film intended to persuade a lay audience to support some kind of action. Facts and figures presented *in the sound track may be completely forgotten.* A few graphic statements, presented in the form of maps or animated charts, may be remembered because of their visual form. But the lay viewer tends to forget quantitative content because of its abstract nature, while he is inclined to remember scenes portraying human beings and their living problems. Moreover, facts are not necessarily persuasive. If an issue requires an extensive presentation of facts and figures to be made clear, then perhaps the nature of the subject is inappropriate for a persuasive film or television program intended for a mixed audience. It is natural to want to reach millions of television viewers with an important message, but if the viewers are not watching at the other end, or if the message is cast in a form having little persuasive effect, then the propaganda film might as well never have been made or broadcast. Film and television programs intended to influence a cross-section of the population should present a problem in terms of what the subject and the viewer have in common—their humanity.

The common-ground approach should be extended, if possible, to show many cultural similarities between the human subjects of the film and the target audience. These similarities should emphasize likeness of traits and behavioral patterns, likeness of religion and life style. The greater the similarity between the subjects of the film and the audience, the greater the likelihood the viewer will identify with their problems and be persuaded to act on their behalf. An example of this cultural identification is found in the support given by Americans of Jewish faith to the cause of Israel, a support motivated by the bond of a shared religion.

EMOTIONAL TRANSFER

The emotional transfer of one subject having known emotional associations to a second subject of neutral association is the essence of propaganda. By pairing them together in an appeal to the emotions, rather than to the intellect, a common denominator of similar emotions may be spread to the second subject in the mind of the viewer.

A simple example of the use of emotional transfer is in the display of the American flag, a symbol which tends to evoke feelings of veneration and loyalty in most Americans. Politicians appear on flag-draped platforms in order to transfer the emotional associations of the flag to themselves in a way that will win votes in an election. Conversely, the symbols of a hostile ideology, such as the swastika or the sickle and hammer, may tend to evoke anger and hostility in the viewer and be used for their negative values to damage otherwise neutral subjects. In Communist and other nations hostile to the policies of the United States, the emotional associations of the viewer may be exactly the reverse, with veneration and loyalty aroused by the sickle and hammer and hostility by the stars and stripes.

Objects, too, have propaganda value, depending upon the context in which the scenes are placed in editing. A scene depicting a pan of maggot-filled beans is merely disgusting. But when presented as the food eaten by a hungry child, it becomes outrageous. When presented as the food eaten by a child because of the economic exploitation of his family

CZECHOSLOVAKIA, 1968. Emotional transfer. *Denis Sanders and Robert Fresco.*

by a third party, that scene of maggot-filled beans has become a powerful weapon of persuasion and propaganda used to aim the anger of the viewer at the exploiter, as was the case in the classic exposé of living conditions among migrant workers, *The Harvest of Shame.*

THE EITHER-OR FALLACY

Presenting a phony dilemma—the "either-or fallacy"—to commend or condemn a proposition because of its supposed consequences to the viewer is a common practice at election time when bond issues, new laws and propositions are submitted for ratification or rejection by the voters. Those whose vested interests may be gored by voter approval of a given proposal frequently launch a propaganda campaign based upon the either-or fallacy in which passage of the bill is presented in terms of the direst consequences to the voter himself, regardless of whether there is a cause and effect relationship or, indeed, any relationship at all.

A classic use of the either-or fallacy occurred after the publication of *Silent Spring*, in which Rachel Carson alerted the public to the difficult and critical problem of contamination of the environment caused by the heavy indiscriminate use of chlorinated hydrocarbon pesticides. The chemicals industry, sensing the threat of an informed and aroused public against their vested interests, first launched a campaign of personal and professional denigration against Miss Carson, and then publicized the either-or fallacy that the choice we faced was between "birds or people," and that the cost in the death of wildlife was more than compensated by the savings of human life. As is now common knowledge, the pesticide contamination problem is a matter of death to birds *and* people, not birds or people, but the industry's use of the either-or fallacy served effectively for a time as a delaying action against legislation to restrict the production and indiscriminate use of DDT.

CINEMATOGRAPHY TECHNIQUES

Cinematography techiques may be used to interpret a subject in ways that will be pleasing or displeasing to the viewer at a level of awareness so low as to be nearly subliminal. A subject may be composed with the top of his head barely touching the picture frame, known for some reason as a "Warner Brothers haircut," or from an angle that will emphasize unattractive physical features such as heavy jowls, a big belly or a bulbous nose. A subject lighted with a harsh key-to-fill ratio or from an unnaturally low angle may also appear irritating or disturbing. A clever cameraman can easily interpret his subject in such a way as to persuade the viewer to like or dislike that subject.

KINESICS

Communication through bodily and facial movements—kinesics— plays an important role in film propaganda, especially when an important person is presented on television for the close scrutiny of the viewer. The humility or arrogance of his eyes, the lifting of a brow, the way he walks and stands, his attitude toward greater and lesser persons, can play a powerful role in shaping that person's image for the viewer, an image that the filmmaker in turn can help to shape by the scenes he selects for inclusion in the film.

EMOTIONALLY LOADED PICTURES AND WORDS

Emotionally loaded pictures and words are those that touch the life space of most viewers and arouse them. A scene of a child killed or wounded is an emotionally loaded visual, as would be the maiming of any human being, and often, the killing of birds and animals. If a scene of atrocity to living things is attributed to some person, organization or nation, any outrage stimulated in the viewer by the scene will tend to be directed toward the alleged perpetrator of the crime. A common propaganda trick is to present scenes depicting the abuse of human beings and other living things and attribute them to one's enemies, regardless of whether they committed that crime or any other like it, because rebuttals and denials are feeble answers to an accusation supported by emotionally loaded scenes. And usually, the first presentation on any subject tends to win the viewer's support.

An example of the propaganda use of emotionally loaded scenes was found in a North Vietnamese film which showed the alleged effects on South Vietnamese villagers of American spraying of defoliants and other herbicides to reduce the protective cover used by the Communist fighters. The scenes showed women reduced to skin and bones, babies deformed, children suffering mental derangement, forests denuded, crops destroyed, cattle dead, birds drowned and fish floating belly up in the water. All this was attributed in the sound track to the spraying of chemical herbicides. Coming at a time when general concern over chemical pollution of the environment was widespread in the United States, the propaganda effect of this film was devastating, and the formal rebuttal expressed in words after the film presentation was just as a bubble blown into the air to be popped by the sharp memory of those emotionally loaded pictures.

SCENES OUT OF CONTEXT

Film scenes selected out of context to prove a point may be suspect to the alert viewer, but are nearly always damaging to some degree. Rarely does a single scene present a balanced interpretation of an event;

more often, many scenes must be edited into a longer documentary statement before the viewer may be given an essential truth. A solitary scene presented as "proof" of what occurred during a given event should be regarded with grave suspicion, as should any disjointed sequence whose loose continuity may indicate that the film could not be edited smoothly without using additional scenes that might change the viewer's interpretation of what happened during an event.

Film footage photographed during riots and demonstrations, for example, is frequently lifted out of context to ascribe guilt to one side or the other. Those who sympathize with the cause of the demonstrators may present a single scene of a policeman beating a participant without showing any of the provocations or destructive acts that preceded the violence. Supporters of the other side may present a scene showing only the provocations and property destruction by the demonstrators and almost nothing of the violent police reaction. A common ploy, under such circumstances, is for a propaganda cameraman to prowl around and photograph someone carrying a banner displaying symbols of a hostile ideology, such as the swastika or the sickle and hammer, and thereby damn a legitimate demonstration with evidence selected out of context, when such extremists may be only peripheral hangers-on exploiting an unrelated situation for their own aggrandizement.

Omission may be a particularly insidious form of propaganda because the scenes included in the film constitute a factual *aspect* of the truth, and the filmmaker cannot then be accused of presenting an unvarnished lie. If someone protests his selection of scenes to interpret a given event, the filmmaker may innocently turn up his hands and insist he is telling the truth as he sees it, and if pressed hard enough, may resort to the sophistry that only the inclusion of film footage of everything that occurred could present the whole truth, and even this would be subject to the selective judgment of the cameramen. Television news commentators are frequently (and often unjustly) accused of presenting film clips whose sum total meaning does not render a balanced picture of the truth, but instead only those aspects of an event that are editorially expedient.

JUXTAPOSITION OF SCENES TO CONVEY MEANING

Juxtaposition of scenes to convey a meaning not inherent in the scenes is a propaganda editing technique whereby unrelated scenes are brought together to create an event which may never have occurred, or may have occurred in a different chronological sequence than that presented in the film. If the contents of different scenes are related logically, they may be edited into a propaganda sequence whose sum total meaning is unrelated to, or even contradictory to, the original circumstances in which the individual scenes were actually photographed.

An effective example of editing technique used to create a nonevent was found in a North Vietnamese film which portrayed the strafing by an American fighter plane of a group of peasants working in a rice paddy. The scenes were as follows: an establishing shot of the Vietnamese peasants transplanting rice in a paddy; a full shot of an American plane flying overhead; a closeup of a peasant's face looking up; a long shot of a plane diving down; a closeup of machine guns firing from an airplane's wing; and a full shot of crumpled bodies lying in shallow water. A perusal of each of these scenes reveals that there is nothing in any of them to prove that an American plane strafed those peasants as the edited version would indicate; and indeed, subsequent analysis indicated that the film grain varied from one scene to the next, suggesting that the scenes were photographed on different kinds of film stock at different times and places. Although such atrocities may have occurred during that protracted, embittered conflict, the film shown was not a portrayal of one of them.

Changing the juxtaposition of scenes may also be used to change the chronology in which events actually occurred. In *Operation Abolition*, a film purporting to document an allegedly Communist-inspired riot against the House Un-American Activities Committee in San Francisco, scenes showing known Communist leaders speaking and passing out leaflets were placed at the beginning of the film to support the accusation that they had agitated the riot that followed. In reality, these scenes of the leaders were photographed several days *after* the riot was over, but were edited into the beginning of the film to assign culpability to the Communists.

MISREPRESENTATION

Misrepresentation constitutes an out-and-out lie on film, done with the full cognizance of the producer. The propaganda filmmaker may misrepresent the facts in a number of ways: He may fake an event before the camera and present it as factual; a television commercial once advertised a brand of ice cream by presenting it as "so richly textured and delicious" that the viewer was urged to emulate the lip-smacking enjoyment of the actor—who was eating colored mashed potatoes. Or, the filmmaker may restage an actual event in order to change some of the relevant facts and thereby affect the viewer's interpretation of what took place. In the Russian film *Stalingrad* many of the battle scenes presented as documentary combat footage were actually staged with small models of Russian tanks and airplanes in order to cover up the fact that the great battle was fought largely with American Lend-Lease equipment sent to the Soviet Union during World War II.

Another form of misrepresentation relates again to editing: A scene documenting one event may be used in a film presenting what occurred at another, but similar, event. A scene depicting a crying Chinese baby, presented as having been abandoned beside a railroad track during the Japanese invasion of China in the early 1930s, later appeared in a film allegedly documenting Chinese Communist atrocities in the civil war of the late 1940s, and then appeared still later in a film presenting Chinese Nationalist atrocities in the same civil war.

USE OF THE CONFIDENT MANNER

This propaganda technique assumes that the viewer does not know who the speaker is, but will infer from the speaker's important appearance and self-assured manner that he knows what he is talking about and is therefore worth listening to. The confident manner is commonly used on television commercials to impress the potential customer with the excellence of a product. The impressive spokesmen for these commercials are usually aspiring or aging thespians, schooled in method acting and capable of identifying themselves emotionally with a bottle of deodorant "so masculine that it is not recommended for women."

Appearance is important in the use of the confident manner. These actors and actresses should be visual stereotypes of the kinds of roles they represent because their appearance on the television screen is so brief that the viewer must be able to tell who and what they are at a glance. Older men are mature, craggy-faced, white-headed men of the world, and older women are the quintessence of motherly maturity and wisdom. Young men are urbane, finely chiseled boulevardiers, and young women are sleek and honeyed creatures of high fashion. And each must speak as if he were the sole repository of all wisdom relating to whatever product is being sold.

PROOF BY REPEATED ASSERTION

Proof by repeated assertion echoes Joseph Goebbel's dictum that "If you tell a lie long enough, it will become the truth." He apparently meant this in the context of a closed totalitarian society where people are presented with one-sided information on a subject all their lives to such an extent that if they are ever presented with proof to the contrary, selective perception and the boomerang effect come into play and they reject the truth as a lie.

Proof by repeated assertion, however, is also effective in a free and open society, particularly when sustained over a long period of time or in a saturation campaign. Most television sales campaigns are planned for the cumulative effects of proof by repeated assertion.

In political campaigns saturation rather than a long, sustained appeal is the primary method; repeated assertions are made in which the incumbent candidates point with pride and the aspirants view with alarm. Each side documents its case with film clips, presented at frequent intervals, which depict stunning achievements on one side and slurs on the other, and whose only real proof, in many cases, is that of repeated assertion.

The Sound Track in Propaganda

The sound track in propaganda film may be used in a wide variety of ways to influence the viewer's interpretation of the visuals. It can give meanings to scenes that are not inherent in the scenes themselves, at levels that range from subliminal sound effects and background music to lies and abusive name-calling.

Narration may be used to state that a given scene was photographed under certain circumstances, when it was not, that the circumstances were caused by the actions of a third party, when they were not, and to relate the scene on the screen to something that occurred earlier, when no such relationship may exist. *Music* may be used as a theme to disparage people and organizations, as irony through the use of distorting filters, as humor and satire by synchronizing ridiculous music with

movements of subjects that might otherwise have dignity, and as communication to add elements of culture to the background. *Sound effects*
may be used similarly as mood, theme, irony, humor, satire, counterpoint and transitional device.

In the propaganda use of the sound track none are more thorough
and obvious than the Communist filmmakers of the German Democratic People's Republic, who, quite literally, tell their viewers what to
think and how to interpret the visuals by their rendition of the sound
track.

In *Berlin Wall*, a film produced by the East Germans to justify their
building of a wall to cut off the exodus of their own people to the West,
the sound track of the English-language version interpreted each and
every sequence as follows: The music of Bach, Beethoven and Brahms
accompanied all scenes portraying Communist officials, armed forces,
industrial developments and people of the GDR, to transfer the dignity,
majesty and cultural glory of the old order to the new. The music
played over scenes of the West, on the other hand, was loud, brassy,

BERLIN WALL. Anger-arousing symbolism. *Wolfram von Hanwehr.*

vulgar popular music—apparently run through several filters to assure its offensiveness—and at a decibel level that was physically painful. Moreover, when presenting scenes of American soldiers, the music was synchronized in a ludicrous fashion to the tempo of their marching feet and the chomp of their jaws chewing gum. To emphasize the contrast, two narrators were used: The narrator for the East spoke with a precise, articulate British accent, using good grammar and no slang. The narrator for the West spoke with a nasal American whine, using bad grammar and slang.

Such heavy-handed use of the sound track may have propaganda effectiveness in a closed society, where there are no other media sources and little basis for comparison, but in an open society this ponderousness may be considered absurd or offensive, and therefore ineffective. But employed circumspectly and with a light hand, such techniques may have a telling effect in films for an open society, especially at crucial points where the filmmaker may want the viewer to laugh at someone.

Other Propaganda Devices

There are a number of other propaganda devices. The Institute for Propaganda Analysis describes seven allegedly spurious forms of persuasion used in other forms of communications as well as in film and television:

1. The Name-Calling Device
2. The Glittering Generalities Device
3. The Transfer Device
4. The Testimonial Device
5. The Plain-Folks Device
6. The Card-Stacking Device
7. The Bandwagon Device

Most of these terms are self-explanatory or have been discussed in their applications to film and television. The *name-calling technique* is commonly used to tarnish someone's reputation with the unsavory connotation of a word representing something repugnant to the people. *Glittering generalities* are a function of narration and dialogue in which broad statements are made that gloss over unacceptable specific details. The *transfer device* is essentially a visual concept in which a subject having known emotional qualities transfers those qualities to another subject, a technique commonly used by politicians who have themselves photographed shaking hands with the President in order to transfer the prestige of his office and person to themselves. The *testimonial device* entails having someone of high status endorse a product, person or organization, and thereby extend the halo of his prestige and spoken endorsement to the new subject.

The *plain-folks device* is an attempt to identify a person aspiring to public support with the common people, by emphasizing that in essence there is little difference between the man and the masses. The *card-stacking device* consists of presenting only those facts that will support one's own point-of-view, while leaving out all telling contradictory facts, and presenting the favorable facts in an order that will convey an impression contrary to the truth. The *bandwagon device* appeals to the viewer to join up with whatever is being presented because it is sure to win; he will thereby be on the road to success and share in the laurels of victory.

A basic objection to these classifications is that they are so simplistic and generalized that they may apply in many respects to honest persuasion as well as to dishonest propaganda films. Although there will always be a certain amount of gray area between the two extremes, the term "propaganda" should be reserved for those presentations that are clearly contrary to the truth.

Wartime Propaganda Themes

A close relative of the hard-line propaganda film is the wartime documentary and agit-prop film. It should be noted that a *declared war* in modern times may raise the question of the very existence of the nations involved, and it tends therefore to become a sacred cause to the peoples involved. Civil rights are suspended, freedom of speech and the press are curtailed, censorship is imposed to control sources of information, and a nationwide propaganda campaign is launched to weld the people into a weapon of unified war against the enemy.

Research by Bernard Berelson has revealed that every major film-producing war-making nation in the world has certain identical themes running through its wartime propaganda films. These are: Our ultimate victory will make possible a better world for all mankind. We detest the enemy who has forced us, a peace-loving people, into an unwanted war. We are confident of our ability to triumph in the end after a hard and resolute prosecution of the war. We have confidence in the integrity and fighting ability of our allies, who share our virtues and goals. We are up against an unscrupulous foe who will stoop to crimes of inhuman enormity to win and we are therefore justified in the use of a few dirty tactics of our own.

The foregoing themes have been found in the films of fascist, Communist, monarchist and democratic nations alike, and should be considered as tactics of domestic indoctrination common to all nations at war.

The Dramatic Form

The dramatic form in propaganda films, with actors and actresses speaking written lines, seldom works effectively in an open society when the real intent is to achieve some kind of political, social or economic change. This is true because the film most often becomes a self-conscious polemic in which actors spout noble principles and ideology instead of behaving and acting like believable human beings. Viewers seldom mistake the dramatic presentation for the reality of a documentary film, and tend to view dramatic attempts to that effect with skepticism, if not with derisive laughter.

Sometimes, however, a dramatic film may exquisitely sum up the essence of a historical moment in which human beings are caught up in the sweep of events and the consequences to them are such as to have a propagandistic effect, as was the case with the classic film *The Grapes of Wrath*. Such successes, however, are nearly always the by-product of an attempt to create absorbing drama rather than propaganda. Under most circumstances, the dramatic form is subject to so many variables unrelated to the message of a propaganda film—a good script, skillful acting and directing, production quality and so forth—that the filmmaker who wishes to advocate some kind of political, social or economic change is usually better advised to forego the dramatic form and use the more credible documentary form.

National Attitudes

Propagandists must take care not to abrade national attitudes that affect the reactions of the viewer. Every cohesive nation has cultural characteristics that bind them together. These national attitudes most often derive from a common language, geographical area and influences, historical experiences, political, social and economic values, a set of concepts about human relationships and certain convictions about what constitutes the right and wrong way to do things. The propagandist who runs against the grain of national attitudes is courting a boomerang effect. Several sociologists, anthropologists and psychologists have systematically studied the recurring values evident in the dominant Judeo-Christian American culture, which are broadly and simply summarized here.

INDIVIDUALISM

Individualism is an important strand in the American fibre, placing the responsibility for a man's success or failure upon his own efforts, stressing the primacy of self-reliance, ambition and enterprise in achieving his economic, social or political destiny. Nearly all aspects of personal, entrepreneurial and governmental actions are judged in terms of their effects upon the welfare of the individual. Competition between individuals for any prize is considered the fairest way to determine who is most deserving of it, who is the better man. Although actually collectivism in the form of organizations representing the political, social, religious, ethnic, racial and economic sectors of the nation dominates American life, the ideal remains one of personal independence centered on the achievements of the individual. The sight of a determined individual struggling against great odds tends to evoke admiration in the American viewer, and may tend to arouse sympathy for the individual's cause, regardless of whether that cause has any merit. A political aspirant running for office will tend to appeal to American underdog sympathies by claiming he is running alone against the political machine of his opponent, even if he is himself supported by a political machine.

THE DEMOCRATIC ETHIC

The democratic ethic pervades the American's judgment of other men. He favors equal opportunity to rise by merit and enterprise rather than by birth, and tends to admire the man who has come a long way by his own efforts. Any public slur on a distinguished man's origins is certain to be offensive, because personal achievement is considered the measure of the man. Politicians, entertainers and businessmen alike often exploit this log-cabin-to-White-House tradition by boasting of their humble origins; but no matter how high a man may rise in American national life, he is expected to retain his humility and the common touch. Senator William Fulbright, chairman of the Senate Foreign Relations Committee and as urbane a man as has ever trod the national scene, runs for office in Arkansas by appearing on television in shirtsleeves and suspenders, while whittling a stick of wood to the accompaniment of hillbilly music, to show his constituents that he is still Just Plain Bill. Those politicians born with the proverbial silver spoon in their mouths do not flaunt their affluence, but instead release publicity films of themselves eating chicken drumsticks with the plain folk at country fairs, playing touch football, walking barefoot along a beach with a pet dog, unspoiled by the burden of unearned wealth.

SUCCESS

Success is an extension of the democratic ethic in judging the worth of an individual, success as measured by such evidence as vocational achievements and status, the accumulation of wealth or power, and public recognition. Material success, if achieved by personal effort and not by inheritance, is considered evidence of intelligence, hard work, efficiency and perseverance, and those who achieve it by unearned means often pretend to have done it the hard way in order to enjoy the prestige that comes with individual achievement. "Getting ahead" through personal initiative and merit is considered something nearly everyone should aspire to, and those individuals who do not try are considered deficient in some respect. A commonly used propaganda ploy among political candidates having a rich adversary is to point out how much money the other candidate is spending on the campaign and accuse him of trying to buy the election, a slur which implies that the rich man is trying to achieve success without earning it, an offense to American values that sometimes bears fruit in the voting booth.

POLARIZED MORALITY

Polarized morality, the tendency to judge people, institutions, events and objects as good or bad, right or wrong, ethical or unethical

—without intervening shades of gray—derives from a puritan attitude based on early American culture and manifested by many Americans today. Nearly any event may evoke a polarized moral judgment for or against the event and its originator. And whatever the private life and habits of the American citizen may be, he will publicly tend to espouse the ascetic pioneer virtues of sobriety, honesty, thrift, abstinence and industriousness, and insist that his political, social and economic leaders exemplify this saintly ideal, however much he, the viewer, may not. Until very recently, any evidence of personal immorality or financial impropriety in an American leader was enough to ruin his career; and even in the more liberal atmosphere of our time no aspirant to high office can afford to have a skeleton in his closet or it may eventually be discovered by his adversaries and used to discredit him over television.

FAIR PLAY

A related element of polarized morality is the strong sense of fair play in most Americans, a resentment of obviously underhanded tactics that can severely boomerang against the offender. During a gubernatorial election campaign in California between incumbent Edmund G. "Pat" Brown and former actor Ronald Reagan, a television film clip presented a scene of Governor Brown saying to a little Negro girl, "You know, Abraham Lincoln was killed by an actor." Since television is essentially a one-way communication device, the sponsors lacked the immediate feedback to realize how offensive the presentation was until there arose a tremendous swell of public outrage. The offending clip was taken off the air only after it had been seen by most of the people, and the voters elected Ronald Reagan, the former actor, as the new governor of California. Although there were many other issues and considerations in the election, there seems little doubt that the presentation of this television clip, coming a few days before the election, was a contributing factor in swinging many voters to Reagan through an offended sense of fair play.

SOCIAL VALUES

The social values of the American relate primarily to his friendliness and to the sanctity of the family unit. The string of admired social virtues begins with ambient friendliness and continues with generosity, kindliness, sociability, gregariousness, sincerity, knowing how to play the game and being a good sport in success or failure. The importance of geniality and amiability may be seen in the fixed smile frozen on the visage of someone seeking the goodwill of the viewer; the warm attitude of the viewer toward a public figure presented over the media will chill quickly at any evidence of coldness, testiness, meanness or poor sportsmanship.

The Importance of the Family

The family unit is an important extension of social values, although perhaps this is less true than formerly. The average American likes a good family man who loves and indulges his wife, loves but does not indulge his children, and is willing to make great personal sacrifices on their behalf. One of the more effective ways to damn any person, organization or system—and generate hostile action by the American viewer —is to demonstrate their responsibility for damaging human consequences to a family.

Political and Religious Values

Political and religious values exist at two levels: the personal socio-economic-political milieu discussed in "Cinema-Television and the Viewer" and the national values concept.

Although the United States is beset with interlocking and unresolved conflicts, most contemporary Americans believe that in a context of personal freedom, their form of political democracy has made possible a higher standard of living for the greatest proportion of its people than any nation in the world; they believe that the two-party congressional system, with its check and balance functions, is the best governmental system of them all, and one that should be continued. Most Americans regard Socialist-Marxist movements as implacably hostile to a free society, and of all the pejorative terms that can be used to damn an adversary, few are more telling than the word "Communist." Any person or organization accused of undermining the American political system, overtly or covertly, will be in trouble with most American viewers.

Paradoxically, the governmental structure tends to be considered inherently inefficient, inevitably corrupt to some degree, and something to be kept out of private production enterprises.

Religion is considered to be a man's own business as long as he believes in some form of religious expression. Americans have solved the problem of religious differences by taking religion out of politics and politics out of religion. The last ghost of religion as a political issue may have been laid to rest with the election of a Catholic, John Fitzgerald Kennedy, as President of the United States. Religious expressions of a positive nature, such as scenes revealing a person going to a church or synagogue, may be used to enhance the general stature of the person, but the slightest slur on a man's faith is certain to boomerang.

The foregoing summaries of American national values do not pretend to be complete, or to treat except in a generalized and simplistic way the ramifications, overlays, interplays and nuances that would exist when these values are activated in any dynamic communication situation. A complete statement would be vast, detailed and subject to variables which exceed the scope of this book. Nevertheless, these are important basic areas of American national character which are mediating influences—subject to emotional transfer uses and abuses in the classic documentary film, the propaganda film, the television documentary program and the television commercial.

18

The Television Commercial

The day has passed when an automobile manufacturer can get away with saying, as Henry Ford did, "The public can have any color it wants—as long as its black." He made his dictum stick for twenty years because there was a great need for reasonably priced automobiles, and having a car was so important to the people that they were in no mood to quibble about its color. Today the fundamental need for automobiles has been met, as has the need for so many products and services in the United States. Virtually all goods and services must now be designed to cater to the consumer's wants and whims, some of which may themselves be created by advertising.

The very survival of many companies now hinges upon the success of their media advertising campaigns. The price of failure is reflected in the products we no longer see or hear about—Chlorodent toothpaste, Glass Wax, Swansdown Cake Mixes, Studebaker automobiles, to name only a few. These companies may have withered away from a number of contributory causes, but foremost among them was the failure of their advertising campaigns to persuade the public to buy their products. Advertising, then, is an important key to corporate survival. The viewer must be successfully urged to satisfy his needs and wants through the purchase of a sponsor's products.

The film and television commercial is only one facet of the much larger subject of marketing; the advertisement can be likened to the tip of an iceburg protruding from the surface of the sea—it is only a small visible part of a huge supporting system. Ultimately, however, the visible tip of advertising is the part that counts, because the marketing system is fed and sustained by the revenue generated by the successful commercial. And the success of advertising is in turn measured by the ability of the commercial to persuade the viewer to purchase goods and services, which then yield a profit for the sponsor. If the sponsor does not sell his product or service, everyone concerned may be out of a job. The commercial, then, is the cutting edge of the free-enterprise consumer-oriented marketing system, by which goods and services are created, produced, distributed and sold to the American people.

The Viewer as Consumer

NEEDS AND WANTS

Goods and services must be sold to the viewer under the guise of meeting some need or want. The average human being *needs* food, clothing, shelter, recognition, recreation and sexual fulfillment. If the viewer lacks (or thinks he lacks) any of these necessities, a basis exists for selling him a product. By appealing to fulfillment of one of these needs through an offer of delicious food, attractive clothing, luxurious articles for the home, prestige symbols, entertainment and increased attractiveness to the opposite sex, the viewer-consumer may dig into his pockets to buy gratification through the sponsor's products.

Wants are not needs and are therefore nebulous. The human race can get along very well without popular records, granny boots, rising and falling hemlines, high-horsepower automobiles, chromium trim and electrically powered toothbrushes. The viewer tends to respond in a predictable way to appeals to fundamental human needs and instincts. But his wants, on the other hand, are vague, variable, complex, numerous and vulnerable to manipulation.

The mercurial nature of human wants may be exemplified by the fad of the hula-hoop. For a year or so there was a national frenzy of hip-twirling hoops—hula-hoop contests, hula-hoop champions, articles praising and condemning hula-hoops, scholarly studies to determine its value as exercise and emotional therapy, and deep theorizing about its underlying sociological importance and place in the grand design of the

Cosmos. Then the public became bored with it all. The "want" vanished inexplicably—overnight—leaving manufacturers with a stock of hula-hoops probably adequate to meet all human demands for the toy for all time.

ANALYSIS OF THE VIEWER

Understanding of the viewer as a consumer is a first consideration in planning the television commercial. Who buys the advertiser's goods and services? What time of day does he or she watch television, and under what circumstances? What kind of programming does the prospective customer prefer? And most importantly, what is the age, sex, level of formal education, socioeconomic milieu and life space of the viewer? Knowing the characteristics of the target viewer may be the most important basis for creating a successful commercial. The advertising filmmaker should remember that he is not broadcasting to millions of potential customers, and should dismiss the notion of a "mass audience." He is making a personal appeal to one person to buy a given product, and since the commercial will be watched in ones and twos, or by a small family, there is very little group psychology involved. Every commercial is presented to only one viewer, although that one may be multiplied by millions.

Many of the characteristics of the viewer as respondent to film and television programming have been discussed at length in earlier chapters. One viewer research tool, however, has become important in marketing and advertising—demographics.

DEMOGRAPHICS

Demographics is an audience analysis technique which consists of defining consumer characteristics in terms of their viewing habits: what times of day they watch television, and what kinds of programs they prefer. Cooperating families and individuals fill out a diary of their viewing activities. Age and sex have been the viewer characteristics heretofore emphasized, with such factors as education, socioeconomic milieu and life space now under study. Demographics evolved from the need of advertisers to know who watched what kind of program at any given part of the day so that the right kind of commercials would be presented to the intended target audience. It would make very little sense to advertise trucks and after-shave lotion at a time of day when most viewers are housewives.

An audience profile by "day part" is an important result of demographic analysis. Inasmuch as the housewife manages the money in most families, in addition to watching television the greatest number of hours of any audience group, she is a primary subject of demographic analysis. One audience profile of housewives, collated by personal interviews with a representative sampling of approximately ten thousand housewives, revealed the following demographic results:

Daytime television viewing—10 A.M. to 5 P.M.—appeals most to the housewife under twenty-four years of age and over sixty-five, with low-income families having a strong bias.

Early evening viewing—5 to 7 P.M.—is the peak viewing time for the young housewife, again primarily in the low-income bracket.

Prime evening time—7:30 to 11 P.M.—appeals to all age groups, but peaks with housewives in the middle-income group, and after 10 P.M. younger housewives in the high-income group have a bias.

Late-evening viewing—11 P.M. to 2 A.M.—is done primarily by young housewives, with primary emphasis on those in the high-income category.

This audience profile has clear implications for advertisers. Inasmuch as daytime viewing is watched so intensively by young housewives of child-bearing age, in an income group more likely to do laundry at home than to send it out for cleaning, daytime viewing hours are obviously the time to sell soap, detergents and other household maintenance commodities. Since prime evening time and late evening are the selected hours for television viewing by women in higher income brackets, that is the time to sell more expensive and prestigious items. The audience profile is utilized by advertisers to purchase sponsorship of individual shows, matching the programs to the known tastes of the viewer, getting maximum effectiveness for their media dollars.

The demographic pie may be sliced another way to reveal seasonal variations in viewing. Using the housewife once again as an example, we find that set tuning information yielded by Nielson's national Audimeter sample revealed the following audience seasonal profile:

Peak television viewing by housewives occurs during the coldest weather months, December through March.

The lowest television viewing levels occur during the hottest summer months, July and August, falling from an average of thirty-five to fifty percent below the peak winter viewing levels.

Viewing during the spring and fall strikes an average between the two extremes.

Late-evening viewing is the most stable at any given time of year, with summer viewing by young well-to-do housewives dropping only an average of ten percent below the peak winter months.

Demographic data may be utilized for analysis of cost relationships. The cost-per-thousand-viewers in reaching a given target audience is very important, with expense factors which include such elements as the cost of actual program and advertising production, purchase of television viewing time distribution of commercials to stations, residuals for talent and the sales price of the goods and services being sold. Another cost factor is the relationship between the audience-income profile and viewing patterns during daytime, early-evening, prime-evening and late-evening viewing times, at different months of the year. Another dimension is the frequency-of-viewing profile. All these cost factors combine to determine what kinds of programming (as well as advertising) are offered at different times of the day, during different seasons of the year. Talk shows and movies are presented during the late evening hours because that is what young people in high-income brackets like to watch during those hours, as revealed by demographic analysis. Soap operas and game shows are offered during daytime viewing hours, because that is what demographic data has shown to be the preference of young housewives in lower income brackets.

The housewife is not the only subject of demographic analysis. The sampling techniques used to determine audience profiles, viewing patterns and cost-per-thousand-viewers are now applied to virtually all consumer segments of American society in order to maximize the exposure of programs and advertising to the intended target audience, and to present advertising in forms having the highest levels of viewer identification.

Once the target audience for the product has been defined, a few other questions should be answered: What proportion of the consumer population is aware of this product? Did they form their perceptions of the product through advertising, purchases or word-of-mouth recommendations? How do they perceive the product in relation to competitive products? By knowing what the target audience believes and perceives about the product, the filmmaker has the kind of research that is far more valuable as the thematic basis for a television commercial than brainstorming or playing a hunch.

Product Analysis

Next, the filmmaker must analyze the product he is selling and ask some hard questions: What is distinctive about the product in terms of consumer benefits, and how does it really differ from competitive products? Can the difference, if any, be visually demonstrated? What segment of the consumer public uses the product, and what needs or wants of that target audience does the product meet?

Since most competitive goods and services are quite similar, the advertising filmmaker should investigate the product thoroughly in order to develop a selling theme that may offer an advantage over the competition. How is the product made? What uses does it serve? What are its strengths and weaknesses? Is there some aspect of the product's manufacture or utilization that makes it work better, in some way, than competitive products? What selling theme can be derived from a special ingredient of the product?

Almost as important is knowledge of the competitive products—their unique advantages and disadvantages, their share of the market, their selling themes and performance claims.

Viewer Appeals

Appeals to ambition and anxiety are primarily what sell goods and services, once basic physical needs have been met. There are as many kinds of appeals in advertising as there are human desires; and through the promise of fulfillment of those desires, innumerable products may be sold:

Appeals to *pride* and *ego* are the basis for selling such things as jewelry, expensive automobiles and luxuriously furnished homes. The viewer is buying visible success.

The desire for *love* and enhanced *sexual appeal* have sold billions of dollars' worth of cosmetics, deodorants and shaving accoutrements. The viewer is buying passion.

The *fear of personal injury*, and threats to home and family security, have sold tires, insurance policies and windshield wipers. The viewer is buying security and peace of mind.

The yearning for buoyant *health* and *youthful vigor* has sold countless containers of orange juice, breakfast foods and vitamin pills. The viewer is buying a second youth.

Admiration for a celebrity or distinguished person has sold every kind of service and product so the viewer could have something in common with him. The viewer is buying prestige.

Sensual appeals to *pleasure* and *comfort* have sold every kind of product that could be put into, onto and around the human body. The viewer is buying gratification.

Identification with some human aspiration—not facts and figures— is the primary basis for selling goods and services to the average viewer. The viewer must become involved with the product through the logic and appeal of the television commercial.

Many of the other factors of persuasive media appeal applicable to television commercials are also found in other film and television forms, and have already been analyzed in earlier chapters.

Commercial Forms

Television commercials are comparatively brief: ten-second, thirty-second, and one-minute spots are the most common time spans. Within these brief time spans the commercial must catch the viewer's attention, interest him in the story, entertain him, present the sponsor's message and motivate the viewer to buy the sponsor's goods or services. For all its brevity, the television commercial must be tightly organized, with a basic selling idea presented logically in a short story that has a beginning, a middle and an end. To avoid joining the eighty-five percent of advertising which allegedly goes unnoticed, the commercial should present its message with taut simplicity and ringing clarity.

The first cinematic concern of the television commercial is to arrest the viewer's attention; this means intruding into the ongoing program at whatever degree of visual and verbal intensity necessary to make him watch the sales pitch. The second concern is to hold his interest by involving him emotionally, by some appeal to a need, ambition or worry with which he can identify. The third is to move him to buy the sponsor's goods and services by a promise of fulfillment. To meet these demands, the television commercial has evolved into several identifiable forms and genres, each having distinctive characteristics and requirements: the *spokesman approach*, the *testimonial*, the *demonstration*, the *problem and solution vignette*, the *story line*, the *funny commercial*, the *mood piece*, the *special effects form* and the *animated film*.

THE SPOKESMAN APPROACH

The spokesman approach to selling goods and services derives from the days of radio, and is almost entirely verbal. The tenor of the sales talk may range from the intimate, personal, soft-sell technique, to the brassy fast-talking high-pressure approach, but the essence of the spokesman approach is an attempt to talk the viewer into buying the product with promises of quality and satisfaction. The success of the spokesman approach is dependent upon the personality of the spokesman: If he is warm, charming, likable and convincing, he may do an effective job of selling the sponsor's product. One need only remember the decades that Arthur Godfrey was on radio and television to realize how persuasive a friendly talk by a likable personality can be.

Personality likes and dislikes, however, can be a chancy thing in television commercials. Style and delivery are important. For every spokesman who is liked by everybody, there are many more who are liked by some viewers and disliked by others. A controversial personality may lose as many customers as he gains. With time and the jading of television viewers, it has become increasingly difficult to sell a product by having a spokesman hold up a box of corn flakes and convince the viewers, on his word alone, that they should buy a tasty bowl.

In the spokesman approach premium is placed on the quality of the copy; it should be written in a pleasant conversational style, with only a few ideas and simple sentences that will sound extemporaneous and believable. When the spokesman approach is used today, it is increasingly employed in conjunction with such low-cost visual reinforcement as simple demonstrations and chroma-key backgrounds, unless time is so short or the budget is so tight that nothing can be incorporated beyond a charming talk.

THE TESTIMONIAL

The effectiveness of the testimonial by well-known figures has been analyzed at length in the chapter on "The Propaganda Film." The testi-

TOYS ARE FUN IN '71. The spokesman approach. *Hanna-Barbera Productions.*

monial may be more effective in sales, however, than in propaganda. The average viewer may be more easily influenced to change his brand of beer or choice of shaving cream than to modify a deeply rooted attitude on issues of race, religion or politics through the testimony of a prestigious person. There must be an obvious correlation between the expertise of the person giving testimony and the product being sold. A golf champion who endorses a given brand of clubs will probably stimulate the sale of those clubs. On the other hand, to have a football star endorse a set of encyclopedias, or a university president a brand of track shoes, would be patently incongruous and probably ineffective.

Moreover, if a prestigious person gives his endorsement to a wide range of products within a brief span of time, his testimonial value may drop with his credibility level.

Unknown persons may have testimonial value if they are representative of a group of viewers, and if a hidden candid-camera technique is used. A housewife, with whom other housewives can identify, who sincerely responds to questions with unqualified approval of a product is likely to sell that product. The sincerity shows through. Soap, beer, insurance, gasoline, all kinds of products can be sold through the testimonial given by an unknown person with whom the viewer can identify. One popular gimmick to elicit a ringing endorsement is to criticize the product; given the contrariness of human nature, many persons will immediately take the opposing view and give a ringing defense and endorsement of the product—selling it to the viewer.

Similarly, an unknown actor or actress may be used to endorse a product if dressed to conform to a stereotype and a role. The surrogate doctor, housewife, appliance repairman, industrial executive, who looks like the popular image of a class of people, may sometimes effectively endorse a product. The talent, however, must be carefully typecast; miscasting may result in a breach of credibility and viewer antagonism.

THE DEMONSTRATION

The demonstration commercial tends to satisfy the viewer from Missouri, and many other kinds of commercials also contain some form of a demonstration. Seeing is believing; man is a visual animal who believes what he sees above all other forms of evidence. All research studies in advertising (and every other form of media communication) agree that nothing convinces a viewer more quickly than showing him that a product can do what it claims to do: Gasoline companies stage endurance contests using the same kind of automobile, but different brands of gasoline, to prove that their petrol offers more mileage to the gallon. Tire companies put their products through torture tests to prove their resistance to punctures and blowouts. Watches are soaked and shaken and pummeled without mercy, but tick inexorably on and on. Shirts soaked in axle grease and coal dust are washed in the sponsor's detergent and brand "X" to prove to the credulous housewife that the dirt can be removed without dissolving the shirt, now clean and fit to wear to a formal dinner.

The demonstrations must be what they allegedly represent: mashed potatoes can no longer stand in for ice cream under hot lights without running afoul of the Federal Trade Commission.

Demonstrations should be staged simply, because viewers have been fooled so often by misleading advertising claims that they tend to be skeptical. We need only recall the *Rapid-Shave* commercial in which shaving cream allegedly demonstrated "moisturizing power" so effective it could loosen sandpaper for shaving, when the razor was actually shaving off grains of sand lightly adhered to plexi-glass with Vaseline, to realize why even simple demonstrations are sometimes viewed with a jaundiced squint.

The technique of the demonstration is essentially that of the process film: Tell the viewer what he is going to see. Show him the complete process, with repetitions, using closeups to reveal important changes and transitions. Describe the demonstration while it is in progress. Tell the viewer what he has just seen. Summarize the product's effectiveness

THE MONEY TREE. The demonstration. *Hanna-Barbera Productions.*

in achieving the demonstrated results. And be candid. Blunt honesty is mandatory from the beginning to the end of any such demonstration. If there is even a hint of cinematic trickery, through time-lapse photography or dissolves, the viewer and the Federal Trade Commission may become skeptical of the demonstration's authenticity.

THE PROBLEM AND SOLUTION VIGNETTE

The problem and solution format is possibly the most widely used television commercial framework because it purports to meet a viewer's need, or a want he may believe he needs. A classic example was a delightful Alka-Seltzer commercial which presented a middle-aged man seated on the edge of his bed, miserably groaning: "I can't believe I ate the w-h-o-l-e thing." Eventually his wife snapped from under her blankets, "Take an Alka-Seltzer." This was followed by a closeup of a glass filled with water and a fizzing Alka-Seltzer tablet. A fast dissolve again revealed the man seated on the edge of his bed, then smiling happily as he sighed: "The w-h-o-l-e thing."

The problem—upset stomach. The solution—Alka-Seltzer.

The problem and solution tactic should follow certain principles:

The problem should be genuine in the sense that the viewer recognizes it from his own life space experiences. Neither the problem nor the situation ought to be exaggerated except for satirical or humorous effect; and if so, the viewer should know of this intent.

The product's capacity to solve the problem should be presented visually and graphically, by demonstration if possible. The average viewer tends to believe what he sees rather than what he hears, and the primary message should go to the eyes. Present only those qualities of the goods or services being sold that relate to the solution of the problem. Bringing in information not relevant to the solution of the problem, or characters unrelated to the problem, may distract the viewer's attention from the persuasive example of a problem solved.

Keep the spokesman for the product in character. To have an appliance repairman tout a laundry detergent by citing chemical formulae and empirical studies, obviously beyond the scope of his expertise, is patently contrived, and may arouse skepticism in the viewer about the product.

The solution to the problem should clearly derive from the unique advantage of the product being claimed and demonstrated. If the problem is one that the viewer can relate to and understand, and the solution to the problem is credible and unique to that product, he will probably be motivated to make a purchase.

The problem and solution format is applied to most needs and wants for goods and services: automobiles, tires, windshield wipers, toothpaste, floor wax, oven cleaners and deodorants. Sometimes the "problem" and its solution are pushed to the point where they lack credibility, as in the ubiquitous laundry soap and detergent commercials: A housewife wails in despair that her husband's shorts lack a certain lustre after being washed by the other soap or detergent. At this point a wonderful neighbor or girl from the bridge club, knowing mother-in-law or animated genie sallies forth to provide a solution to this desperate situation. (Pushing the problem to the point of laughability apparently continues to induce some viewers to buy the product.)

The problem and solution format works with almost every kind of product and service, but if aimed at discriminating viewers, the filmmaker should keep certain considerations in mind: The problem itself must seem important to the target audience, and not a transparent contrivance; to become a manic-depressive case over the issue of bright, clean underwear is simply not credible. The solution to the problem should be believable; to have a girl from the bridge club announce that this soap is superior because of comparative statistical analyses, which she cites to the degree of two standard deviations, is not credible. And the consequences of using said detergent should also land somewhere within the realm of reality; to have the husband so happy over his radiantly white shorts that he takes her on a second honeymoon is not believable.

The satisfaction of using the product should be painted in glowing smiles on the faces of the users in the television commercial. Using that brand has solved the problem and all is well with the world. Moreover, rewards may come in the forms of the approval and admiration of others: When the housewife uses the advertised brand of cake mix, she becomes the center of her children's love, her husband's passion, her mother-in-law's grudging respect and her neighbor's admiration.

Reinforcement may be added at secondary and tertiary levels: Her children become more popular and sought after as companions through the tastiness of her cake. Her husband's boss, invited to dinner, is mightily impressed with the good judgment of his employee in selecting this marvelous cook as his wife and consort, and so forth. The more levels of reinforcement, if subtle and within the bounds of credibility, the better. The commercial is not only selling cake mix, but the prestige of being a successful housewife. And all of these rewards should culminate in one dazzling image—the product's name.

THE STORY LINE COMMERCIAL

The story line commercial is a miniature dramatic conflict, with a beginning, a middle and an end. Although the story line is seldom more than a minute long, it usually has such elements of dramatic structure as joining the conflict, ascending crises, an obligatory scene and a climax. For example: A Texaco commercial began with a medium shot of a little girl who lost her ball upon opening the door of a parked car. As she got out of the car to pursue it, the ball bounced away from her, rolling over, under and through a series of obstacles, to elude her. Then it rolled to the feet of a uniformed man; a hand reached down to pick up the ball and give it to the little girl. A quick cut to the smiling face of the thankful girl, another cut to the helpful man—a Texaco dealer— followed by a long scene of the Texaco sign. A complete story line was presented, with dramatic structure, without a single spoken word.

The cinematic interpretation of the story line commercial closely follows the narrative forms of dramatic film and television programming rather than the format of flashy special effects. The opening scene usually begins with an establishing shot to create mood and context, full shots to introduce characters, closeups for reactions, with all meaning ascribed to events by the reactions of the viewers. Editing techniques and tempo also reflect the dramatic form, with progressive shortening of scenes as the story line progresses toward the climax. The payoff, of course, relates the climax to the sponsor's product.

Suspense is an element that may be added to the story line form, the demonstration or to almost any kind of commercial that can be shaped around a situation that creates the question—What will happen? Who will catch the ball pursued by the little girl? Will the battery be strong enough to start the car and take the family home on the darkest, coldest night of the year? Will the automobile resist a blowout after running over lava rock, broken glass and a barrel of nails? The climax provides the answer and the hero—the sponsor's product.

The techniques of suspense are essentially those discussed in the "Action Films and Psychodramas": shifting points-of-view and levels of uncertainty; progressive pacing from long shots to closeups, or repetition of scene sizes until near the end, and then a radical change for the climax. Suspense may be enhanced by holding back the name of the product: A mysterious-looking object turns around slowly to reveal, eventually, the name of the sponsoring product. Weird sound effects and music may also enhance the feeling of suspense.

THE HUMOROUS COMMERCIAL

The humorous commercial is difficult to create, in part because humorists are born and not made, and in part because the way is fraught with pitfalls. The elements of comedy and humor discussed in "The Comedy and the Musical" also apply to the television commercial, with some modifications and exceptions.

Comedy deals with universal human foibles and pretensions, and as such is universal and nearly timeless. The animated commercial that presented a quarrel between a man and his stomach over the kind and amount of food the latter was eating will probably always be funny to everyone who has overindulged in too much of the wrong kinds of food—which means everyone. Husband-wife grouches and the battle of the sexes, boy-girl romances, mother-daughter tiffs, are all timeless verities which provide a rich source of ideas that are universally funny.

Humor, on the other hand, is topical, narrower in its target audience appeal and short-lived. The commercial based on a parody of soap operas, talk shows, politicians, popular movies and the latest flight to the moon may be hilarious to those viewers who are knowledgeable enough in the subject to get the point of the humor. On the other hand, it may not be the slightest bit funny to the viewer who knows little or nothing about the subject being parodied.

Satire, the highest form of humor, carries with it the potential danger of a boomerang effect. Some viewers do not consider certain things appropriate subjects for satire, and especially not a satire used to sell a product. Satire should be rendered very broadly so there will be no danger of its being taken literally. An angry reaction to a parody on a subject the viewer takes seriously may transfer to the sponsor's product, perhaps costing him customers he already has in addition to those he hopes to win. Cruelty, tastelessness or insults may come at a high price in the satirical commercial, possibly in the form of litigation.

A pitfall in the funny commercial is the possibility that the sponsor's name may be drowned in laughter and forgotten. In the funny commercial the essence of the comic or humorous situation should be integral with the function of the product, rather than added as unrelated sugar coating. A fine example of laughter integrated with the function of the product was the Alka-Seltzer tablet given to the man who could not believe that he ate the w-h-o-l-e thing. The sales message is the reason for the commercial's existence; the wit must make its point in support of the sponsor's goods or services.

THE MOOD PIECE

The mood piece commercial avoids verbal claims or visual demonstrations and seeks to identify the product with a time of happiness in the mind of the viewer: The fishermen return to their cabin at sunset with a good catch and crown a glorious day on the lake with a can of delicious beer. The lovely woman enjoys a tête-à-tête dinner at a fine restaurant, with candlelight, flowers and quavering violins, consummated with a glass of the sponsor's wine. Teen-agers gambol like healthy animals at the beach, swimming, surfing or just walking hand in hand through the spindrift, to end their day with a thirst-quenching soft drink. Hikers stride through flowered meadows, forests and mountains, and pause for lunch carried in (bio-degradable) plastic bags. The essence of the mood commercial is the transfer technique used in the propaganda film—an attempt to associate the emotions generated by a given environment with the sponsor's product.

THE SPECIAL EFFECTS FORM

The special effects commercial is one way to circumvent the tendency of many adult viewers to tune out mentally when the television commercial tunes in. Its purpose is to present a situation so bizarre that it arrests the viewer's attention long enough to sell him goods or services. Sometimes the situation alone is sufficiently extraordinary to catch the attention, such as displaying a new vacuum cleaner in the Louvre as an *objet d'art* (between the "Mona Lisa" and a Rodin sculpture) or showing a white knight in armor bright, thundering through suburbia to transform dirty laundry into whiter-than-white with a touch of his magic lance.

Other forms may involve the manipulation of some element of reality through technical special effects. One commercial had a miniature salesman walk out from behind a pitcher in a formal table setting. He strolled before a bouquet of flowers and stood before a knife and fork to speak to the viewer. So realistic was this commercial that the minuscule salesman and the apparently gigantic table setting threw shadows of approximately the same length (an effect achieved by the Technimatte process) in a credible setting of the incredible. So outlandish but realistic were the relationships between the formal dinner tableware and the man that the viewer felt compelled to watch and listen as the tiny man made his sales talk.

Another commercial sought to illustrate the quietness of the Ford automobile by special effects of sound as well as sight. The vignette began with a montage which presented the clattery clang of a noisy city: traffic lights, milling crowds, bumper-to-bumper traffic, whistles, noises, din. The Ford automobile was parked at the side of a crowded street in San Francisco with traffic streaming around it. The special effect required was a total stop-action of all sights and sounds except those of the salesman.

The passing people and traffic were immobilized and silent, while the speaker walked completely around the automobile, stepping over a sleeping dog and between static pedestrians, pointing out the advantage of quietness in the Ford automobile. After he had walked around the automobile and opened the car door, all the traffic and pedestrian movements began again, as if the moment of suspended time had never occurred. This incredible special effect was achieved through a fusion of film and electronic techniques. The scene in San Francisco was photographed on film. The scene to be frozen in time was transferred to disc on the HS-200 Special Effects Recorder. Then an automobile was parked in a videotape studio in a position which exactly matched that of the car parked on the street; the spokesman walked around the car, stepping over the nonexistent dog, while he explained the advantages of the Ford. The two scenes, city street and quiet studio, were then combined by the Technimatte process.

A special effects commercial holds a major pitfall: Unless great care is taken to make the effect integral with the product's function or the sponsor's name, the viewer may remember the gimmick and forget the message. The special effects approach offers the filmmaker the fullest opportunity for self-expression through the design of shapes, forms, colors, movements and sounds—and enough rope to hang himself. A stunning award-winning commercial which provides a rich and exciting viewing experience—but fails to sell the product—has negated the reason for its existence. Every visual and sound effect should be carefully weighed in terms of its relationship to the sales message. If the special effect sells the product, use it. If the effect distracts the viewer's attention from the product, however pleasing it may be, discard it.

THE ANIMATED FILM

The animated film is perhaps the catchiest of all the forms of television commercial, because the form lends itself to any flight of fancy an artist's mind can create. The commercial which portrayed an acrimonious debate between a hungry man and a disgruntled stomach about the kinds of food the former shoveled into the latter was so hilarious, and became so popular, that it not only sold the product, but made the program it interrupted seem mundane by comparison. The animated aerosol can that conducted its Raid against thief and hoodlum insects made graphic its killing effectiveness in a way that desensitized its extermination function, and sold the insecticide. And the public relations commercial which revealed how new ideas, and men with new ideas, are respected at the 3-M Corporation, expressed an abstract concept that could only find form in animated films and videotapes.

There is scarcely a television commercial that does not use animated forms in some way; titles, objects, people and cartoons are often mixed together for maximum visual novelty. A common technique is to combine animated cartoons with live-action backgrounds; an animated figure may hop around an automobile engine, pointing out the mechanical advantages of this particular engine or revealing what corrosive disasters may occur if the viewer does not buy a given brand of lubrication. Or, if madam's garbage disposal does not work, a cartoon gremlin can hold his nose and descend to the abyss to explain to the live-action housewife, and watching viewer, how a given brand of drain cleaner can solve the problem. Anything goes if it visually captures the attention of the viewer, so that he or she will be motivated to listen to the sales talk and buy the product.

Classifying television commercials into categories is as arbitrary as defining their emotional appeals, because there is a continuing process of cross-pollenation. In practice, a commercial may at once appeal to several levels of human desire, using almost every kind of film and videotape television technique to drive home the sales message. In most commercials, however, the filmmaker will select one primary appeal to a given target audience: pride, fear, ambition, sex appeal. And he will then select the media technique that will most effectively drive home that appeal: demonstrations, special effects, animation. The characteristics of the products and the target audience determine the means of selling the sponsor's goods and products.

Longer commercials are not necessarily more effective than short ones. Relevant advertising research has established the following generalizations: Shorter commercials are watched and better liked by most viewers. Commercials that are thirty seconds long may be ninety percent as effective in selling the sponsor's goods and services as sixty-second commercials. When a commercial exceeds a hundred seconds in length, its effectiveness falls off rapidly. The secret to effective selling in a television commercial is evidently not how long it is, but how cleverly it is packaged in qualities of human appeal.

Educational and Research Forms

19

Teaching with Films

In 1910 Thomas Edison wrote: "I believe that the motion picture is destined to revolutionize our educational system, and that in a few years it will supplant largely, if not entirely, the use of textbooks in our schools." These and other breezy generalizations about "at last getting rid of teachers" did little to endear him to the educational community of his time. His wishful thinking was understandable in the light of the fact that he had been expelled from school for being unable to learn, and perhaps forgivable in the sense that his words had something of the ring of prophecy. At the time he wrote, 1910, the first educational film catalogue had already been published, listing more than five hundred titles. Since then the production of educational films has flourished steadily, largely without publicity, finding enrichment and instructional uses in schools at all levels, as well as in business, industry and the armed forces. With the advent of television as an incomparable distribution system and the development of videotape for quick, low-cost productions, educational film and television programs now permeate almost every aspect of American society.

Learning Characteristics

The learning characteristics of the target audience are a primary consideration in films produced for teaching purposes. They are important not only because pupils must have the proper educational background in order to understand what is being presented, but also because students' capacity to learn from films and television programs varies widely with maturation.

Films and television programs created for the primary grades presume nothing in terms of previous instruction, because these grades are considered the child's first exposure to education. In reality, children from some well-to-do areas have had preschool training and parental tutoring to give them a head start, while others come from homes in which education is not valued and are almost blank slates in terms of their formal education. Because of the numbers of disadvantaged children, the primary students are treated as if they are all attending school with the same educational background—none at all.

Films are held to a length of five to ten minutes to match the attention span of young viewers, with each scene held a long time on the screen because of the relatively low film literacy level of children. Narration is minimal, with short sentences, few new words and each concept repeated several times. As much as possible, the content is visualized rather than explained.

In the primary grades almost any given subject is introduced and interpreted as if it were being presented for the first time. Such factors of apperception as film literacy, formal education and predisposition toward the subject are presumed to be nonexistent.

Subjects presented during the first three grades are concerned with physical things and with matters of safety, such as how to cross the street and how to act in a fire drill. Science is introduced in terms of "Wonders in Your Own Backyard" and "Collecting Specimens from a Tidepool." Art films teach how to make collages and finger paintings, those on social studies treat such subjects as "Your Friend, the Policeman." And all of the stories portray children the ages of those in the audience, doing the activities typical of the viewer's own everyday experiences. Abstract concepts are seldom taught at this age.

Films for the next five grades, the intermediate elementary grades, presume a certain film literacy and a curricular level of formal education. With higher film literacy the tempo quickens, camera and editing techniques become sophisticated, the average film lengthens to eleven to fourteen minutes. Both male and female students tend to identify with a representative boy about twelve to fourteen years old. Vocabulary levels become important and terms are used which derive from curricular offerings.

The range of subject matter broadens and a transition begins from physical things to abstract concepts; animated films are used to clarify mathematical concepts and teach desensitized forms of anatomy and hygiene. Masculine and feminine spheres of interest develop and the gang instinct becomes strong. Personal identification with peer groups becomes increasingly important, and peer group mores must be reflected in social studies films or such films run the risk of a boomerang effect. Whereas films for the earlier grades were concerned with personal safety, those designed for the intermediate grades are concerned with civilized behavior in the interpersonal relationships of the classroom and the playground. Science, mathematics, language arts and social studies are presented in more abstract terms, with students expected to make visual analogies and interpret basic kinds of schematic animation.

Film literacy reaches its peak in teen-agers enrolled in senior high school. At this age pupils learn more quickly from films than do adults (probably because of "adult discount"), and the most sophisticated cinematic techniques may be used. The average film length of a hard-content subject increases to sixteen to twenty-two minutes and the narrative absorption rate becomes as high as it will ever be.

As massive hordes of hormones begin to surge through the veins of the teen-age viewer, the messages of films are more specifically addressed to "him" or "her," with those intended for the life space of one sex often being of marginal interest to the other sex at a given stage of maturity. Male and female role identification factors become important as the pupils begin to identify with the functions assigned by society to each of the sexes. Film subjects now emphasize the study of hygiene, the sciences, physiological maturation, social studies, personal and vocational guidance, and the menace of narcotics, alcohol and tobacco. At this point the boomerang effect looms in every social studies film produced, and if what is taught in school is an obvious attack on the mores of the peer group or the values taught at home, many students may reject the new concepts and leave with their prejudices reinforced.

The spectrum of human knowledge that lends itself to media communication may now be presented in their most abstract forms. Mathematics, the physical and biological sciences, projections of the most abstruse concepts, may now be rendered in the media, subject only to the age and intelligence of the viewer and his level of formal education. With each passing year, however, the spread of intelligence and capability becomes more pronounced, and age itself becomes an intrinsically less important factor. The older the target audience, the more specialized becomes their interests and abilities, and the more specialized must be the film and television program designed to teach them. After high school the content of teaching films seems to break down into two categories: general-interest films to be viewed by everybody, and special-interest films to be viewed by those having a sophisticated background in the subject presented.

Every kind of film technique and special effect may thereafter be used—multiple images functioning independently on the screen, subjective editing techniques with kaleidoscopic images and esoteric interpretations, animation combined with live action and special effects, all rendered with flashing tempo and subtlety to the flicker of an eyelash. The years of maximum film literacy are followed by a dulling (alas) in everything. Perhaps this is due to physical and physiological decline, or perhaps to adult discount—the tendency to take everything with a grain of salt. With maturity and skepticism come a resistance to change, and a corollary resistance to learning.

Producing an Effective Teaching Film

There are several concerns the filmmaker must keep in mind if he wishes to produce an effective teaching film. These are: *behavioral purpose, target audience, subject matter, core idea, cinematic form, story line* and *identification.*

BEHAVIORAL GOALS

Behavioral goals refers to what the viewers are expected to know or do as a consequence of what they have learned from the film. Moreover, it refers also to how that learning will be measured; whether by classroom discussion, a written test, a performance skill or insights revealed in essays and research assignments. All the other concerns in making an instructional film are directed toward its behavioral objective—measurable learning.

A film made with one educational objective in mind not only hits its mark, but often finds other unanticipated uses as well, because the content and its interpretation are specific and not bogged down in vague generalizations. Conversely, a film produced to serve several educational purposes at once seldom achieves more than marginal success and often fails to hit any mark at all. The filmmaker should select one primary objective—one behavioral goal—and relate all the other concerns of the film to that educational objective.

THE TARGET AUDIENCE

The characteristics of the target audience must be known to the filmmaker before he can make a film to influence it. As discussed earlier, the teaching film should ideally be conceived and produced for an audience of a given age, sex, intelligence quotient, level of formal education, film literacy, lifespace and socioeconomic milieu. These factors apply most emphatically to films produced for pupils up through the high school years; thereafter the distinctions soften, demographic interests develop and the factor of adult discount sets in.

During the school years, however, it is essential that the filmmaker understand the characteristics of his target audience in every phase of production from script to screen, and keep these questions in mind at all times: For whom is the film intended? What viewer characteristics should be taken into account when writing and producing the film?

Common sense would dictate that any filmmaker intending to produce an educational film on a given subject investigate the curriculum of the school system to find out at what age and grade level a given subject is taught, and what behavioral goals and forms of content are best served by his proposed film. Moreover, such matters as attention span and vocabulary level have an important bearing on the interpretation of a subject at a given age level. A motion picture treating sex education which is slanted toward a sixth-grade audience, when the subject is taught in the ninth grade, would be unacceptable in either classroom.

SUBJECT MATTER

Selection of content is the third concern. The reason for considering content third instead of first is that once the behavioral goals have been defined and the characteristics of the pupils determined, it becomes easier to select the most effective form of content. A film intended to ameliorate racial prejudice in the high schools of a given region will have a better chance to succeed if its objectives and the prejudices of the audience are understood from the beginning. The filmmaker will then select the specific forms of content that will be persuasive and not trigger a boomerang effect. Obviously, the filmmaker will have a general area of subject matter in mind when he plans his film, but the selection of specific content should await definition of behavioral goals and analysis of the target audience.

THE CORE IDEA

The core idea is what the filmmaker (or sponsor) has to say about the subject. The core idea may be the very reason for making the film— someone has a compelling need to speak out about some aspect of the human condition—it is this message which provides the intellectual framework of the production and permeates every aspect of cinematic interpretation. In films made for the classroom, in which the curriculum dictates much of what is presented, it makes a difference if the filmmaker can find some aspect of the subject or its purpose to which he can make a personal commitment.

CINEMATIC FORM

The cinematic form should be the fifth consideration, rather than first or second, because the decision of whether to produce the film in the form of a drama, a documentary or as animation depends upon the purpose of the film, the background of the target audience, the nature of the subject matter and the core idea. If the educational purpose is to change self-destructive habits in the target audience, then an appeal to the emotions through the dramatic form may be preferable. If the purpose is to reveal the roots of civil discontent, then the documentary form may be best. If the purpose is to render mathematical relationships in a form the students may see and understand, then animation may be used. The cinematic form should be selected only after the other decisions are made.

STORY LINE

The story line, or plot, is the organization of film content. The way the material is presented and interpreted relates, always, to one primary goal—the instructional purpose of the film. Every scene and every item of content should relate to that purpose in some way or be deleted from the film. The way the content is organized derives from its cinematic form. For example, a dramatic educational film would join a conflict and build through crises to a climax and obligatory scene, with modifications in the dramatic structure to suit its educational purpose. A documentary would present its idea in terms of human consequences, and lead the viewer toward an inescapable conclusion. The same organizational principle holds true in the teaching applications of all the film genres.

IDENTIFICATION

Identification is the last but not the least of the filmmakers' conceptual concerns. A viewer's interest in a film is determined to a large extent by the degree to which he personally identifies with the life on the screen and perceives its content to be relevant to himself. In practice, this means including representative individuals, or symbolic items, as vehicles of identification in the film for the viewer. A film intending to persuade high school seniors to pursue forest genetics as a life's work would probably include a young man of that age studying that vocation. A film that teaches kindergarten children how to make paper collages would include boys and girls of kindergarten age making collages. Identification may be aroused by inclusion of religious or political symbols, styles of clothing, rituals or authentic ways of doing things, anything relevant to the viewer.

Teaching Forms and Formats

All of the major motion picture forms analyzed thus far in this book—the languages of film and videotape, dramatic structure and character development, documentary and propaganda films—find some form of application in the classroom in almost every kind of subject matter. Often, however, they are modified in some aspects of their conception and execution to meet the specific needs of education. There are six major film applications to the classroom: *the single-concept film, the modified dramatic film, the documentary film, the animated film, the process film* and *the programmed instruction film.*

Single concept film. *Convair Aerospace Division: General Dynamics.*

THE SINGLE-CONCEPT FILM

The short, silent single-concept film was the first application of motion pictures to the classroom. Films produced around the turn of the century consisted of a few minutes' viewing of leverage used to hoist large weights, birds beginning their fall migrations and magnets attracting iron filings. The teachers lectured on the subject during the silent-film showing, and the pupils were free to speak up and ask questions. This brief and handy form of film was eventually eclipsed by the longer sound motion picture and eventually by television, but has recently begun to enjoy an instructional renaissance, thanks to the development of the cartridge-loading projector and console, and the insistence of teachers who want to do their own teaching.

The uses of the single-concept film in the classroom differ so widely that few hard and fast rules can be laid down regarding its characteristics. In projection time, it usually lasts from one to three minutes. Its subject matter commonly involves a process needing visual presentation to be understood: chemical reactions, living creatures in their environment, animated diagrams, functioning machines and other forms of content in motion. Often the time scale is changed so that transient phenomena are slowed down or stopped for detailed study, or slow phenomena are speeded up to make their movements perceptible. The single-concept film offers three advantages: The teacher can do his own teaching, integrating the film into his lecture and curriculum. And the pupils can ask questions while the demonstrations are in progress.

THE MODIFIED DRAMATIC FILM

The dramatic form appeals primarily to the emotions of the viewer through identification with characters in a conflict situation. To serve educational purposes, however, the classic dramatic structure often needs to be adapted and modified. The educational form is frequently missing one or more vital parts of the plot structure in order to stimulate thought in the viewer and discussion in the classroom. The early portions of the drama are usually the same as those in theatrical films—joining the conflict, building suspense through a series of crises ascending to the obligatory scene and the climax. At the end of the educational dramatic film, however, the climax is often omitted. This leaves the viewer up in the air about what the climax should have been, and provides the basis for discussions among the students. This format is called the "open end" film.

Phoebe, for example, tells the story of a nice teen-age girl who has let her passion for her boyfriend get the better of her common sense. The film revolves around the memories of her passion, and her fears of the possible reactions of her boyfriend, her parents and school officials when the time comes to tell them she is pregnant. In each instance Phoebe fantasizes a gamut of reactions ranging from joy to contempt, ending with contempt. The obligatory scene of the film is, of course, when she must break the news to her boyfriend, and here the film ends—without a climax. *Phoebe* ends and the lights come on for discussion among the teen-age female viewers about premarital sexual relations.

The dramatic form may be used for several specific educational purposes: *To attack racial, religious and ethnic prejudices; to breed tolerance for differing ways of life; to change self-destructive social habits; to offer insight into historically important persons and events; to inculcate ideologies;* and *to sugar-coat the teaching of a process or a theme.*

To attack racial, religious and ethnic prejudices is a tricky business because of possible boomerang effects on the target audience. A Canadian film, *A Day in the Night of Jonathan Mole*, treats the issue of racial and ethnic prejudice by presenting it in the form of a farce. Mr. Mole, the quintessence of blind prejudice against Jews, Indians and immigrants, goes to sleep one night and dreams of the opportunity to be a judge passing sentence on these minorities for the alleged crime of wanting to better themselves. The witnesses against the accused are caricatures of various forms of sophistry in defense of prejudice: The social snob insists "they will be happier with their own kind." The gregarious go-along supports the prejudices of his fellows in order to be considered a nice guy. The failure in the eyes of his wife, his boss and himself rationalizes his shortcomings by attacking these minorities who, for some undefined reason, are responsible for his lack of success. By caricaturing these prejudices in a ludicrous way, the problems of prejudice in a subtler form are exposed for serious discussion.

The characteristics and life space of the target audience must be carefully considered when launching this kind of satirical attack. The author showed *A Day in the Night of Jonathan Mole* to a group of

PHOEBE. Open end film. *National Film Board of Canada.*

university students, who were delighted by the farce because the caricatures made fools of older prejudiced adults. The same film presented to
an evening class of adults had a boomerang effect because the barbs
were aimed at them. Conversely, dramatic films revealing the bigotries
of youth are resented by the young, while delighting the adults with
their objectivity. Each group is willing to laugh at the shortcomings of
the other, while bristling at attacks on themselves. It would appear that
one way to attack irrational prejudices in one target audience is to point
out these failings in another.

To breed tolerance for differing ways of life is a worthwhile use of
the dramatic form in education. On the premise that knowledge breeds
tolerance and understanding, Canada has assigned its National Film
Board production teams the continuing task of producing dramatic and
documentary films about its racial, religious and ethnic minorities for
distribution to all the peoples of Canada. Brief dramatic films provide
insight into the family lives, work habits and religious beliefs of those
Canadian minorities who, through choice or circumstance, live outside
the mainstream. The dramatic form is similarly used to engender insight
into the lives of the peoples of Asia, Africa and other parts of the world,
because of its intimacy and emotional appeal.

Viewer identification with characters in the dramatic form is important in *changing self-destructive social habits.* One major social problem
derives from those young persons who drop out of school because they
dislike academic life and classroom discipline, without realizing that
they may be heading for dead-end menial jobs. *You're No Good* is the
story of the dreary career of a high school dropout who dreams of being
glamourous and important, but whose work consists of delivering sandwiches for a food-to-go café. The film's purpose is to point out the
consequences of not having an education without ever touching upon
the subject of education. The boy's story is a tale of continuing humili-
ations—because of his humble job and lack of an education—culminating in his impulsive theft of a motorcycle to impress a girl friend. Once
he steals the motorcycle and is identified as a thief, it is downhill all the
way—he is rejected by his girl friend, avoided by his friends, afraid to
go home—until, at the end, he awaits the police. Any teen-age boy with
a proclivity toward "dropping out" is given something to think about in
You're No Good.

To offer insight into historically important persons and events is
another function of the educational dramatic film. Historical lives and

events, when read about in books, seem to many pupils to be dry and musty occurrences that could never have been lived in the heat of blood. The historical dramatic film may enable the viewer to subjectively experience what happened in the past, as if it were taking place today, through identification with the characters involved in the struggle.

Many educational historical dramas are produced to illuminate the great events of the past and offer insight into the motivations of men who shaped the events of their time. The interaction of men and important events tends to engender greatness or venality, and what men have done to present their posterity with solutions or problems may be given vivid form and contemporary flavor by dramatizing the conflicts as if they were occurring today. The Golden Age of Greece, the rise of Rome, the spirit of medieval yearning for peace and unity, may be dramatized as personal-professional crises in the lives of Socrates, Caesar and Charlemagne. Care needs to be taken in historical dramas that the characters act and speak as human beings; at times, the difficulty of revealing relatively abstract cause and effect relationships in history creates the temptation to put unnatural dialogue in the mouths of great men.

Not all educationally successful historical films have been made for educational purposes. Feature films, such as *The Battle of Algiers* and *The Ox Bow Incident*, have been adapted for classroom use. And many dramatic historical films made for national television broadcast ultimately found their way into the classroom. Probably the finest ever produced for American television have been such Wolper Production specials as *Surrender at Appomattox* and *They've Killed President Lincoln!* In the latter film, for example, most of the important historical enigmas relating to President Lincoln's assassination were raised and explored in dramatic form: Why did the President's bodyguard leave just before the arrival of the assassin? Why was the assassin's escape route, the only road out of Washington, left unpatrolled? Over a century after Lincoln's assassination, when history seems to be repeating itself, the question of coincidence or conspiracy still haunts our history, with the issues dramatically presented for discussion in *They've Killed President Lincoln!*

Propaganda, the *inculcation of ideologies*, is a related use of the dramatic form. Many nations are embarrassed by certain bloody and treacherous pages in their history, and produce dramatic films to revise the events of the past and the circumstances in which they occurred to polish their own traditions in the minds of the young. It is not uncommon for democratic nations, at some times, and totalitarian nations, at all times, to convince the younger generation that good was bad, and vice versa, thereby subverting the realities of the past to serve the politics of the present. For years American dramatic films interpreted the white man's relations with the Indians in the simplistic terms of the noble pioneer fighting the dirty redskins. Today, this relationship is reversed in dramatic films, with the Indian portrayed as nature's nobleman and the pioneers as unscrupulous brutes. Both dramatic interpretations are propaganda, since there is no such thing, historically, as all the good being on one side and all the bad on the other.

The dramatic form is sometimes used *to sugar-coat the teaching of a process or a theme* and thereby make a dull subject palatable. This kind of film is usually made specifically to meet a teaching need and is seldom adapted from a feature film. *The Grievance*, for example, teaches industrial workers in an automobile assembly plant what kind of con-

THEY'VE KILLED PRESIDENT LINCOLN! Recreation of historical events. *Wolper Productions.*

STILL A BROTHER. Minority studies. *Contemporary Films/ McGraw-Hill*.

flict constitutes a legitimate grievance against the company and how to prosecute that grievance in a legal way compatible with their status as union employees. The conflict is joined when the metal of a truck cab comes out of a paint-drying oven too hot to touch. The worker assigned to the next phase of assembly refuses to handle it, even at the insistence of the company foreman. The worker walks off the job and seeks out the union steward. The two men filed a formal grievance against the company and the subsequent grievance procedure then becomes part of the dramatic structure. Each level of complaint becomes another dramatic crisis, all the way up to the final arbitration. As is true of this kind of dramatic process film, the outcome is left open-ended—for discussion, and so the viewer does not get the idea that by following the correct grievance procedure he will always win a victory.

The Documentary Film

The documentary film has been discussed at length in the section treating the characteristics of that genre. Documentaries produced for network television broadcasting and other purposes eventually find their way into the classroom. They are used for enrichment in United States and world history, civics, drug abuse education, ecology, fine arts, minority studies, social and personal guidance, psychology and an infinite variety of other courses. The documentary form finds so many uses at every grade level from elementary school through graduate school, as film and television programming, that its applications are almost beyond enumeration.

The documentary film originally produced for other uses may not find its way into the curriculum without modification. Often large sections of a documentary film contain subject matter extraneous to the needs of a given course, and these are simply deleted from the film by the distributor, often to the anguish of the producer. Or a film may be too long, so it is chopped down in draconian fashion to fill the scheduled class time. Sometimes, unfortunately, the content is considered too yeasty for young intellects, or its ideas too controversial, and an excision may be performed to prevent a film from raising any mental dust or parental ire. A fine television documentary, *The Tenement*, dealt openly with such discomforting realities as illegitimacy among teen-age Negro girls, but these segments were deleted before distribution to the schools, apparently to make it a "safe documentary."

The Animated Film

The instructional uses of the animated film are many, and have been discussed in the chapter on "Animation: The Eye of the Mind." Its function in teaching is to present nonrealistic ideas and abstract ideas in their true and understandable relationships. The current applications of animation are for the revelation of invisible forces, depiction of processes, simplification of processes, desensitization of subject matter, creation of visual projections and generalizations, re-creation of the past, progressive presentation of related elements, offering of visual cues and visual analogies, and the tangible visualization of ideas.

The process film. *United States Navy.*

THE PROCESS FILM

The process film is a specialized instructional form used to teach the viewer how something works. The process concept falls into three teaching categories: *achieving a performance skill; the managerial process film;* and *the overview of a process.*

Achieving a performance skill requires a one-to-one relationship between the film or videotape presentation and the viewer. The program is a teacher addressing each viewer, and the student, after seeing the program, should be able to turn around and begin to practice whatever skill has been taught on the screen. Teaching a performance skill—how to assemble a jet engine, fight the fire of a burning airplane, repair an electron microscope—requires unique teaching principles and atypical cinematic techniques.

The teaching of new concepts and skills in a process film is enhanced if the content is presented visually, labeled and spoken: a concept called "multiband learning." If the viewer is studying gross anatomy, for example, he will learn more quickly if he simultaneously sees a tibia bone, reads the word label adjacent to it and hears its name spoken. Multiband stimuli joins all the related information simultaneously, in space and time, and thereby reinforces all the viewer's levels of perception.

The length of the film itself should be brief when teaching a performance skill. One skill taught and quickly implemented is a skill learned. In practical terms, this means a single process presentation should be five to ten minutes long, depending upon the complexity of the skill and the preparation of the viewer.

The pacing of content should be far slower when teaching a per-

DEEP SEA DRILLING. Overview process film. *Scripps Institute of Oceanography.*

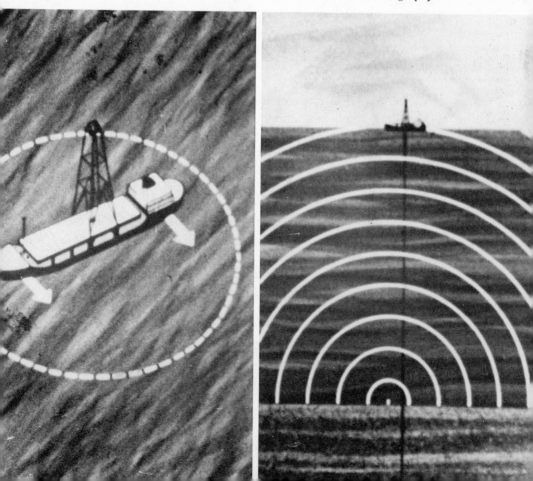

formance skill than in any other film form, because learning a physical skill takes time, and the more difficult and complex the skill to be learned, the more time it is likely to take. The viewer must psychologically orient his limbs to the relationships portrayed on the screen and mentally learn a physical skill that he can implement only after the film is over. The already slow pacing should slow down even further under the following circumstances:

Whenever new and unfamiliar objects or ideas are introduced for the first time to the viewer, they should be held a long time on the screen. The less experience he has had, the fewer apperceptions he brings to the subject, the more time he will need (within reason) to familiarize himself with whatever is new. This means, of course, that the overall pacing of the film will seem impossibly slow from the entertainment point of view.

Whenever there are new words to be identified with new objects, the pacing should decrease. It is sound teaching practice to show the new object, label the new object and speak the name of the new object, so the viewer can see, read and hear it all at the same time.

Whenever the content is inherently difficult to understand—with complex, quantitative or abstruse relationships—the pacing of content should slow to a merciful crawl.

The cinematic techniques used to slow down the pacing of content are as follows: If no movements are involved, the scene may simply be held on the screen long enough for the viewer to learn its content. If movement is itself the subject, such as the twist of the body in a tumbling exercise, the preferred film technique may be slow motion. If one phase of the movement is so crucial or difficult that it deserves careful scrutiny and analysis, the movement may be stopped in mid-phase in a freeze-frame.

Camera angles and closeups serve unique functions in the manual skills film. It is best to teach a skill involving some kind of assembly from the subjective point of view—through the eyes of the viewer, as he will see the assembly when he turns from the film to try the skill. This often means photographing the manual performance from so subjective an angle that two hands apparently come in from opposite sides of the screen to do the work. By presenting the identical point-of-view from which the viewer will eventually implement the skill, the filmmaker reduces the likelihood that the student will make errors. In a sense, the viewer memorizes the visual patterns of the hands in motion.

A closeup should be used in a skills film whenever there is a changing physical relationship. For example, if a process film were teaching the viewers how to thread a film projector, a closeup would be used whenever the film was being engaged in threading sprockets, the film gate or at any other point along its path that differed from its handling procedure at any preceding point. The closeup alerts the viewer to something new and important, and simultaneously gives him a careful look at the new physical relationship.

It is important to show possible errors in performance process films to avoid confusion, and possible injury or death, in the implementation of that skill. When the United States Navy uses films to teach how to fight the fires raging in a downed aircraft, it includes all the things that could go wrong—such as an explosion—so the student will not have any sudden surprises when he goes out there to put down the blaze.

The student tends to remember best the first and the last items of a skills film, the intervening items least. The way to sharpen the fading center of the memory curve is to make the visual characteristics of the middle items distinctive from those of the beginning and end by a change of color codes, thematic sounds, unusual cues and designs, or by providing some cinematic change of pace.

The second type of process film is the *managerial process film*. This is one degree of abstraction removed from the skills performance film in the sense that the viewer would be able to follow all the phases of a process, relating the parts to the whole, without necessarily being able to perform any of those phases himself. The managerial film usually involves a presentation of all the stages of a scientific or industrial project in sequential order. For example: The procedural phases of a projected rocket mission to the moon are often filmed in advance by a process film which shows, through simulated firings with models, animation and simulated environments of minimum or no gravity, all the phases of the actual firing. The managerial process film presents the closest possible approximation of reality in the form of a film simulation, thereby reducing confusion at the time of the real mission.

The principles of multiband learning still apply to the managerial process film, as does the need for a closeup to reveal any changing physical relationship. The duration of the managerial form can be longer, however, and the tempo of the editing can be increased, because no manual learning skills are involved. The pacing of content is quicker, because the content is more generalized, and any viewer at the managerial level brings apperceptions born of training that enable him to give quick scrutiny to a difficult phase that would have to be studied slowly by the viewer of a skills film. Every phase of the process should be presented in the sequential order of its real occurrence to reduce the possibility of viewer confusion when he confronts reality.

The *overview process film* is a generalized information film often used in the form of a report. The overview process film is produced without any strictures of form, pacing, point-of-view or editing, so long as the lay viewer can understand, in a general way, what took place. It can be as dynamic and fast-moving as an entertainment film. *Deep Sea Drilling Project*, produced for the National Science Foundation, portrayed the activities of an expedition sent out to test the ponderous theory of continental drift by drilling core samples in the undersea crusts of the ocean. The project itself, a tedious process, took years to plan and implement, but the twenty-minute film reporting its methods and findings was presented in the forms of animation, live action, multiple-panel effects and editing dynamism that was every bit as exciting as a science-fiction action film.

THE PROGRAMMED INSTRUCTION FILM

Programmed learning is a teaching system in which content is taught by the question and answer method, with the content presented in a series of small increments of increasing difficulty. In theory, programmed instruction attempts to present the content in increments so small that the student can scarcely make a mistake, and to reinforce his learning by providing him with immediate knowledge of results. This system of operant conditioning may be regarded as a threefold process: simplification of content; reinforcement of learning; reshaping of simple responses into complex ones.

Programmed instruction originally consisted of written questions and answers in both linear and branching techniques, usually in the form of programmed textbooks, with page-turning for the next question.

"Teaching machines," originally mechanical page-turners, soon evolved into electrically operated units utilizing motion pictures, slides and videotapes. Electrically operated teaching machines can assure that the student obeys operating instructions, makes an overt response (or the program will not advance) and controls the presentation of content in a way that virtually eliminates cheating. The teaching machine does not teach, but merely presents each sequence of instruction in a controlled sequential order to the student; it is the program that teaches.

The film and videotape applications to programmed instruction usually involve a console containing a viewing screen and rows of student response buttons. This console presents sequences of Super-8 or 16-mm. images (loaded on loops or cartridges) on the viewing screen, or sequences of videotape containing similar content, which can be pre-programmed to stop automatically on any selected frame, and can be stop-framed or reversed by the student. An active response to multiple-choice questions is provided for by pushbutton, with the student's answers recorded on punched tape. The student may proceed at his own pace, each question and answer building upon the knowledge acquired earlier in the program. Immediate knowledge of a correct answer provides reinforcement of that knowledge. If the student gives an incorrect answer, the system can provide him with remedial material to help him find the correct answer on his own.

Computer-based teaching machines currently provide the ultimate system for programmed instruction. An enormous range of instruction may be presented to the student through animated film, live-action film, videotape, film-strip, synchronized tape recorders or written text. Similarly, the form of the student's responses may be written, spoken or a performance activity, with the computer evaluating each response and selecting the increments of instruction based on the student's subsequent performance. It seems only a matter of time until the Random Access Videotape Editor (see "Videotape and Film: The New Synthesis"), with its information storage on magnetic discs and instantaneous retrieval at the point of a light pen, will provide the heart of a revolutionary new system of accelerated learning through programmed instruction. And the step beyond that may be the combination of RAVE with animation software created on the analogue computer (see "Animation: The Eye of the Mind").

20

Teaching by
Television

Television was first used for classroom education in the United States on May 19, 1938. A program lasting forty-five minutes was presented over twenty-five sets in the RCA building in New York to 250 students of the New York University School of Commerce. The image of the instructor appeared on every screen and a two-way radio system permitted questions and answers. Similar instructional television programs proliferated in higher education until, today, there is scarcely a college or university that does not offer videotaped lectures and courses over a closed-circuit television system. The public schools, both elementary and secondary, have kept pace with this instructional television development.

Meanwhile, outside these educational institutions, business, industry, government agencies and the United States Armed Forces have utilized instructional television in one form or another for training programs and adult education. As early as 1942 television was being used by the government to train air-raid wardens, and the armed forces have since become leaders in research and development in the practical uses of television as a training medium, as they were earlier innovators in the instructional uses of motion pictures.

Given the availability of many new educational television channels through cable transmission, it is only a matter of time until many Americans can acquire a higher education while attending television lectures in their own homes, unhindered by such liabilities of the past as lack of money. Instructional television may bring true educational democracy to America, if the medium is effectively used.

The advent of commercial television has opened up a window on the world for virtually every household in America. The image empires of the broadcasting networks have become "educational" in their revelations to the average citizen of the great events of our time. The viewer is not really an outsider, but almost a participant in these events. In addition to its timeliness and immediacy, television conveys a sense of spontaneity, of being where the action is. Television brings great events home to the viewer before they become history. With the advent of satellite broadcasting, the visit of an American President to China can be watched in any town in America at the time of its occurrence—a true conquest of time, space and ignorance. The commercial television networks, for all the criticism that may legitimately be leveled at them, have created as enlightened a common denominator of public opinion as may be found in any nation in the world.

Moreover, seeing what is being done in other parts of the nation has raised the public's taste and discrimination in isolated communities to a level not significantly different from those of the urban centers. The local yokel of joke and legend has all but disappeared. The man on the street in Buffalo Wallow is about as well informed as the man on the street in New York or Los Angeles.

Educational and Instructional Television

The terms educational television (ETV) and instructional television (ITV) have acquired different connotations. Educational television refers to education in the broader sense of enrichment, of contact with every aspect of the world that might go beyond the content of a given curriculum. Concerts, political conventions and interviews fall within this purview. Instructional television, on the other hand, is specifically concerned with content to be included in a given curriculum and presented to a specific class. Lectures, demonstrations and the like fall into this category. Educational television is undefined in what it may encompass, while instructional television is defined specifically in terms of teaching the factual information, skills and concepts of a prescribed course of study.

NORMAN CORWIN PRESENTS. Cultural presentations. *Group W Productions.*

Educational television has brought new forms of culture into American life. The enjoyment of listening to great music at home is enhanced by the pleasure of watching the conductor and the musicians perform. Exhibitions of sculpture and the other arts can be brought to the distant viewer, who acquires new tastes and sensibilities by viewing them. A United Nations debate presents a world issue to the individual viewer. Poets read their works, great men speak, and the viewer can listen and watch as he develops new insights. Erik Barnouw described the effects of educational television: "Over television, quietly and informally, great men of the age have talked to us. A Robert Frost or Frank Lloyd Wright tells us about his life and work. There is astonishing intimacy. Throughout the great man's life, few human beings have looked on his face so long and closely as does the television viewer during such a program. Here intimacy and simplicity help give narration the most dramatic impact it can achieve." Thanks to the remote television camera, any visual or verbal form of cultural life occurring anywhere in the nation can be brought to all the viewers watching everywhere in the nation.

Instructional Television Functions

In the schools educational television is used primarily to extend and enrich the curriculum by providing vicarious experiences that relate to the subject matter taught in the particular courses. Subject matter taught by instructional television ranges from accounting through zoology, with hundreds, perhaps thousands, of other subjects in between. The grade levels taught begin with kindergarten and end with university graduate schools and adult education classes. The courses selected for instructional telecasts at any particular level of schooling have been dictated by the specific needs of the school systems, institutions and professional schools that are using instructional television, and no generalized yardstick for application exists.

The extraordinary breadth of curricular offerings by television has led, in some circles, to overselling television, as the medium for all forms of teaching at all levels. This reflects naïveté about the nature of media as a means of teaching—there is no one communication system that provides the answer to all the questions in the educational process. We do know, however, that instructional television can be used to teach an extremely wide range of subject matter, skills and insights.

The functions of instructional television, in terms of control of time, space, size, distance and perspective, may be exemplified by its successful use in medical schools. These functions are *image magnification, image multiplication, viewpoint control, image transportation, multiple-image presentations* and *image transformation*.

IMAGE MAGNIFICATION

Image magnification is by far the most widely cited use of television in medical teaching. Specimens of gross anatomy may be enlarged to permit students to see minute details, and the images held on the screen indefinitely to permit the instructor to point out relationships. A histology slide under a microscope may be magnified to provide examples and visual cues for students working at their own microscopes.

IMAGE MULTIPLICATION

Image multiplication, the dissemination of a key scene to many television receivers in many classrooms, is a capability unique to television. The same crucial operation, such as a heart transplant or some other rare surgical event, may be watched simultaneously by every medical practitioner, teacher and student interested in witnessing the event. Image multiplication is perhaps the most persuasive reason for nation-wide installation of television systems in every kind of school.

VIEWPOINT CONTROL

Viewpoint control to optimize the student's opportunity to witness a demonstration is a universal application. This adaptation may range from simulation of a surgeon's single point-of-view during an appendectomy, to the use of several cameras and monitors to provide classroom students with multiple viewpoints during the surgery demonstration.

Television is far more practicable than film in offering observation of such hard-to-view demonstrations as brain surgery or dental repairs. Two or three television cameras may be trained on the demonstration, each equipped with a lens of differing focal length, to provide a simultaneous medium shot, closeup and extreme closeup, for concurrent viewing on three television monitors. In an adjacent room having such monitors, all three scene sizes may be concurrently viewed, analyzed and discussed by students and teachers without disturbing the demonstration in progress. Another advantage is that the demonstration may be viewed at a distant location, and if it is a rare event, may be video-taped on all three monitors for replay again and again. Students tend to prefer direct observation of demonstrations to television presentations, but their learning from the televised concepts is equivalent. Three-tape demonstrations edited into one videotape in the manner of film may subsequently be used as an instructional television program or in a video-viewing console under the direct control of a classroom teacher.

IMAGE TRANSPORTATION

Image transportation from an experiment conducted in isolation to a distant classroom permits a demonstration to take place undisturbed by the presence of teachers and students. The treatment of a paranoid patient by a psychiatrist, the countermeasures taken by a physician in a drug overdose case, the injection of a deadly virus into a rat by a microbiologist, may be televised in isolation and the images transported to a remote location and studied without upsetting the original experimental relationship.

Multiple-Image Presentations

Multiple-image presentations on separate monitors may be used to simultaneously televise component elements of a demonstration or experiment. During surgery on a spinal column, for example, one monitor might reveal the gross manual actions of the surgeon, the second could present minute renditions of the incisions and a third would offer fluoroscopic images of subsurface relationships. This three-dimensional viewing permits a greater understanding by the viewer of all contemporaneous elements of the operation.

Image Transformation

Image transformation is a recent trend. Image intensifiers are being used in conjunction with television to sharpen up otherwise obscure images, particularly in radiology and cardiography. Ultraviolet visual inspection of tissues in perspective is made possible by means of three-channel viewing through black-and-white videotubes in a color camera, enabling medical practitioners to locate tumors and count cancer cells through line-by-line television scanning. Some medical schools have tested fibre optics stereofluoroscopy, image addition and subtraction, to further extend the image transformation capabilities of television as a teaching and diagnostic tool.

Videotape Television Functions

The use of videotape adds to instructional television's capabilities a number of other advantages. These are *immediate playback, teaching of performance skills, reinforcement through repetition* and *vicarious visits to remote locations.*

IMMEDIATE PLAYBACK

Immediate playback is a unique advantage offered by videotape recording, a capability which lends itself to a wide variety of instructional television uses: A high diver may practice his acrobatics from board to water before the lens of the electronic camera, and get out of the pool to play back the videotape immediately for an appraisal of his performance. Before the diver is dry, he can go through his routine again, incorporating modifications based on what he has just observed in playback. The same playback and critique system may apply to teachers who wish to upgrade their lecture and demonstration skills, actors who wish to appraise their performances, speech students who need immediate feedback, psychiatrists who want to review a patient's once-only reactions and medical students who wish to study a rare example of surgery. There are no flat and firm generalizations about when and where to use the playback capability of videotape, because its possibilities are almost infinite. It was the immediate playback capability of videotape that first led to its adoption for comedies and dramas on commercial television; the cast and crew could view the performance immediately and decide whether another take was necessary.

TEACHING OF PERFORMANCE SKILLS

Teaching performance skills of various kinds is a televised extension of the process film. With the advent of videotape, quickly erasable and revisable, in-house production of low-cost presentations to teach basic skills becomes practicable. In schools, factories and armed forces alike videotapes teaching such perceptual motor skills as laboratory techniques, physical education, foreign language vocabulary, electronic assembly, aircraft repair, military tactics and safe driving habits may be produced at the point of use to meet the needs and characteristics of a known target audience. Moreover, with direct control over the playback facilities of a closed-circuit system, the presentation of the content may be halted at any time to permit the learners to practice the skills presented up to that point, before proceeding further.

REINFORCEMENT THROUGH REPETITION

Reinforcement through repetition is an effective way to enhance learning. The repetition may take the form of replays of a videotape television program, or by means of practice, workbooks, study guides, programmed instruction or discussions led by qualified teachers.

VICARIOUS VISITS TO DISTANT LOCATIONS

Vicarious visits to distant locations and past events may be made in the classroom by means of the television remote unit and videotape. Field trips to museums, atomic energy installations, oceanography expeditions, ecological crisis areas, may be videotaped and brought to the classroom for study and discussion. Historical events may live again through replay on videotape. The funeral of President Kennedy provided a classic example of the opportunity television offers for simultaneous viewing of a single event by millions that would otherwise have been witnessed by only a few thousand, an event preserved for posterity on film and videotape. This visitation capability may be used to bring all kinds of cultural and political events to the classroom.

Pupil Interaction Problems

Pupil interaction with the television teacher, and with other students, has often been lacking in instructional television. If the program has been recorded on videotape, then the only interaction possible is with the classroom supervisor. If the originating program is live, however, then electronic interaction is possible. Two-way communications systems may be used between the teacher and the remote students, and, sometimes, between different classes in separate locations. When a student in a remote classroom has a question, he may press a button which turns on a light in the originating studio. The television teacher then turns on the talk-back control panel to hear the question. He can either answer it, or, if he chooses, he can call for an answer from a student in another location. If a second student volunteers an answer by pressing the button in his location, the television teacher can bring in the voice of the answering student through the talk-back control panel. This system brings a degree of pupil participation into the television teaching system that works as long as there is not a flood of questions coming in from all the remote classrooms.

What a videotaped television program cannot provide, however, is the face-to-face motivational power of a teacher present in the classroom: a friendly word of encouragement, a phrase of clarification, an articulate discussion about an obscure point in the lecture, may stimulate pupils to study more effectively than the most carefully packaged television program. Whenever the interactive human touch is needed—and it is required in a large part of the educational process—there is no substitute for that tweedy anachronism, the teacher.

Moreover, certain kinds of verbally abstract ideas are fragile and subject to misinterpretation unless thoroughly discussed with students. The television teacher may deliver what he feels are lucid lectures on the concepts of existentialism to his remote classes, but unless he can discuss the concepts of Sartre and Merleau-Ponti with his pupils, he has no way of knowing whether they have intellectually digested them. Abstract relationships, on the other hand, such as those of mathematics, can readily be visualized in animation and broadcast over television.

Other inappropriate but not impossible uses for instructional television are seminars and psychotherapy sessions. These are mind-to-mind and emotion-to-emotion confrontations whose educational purposes are best served by interpersonal communication. It can be argued that two-way communications devices may be used to unite a teacher and students separated by distance or circumstances, but using television in this context means making the best of an awkward situation.

Producing Instructional Television

The first concern in teaching by television is to determine the program's relationship to the established curriculum. Will it serve as enrichment for a conventional class? Will its role be that of collaborative teacher, with a television teacher presenting part of the content and the classroom teacher doing the rest? Or will the television program present total instruction for a given course?

With television's function defined, the next concern is for the objectives of the curriculum and the individual courses. The official curriculum and its content are stipulated by state and local educational departments and the behavioral objectives of any instructional television program must advance those requirements. Subject matter experts and administrators then relate the capabilities of televised teaching to the stipulated text materials, assignments and examinations of a given course, and decide which aspects will be the responsibility of instructional television. Finally, the subject matter assigned to television is broken into topic lessons, per program, in consultation with curriculum consultants, subject matter supervisors and classroom teachers who are specialists in the age and grade level characteristics of the students.

At this point the television producer begins work to produce instructional programs having the stipulated content. Because of the long chain of administrative command, the instructional television producer often has less control over the objectives, content and interpretation of his program than does his counterpart in educational film.

The conceptual outline of an instructional television program follows a pattern similar to that of instructional film:

The objective of the lesson is defined in terms of its behavioral objectives: What is the student expected to learn from the program, and how is that learning to be measured?

The content selected for the program is related to the overall objectives of the curriculum, deriving from the class that preceded the program and building toward the lesson to follow.

Those forms of content requiring visuals to be understood are graphically illustrated with film clips, slides, animation, models, charts, maps and so forth, to be clearly presented on camera when discussed.

The organization of material for instructional television is subject to the same disciplines as for instructional film. Whenever a demonstration is presented in instructional television, it is best organized like a process film: Relevant introductions should be made, telling the viewer what he is expected to learn from the program. Repetition of important concepts and sequences should be interwoven in the program. Summaries should relate what is being presented to what has gone before. The rate of presentation should be slow enough for the viewer to learn the material as it is being shown. If the demonstration presents a performance skill to be learned by the viewer, common errors should be shown, as well as how to correct them. And finally, the subjective camera technique should be used to teach performance skills, whenever possible.

The pacing of the instructional television program should be appropriate to the age and attention span of the pupils and the nature of the subject matter.

The camera position and movements should be preplanned and rehearsed before videotaping, as with any other switch-panel program, and integrated with other contributory visuals.

The learning of the students should be reinforced after viewing by tests, discussions, reading and homework assignments, or by performance of the skills taught in the instructional television program.

Television teachers are content specialists who must be generalists. They work with curriculum specialists and supervisory committees doing research, writing scripts, collating and organizing visual materials, planning production and presenting their lessons with minimum rehearsal before the camera. New York allots a television teacher about one week to plan a twenty-minute program, and two hours of stage time for setting up visual aids, rehearsal and videotaping.

The length of television programs, like that of films, is determined by the age and attention span of the pupils and by the nature of the subject matter. The attention span of young children is very brief, but lengthens with age—up to a point. Instructional television programs last from five minutes to two hours, depending upon the factors of age and preparation.

Programs produced for the first three elementary grades average from five to ten minutes in length, and for the next five grades range from fifteen to thirty minutes. Lessons for high schools average from thirty to fifty minutes in duration, and those for colleges and universities from forty-five to ninety minutes. Longer programs are usually produced for enrichment, and take the form of televised field trips, concerts and dramatic performances. With experience, those associated with instructional television have learned not to pad television lessons to fill out a time slot, in the manner of commercial television, but to accept dead air time as an opportunity for classroom discussion.

Almost two-thirds of the instructional television programs in the American classroom fall into four content areas: science (nineteen percent); foreign languages (fifteen percent); social studies (fourteen percent); and English and language arts (fourteen percent). This apportionment of subject matter parallels the national norms, except that English and language arts are represented on instructional television by more than twice their percentage in the national curricula.

Production of an ITV program is essentially that of the three-camera switch-panel approach discussed in "Videotape and Film: The New Synthesis," with modifications for its applications to education. The staging relationship of the television teacher to the electronic cameras, and to the audio-visual materials, should be carefully planned and rehearsed. Floor marks and props can be used to assure that cameras and teacher will be at a given point in the staging area for electronic photography when the lecturer is discussing a given topic. The television teacher usually works closely from scripting through production with a skilled director, who knows where and how to obtain the necessary audio-visual aids. At all times the primary consideration of an instructional television program should be what the viewer will perceive, a factor which sometimes leads to friction between content and communications experts.

Instructional Television Formats

Educational and instructional television have evolved into certain teaching forms and formats based upon the low-cost production method of the three-camera switch-panel technique. These forms are the *lecture-demonstration, the interview, the panel discussion program, the dramatic performance* and *the motion picture.*

THE LECTURE-DEMONSTRATION

Instructional television producers use one primary teaching format: the lecture and demonstration method. When television was introduced to the classroom, and the teacher was introduced to the electronic camera, it seemed most natural to have the teacher lecture to the camera as he had formerly lectured to his classes. Many subjects lend themselves to the lecture method because their content is intrinsically verbal. History, English, political science and literature are typical examples of what may suitably be taught by the straight lecture method, recorded on videotape and played back on television. Through the "halo effect" (the dignity accorded a person and his ideas through his presence on the media) the television teacher and his subject are endowed with a breadth of authority transcending the influence of the ordinary teacher. A teacher giving the same lecture over television that he gives in the classroom tends to seem more authoritative when viewed on the screen.

The television lecturer, however, does not have the sense of timing that the teacher has when facing a live class. Lacking this feedback from students, the television teacher needs to be careful to proceed deliberately with the content, and not try to cover too much ground. Somewhere out there a student may be yearning to raise his hand because he does not understand, and there is no practicable way to stop the videotaped lecture to clarify the point of confusion. True, a classroom supervisor may explain it after the program is finished, but the student may have been lost from that point in the lecture to the end of the program. The pacing and thoroughness of the teacher's lecture should be determined by the difficulty of the content.

The lecture method soon evolved into a broader system which integrated other audio-visual aids: Graphs were hung on scenery flats and flip-charts were mounted on tripods. Three-dimensional models of molecules and skeletons were set on pedestals to be turned around and pointed to. Dioramas of cities and other developments were set on tables to be perused and scanned by the zoom lens of an electronic camera. Process screens waited mutely in the background to receive their rear-screen projection of a slide at the desired point in a lecture. Film clips were threaded on telecine systems to be intercut with the studio scenes from time to time during the lecture, to introduce content from outside the studio and to emancipate the program from the closed-in quality of the studio demonstration. And finally, puppet animation, traditional animation and computer-produced animation were introduced, on film and videotape, to bring the world of the imagination to the studio. Such program series as *Sesame Street* and *The Electric Company* abound with stimulating uses of puppets and animation.

The lecture and demonstration method consists in principle of having the teacher talk to camera number one with eye-to-eye earnestness, then demonstrate the functional aspects of his lecture with a Bunsen burner or some other object for camera number two, and then relate principle and practice on a chalkboard for camera number three. The lecture-demonstration is usually recorded and edited on videotape while the program is in progress (the switch-panel mode).

A kind of dramaturgy has evolved in instructional television to brighten the visual sameness of having a teacher drone his lecture at the camera. All of the related audio-visual materials are arranged about the staging area in ways that provide motivation for movements by the teacher. These movements are rehearsed and the pause points marked for teacher and cameras, as they are for any other kind of three-camera switch-panel program. The various exhibits are often kept in the dark until the teacher makes a given point in his lecture; at the appropriate time each is illuminated dramatically by a spear of light, and then is darkened afterwards. The process screen may suddenly fill with luminous images, or the voice of the teacher may continue over films and animation cut in from outside the studio, such as in *Mr. Wizard* science experiments. If the producer has the financial resources, chroma-key and other electronic effects may be introduced, as in *Sesame Street* and *The Electric House*. The finished videotape is now being used to synthesize all the other media into a rich, meaningful instructional program that transcends the original lecture format.

Having mentioned the weaknesses of the lecture method, let us examine its strengths. If the television teacher has a magnetic personality, knows his subject thoroughly, has an exciting point-of-view and knows the characteristics of his target audience, he can offer vital and illuminating instruction over television. One need only remember the brilliant British series *Civilisation*, based largely on lectures by Kenneth Clark, to realize what the television teacher can contribute to education. Television, however, is only a channel for transmission, and a mediocre teacher is somehow even more drab over television than he is in the classroom, where he can make up for his shortcomings by personal consultations with the student. The good teacher, on the other hand, with the aid of specimens, slides, models, charts, graphs and film clips, can project an intimacy over television which may excite his students

SESAME STREET. Muppets and people. *Children's Television Workshop.*

and make him far more effective than he would be in a large lecture hall.

At the next step away from the lecture-demonstration method, however, resistance sets in with regard to giving visual forms to abstract ideas. Some content specialists and instructional television producers have the notion that departing from the lecture-demonstration format is a kind of intellectual slumming, prostituting academe. It flies in the face of common sense to have a teacher give a verbal explanation of such visual concepts as mathematical relationships, neurological response modes and electrostatic relationships, yet it is not uncommon to see the use of animated films and models swept aside disdainfully in favor of an obscure lecture.

THE INTERVIEW

The interview is more common to educational television than to the instructional form. The interview consists of bringing some distinguished person into the studio and asking him a series of relevant questions about an issue or his area of expertise. Statesmen, politicians, artists, philosophers—the spectrum of talent and intellect—may be interviewed in the studio for the edification of millions of viewers. Controversial figures, too, may present their points-of-view for consideration, as in *Meet the Press* and *Face the Nation*.

The interview may be structured somewhat through the preparation of probing questions designed to elicit specific answers, but the educational value of the program depends upon the quality of those answers. Some politicians are so clever about answering awkward questions that they manage to reveal very little ("I'm glad you asked me that—"). Artists may be disappointingly inarticulate outside their chosen medium of creative expression. Philosophers may speak over the heads of most of the viewers and leave them with only snatches of understanding. Nevertheless, with good probing questions and candid, revealing answers, the interview may have educational value.

THE PANEL DISCUSSION PROGRAM

The panel discussion program involves bringing several distinguished persons into a studio and gathering them around a table to discuss an issue or several issues from each of their points-of-view. A typical example of this is the *CBS Round Table Discussion* on national and international affairs, conducted at the end of each year by reporters brought in from around the world. Usually a moderator presents each issue or aspect of an issue, and the opportunity to address himself to the item then passes in turn to each panelist. When all the remarks have been made, the moderator attempts to synthesize the opinions of panelists into some kind of consensus or statement of dissenting positions.

During the panel discussion show it is the job of the three electronic cameramen to keep their lenses focused on the moderator and the speaker presenting his remarks, with the third camera used to record spontaneous rebuttals to the speaker by one of the other panelists. The director issues his commands based upon the speaking sequence of the panelists, and improvises if the discussion becomes heated.

Like the interview, the educational value of the panel discussion show depends upon the probing nature of the questions, the intellectual and speaking capabilities of the panelists and the validity of the answers.

An apparent weakness of the panel discussion program is the tendency to seek a common denominator of agreement among the participants. The moderator and the panelists are usually concerned with presenting a serene television image. Controversial frictions that could erupt into contention and send sparks of illumination flying to the viewer are carefully damped down. Everyone wants to look good. Moreover, the panelists are often limited in their speaking time and are therefore unable to explore points in depth and clarify them; each discussant says a few words, and then defers to another panelist, who does the same. And the moderator, struggling to remain impartial, becomes a clock-watcher and smoother of ruffled feathers. As a rule, less in-depth understanding emerges from a panel discussion show than from an interview with one person who is an expert on an issue.

The Dramatic Performance

Videotape has made the dramatic performance practicable in terms of time, trouble and expense. One-act plays, short scenes from long plays, puppets, marionettes, reenactments of episodes from history, skits and farces of every kind, can provide students with a wide range of educational values. The use of a host speaker to provide an introduction and background to a dramatic scene from history, and to close the program with a discussion of the historical aftermath of the episode just seen, is an excellent dramatic production technique unique to television.

Certain subjects and situations lend themselves better to the educational use of the dramatic form than do others. Drama, the social sciences, psychology and history are suitable. Scenes that can be staged within a small studio are appropriate. Dramatization is justified in education whenever pupil identification and experience are central to understanding the message. Many classic and contemporary plays from the theater are now locally produced in schools on videotape by drama students. Others are rendered on film and television by National Educational Television and distributed nationally for study in drama and literature classes.

Attracting ethnic and racial minorities to dramatic educational television programming has been a continuing problem, particularly among the adults. Most ETV programming has been culturally oriented toward middle-class whites who already have a fairly high level of education and artistic sophistication, and is seldom watched by such minority groups as blacks and Chicanos.

A different tack was taken in Los Angeles, where an attempt was made to attract the Spanish-speaking citizens of the *barrio* to dramatic programming on educational television through a series called *Cancion de la Raza* ("Song of the Race"). The format was frankly patterned after daytime soap operas, but with themes of social change: unemployment, job retraining, welfare problems, school protests, financial problems, the irritations of rebellious teen-agers and aging relatives—all were presented in the weepy-eyed dramatic situations of the daytime tearjerker.

The Ramos family, their relatives and their friends managed to suffer most of the slings and arrows of outrageous fortune flung at the Chicano community, and they confronted and surmounted them with courage, resourcefulness and common sense. In so doing they set fine examples for their viewers and broadcast constructive ideas: Help yourself by hard work. Help your family and friends. Find out what needs to be done in your community and do it—get involved. The success of *Cancion de la Raza* suggests a model for dramatic educational television programming aimed at other minority groups of Americans.

THE MOTION PICTURE

Motion pictures of every kind and description are threaded up on telecine systems and used for instructional and educational television.

ODYSSEY IN BLACK. *KLVX, Las Vegas, Nevada, and Great Plains National ITV.*

Any 16 mm. film produced for any purpose whatever can also be used for closed-circuit and broadcast television: documentary films presenting in-depth reports, slice-of-life films, interviews, biographies, general information programs, historical compilation films, ethnographic studies, nature films, all find their way into instructional television. Dramatic films are used for the many educational purposes discussed above. Process films of every kind and purpose can be sent over channels of learning. Animated films serve their function of giving graphic forms to the realities of the mind. And even the short single-concept film can be used for a single-concept lesson on television. Television is a marvelous media synthesizer. Moreover, the content of the film is transmitted through the medium of television without the slightest change of message.

Advantages and Restraints to Further Development

Sesame Street, an enormously popular instructional television program for young children, interweaves solid content with entertainment gimmicks by synthesizing all the techniques of film and television. The approach is essentially that of hard-sell advertising. Most viewers tend to pay more attention to stimuli that is loud and colorful than to stimuli that is soft and bland. *Sesame Street* exploits this tendency when it pops on a big red vibrating "A," or sends "2 plus 2 equals 4" flashing across the screen in wild, psychedelic, computer-animated colors. Children certainly pay attention to the program, which, salted with content worth learning, is a step in the right direction.

Viewer identification with the program is an important reason for the success of *Sesame Street.* The films, songs, dances and little dramas are sprinkled with words, expressions and cultural experiences recognized by the young urban viewer, which makes the child feel that the content is relevant to him. Moreover, when a character on the show turns toward the lens of the camera (establishing eye-to-eye contact with the viewer), and praises him for being "smart" enough to follow the program, he is giving social reinforcement to the viewer which probably enhances learning and certainly builds a devoted audience.

Moreover, vicarious learning probably takes place among the viewers of *Sesame Street.* If a child on the show knows the right answer, and is praised accordingly, the viewer who identifies with that child may imitate him by learning the correct answer too.

This indirect form of reinforcement, however, has less effect than the direct reinforcement of the viewer offering the right answer himself and being told, "You're smart!"

Sesame Street also presents what might be called "mixed reinforcement." Entertainment is mixed with subject matter in order to establish associations of pleasure with learning in the mind of the child viewer that will persist after the electronic fireworks have faded into memory. Some educators have denounced the puppets and Big Bird as being instructional crutches. And they probably are. Nevertheless, when the learning of academic material is made delightful to ghetto children—by whatever means—they are more likely to develop an intrinsic interest in learning than if they are bored with education right from the start. Hopefully, with pleasure in learning established as a continuing possibility, young minority children will be less likely to drop out. At a time when many people who attend school fail to learn to read and write, and leave school at the first opportunity, a program like *Sesame Street*, which conditions children to think of learning as fun, deserves only praise.

Since its inception instructional television has held up the promise of a free advanced education to all Americans, regardless of race, creed or financial resources. Whole courses taught by master teachers could be videotaped and filmed and made available at home to deserving

SESAME STREET. Fun and learning. *Children's Television Workshop.*

students, enabling poor but intelligent and ambitious students to rise as they should in our society. The promise is still there, but remains unfulfilled for three primary reasons:

First, the school population is not truly homogeneous in terms of intelligence and preparatory education at any grade level; even in kindergarten the children of the ghetto, the suburbs and the rural areas come to a given program with widely differing backgrounds and perceptions. The content and organization of material that would be effective with the children of one area would probably be ineffective with the others, a pattern that continues through all age levels and grades.

Second, the same subjects are taught at different grade levels, with emphasis on different content, in the different regions of the United States; it is quite possible for a child whose family moves about frequently to study Columbus' voyages several times over, or not to study them at all. For massed courses to be successful, the entire nation's school population, or at least that of a given region, would need to adopt a lock-step curriculum, an approach basically incompatible with local control of the schools.

Third, courses requiring cumulative knowledge, such as physics, mathematics and chemistry, would need to be presented progressively on videotape from semester to semester on an all-or-nothing basis. This would tend to reduce the importance of the classroom teacher.

Yet the promise of instructional television remains valid—it can partially resolve the civil disorders deriving from educational inequities and bring a true democracy of opportunity to America. But the vested interests of some educators will have to be sacrificed—they must let go.

Instructional television has found wide uses outside the world of formal education. Industry, for example, uses films and videotapes for sales conferences, training purposes and data analysis studies; in-service instructional television programs are used to train employees in various skills and assembly jobs, increasing their competence in new techniques and technologies. The armed forces are among the leaders in experimentation with teaching forms and formats; films and videotapes are produced for every kind of training purpose, from the take-down and cleaning of a .45 semi-automatic pistol, to simulation of aerial combat, to documentaries on the effects of improper conduct in foreign countries.

21

The Teaching
Effectiveness of
Film and Television

The first euphoria among teachers over the potentialities of film and television in education has passed, and been replaced by a degree of humility. For the first few years "economy" was the magic word; the media would end the (then) teacher shortage and make education less expensive for the student. It became apparent to educators, however, that the media were cheaper only when the soaring costs of equipment, producers, technicians and software were paid for by the Ford Foundation. Next "superior education" became the maxim of the day, and it was envisioned that television would bring the great minds of the world to pupils in the remotest classrooms of the nation. Then it was found that there was no significant difference, under most circumstances, between what the pupils learned from the great man on television and what they learned from Mrs. Bristlebottom in person. Now "enrichment" is the bright new slogan, chanted bravely in the face of fading dreams of 1984 in education. Perhaps once the pipe dreams are completely blown away, educators in film and television will take heart from the extraordinary things that media *can* do that teachers cannot—as proved by research.

Research on film effectiveness was at first concerned with the moral effects of movie entertainment upon our youth. DeMille's formula of eleven reels of glorious sin and one reel of retribution was sure-fire at the box office, and these voluptuous cinematic revels stirred academia of the 1920s to ascertain whether movies were corrupting the moral fibre of the young with their appeals to sex and violence. The conclusions of the Payne fund studies were that the effects were pervasive, deep and persistent, and the researchers inferred that children might indeed be going to hell in a basket. All subsequent research indicates that this trend in film continues, but somehow the Republic endures.

Research on the teaching effectiveness of film began with occasional experiments in the 1930s. Intensive research began in the 1940s, supported by Defense Department grants and later by philanthropic foundations, to determine in scientific fashion the educational effects of different aspects of film production and utilization. The film evaluation studies culminated in 1951 in the Instructional Film Research Program at the Pennsylvania State University; the conclusions of this testing program provided a summing up of the teaching effectiveness of the projected classroom film. From 1951 to the mid-1960s most of the media studies were concerned with instructional television, usually involving comparative studies between televised and classroom instruction. From then until recently the emphasis has been upon computer-based and computer-assisted instructional technology in visual and verbal forms, and the implications of satellite televised educational programming.

The present chapter on the teaching effectiveness of film and television is based primarily upon experimental studies carried out under controlled conditions. No generalizations can be derived from historical or descriptive studies because they seldom relate directly to instructional purposes and vary so widely from one to the other in their essential characteristics. The experimental study, with its controls over the number of subjects tested, criterion instruments, validity and reliability data and so forth, seems the least dubious method of analysis in a field characterized by fluidity.

The majority of experimental studies in media teaching attempt to compare the effectiveness of film and television with that of the classroom teacher. A review of the research done reveals an immense array of instructional studies at the elementary, secondary and university levels, with comparable analyses made in business, industry and the armed forces. The subjects tested in media virtually encompass the range of content being taught in the classroom—the physical and biological sciences, psychology and the social sciences, the humanities, mathematics, physical education, military training, electronics—a list that seems beyond counting. Variables of film and television production that have been tested for their teaching effectiveness in dramatic, documentary and process films include camera angles and scene sizes, points-of-view, pacing of content, narration, music, special effects and animation.

The length of these comparative studies varies from one or two classes, with small experimental and control groups, to entire curricula extending over several semesters. Although the circumstances under which the tests were made vary widely, one result emerges repeatedly when the teaching effectiveness of media is compared to that of direct instruction: "No significant difference." Under most circumstances the media can be used to teach as well or better than the average classroom teacher. The corollary implication is, of course, that many teachers of basic courses could be replaced by filmed and videotaped courses. Many classroom teachers, as a consequence, fervently resist introduction of the media to their content areas.

The "no significant difference" result of so many experimental studies, however, is ironically misleading. Most such results derive from television experiments in which a videotape of a teacher, lecturing and pointing to a visual aid, is compared to a live classroom teacher, lecturing and pointing to a visual aid. Since the elements of communication are identical, there is no significant reason why there should be any significant difference. Over a billion dollars in research funds has been spent to realize this blinding truth. When the media are used to render the content *visually*, on the other hand, instead of *verbally*, there are often significant differences. These significant differences were revealed in experiments on *variables of production, variables within the viewer* and *variables of utilization in the classroom.*

Production Variables

Such production variables as camera angles, scene sizes, narrative and implicit editing, the relationships of image to narration, dialogue, music and sound effects, and the functions of animation and special effects have also been the subjects of educational research. The substance of this research has already been presented in the first section of this book, in those chapters dealing with "The Language of Cinema-Television," "The Grammar of Cinematography," "The Syntax of Editing," "The Punctuation of Sound," "Animation: The Eye of the Mind" and "The Concepts of Special Effects." The elements of cinematic communication treated in those chapters apply equally to educational film and television, with the following qualifications.

THE SILENT FILM

The silent film is as moribund in education, one might think, as it is in entertainment. Not so. Tests conducted by the Australian Office of Education comparing the educational effectiveness of silent and sound films found that their technical students learned more from silent films. But the silent films actually were accompanied by narration—while they were being projected a teacher discussed the content and related it to what was being taught in the curriculum, and the students were able to raise questions and receive answers during the projection. The sound film, with its integral optical track, was a complete communication package that teacher and students could not tamper with until finished. The silent educational film is enjoying a flourishing renaissance in the United States in the form of Super-8 film clips and loops and cartridges used in viewing consoles. Many teachers prefer the silent film for the dual reasons that they can easily include it in their own presentation of the course work at a time of their own choosing, and it seems less of a technological threat than program television.

COLOR

Color films and television programs are often more enjoyable than they would be if produced in black and white. Color is therefore often presumed to be more effective in teaching. Not so. All the research done since 1951 comparing the teaching effectiveness of color versus black and white indicates that there is no significant difference between them, regardless of whether the program is of a dramatic, documentary or process nature. Viewers tend to perceive shapes and forms more in terms of their light and dark values and less in terms of color. There is one notable exception—color used as a code or identification device. Color serves as an expository technique for communication when used to distinguish between different parts of an organism, such as a schematic cutaway of the brain. Similarly, color can be used to represent organizational differences, such as distinguishing between states in a map of the United States or in a flow chart revealing the different functions of departments within an organization. Otherwise, color seems to contribute only pleasure to the learning process (which is justification enough).

SPECIAL EFFECTS

Special effects appear to have no positive effect upon learning unless there is a specific content relationship. One example of a specific content relationship that is educationally effective is found in the Scripps Institute film *Deep Sea Drilling*. Multiple images on the screen present the following actions simultaneously: shipboard drilling activities, in live-action footage; the coring operation into the ocean floor, in animation; the sonar communications system between ship and coring device, in animation; and the computer readouts of the total relationship, in live action. This special effect allows individual aspects of a single operation to be presented simultaneously for a more complete understanding of the whole process by the viewer. Special effects used for their own sakes, however, or for supposed enhancement of viewer interest, apparently contribute little or nothing to learning.

MUSIC

Music, like special effects, contributes to learning only when it has a content relationship. Music used in a film about music, obviously, is an educational experience. In an anthropology film about the Cocopah Indians, for another example, songs sung on occasions of birth, marriage, death, planting and harvesting may be presented with those events to add to the viewer's understanding of that culture. Music may also be used to signal a transition to another time, place or form of subject matter. On the other hand, music used for aesthetic and emotional enhancement in a documentary, dramatic, or process presentation adds little that is measurable to the learning experience.

ANIMATION

The animated film is the only effective means of giving graphic visual form to such nonrepresentational relationships as mathematic and scientific concepts, and to a number of art forms. Animation is used in some form (as a segment) within more than one-third of all live-

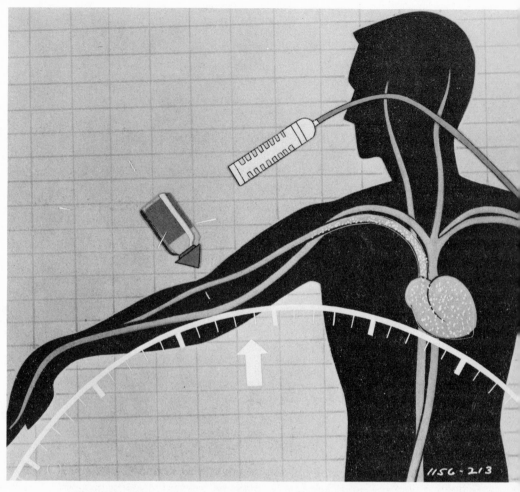

OUR FRIEND THE ATOM. Animation of processes. © *Walt Disney Productions.*

action educational films. Through animation, internal processes may be depicted which cannot be visualized by live-action cinematography, functions may be lifted out of context for closer examination, ideas and processes may be presented in simple graphic form, visual projections and generalizations can be made, and visual cues may be used to point out what is important and to eliminate or subordinate what is unimportant. Animation effectiveness is difficult to measure, because its validity and clarity are dependent upon the skill and creative ability of the animator, and tests sometimes tend to measure him rather than the medium.

In the few extensive tests on animated film, made by the United States Navy and the Human Resources Research Laboratories, the student "groups having the animated film learned significantly more than the groups having the non-animated film, regardless of pretesting, or number of examples. . . . This was true for trainees of both above and below average intelligence." The value of the animated film in teaching abstract concepts to retarded children was studied at length by John Driscoll, and he found animation significantly more effective than either live-action film or television teaching with visual aids. Given the new low-cost analogue-computer animation techniques, it seems probable that the future will witness an expanding educational use of animated films.

THE ROMANCE OF TRANSPORTATION. Animation in education. *National Film Board of Canada.*

FILM STRIPS AND SLIDES

Filmstrip and slide presentations sometimes outdo the motion picture in educational effectiveness, but the difference has an important relationship to the nature of the content. Slattery ran a series of comparative tests in a Catholic elementary school in which he found that if the content did not intrinsically require movement to be understood, the film strip was more effective than the sound film. Other factors were operating, however—a teacher provided narration during the film-strip presentations, and the direct control of pacing permitted him to stop and answer questions and to carry on discussions with the students for as long as necessary. Motion pictures should be used whenever movement is an integral element of the content, but as was noted in the comparison between silent and sound films, there need not be a sound track. If movement is unnecessary, common sense and economy would suggest the preferred use of the film strip.

EXPLICIT PRESENTATION

An explicit presentation of content—stated in the baldest factual terms—is the most effective approach to instructional film and television. If the content requires inference, is sketchily treated or carries much of its important information in narration, the learning level may be very low. This has implications for two popular forms of educational technique—the dramatic form and the panel discussion show. Dramatic and situational programs are most often effective when the situations portrayed relate specifically to actions the viewer is expected to learn, such as riot control tactics, simulated combat, teaching of drama techniques and so forth. The panel discussion show and the interview are no better than the questions asked and the answers given; if these are tightly organized to elicit the desired content the student is expected to learn, fine. Too often, however, the panel discussion program is a sprawling affair, easy to produce and pleasurable to dignify with the term "educational," but too often leaving the student with little residual knowledge.

Viewer Variables

The variables within the viewer constitute the second area of elements affecting his ability to learn from educational film and television.

He brings to an instructional program the same characteristics of age, sex, film literacy, level of formal education, socioeconomic milieu and life space that he brings to dramatic and documentary films, and these filter his interpretations. The research relating to these factors has been discussed in "Cinema-Television and the Viewer," and the chapters dealing with "The Classic Documentary Film," "The Television Documentary Film" and "The Propaganda Film," as well as in those chapters on "Cinematic Development of Characters," "Dramatic Structure in Cinema-Television" and "Adaptation: Novels and Stage Plays into Cinema-Television." Additional media-learning factors in the viewer include intelligence, previous conditioning to learn from media, motivation to learn and faculty-student attitudes.

INTELLIGENCE

Intelligence is an essential factor in learning from educational films and television. As one might expect, the proportionately greater the viewer's intelligence (given suitable preparation), the more he is able to learn from media presentations. The popular hypothesis that dull students learn more from films and television than bright students is a misinterpretation of certain studies dealing with retarded children. Studies by John Driscoll and others revealed that abstract concepts could be taught to exceptional children through the graphic use of animated film, time-lapse photography and other cinematic techniques that otherwise could not be communicated at all. Mathematics and scientific principles could be brought within the children's comprehension through a more visually valid presentation of the content than was practicable by means of the classroom teacher using visual aids and verbal explanations. At all levels of learning, however, the greater the viewer's intelligence, given an adequate educational background, the more able he is to learn from films and television.

PREVIOUS CONDITIONING

Viewers must be conditioned to learn from the media. Those who view entertainment films and television programs soon develop a high degree of film literacy which enables them to comprehend cinematic content at a high level of sophistication. Many of them are not conditioned, however, *to study the film.* The lay viewer brings to the instructional presentation an attitude of "amuse me," and settles back to be amused; if the program lacks the entertainment value to which he is accustomed, it is a dull film, and therefore a bad film. Learning and amusement, however, are not necessarily synonymous, all attempts to make education enjoyable notwithstanding. For a viewer to learn from the media, he needs to discard his amusement expectations and face the program with the same seriousness of purpose he brings to a textbook. Those viewers who have had educational films in the classroom from the earliest grades consistently learn the most from film and television programming.

MOTIVATION

Motivating students to learn is half the battle in teaching them. Ever since film and television were introduced into education, teachers have hoped that the media would have some magic ingredient, some transfer of glamour, to make learning delightful. Research has indicated that certain media-related concepts and techniques are indeed effective in motivating students, but the variables are as often in the student as in the media.

Perceived usefulness of the film's content is a primary reason for learning it. If the viewer can see how it will serve his interests to learn, he is more apt to pay careful attention to the program. This is less of a problem in subjects related to the viewer's professional or personal interests because then he is viewing a film whose content interests him. In those subjects outside the viewer's purview of interests, however, other techniques may be needed.

Anxiety is a stimulus to learning. The announcement that a film or television program will be followed by a written examination on its content tends to make most students watch more carefully. Ideally, learning should be a joyous experience unalloyed by terror tactics, but realistically, it is true that many students take courses in which they lack the slightest interest because they are required to do so, and are enrolled in higher institutions because the college degree is considered a guarantee of economic security.

Students should be told firmly what they are expected to learn from the film and that they will be tested on its content. Pretesting and posttesting, and introducing the film and stating the purposes and importance of its content may hone the student's motivation to learn. Study guides, used before and after the showing, will enable the student to learn more. Note-taking should not be encouraged during a film presentation because it interferes with attention, and hence with learning.

Novelty is motivating under certain circumstances. If a student feels he is participating in some kind of experiment, he may learn more than he might have learned in a standard teaching situation. The United States Navy discovered this by employing a little trickery. When instructional television was first being introduced into the service, the Navy ran what was ostensibly a comparative test of the teaching effectiveness of film and television, using a spurious kinescope (filmed television program) to represent television. In actuality, the so-called kinescope was a black-and-white print of an instructional film, not a television kinescope. The original instructional film and the black-and-white print of it, identical in every respect other than color, were presented to two different groups. The result was that those watching the spurious kinescope learned more than those watching the instructional film, apparently from the novelty of believing they were the first to be tested with television.

Viewer interaction with a filmed situation—simulation—has been found to reinforce learning. The Air Force has used simulation since World War II in training combat pilots by forcing them to react on mockup airplane controls to combat situations projected on film. If they are shot down too often on film, they may never get off the ground for real combat. Simulation is being widely used, wherever applicable, to teach every kind of process from safe driving in high schools to riot control for police forces.

Viewer participation in some form reinforces the viewer's learning of the program's content. This participation can take the form of practice sessions, written examinations or analyses of the content, alternated with sections of the film. Overt or covert participation by the viewer appears to result in consistently better learning performance, through reinforcement, than does simply viewing the program. This interaction with the medium is less practicable on television, where the program usually must run its full course.

Negative motivation—a defensive avoidance of the filmed content —may occur when strong fears are aroused by the film's form or content. Filmmakers who feel that such problems as drug abuse and careless driving can be resolved by the most gruesome presentations of their dire consequences may be deceiving themselves. Those viewers at whom the brutal content is directed are often the first to tune it out, mentally. Once the threshold of fear is crossed the viewer may be "gone" for the rest of the film.

The boomerang effect is a form of negative motivation. As described in "Cinema-Television and the Viewer" and "The Propaganda Film," the boomerang effect occurs when the content of a film or television program directly attacks the value system of the viewer in a way that makes him angry, and thereby reinforces the ideas the film was intended to change. Once the boomerang effect has occurred, the viewer may be more resistant than ever to change on that particular issue.

Humor is popularly thought to motivate learning by making hard content more enjoyable. Repeated studies over the years, however, suggest that just the opposite is true. Humor tends to distract the average student from a serious consideration of the content, softening his focused state of mind, and sometimes important points are lost in laughter. Moreover, humor is fragile, quickly dated and strongly related to the life space of a target audience. As desirable as it may seem to add joy to the classroom, learning and laughter do not generally mix.

An *immediate answer* to a student's question tends to reinforce learning. This immediacy is one advantage of using film and television as supplementary aids to the classroom teacher, rather than teaching with filmed and televised courses alone. The inability of a learner to clarify some important point in the content may leave him confused about everything that follows.

Film projection offers one important advantage over television programming as a teaching medium—its projection is *under the viewer's control* at all times. A film may be stopped for discussion, backed up and replayed for a more careful examination of a given segment, or replayed in full as often as desired. A broadcast television program is, of course, locked into a time slot, and continues on inexorably regardless of the wishes of the students and the teacher. This direct control of film offers great promise for the future of filmed courses released on film or videotape cartridges for console viewing devices. These filmed courses could be checked out like library books, or rented at low cost, and studied at home as often as necessary, offering the advantages of further formal education or professional retraining to anyone with the will to pursue them.

FACULTY-STUDENT ATTITUDES

A large body of studies is concerned with student and faculty attitudes toward learning from film and television. Student attitudes toward the media are affected to some degree by teacher attitudes, and faculty attitudes are in turn often affected by the fear that the technological revolution in education may cost them their jobs. For the most part, there is a difference between attitudes toward film and television. Film is liked, while television is not. This may be a result of the teachers' control over a film presentation, with the film serving a supportive role, and their lack of control over a complete television program. In other words, television may appear to be more of a direct threat. Or, the preference may be due to the more graphic presentations of content usually made in cinematic form, with greater care given to every aspect of production. The instructional television practice of having a teacher talk for a solid hour was discarded decades ago in educational film in favor of the visual rendition of content.

Utilization Variables

Utilization in the classroom constitutes the third major area of research to determine the educational effectiveness of the media.

Multiple viewings of the same film reinforce the learning of its contents—up to a point. The first presentation of a good film or television program offers a degree of novelty and a new story line that the students may follow with interest. While following the main threads of the presentation, however, the viewer may miss important subordinate aspects or mentally tune out from time to time. A second viewing permits the viewer to grasp what he may have missed the first time, because he is less entranced by the story line and can concentrate on specific facts and relationships. A classroom discussion between showings, moreover, may redirect his attention to those elements to which he had not earlier given his serious consideration. Two projections of the same film are enough. Three or more showings contribute little more in the way of learning and invite viewer rebellion.

Massed sequential media presentations, with a high degree of repetition, seem effective in producing changes of opinion and attitude, particularly if the viewer is called upon to demonstrate his change in a behavioral way.

The *number of teaching objectives* should be fewer when teaching a performance skill than when presenting general information. The memory of skills portrayed tends to fade quickly if too many objectives are attempted, or if unrelated material is introduced before the earlier skills have been exercised.

Introductions should precede the portrayal of content to alert the viewer to what he is expected to learn, and therefore to seek this in the film. If not cued in advance, the viewer may watch distracting elements of little consequence while the key content slides by. It may be advisable to tell the viewer what he will be expected to do after seeing the film, and to warn him he may be tested.

Repetition helps to reinforce learning. Each major phase of content should be repeated two or three times, more if the skill or content is complex.

Summaries of preceding content, presented during the middle and latter portions of the film, may refresh the viewer's memory and add the reinforcement of repetition. Narration summaries may also serve to relate what is on the screen to what occurred earlier.

Showing the student the errors he is likely to make, surprisingly, is a good teaching technique, one based upon known psychological responses in the average viewer. If a process film teaching a complex technique presents it as if nothing could ever go wrong, the student who tries it and makes a common error may become discouraged and quit. This is particularly true when dealing with the undereducated, for whom films to teach process skills are so often made. Showing possible errors, and how to correct them, serves the twofold function of reassuring the viewer and enabling him to cope with whatever problems may arise.

Rigid television time segments offer serious instructional problems in *matching content to program length*. Ideally, the program should be no longer than is necessary to effectively teach the content, and the students would then have discussions with the teacher and practice. The fixed time sequences of television programs, however, chop all subjects into the same sizes, regardless of the nature and difficulty of their content or the attention span of the target audience. Since the time segments are longer in most cases than is appropriate for the material, the usual television answer is to fill in the extra time with talk, and in the process obscure what has just been taught. A partially successful solution to the time slot problem is the closed-circuit television system, in which the program is produced, like a film, to be only as long as needed, and the set turned off when the concept has been taught. In programs produced for syndication, such as the immensely popular *Sesame Street*, the alternative solution has been to break up the kinds of subjects presented within the segments, presenting animation for five minutes, dramatic skits for ten minutes and so forth. Nevertheless, those concepts presented early in the program are likely to fade in the viewer's memory when new subjects are introduced, unless they are reinforced during later phases of the program.

Programmed instruction, applied to instructional television, was evaluated experimentally by Gropper and Lumsdaine. The subjects taught were "the laws of motion," "levers" and "how movies work." The content was broken into small increments and televised. At the end of each increment the students were asked to answer a question. A second group of students, to which the programmed instruction group were to be compared, simply watched a straight ITV lecture of the content, and was tested after viewing the complete uninterrupted programs. Analysis of variance tests revealed that the group taught by programmed instruction television had significantly higher achievement scores than those who had simply watched the ITV program. Similar experiments with programmed motion pictures, requiring active student responses after viewing brief film increments, brought similar results.

The *shortened time-learning relationship* is a commonly overlooked factor in favor of extensive film and television teaching. In one experiment a ninth-grade biology course was taught by forty-four sound films alone, and compared with a standard lecture-demonstration-discussion course taught by a classroom teacher. There were no significant differences in student performances between the two groups, and no significant differences on delayed recall tests after three months. The group with films only, however, completed the course in *twenty percent less time* than the classes taught by the teacher. This reduced time-learning factor appears again and again in other research relating to film and television teaching, and to programmed instruction as well.

Accelerated learning may derive from the more careful organization that usually characterizes a media production, or from the greater alertness on the part of the student, who realizes that he cannot ask questions and thus pays more careful attention to what is presented. Whatever the reason, this twenty-percent time reduction in learning equivalent material appears repeatedly in media research. If the media were applied broadscale to elementary, secondary and higher education, in those subjects that lend themselves to media teaching, it would appear that the average student could complete his formal education in less time, or that more content could be taught within the same time span. Given the accelerating information explosion, the reduced time-learning factor alone seems reason enough for the expanded use of film, television and programmed instruction in education.

Criticisms of Teaching by Film and Television

There is a fourth aspect of film and television effectiveness that should be included here—the criticisms classroom teachers have voiced over the years with regard to educational media. Most of their ten major complaints relate to selection and organization of content, as follows:

1. *The program tries to cover too much ground.* This is in part a result of the lack of immediate feedback from the viewer. Both film and television media are essentially one-way communication systems in which the producers do not really know when their program contains more hard content than a given group of students can absorb at a sitting. This is less true of educational films because a teacher is usually present to answer questions and relate the film content to other things being taught, and a protest from the students can bring a temporary halt to the film. In educational television, however, if a chemistry program is scheduled for 2 to 2:50 P.M., it will grind inexorably on, sometimes long after the students can retain what they see and hear. The length of an educational program should be determined by the difficulty of the content, as well as the attention span and learning characteristics of the students, rather than an arbitrary time slot fixed for administrative convenience.

2. *Too much unrelated material is dragged in.* This problem may arise from any of several causes. Most commonly, the inclusion of unrelated materials occurs because the sponsor or educator wants one film to achieve too many goals. The use of the shotgun rather than the rifle approach usually results in the film doing nothing well. Instructional film and television programs are most effective when they are designed to achieve a narrow set of specific behavioral goals with a given target audience, and all materials unrelated to those behavioral goals are de-

leted. A secondary reason for the inclusion of extraneous materials is the pursuit of aesthetic rather than social goals by the filmmaker; he becomes obsessed with effects for their own sake and drags in anything that will make his film more cinematic, more exciting and enjoyable.

3. A third problem is *simple ignorance*; the education field is filled with "experts" who believe that the secret of media effectiveness is to point a camera at someone talking. The director of an instructional television program once said, in defense of a videotaped lecture, "The human face is the greatest audiovisual communication device ever invented." It would be amusing to watch him render the metamorphosis of a caterpillar into a butterfly with his face.

4. *The pacing of content is too fast.* Here the media split: film is often too fast in its pacing, and videotape is sometimes too slow. Films are created on the editing bench, with the elimination of all superfluous movements and actions to create cinematic time and distance and strip the subject to its essence. Once a film is finished, there is little recourse for the student who wants to raise his hand and say, "You're going too fast" or "Would you repeat that—I didn't get it the first time." A secondary reason for overaccelerated pacing in educational films is the influence of the entertainment film. The only sure way to pretest the pacing of content in an educational film is to photograph or videotape a story board at the intended speed and present it to a sample of the target audience, accompanied by spoken or recorded narration.

The pacing of content in educational videotape tends to be too slow because the medium content is locked into real time and real distance. Videotape may be cut and spliced in the physical manner of film to remove mistakes and some superfluous actions, but editing in the cinematic sense is impracticable because the original conditions of production require that the director direct, record his visuals and roughly edit the production simultaneously—a system that limits the editing which may be done afterwards. However, the slow nature of live videotape production makes it suitable for the slow pacing of content so often required in teaching.

5. *The content does not fit the curriculum or the intended audience.* This complaint relates less to film and television producers than it does to the grass-roots control of the American educational system—every school district has its own schedule for introducing content courses into its curriculum. And a given media communication on almost any given subject is likely to fit poorly into the curriculum unless it is produced for

inclusion in a specific district's program. In a nation where there is a three-year time difference between states in the introduction of the same subject, as there is between New York and California in the teaching of American history, the complaint that the content of an educational film or television program does not fit the curriculum is likely to go unremedied until there is either some national coordination of curricula or each school district has its own film and television production teams.

6. *The film is unsuitable for the course being taught.* This complaint applies more to educational films than to television. Company-sponsored films are often stocked in educational film libraries because their subjects seem to relate to certain courses, such as a film treating oil production used in a class in geology. Such public relations films are frequently created by commercial firms and rendered like extravaganzas, but they are seldom produced with the classroom in mind, and even more seldom produced from the goodness of the corporation's heart. These films are produced to advertise their sponsor's firm, not teach hard content in the classroom. And communicating content, in its various forms, is the primary reason for using films in the classroom. Another reason that films are sometimes unsuitable for the courses being taught is that the filmmaker becomes more concerned with aesthetic than teaching goals, and the teacher in turn becomes enamoured of the cinematic fireworks and uses it in the classroom.

7. A number of studies have assessed *students' emotional reactions to being taught by mass television courses* and reported these findings: Many students felt insecure in the kind of huge television classes that are found in some large universities; they experienced a loss of identity, a loss of contact and rapport with a teacher. (This loss of identity in large classes, some teachers reported, also offered greater opportunities to cheat in tests.) The lost opportunity for emotional release by participation was more keenly felt by younger students, particularly in the elementary grades. The impersonality of the televised classroom situation affected the interrelationships of the students, and many reported less interaction among themselves. Last but not least, from an American values point-of-view, there is far less emphasis on teaching students as individuals in televised instruction.

8. *Administrative complaints* about television are common: It is difficult to schedule with classes—television does not fit into traditional patterns of teaching that use media as a supplement. Television is also difficult to fit into the curriculum of existing courses, but lends itself to

all-or-nothing incorporation into reorganized courses. Finally, television is difficult to utilize in existing classrooms; new classrooms need to be planned with educational films and television in mind.

9. Two complaints are closely related: *The organization of content is bad.* And, *there is no central theme to the presentation.* The poor organization of content and lack of central theme may relate to the sloth or incompetence of the filmmakers, or both. Sloth, like death and taxes, is with us always, and outside the purview of this study. Incompetence may relate to the lecture syndrome, the unwillingness to transmute content into graphic form, lack of training or simple inability to function in media communications. Having a central theme is a matter of deciding in advance of production what content is to be communicated, and relating everything in the production to that idea.

10. Complaints relating to *production quality* fall into three categories: poor sound recording quality and too much narration; bad acting by performers in an educational drama; and overlong presentations. Poor sound recording is both a technical and an aesthetic problem. Too much narration has been discussed. Bad acting may be due to the lack of funds to employ competent talent. And the excessive length of programs in relation to content difficulty will continue as long as broadcast television is geared to inflexible time lengths.

No one medium is the answer to all educational and instructional problems. For some forms of content and some students the film or television program may prove an effective teacher. For others it may be programmed instruction, film strips, slides, still photographs, computer-assisted instruction, or a communication systems approach comprising them all. From time to time, the best educational team may even prove to be that quaint anachronism—the book and the teacher.

Television broadcasting systems, despite their draconian time slots and mutilation of content, now offer the most practicable distribution method yet devised. They can extend the best available instruction to many places that could not otherwise afford the best, from indigent blacks in city slums, to impoverished Indians in reservations, to poor whites everywhere. Instructional television can present, through films, every conceivable form of content that may be photographed, and make rare forms of content commonplace that would otherwise be unavailable. And when applied on a full-course semester basis, there is reason to believe that instructional television would offer economic advantages at a time when public and private expenditures for education are rising steadily.

The Open University

The "Open University" is a proposal to offer the courses necessary to complete a four-year university education over broadcast television, with the student coming on campus only to submit his papers and take examinations. Through the mass distribution capability of broadcast television and the nationwide application of the Open University, it should be possible to realize one aspect of the American dream: to give every person an equal opportunity to an advanced education, and thereby an equal chance to rise on his merits. This would end the bitter and justified complaint that poverty begets poverty because it takes money to acquire an education. A nation needs the development of its best minds, regardless of race or economic origins, and America has the resources to make higher education universally available. Educational television on a regional or national basis could be a major instrument for removing the inequities of opportunity that have created so much domestic strife. Equality of opportunity in higher education is not a wild dream, but an American necessity.

22

Science and Cinema-Television

Cinematography and television are integral parts of the vast systems of technology supporting today's sciences. There is scarcely a scientific discipline anywhere that does not make some use of the media for research studies, documentation, illustration and education. The subject of film and television utilization in the sciences would fill volumes, and far exceeds, to say the least, the limitations of a single chapter. What may be presented, however, is an overview of the representative forms of media technique common to such disciplines as *medicine, primatology, aerospace, oceanography* and *technical data studies.*

Medicine

ILLUMINATION

Medicine may be considered representative of the organic sciences in its uses of specialized forms of lighting, film emulsions and electronic photography. Visible light is used, as in other forms of film and television production, for rendering gross physical specimens. Invisible illumination is also used, however, to make visible those obscure and invisible subjects that cannot otherwise be seen with the unaided eye. Although the technical aspects of media are outside the purview of this book, a brief statement is in order about the nature of illumination in order to better understand its specialized applications.

The light that makes vision and photography possible is a form of radiant energy which travels at the incredible speed of 186,000 miles per second. It is made up of wavelengths of frequency and amplitude that fall within the perception of the human eye and conventional film emulsions. Light, however, is only one form of radiant energy that can be photographed. The full spectrum of radiation from shortest to longest wavelengths, consist of the following:

Gamma rays

X-rays

Ultraviolet radiation

Light

Infrared radiation

Radio waves

Most of these wavelengths of radiation are invisible to the unaided eye. Some of them, however, may be made perceptible through the use of specialized film emulsions chemically formulated to be sensitive to the images rendered by (invisible) radiation. The use of X-rays to make renderings of human internal organs and bone conditions is common. Other forms of radiant energy finding scientific uses, in addition to visible light, are infrared radiation, ultraviolet radiation and a variant of the latter called luminescence. The unique photographic properties of these wavelengths will be described in their scientific purviews of application.

SPECIMEN PHOTOGRAPHY

Gross anatomical specimen photography is universally used in medical research for purposes of illustration, documentation and education. Subjects may range from small specimens taken from hospital autopsies to full-size living patients. Pancreatic glands, teeth, skulls, sectioned kidneys, a woman's breasts, a man's torso, a child's full form, are all subjects for research through gross specimen photography.

The photography and illumination techniques are essentially those of conventional photography and cinematography, with variations to delimit areas of interest. Strong cross-lighting is used to emphasize surface textures or body deformities. Shadowless even lighting serves to illuminate smooth lesions.

PHOTOMACROGRAPHY AND PHOTOMICROGRAPHY

Photomacrography is the rendering of specimens too small for an ordinary closeup lens. A simple microscope, one with an objective lens only, is used for photomacrography. A cornea, a gland, the cross-section of an artery, are specimen sizes suitable for photomacrography.

Photomicrography takes up in minuscule studies where photo-macrography leaves off. Photomicrography is done with a compound microscope which uses both an objective lens and an eyepiece to form an aerial image focused at the film plane. This technique is used for studies of the smallest specimens that can be photographed without electronic aid, or the specialized illumination of infrared and ultraviolet radiation.

Infrared, ultraviolet and luminescent photography can render information about a subject or object which cannot be recorded by visible light. The value of these other kinds of illumination lies in the capacity of certain subjects to reflect and absorb the radiation in varying degrees, which makes obscure details and differences visible.

A given lens changes its specified focal length when used for either infrared or ultraviolet cinematography, and often a change of lens is needed for such illumination. When infrared is used to render an image, the focal length of the lens becomes longer. When ultraviolet is used to form the image, the focal length becomes shorter.

INFRARED PHOTOGRAPHY

Infrared photography is used in medical work primarily because this form of illumination can penetrate skin surfaces to render subcutaneous images. The veins under the skin for example, appear much darker (and bluer in color) when rendered in infrared images than when rendered on panchromatic film. The reason for this effect is that venous blood can absorb infrared illumination, while the skin reflects most of the infrared illumination.

The ability of infrared illumination to emphasize concentrations of venous blood make it an important photographic technique in circulation studies. It has been responsible for important discoveries in relation to thrombosis, diabetes and pericardial effusion. A current area of research using infrared illumination is the study of tumors and their blood supply to assess the possibility of malignancy. Pupillography is another notable use, with infrared used to photograph the eyes and their movements without interfering with, or stimulating, visual responses; visibility curves, dark adaptation, response to flash stimuli, accommodation, the effects of drugs and fatigue and the response to sexual stimuli are all photographed by infrared cinematography. And, of course, the "see in the dark" capability of infrared makes possible the photographic recording of the behavior of human and animal subjects in the dark.

ULTRAVIOLET PHOTOGRAPHY

Ultraviolet light cannot be seen by the human eye throughout most of its wavelengths, except for a narrow visible spectrum of radiation from about 400 to 700 millimicrons in length. Ultraviolet illumination may come from many sources, including the sun and artificial illumination. Whatever the source, the camera lens must be covered with a filter which permits a high passage of ultraviolet radiation and precludes transmission of any visible light. Ultraviolet illumination and photography must be used in an isolated form in medical work, because ultraviolet rays are easily scattered by other forms of radiation.

The medical applications of ultraviolet photography are primarily in the fields of dermatology and micrography. Since ultraviolet is strongly absorbed by pigment in the skin, films made for dermatology studies are used to record unusual skin pigmentation by reflected-ultraviolet photography. Conditions of either hyperpigmentation or depigmentation can be recorded by this technique, whereas visible light photography may reveal little concerning pigmentation.

Ultraviolet micrography is a second major medical application. Cinematography through the microscope often requires more resolution and delineation of details than is possible with visible light, and for this reason the shorter wavelength of ultraviolet radiation is used for lighting to enhance the structural differences that may occur in a specimen.

LUMINESCENT PHOTOGRAPHY

Luminescence is a form of light emission created by subjecting certain receptive subjects to shortwave electromagnetic radiation. A luminescent "after-glow" may be excited in a receptive substance by exposing it to such forms of illumination as X-rays, ultraviolet, gamma rays, and some wavelengths of visible light. If luminescence in the subject ends within a brief time after the exciting radiation is terminated, it is called "fluorescence." If the luminescence persists after the radiation ceases (and sometimes it persists for hours) it is called "phosphorescence." A kind of secondary luminescence may be created in some nonreceptive subjects through impregnation with phosphors susceptible to excitation by some form of radiation.

During the time a subject is luminescent, it may be photographed for display on a television screen or on film. The image in an electron microscope, for example, is visible only on a fluorescent screen. X-rays are a form of fluorescent photography. In medical research, fluorescence is used to make photomicrographs of tissue sections colored with luminescent stains like acridine orange and illuminated by ultraviolet radiation. Most proteins and nucleic acids become luminescent after chemical treatment. The movements of internal organs in human and animal subjects may be studied by having the subject ingest luminescent materials which render the forms of the organs visible for photography. Fluorescent microscopy has become important in the study of microorganisms and their movement patterns, and in the early detection of cancer in smears and tissue sections.

Television viewing and videotape reproduction are finding unique application in the fields of *surgery, microscopy, obstetrics and gynecology, pharmacology, radiology, psychiatry, and sex and violence.*

SURGERY

Before the advent of television surgery could be watched only from viewing domes and theaters, and those in the audience were seldom able to see the operations in detail unless they brought binoculars. The only alternative was the clumsy and impractical method of having viewers crowd around the surgical table to peer over shoulders and under arms. Thanks to electronic cameras and their long focal-length lenses, brain surgery, heart transplants, appendectomies, cornea transplants and other medical operations can be studied at the time of their occurrence, or on videotape playback over closed-circuit television, by all interested medical personnel. The magnification of details and the several points-of-view offered by multiple cameras and monitors sometimes reveal more at one time to the viewer than is seen by the operating surgeon himself.

MICROSCOPY

Televised microscopy, photography through the electron microscope, enables scientists to record and study cells at extremely high levels of magnification. The filmmaker can zoom in on a tiny area of a stained slide so that a minuscule part of a cell will literally fill the screen. This can be done with either a television or a motion picture camera. The electronic camera is preferable when low light levels must be maintained and for the quantitative measurement of light absorption in living cells. With television cameras, the electron microscope can be fitted with image intensifiers to transmit more brilliant pictures with better resolution into the closed-circuit system; moreover, the intensifier uses so little ultraviolet radiation that fragile specimens remain relatively undamaged. The image intensifier makes possible the viewing of specimens that could not be seen in any other way. Television microscopy has vastly increased the filmmaker's control over magnification and contrast in minuscule images, and over the spectral range of illumination.

OBSTETRICS AND GYNECOLOGY

The demonstration advantages offered by closed-circuit television are emphasized in obstetrics and gynecology. By using two television cameras, one placed over the patient and the other at table level, the viewer can witness an operation on monitors from the same points-of-view as the surgeon. Moreover, by using zoom lenses to vary the size and magnification of the images, the presentations can be made more graphic to those outside surgery than to those within.

Patient sensibilities are an important factor in obstetrics and gynecology demonstrations. Before the advent of television, it was sometimes difficult to persuade women having disorders of medical interest to submit to examinations by large groups of doctors and medical students. The television cameras tend to desensitize the examination, to assure the woman's personal anonymity and to permit the patient to watch a videotape playback for reassurance that only the affected areas have been televised. Many women will not permit themselves to be photographed in motion pictures or videotape unless they are guaranteed the right of review to preserve their anonymity.

Television has been highly successful in showing the delivery of babies, usually to medical students, sometimes to anxious fathers. It is common practice in the surgical use of television to have a surgical advisor at the side of the television director to tell him what should be visualized at a given point in a delivery or operation. This "technical advisor" sometimes adds to the operating surgeon's commentary to make sure that everything shown on the screen is clearly explained for the understanding of the viewer. When a given operation is being transmitted live to a classroom, this surgical advisor may also answer questions raised in the classroom, thereby serving as a key communications link between the surgeon (who has his hands full) and medical students.

Sometimes one televised operation may be used to teach two different disciplines of study, simultaneously, in two different classrooms. During an operation, for example, one camera and remote monitor may present the surgical process itself, with isolated emphasis on the operation area, while the other camera and remote monitor present the equipment and its functions and relationships to the processes of surgery. In one of the two classrooms a teacher may explain the surgical processes per se, while in the other another teacher may explain the technology relating to that surgery.

PHARMACOLOGY

Pharmacology is a field in which television is increasingly used for demonstrations of the effects of drugs on isolated organs, primarily to teach large classes of medical students. Isolated dog hearts and rabbit hearts, for example, have been injected with various drugs, and the effects studied on television monitors far from the experimental laboratory. To create multiple-image communication, one camera may be aimed at the heart, to which a drug is being administered, a second camera may be pointed at the oscilloscope, which visualizes the responses of an electrocardiogram, and the two images may then be presented simultaneously on separate monitors. Or, the switch-panel system may be used to combine the two images into one, with the white oscilloscope line of the electrocardiogram moving synchronously across the living image of the drug-affected heart.

RADIOLOGY

The field of radiology makes use of remote television cameras to reduce or preclude the hazards of radiation inherent in X-ray work. By viewing a patient's X-ray on distant monitors, the radiation dangers can be virtually eliminated. A vidicon camera and closed-circuit system are used with an image intensifier, with large-screen amplification, to compensate for the low brightness level on the X-ray screen and to enhance through brightness the sharpness of the images. Virtually all of the interior body organs of a given patient can be examined from three points-of-view without any need for a radiologist to be near the patient. Moreover, the television system permits simultaneous viewing, image transformation and videotape recording, so that every desired visual presentation can be made and permanently recorded for further examination, without having to subject the patient to the added radiation of further X-ray studies.

A recent development in the treatment of heart diseases in living patients involves the use of extremely high magnification to present a detailed image of the affected organ on the screen. Small tubes, called catheters, are inserted in a patient's veins. These tubes are then guided through the veins to the very center of the disease itself, in the heart. A dye is then injected into the organ, and the television producer can use a fluoroscope and X-ray device to render an image on videotape. A detail as small as a closeup of a clogged artery can be electronically photographed in this way.

PSYCHIATRY

The field of psychiatry and other behavioral sciences has proved to be a fertile ground for the playback capability of television. Videotaped interviews of patients manifesting symptoms of schizophrenia, paranoia, ego-defense mechanism and other disorders are replayed on the television monitors for evaluation by psychiatrists and as case-study projects for medical students. By utilizing videotape to record an interview with a patient, the psychiatrist can concentrate on the sensitive interpersonal rapport necessary to the two-person psychiatric interview. Later, during the videotape playback, he can study and evaluate the patient's reactions during the interview as expressed in body kinesics, manual gestures and facial expressions, as well as by listening to what he says.

The television playback system was a vast improvement over the earlier case-study method of having a few observers crammed into a small room behind one-way glass, to later tell the psychiatrist what they had seen. Now, hundreds of psychiatrists and medical students can watch and discuss a single presentation on monitors. Moreover, it can be done in closeup, with one lecturer applying professional terminology and rationales to one patient in one case-study situation.

A matter of medical ethics is involved in videotaping an interview with a patient. The confidential nature of the doctor-patient relationship, and the confidential status of hospital records, is extended to videotape interviews, with only those persons given access to the videotape records who would have access to other medical records. Nevertheless, some patients are apprehensive about being videotaped and subsequently studied. Permission is always asked of the patient to be interviewed before the electronic cameras; in cases of indigent patients treatment is sometimes given in exchange for consent to be videotaped. By way of reassurance, the patient is introduced to the studio setting of cameras, crew, bright lights and monitoring facilities, and given a description of the viewers who will be studying the interview in playback. The patient has the option of refusing to be recorded on videotape, even though, in most instances, the persons who will see the playback are medical personnel and students.

A new technique in psychotherapy is to confront the patient, or group of patients, with a videotape playback immediately after a recording session. The effect on the patient is often electrifying. By viewing the living image of himself interacting with others, he sees how others see him, and sometimes the shock serves as a more effective motivation to change than months of discussions, interpretations and exhortations.

SEX AND VIOLENCE

Films are widely known for stimulating the emotions of the viewer. What is less widely known are the scientific uses to which the stimulus functions of film are applied in psychiatry for research, testing and therapy. Perhaps the most intensive use of film as a stimulus has been in the area of human sexual behavior. The subject matter of these films consists of the graphic depiction of most kinds of sexual activity, with its scientific uses consisting of testing the viewer's responses to the scenes of sexual activity.

Dr. Kinsey and his associates were the first to obtain comprehensive empirical data, based upon interviews, on erotic stimulus functions of film among the general white population. These film stimuli, as collated by Cairns and others, were portrayals of attractive nude figures, genitalia of the opposite sex and sexual activities between a man and a woman.

Women tend to respond less to erotic films and more to erotic literature. This finding by Dr. Kinsey was later retested by Mosher and Greenberg: Seventy-two college females were divided into two groups according to a pretest which measured their degrees of high or low sex guilt. They then read an erotic passage from the novel *Eternal Fire* by Calder Willingham, under two different contexts, and were given a post-test. Results indicated that reading the erotic passage produced significant sexual arousal in the women to a degree not replicated by erotic films, slides or still pictures. This study, and the cumulative evidence of other studies, leads to the conclusion that men and women are often sexually aroused by dissimilar kinds of media stimuli—visual for the male, verbal for the female.

Later studies by Koegler and Kline, Loiselle and Mollenauer, and researchers working for the Presidential Commission on Obscenity and Pornography, reported that women did record a Galvanic Skin Response when presented with sexually explicit films. Since a Galvanic Skin Response measures emotional change of any kind, without distinguishing between them, there is presently no scientific way of knowing whether the response was sexual arousal, as the researchers believe it was, or disgust and revulsion, as many of the women insisted it was. Both affective states are characterized by high arousal. Perhaps there was a bit of both. A change of sexual mores in America has steadily reduced the guilt associated with sex in the Puritan tradition, and many of the women tested during the Presidential Commission studies on obscenity and pornography freely admitted being stimulated by erotic materials.

The most extensive experimental use of color films to investigate the anatomy and physiology of human sexual response was conducted by Masters and Johnson at the Washington University School of Medicine. Their results represent by far the most comprehensive laboratory study of human sexual behavior reported to date, including that stimulated by motion pictures. Although the study comprised a biased sample of males and females—those sexually active persons willing to breach the social taboos against direct observation of sexual activity—the findings were significant in terms of media: both male and female subjects do respond, in terms of sexual behavior, when presented with erotic color motion pictures.

Viewer reactions to sexually explicit motion pictures vary according to age and sex, although there is disagreement among those conducting the research about the validity of one another's experimental techniques. Results indicate that those near sixteen years of age exhibited the most intense responses. Adults exhibited a less intense response, and were sometimes inclined to react critically to the stimuli, perhaps because of a cultural factor. And children under twelve reacted the least, in some cases failing to understand what was going on. The responses of women to sexually graphic films seems to be the area of greatest disagreement.

Infrared cinematography is used to photograph pupillary dilation as a means of testing sexual interest by the viewer. Hess and Polt theorized that in humans the size of the pupil varied with a subject's interest in various pictorial stimuli. They tested their theory with heterosexual and admittedly homosexual males by presenting images of nude males and females to the two groups. They discovered that the pupils of the heterosexual male dilated when viewing a nude woman, and the pupils of the homosexual male dilated when viewing a nude male. Conversely, heterosexual males revealed no pupillary dilation when viewing nude males, and homosexual males were similarly unresponsive to scenes of nude women. A similar technique may be extrapolated from this experiment and applied to women, to test the existence if not the degree of sexual arousal from watching sexually explicit films.

Levitt and Brady tested the sexual preferences of heterosexual viewers to allegedly erotic images in order to establish a scale of erotic appeal. Each male viewer was given the task of rating the image of a six-point scale indicating the degree to which he found it sexually stimulating. The procedure was repeated with other groups and yielded the following scale of visual erotic preference, ranging from greatest appeal to least appeal:

1. Heterosexual coitus in the ventral-ventral position.
2. Heterosexual coitus in the ventral-dorsal position.

3. Heterosexual petting, participants nude.
4. Heterosexual petting, participants partly clad.
5. Heterosexual fellatio.
6. Nude female.
7. Heterosexual cunnilingus.
8. Masturbation by a female.
9. A triad of two females and one male in conjunctive behavior involving coitus and oral-genital activity.
10. Partly clad female.
11. Homosexual cunnilingus.
12. Homosexual fellatio.
13. Sadomasochistic behavior, female on male.
14. Masturbation by a male.
15. Nude male.
16. Partly clad male.

This scale proved reliable in both individual and subject ratings. An interesting inference drawn from related tests given at the same time, the Endurance sub-scale and the Reactivity index, was that persistently hard-working individuals are relatively indifferent to fantasy sexual stimulation.

Erotic color motion pictures are apparently more sexually stimulating than color stills. Corman examined the effects of a film portraying scenes of a man and woman making love in bed with slides of nudes taken from *Playboy* magazine. He presented them in turn to a group of young married men, and tested the increase in their heartbeats during the viewings. Viewings of the slides of a nude woman evoked a barely perceptible change. Viewing of the erotic film increased the heart rates by an average of five beats per minute. It should be noted that the erotic film contained no revelation of genitalia that might be considered "hard-core" pornography.

A similar study by Bernick and Kling measured the sexually stimulating effects of motion pictures compared to slides by using the pupillary dilation system developed by Hess and Polt. Once again, the response to the color motion picture was significantly greater than the response to the slides of nudes.

Levitt and Hinesley conducted a related experiment to compare the sexually stimulating effects of erotic photography with that of erotic paintings and drawings. They found that graphics were less sexually stimulating to the viewer, a characteristic of desensitization in artwork found also in motion pictures, as discussed earlier in the chapter dealing with the animated film.

Films and videotapes are now serving sexually therapeutic purposes under medical prescription and experimental conditions. Married couples having problems of male impotence, female frigidity or just plain sexual boredom with each other are being exposed to sexually stimulating films. Color films portraying sexual intercourse from a wide variety of positions are being prescribed for jaded couples as one might prescribe a stimulant.

Mann, Sidman and Starr tested the effects of erotic color films on eighty-five couples, forty to fifty years of age, who had been married for more than ten years. The couples watched erotic films for twelve weeks and recorded their daily sexual activities in a mail-in log book for eighty-four consecutive days. After exposure to erotic films was terminated, they continued to record their daily sexual activities for an additional four weeks. If their responses were truthful, there was a significant increase in sexual activity. Couples reported that their lovemaking increased in frequency, during the film exposure period, with longer foreplay and a greater variety of sexual techniques, and that their enjoyment was enhanced. The study did not distinguish between the reactions of husband and wife, however, and there is no way of knowing whether the erotic films stimulated the husbands in particular to be more imaginative in their lovemaking. Moreover, no records were kept by the husbands and wives beyond the test period and the results of the experiment did not indicate whether the effects were permanent.

Homosexuality can apparently be started in certain individuals at an early age, triggered by pornographic films and photographs. Davis and Braught implemented a retrospective survey of empirical data to determine the effects of pornography on character and sexual deviance, and discovered that during the early teens—when males in particular are susceptible to sexual arousal by pornography—they may turn to any form of sexual release available to them. They found that in boys' schools and in other circumstances where no female is available for normal coitus, the young males have most often reacted to pornography by masturbation, but have sometimes resorted to sodomy and homosexual fellatio. Once this homosexual pattern has been established, it frequently continues, making normal sexual relations with females difficult to establish.

Even the most graphic forms of filmed sexual activity can become a bore if there is too much of it. The effects of satiation were tested on undergraduate males by research teams of the Commission on Obscenity and Pornography. Howard, Reifler and Liptzen subjected these young college men—at an age when the sex drive is very strong—to five solid weeks of daily exposure to pornographic films, magazines and books. At first the pornography was, by their own admission, sexually arousing. The daily bombardment of multimedia sexual stimuli eventually began to pall, however, and by the end of the five-week test period the most erotic of the stimuli was greeted with a yawn. This desensitizing effect does not seem to endure; a lapse of time restores the sexual appeal of filmed pornography. It appears that a sexually active male would have to subject himself to pornography almost constantly in order to remain desensitized.

It is intellectually fashionable to defend the unrestricted dissemination of pornography to adults on the grounds that it cannot do any harm and that it comes under the aegis of individual freedom. Scientific research indicates, however, that pornography does stimulate sexual activity by the male viewer in whatever form he may have enjoyed sexual gratification in the past: young boys masturbate or find homosexual partners; young men seek out sexual relations with girl friends or prostitutes; married couples have sexual intercourse. To draw the line at this point and insist that rapists do not rape when stimulated by pornography is to make the exception that only rapists do not respond to pornography by following their own precedents in sexual activity.

Similarly, the portrayal of violence tends to stimulate aggressive behavior among some children and certain elements of the adult population. The theory that filmed and televised portrayals of violence allow pent-up emotions to be released harmlessly, as a catharsis, has been largely dismissed by the report to the Surgeon General, *Television and Growing Up: The Impact of Televised Violence*. One of the volumes of supporting research stated in conclusion: ". . . present entertainment offerings of the television medium may be contributing, in some measure, to the aggressive behavior of many normal children. Such an effect has now been shown in a wide variety of situations." Portrayals of sex and violence are not exempt from the stimulus effect of the media.

Primatology

The primates, because of their physical, physiological and emotional similarities to man, have become surrogate subjects in several areas of scientific research. Many medical discoveries, such as the finding of the RH blood factor, were made possible through experimentation with rhesus monkeys. The techniques of transplanting kidneys and hearts in humans was first developed in surgical experiments on apes and monkeys, and significant research is underway to determine the feasibility of transplants of primate organs into human beings. Other roles of the primate in medical research include the study of the electrical behavior of the brain, muscular dystrophy, the effects of hormones, heart and kidney diseases, the study of the possible virus origins of cancer and physiological responses in aerospace studies. Although film and television techniques are utilized in the medical areas of primatology in ways similar to their use in human medicine, there are unique media uses in the area of behavioral studies.

Chimpanzees, gorillas, baboons and orangutans are being studied in order to explore their emotional response patterns to different kinds of stimuli, as well as their intellectual processes, personality traits, kinesic movements, social behavior and social hierarchy. In virtually all of these behavioral studies motion pictures and videotape are being used as the primary research recording systems.

Experimental studies of the reasoning processes and visual discrimination capabilities of primates are usually made by placing a camera, operated remotely, in a sequestered enclosure with the subject. The technique consists of presenting the primate with a task or discrimination problem requiring a degree of rational thought to solve, dangling a banana or some other fruit as a possible reward, and turning the lens of the camera on the subject as he works toward a solution. The kinds of experiments rendered on film and videotape include simple discrimination learning, oddity concept formation, discrimination reversal and learning set (learning-how-to-learn).

Other kinds of nonexperimental activities photographed for subsequent study include curiosity, social behavior, infant care patterns, attentiveness, activity levels at different times of day, locomotion studies and tool use. In all of these studies the camera is ignored by the primates, who act as if they were alone and unobserved.

Experiments in primate affection have taken such forms as raising

SURVEY OF THE PRIMATES. Affection studies. *Robert E. Lee, San Diego Zoo. Appleton-Century-Crofts.*

an infant rhesus monkey with two artificial mothers, under the lenses of cameras: One mother was made of cold wire and gave the infants their milk. The other was made of furry cloth and offered the infants nothing more than something warm and soft to hang onto. Then the infants were deliberately frightened to see whether they would flee to the wire milk-giving mother or to the inanimate but soft-cloth mother. The film footage revealed that virtually every one of the rhesus infants ignored the wire mother and found solace in the folds of the cloth mother.

This experiment, and others like it, was recorded on film and videotape to avoid the intrusive presence of the primatologist, and to obtain a visual record that could be perused again and again. A decade of filmed studies has revealed that the expression of affection in primates takes five general forms: the love of an infant for its mother; the affection of a mother for its child; the protective fondness of adult males for infants; the camaraderie between individuals of a gang of juveniles; and the sexual attraction and love between adults of opposite sexes. (These primate affection patterns sound familiar.)

The social structure and hierarchy of monkeys, however, cannot be validly studied in captive species; the environment and food supply are artificial and imposed, and all predators have been excluded. Primates must be systematically observed in their own wilderness environments, and today scientists from several intellectual disciplines have teamed up to study the intricate structure and interrelationships of ape and monkey societies in their natural environment.

Primatology studies in the field require the patience of Job. Primates in the wild are alert and organized in the defense of their own kind, and the primatologist is just another intruder into their territory—another predator. Cinematography of primates is comparable to producing a natural history film; the scientist must wait with his camera and telephoto lens for something to happen in the primate community. He patiently photographs their activities in short scenes, whenever he has the opportunity, and then studies the results to determine whether their patterns of social behavior bear any resemblance to that of man.

The cumulative film studies of such primates as the baboon in the wild have revealed the following social structures: Infants have prolonged periods of dependency in which they are protected by the adults and instructed in the social patterns of the troop, as well as how to secure food, water and shelter. Peaceful relations between hostile individuals are enforced by dominant males. The powerful adult males cooperate as a fighting force to defend females and infants against predators. And each troop maintains territorial rights and repels any geographic intrusion by others of its own kind. These cinematography studies have revealed social group patterns remarkably similar to those of man.

To date, color film has been the overwhelming favorite in recording the social structures of primate societies, in preference to videotape. This is due in part to the fact that motion picture cameras were first on the primatology scene and have proved quite satisfactory; they are light, portable and rugged, and primatologists are accustomed to using them. Electronic photography, on the other hand, was late in appearing in the primatology world, and has heretofore been limited in its use because of equipment clumsiness and fragility, lack of details in long shots and the absence of color in small units. The immediacy of playback in video-tape, however, offers an advantage of great value to a primatologist in the wilderness—he can see what he has recorded, and, if necessary, rephotograph the same scene immediately. With film he would have to wait until he returned to civilization and had the film processed to see what he had recorded in image form, and if something had gone wrong, there would be no possibility of retakes without organizing another expedition. With time and the development of videotape equipment offering the advantages of the motion picture camera, it seems reason-able to assume that its immediate playback capability will make elec-tronic photography the favorite with primatologists in the wilderness.

The footage photographed in the wild often ends up in documentary films, such as the National Geographic Society's television specials, and in scientific research films produced by such zoological societies as the San Diego Zoo. *Survey of the Primates* is a representative example of the primatology research film. The film reviewed the major families of apes and monkeys, classifying each species according to its geographical location, physical characteristics and manual dexterity. It made a com-parative analysis of the capacity of each species for solving problems, perceiving relationships among objects and events, and making adaptive and creative use of tools. The film further set forth in scientific fashion such social functions as the common defense of the group against preda-tors, social hierarchy within the group, joint protection of the home territory against rival primates, preservation of "law and order" within the primate community, and the rearing of the young to learn social patterns and techniques of obtaining food, water and shelter. Films of this kind are circulated primarily within the scientific community, but are growing in popularity with the general public as the average viewer becomes increasingly cognizant of ecology and takes an interest in his distant relatives, the primates.

Aerospace

Space photography reached extraordinary levels of excellence dur-ing the *Mariner 9* space flight to Mars. In 1971 a spacecraft launched by an Atlas/Centaur vehicle was sent on an orbital mission to Mars to study and photograph the characteristics of that planet. During the first ninety days that the *Mariner* spacecraft was in orbit, about seventy percent of the planet's surface was mapped, the structure and composition of the surface was photographed, and changes in surface markings, such as darkening during the Martian spring, were photographed and broadcast to Earth.

The television experiment, one of six conducted by the *Mariner 9* mission, was the heart of the space project. Its primary objectives were to obtain photographs of "fixed features" and "variable features" suitable for composite mapmaking of the geologic, dynamic and topographic features of Mars.

The fixed-feature assignment was fourfold: to make a more accurate delineation of the shape of Mars; to map the surface physiognomy of that planet, showing structural features, crater configuration and local surface conditions; to determine the heights and slopes of surface features; and to study the surface characteristics of the Martian moons, Phobos and Deimos.

The variable-feature investigation, related to finding conditions suitable for life, was fivefold: to document seasonal darkening variations of the surface; to note the polar-cap and cap-edge phenomena with the onset of a Martian winter; to observe white "clouds" in nonpolar regions; to study the patterns of atmospheric haze; and to record atmospheric and surface fluorescence during the Martian night.

The television system consisted of two electronic cameras mounted on *Mariner 9*'s planetary scan platform. The first camera was equipped with a wide-angle lens having a focal length of 50 mm. (considered wide-angle in space photography), which had a rectangular field of view of 11 by 14 degrees. The second camera had a long focal-length lens of 500 mm., with a rectangular field of view of 1.1-by-1.4 degrees. Both cameras were pointed down in the nadir direction for a direct line-of-sight view of the planet's surface. The cameras provided two simultaneous images of the Martian surface, with the wide-angle pictures of selected points on the planet's surface supplemented by a few television narrow-angle pictures at ten times better resolution.

The television cameras mapped the planet with continuous low-resolution photographs of 1 km. per television scan line, and with high-resolution closeups of 100 mm. per television scan line, to provide detailed reproductions of the areas of greatest scientific interest. The images were electronically recorded in the spacecraft's data storage sub-system tape recorder, and subsequently broadcast back to Earth to be replayed on television monitors and photographed. Within ninety days the two-camera television system electronically mapped seventy percent of the Martian surface, covering some of the areas again a second time to see if any variable-feature changes had occurred.

Meanwhile, back at the world, tracking stations pointed their giant antennae at the *Mariner* spacecraft in orbit around Mars. The main antenna for reception of televised data transmission was the single 210-foot-diameter antenna at Goldstone, California. This center was supported by tracking stations around the world, each equipped with 85-foot antennae, and all providing twenty-four-hour backup reception to the single main antenna in California.

The images are transmitted to Earth by the radio-frequency sub-system to the deep space stations on Earth. Received and transmitted frequencies are in the S-band part of the spectrum. Each line of digital data renders one scan line on the television screen, with the combined individual lines blending to form a continuous picture. Because the *Mariner* spacecraft acquires data faster than they can be transmitted to Earth, the data storage sub-system stored the data in digital form on the tape recorder until they could be transmitted to Earth at the slower rate needed to present the image on a television monitor.

Mapmaking was made possible by taking adjacent pictures every eighty-four seconds on each elliptical orbit. Gaps at the side were filled in on subsequent seventeen- to eighteen-day longitude circuits. Each square of overlapped electronic photography was recorded on the spacecraft's tape recorder and radioed back to Earth. Scientists then assembled the mosaic of photographs into a coherent map of Mars.

Satellites with television transmission capability, similar in concept to *Mariner 9*, are now being used to study the essential elements of the Earth's weather—humidity, temperature, wind and atmospheric pressure. The unblinking eyes of satellites orbiting over our world now contain sensing devices that watch the birth of hurricanes, measure their rainfall, windfall velocity and direction. They transmit the information to computers that digest billions of bits of information and in minutes draw complete weather maps on television monitors.

Television monitors are used to visually render the information received from satellites from a number of sensing devices in addition to that of electronic photography. The three sensing devices most commonly used in space and meteorological documentation systems are *infrared spectroscopy, infrared radiometry* and *ultraviolet spectroscopy.*

INFRARED SPECTROSCOPY

Infrared spectroscopy is used to study the physical movements and behavior of the atmosphere, in relation to the surface of the planet, by measuring the spectral radiance emitted from the atmosphere. Infrared studies, made from a satellite, provide measurements of the moisture content, vertical temperature structure and minor chemical components of the atmosphere, and provide values for the thermal characteristics of the surface of the Earth. The swirling anatomies of killer hurricanes in the Caribbean Sea are watched in this way; color added to a satellite infrared photograph, on the television monitor, charts the storm's moisture content, with the whitest areas indicating the fiercest deluges. Some of the newer infrared sensors may now report on the total levels of such lethal atmospheric pollutants as nitrous oxide, carbon dioxide and sulfur dioxide, so we can keep track of how rapidly we are making the air unbreathable.

INFRARED RADIOMETRY

Infrared radiometry is a valuable satellite system for measuring the temperatures of the sea and the soil over a wide coverage of the planet's surface. Radiometry may reveal warm and cold currents in the ocean, and those points of confluence most likely to offer the best fishing and spawning grounds. Infrared radiometry also reveals "hot spots" in the Earth's surface to indicate sources of internal heat from incipient volcanoes or earthquakes. The resulting radiometer scannings may be converted to pictures on television monitors; moreover, since the radiometers work with both infrared and visible lights, they can produce clear images on the night side of the Earth, as well as the daylit side, making twenty-four-hour global coverage a possibility.

ULTRAVIOLET SPECTROSCOPY

Ultraviolet spectroscopy is used to observe the surface and lower atmosphere of the earth by splitting and measuring its ultraviolet wavelengths. These measurements help to determine local ozone concentrations, and local atmospheric pressure over most of the planet, using the ultraviolet scattering properties of the lower atmosphere. This system also provides data on the composition of the atmosphere as a function of latitude, longitude and time, and data on the distribution and variability of magnet fields. The data are recorded digitally, as before, to be broadcast and translated into scan-line bits of information to form a television map of the variations of the ultraviolet wavelengths.

The National Oceanic and Atmospheric Administration sends meteorological satellites aloft in a northward orbit so that the Earth, in turning, will present its entire surface to the unblinking eyes of the cameras and sensing systems in twenty-four hours. These weather satellites are similar in principle to the *Mariner* system. They contain television cameras which store daytime pictures on tape, in digital form, for broadcast on command from monitoring stations on Earth. They have automatic picture transmission cameras which continuously send cloud-pattern photographs for use by local weather forecasters around the world. They contain infrared sensors to gauge the earth's heat radiation, and an infrared scanner to record the earth's cloud and surface temperatures, both day and night. Every perception device transmits a digital signal to be rendered in a separate picture on a different television monitor. The satellite sensing systems are all powered by three winglike panels which convert the sun's energy into electrical energy.

Television monitors, used in conjunction with computers and satellite systems, are revolutionizing the field of meteorology. The sensing devices enable weathermen to assess the temperatures of earth, sea and clouds to 3° F., to estimate how cold the clouds are, and therefore what kind they are. The computerized readouts rendered in colored-map form on the television monitors enable the viewer to see exactly what kind of weather is occurring and where. These colored television maps have proved extremely useful in early detection of hurricanes and other severe storms, and in making longer-range weather forecasts than has heretofore been possible.

The early discovery that infrared photography can penetrate blue haze to render distant terrain soon led to its adoption for aerial and satellite photography, in mapmaking and for wartime photoreconnaissance. Infrared photography has also proved invaluable because of the way it renders foliage. Trees of different species appear in differing tones, with conifers appearing darker than deciduous trees, regardless of their real colors and values. Crops and orchards suffering blights and diseases can be perceived through the differing tones which emerge in aerial infrared cinematography. Moreover, back on the ground, the condition of the plants themselves can be studied because the internal structures of leaves reflect infrared strongly, appearing much lighter in the film footage than to the unaided eye. Rusts, molds and other plant diseases tend to absorb infrared light and appear on film as very dark, making them easily visible for study. Infrared photography may be valuable in ecology for differentiating soils and plants, and in hydrology for studying water pollution.

Film is presently the preferred medium when photographing the sun and other celestial bodies through the lenses of an astronomical telescope. The definition of data in film is sharper, subtler and more detailed, offering far more information per frame than is possible on the 525-line raster of a television monitor. New scientific monitors with 2000 scan lines or more may change all this. The detailed definition of film made possible the discovery of thunder on the sun, found by accident when Cal Tech scientists examined some footage they had photographed through the telescope. Sound waves were observed undulating outward from sun spots at speeds up to 24,000 miles per hour—1600 miles from crest to crest—through subtle, rhythmic image variations in the motion picture frames. The discovery of this phenomenon opened up a new consideration of the physics of sun spots, a whole new picture of solar energy production. As a rule, whenever finely detailed data analysis by eye is important, and motion pictures are practical (as they would generally not be in a spacecraft), film is preferable to television.

The research uses of film and television made by meteorologists promises to expunge that old adage that everybody talks about the weather, but nobody does anything about it. Discoveries made through the use of media are raising the genuine possibility that man may be able to control the weather for his own benefit.

Oceanography

Oceanography is among the pioneering sciences, and cinematography has become an important means of exploring the undersea world that constitutes the earth's last frontier. For many years the study of deep sea marine life was conducted by using such methods as trawls, fish traps, and nets to catch specimens for study. The sea life pulled up in this way, however, was often killed in the process and could only be studied as a cadaver; or, if captured alive, was placed in an aquarium in which the ecological environment bore little resemblance to its natural habitat. Moreover, the capture of large, active creatures was impractical by these methods. The only valid way to study marine life is to go down to where they live and observe them at home in the freedom of the seas.

Direct observation of undersea marine life became possible with the advent of scuba diving gear, manned submersible vehicles, and ship controlled camera systems. Undersea cameras, blimped for protection against the ravages of salt water, are commonly used by scuba divers in shoreline areas to obtain beautiful sealife footage. For the most part, this is done in the natural light which diffuses down from the surface, supplemented by quartz lights attached to the camera housing.

Farther down, however, the ocean becomes too dark, the pressures too great, and the dangers too threatening, to permit free swimming observation and cinematography. The development of the manned submersible vehicle enabled the oceanographer to go down personally to make observations and to photograph marine life. This system, too, has its limitation: Except for the *Trieste*, which has gone down 35,000 feet to the deepest ocean depth in the Marianas Trench, dangerous pressures limit how far down most submersibles can go. The ability of human beings to endure close confinement is limited to relatively short periods of time. And finally, this means of exploration is expensive because it consumes so many man-hours on the mother ship and on the submersible vehicle for the amount of film footage obtained.

DEVELOPMENT OF THE DEEP-SEA CAMERA SYSTEM

The first deep-water cameras were used for still photography in geological studies of the ocean floor. The cameras were suspended from a wire connected to a ship slowly under way. A "pinger" accoustical system was developed to determine the distance of the camera from the bottom. The camera was hung with its lens pointed down, focused at a known distance from the sea bed, with a predetermined exposure and a fairly constant field of view. As the ship moved slowly the camera automatically took overlapping photographs of the ocean floor, obtaining information for map making and geological interpretation.

At the Scripps Institute of Oceanography this accoustical system of still photography was at first used for observing marine life on the deep ocean floor. Then a more practical alternative was created by the development of what was called the "autonomous deep-sea cine camera system." The Scripps Institute of Oceanography created a still and cinematography unit that could be dropped overboard to photograph marine life on the bottom without any physical links to the oceanography vessel. Ballast takes the autonomous cine camera system to the bottom, but without any connecting wires. The unit descends freely to the ocean floor where it rests in a fixed position. Bait is mounted on the end of an eight-foot bar which lies on the surface of the sea-bed. The camera faces the bait at an angle only slightly raised from the ocean floor, with its lens precisely focused on that bait. Marine life is lured into the camera's field of view, and the camera photographs the denizens of the deep at selected intervals until, at a predetermined time, the deep-sea camera

DEEP SEA CINEMATOGRAPHY. Suspended camera system. *Scripps Institute of Oceanography.*

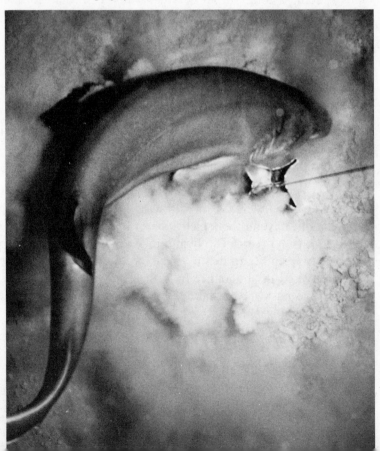

system is recovered. Because the camera can be focused on a subject known to be at a given distance from the lens, the footage will be as sharp and clear as the obscuring sea will permit.

At a predetermined time, the deep-sea camera system is retrieved. The new recovery system dispenses with physical attachments to the oceanography vessel. It consists, instead, of a location buoy, main float, the cinematography instruments, a lighting system, a ballast line, and a wire linking all the component units together at the bottom of the sea. When the time comes to recover camera and film, a release mechanism separates the ballast weight from the remaining buoyant system, and the main float brings the whole system bobbing up to the surface. Once at the surface, the location buoy transmits a pulsed signal for location by radio. The photographic system is located by a finder on the oceanographic vessel and the film is recovered for processing and study.

A major problem in deep-sea cinematography is the absence of light at great depths. The photography system must carry its own lights and batteries to the bottom of the sea. At the present time, the photography area at the end of the bar is illuminated with three tungsten-halogen bulbs yielding a total output of 1050 watts. Fish that normally go deep to avoid daylight will be attracted to the bait despite the illumination of the lighting system.

Water itself acts as an optical system. Objects appear to be one-fourth closer and one-fourth larger than they really are. This illusion may be corrected by using a compensating lens designed to reduce apparent size and distance by one-fourth, thereby rendering the images as if no water were present.

CINEMATOGRAPHY OF UNDERSEA LIFE

These camera systems have brought about major reassessments of the realities of underseas life. It was once believed that the deepest ocean depths, beyond the penetration of light, were almost as sterile and lifeless as a true desert. The living image revealed, however, great numbers of active sea life to depths of 20,000 feet. Free swimming fish have been discovered in abundance in most locations, at all depths, except in an anaerobic basin; even there, several fish were photographed. Sharks have been photographed at depths of 7800 feet, far deeper than they were ever thought to go. Some of these predators were found to be 24 to 30 feet long, so large that the angle of the lens was not wide enough to photograph the entire shark. Arctic sharks have been discovered to be living in temperate oceans at depths whose frigid temperatures approximated those found in their cold waters in the North; the distribution of sharks, it now appears, is as much a function of temperature as geography.

Behavioral studies of fish are now made possible by deep-sea cinematography. Unusual motions and behavioral patterns have been observed during the feedings of marine life that were attracted into the camera's field of view. There was remarkably little aggressive behavior revealed at the dinner table. Each fish fed in turn, and there has been seen only a single instance, to date, of one fish attacking another. Eventually, the collection of more motion picture data may add information about breeding habits, symbiotic relationships, predatory and feeding cycles, and reveal insight into the prevailing deep-sea ecological relationships. There is even talk among research associates of someday trying to program the behavior of fish, as Dr. Skinner has programmed the behavior of pigeons, to establish man-directed patterns of conditioned activity, all photographed on the ocean floor with film and videotape.

Deep-sea photography has yielded other information of scientific interest and potential economic value. The floors of the continental shelves have been found to be covered with nodules of manganese and embedded with other kinds of minerals which could eventually be mined. Vertical migrations of animals have been discovered; as the sun rises and sets, certain species of animals come up and go down in order to remain in the dark. The relationship of sea life to currents has been studied by cinematography, along with other measurements, and their patterns of concurrence charted. Perhaps one of the more important results of deep-sea photography is the revelation of human pollution on the ecology of the sea; the camera reveals clearly the effects of dumping junk, garbage, toxic chemicals, and radioactive waste amid the plankton, fish, and crustacea of the mother sea.

A large scale ocean-atmospheric interaction project is being conducted by the Scripps Institution of Oceanography in the North Pacific in which film plays a modest role in documentation. Deep moored buoys are stationed at critical confluences to measure the strengths and movements of currents, temperature changes, wind speeds and shifts, and changes in salinity. These shifting elements are measured and displayed on dials, which are photographed at hourly intervals. The film is

OCEAN DATA STATIONS. Buoy: film documentation. *Scripps Institute of Oceanography.*

periodically picked up by an oceanography vessel for processing and study by oceanographers.

Motion pictures are made on the oceanography vessel as well as in the deep sea. The shipboard techniques are themselves photographed to provide a permanent visual record of research procedures; much of this footage is subsequently edited into a process film documenting the scientific venture.

Today's oceanographers are the Vikings of science, whose discoveries in the depths will prove increasingly important as the resources of the land are depleted, and men turn to the deep seas for sustenance.

Technical Data Studies

Where does an automobile crumple most severely when it hits a brick wall while traveling at 70 mph? How does gravity affect the velocity of a bullet having a new configuration? How does underwater torque affect the functions of a new tool designed for use in repairing a ship's propellers? What causes malfunction in an automatic welding process? How do water resistance, water pressure and wave formation affect the passage of a new submarine hull design? Why did the second stage of that rocket fail to disengage properly?

HIGH-SPEED CINEMATOGRAPHY

These are the kinds of problems to which technical data studies provide the answer, usually by means of high-speed cinematography. High-speed cinematography is the rendering of images at rates of 250 to 26,000 frames per second, with exposure durations of one-thousandth of a second or less. This tremendously high rate of photography, when played back at the modest rate of 24 frames per second—or stopped on a single frame—converts phenomena and motion into events that people can see, study and understand. Transient phenomena lasting only a fraction of a second may be projected on a screen and analyzed frame by frame at a rate convenient to the human eye. Sometimes the films are played backward, to reverse the event and relate effect to cause, to offer even more information. The versatility of high-speed cinematography makes it extremely valuable in today's world in the fields of aerodynamics, hydrodynamics, physics, ballistics and any other discipline in which events occur too quickly to be comprehensible to the unaided eye. In some extreme cases it is possible to use a high-speed framing camera in conjunction with a microscope to obtain 26,000 pictures per second of a subject enlarged 1000 times.

TIME-LAPSE PHOTOGRAPHY

Time-lapse photography is the reverse of high-speed cinematography. The time-lapse technique is the rendering of individual frames of motion picture film at widely separated intervals of time, ranging from a tenth of a second to a frame every few hours, or even days. Its purpose is to render movements and developments which normally occur at so slow a rate of speed that the changes are undetectable to the unaided eye. Typical subjects for time-lapse work may be the growth of plants or fungi, the apparent movement of stars and other astronomical phenomena or barely perceptible chemical transformations. When these extremely slow changes are photographed at widely separated intervals, and projected on a screen at sound speed, the movements are apparently speeded up in a way that makes them comprehensible to the unaided eye.

THE CONTRIBUTIONS OF INDUSTRY

Many industries are responsible for the technical implementation of government programs in aerospace and oceanography, and actually do much of the film and television studies needed to document these experiments. The Convair Division of General Dynamics, for example, has been involved with federal research in aerospace studies and oceanography almost from the outset of government sponsorship. In the space program Convair has been largely responsible for the documentation of missile firings, for the rocket-borne cameras which photograph the earth as it recedes in the distance, and for the documentation as the stages of the rockets separate, so that internal malfunctions may be studied.

In another aspect of their representative contributions vacuum tanks were used to simulate a space environment, and astronaut clothing and other artifacts were tested within it by withdrawing the air to the point of a near vacuum. Conditions in space were further simulated by subjecting the artifacts to searing arc-light heat from one side and intense cold from the other, with all subjects studied by media for possible cracking or chemical change. Some of Convair's other specialized areas of technical data processing include: simulated space vehicle flights in a nearly closed ecological environment; recoverable space photographic systems; Photoelastic stress studies; gravity conditions from 0 to 50 gs.; trajectory data study in wind-tunnel testing; cryogenic studies to $-420°$ F.; underwater instrumentation and cinematography; vibration tests with Chadwick-Helmuth slip-sync techniques; high-heat ablation tests; cineradiography and X-ray television systems; photo-optical and television instrumentation for thousands of tests of solids, liquids and gases under all types of conditions; and precise testing of new ship hull designs by photographic analysis of wave formations and water resistance.

More and more industrial plants are becoming increasingly concerned about the properties of compounds, materials and components when subjected to the stresses of movement and chemical changes. Typical areas of media emphasis are found in electronics, pharmaceuticals, plastics, ceramics, metalworking, criminology, computer data processing and other fields almost beyond counting. Most of those industries making technical data studies utilize those techniques, in addition to high-speed and time-lapse photography, found in the sciences: infrared, ultraviolet, X-ray and luminescent photography; macroscopic and microscopic enlargement; radio signals to render a remote image; remote viewing by closed-circuit systems and videotape playbacks; acoustical signals to control the distance of a camera from its subject and remote focusing of the lens.

Quite often, three cameras are used simultaneously during the development and testing of an industrial product, each rendering the subject at a different rate of speed. The resulting footage may then be used for technical data studies, managerial process films, reports, training films and documentaries. The scope of film and television utilization in industrial research and technology is enormous and is spreading rapidly, an integral part of science and the media in the service of the nation.

Bibliography

Books

Arnheim, Rudolph. *Film as Art*. Berkeley, California: University of California Press, 1958.

Arons, Leon, and Mark A. May (eds.). *Television and Human Behavior*. New York: Appleton-Century-Crofts, 1963.

Barnouw, Erik. *The Image Empire*. New York: Oxford University Press, 1970.

——. *Mass Communication: Television, Radio. Film, Press*. New York: Rinehart & Co., 1956.

——. *The Television Writer*. New York: Hill & Wang, 1962.

Belson, William A. *The Impact of Television: Methods and Findings in Program Research*. Hamden, Conn.: Archon Press, 1967.

Benton, Charles W., Wayne K. Howell, Hugh C. Oppenheimer, and Henry H. Urrows. *Television in Urban Education*. New York: Frederick A. Praeger, Inc., 1969.

Berelson, Bernard, and Morris Janowitz (eds.). *Reader in Public Opinion and Communication*. New York: The Free Press of Glencoe, 1953.

Berlo, David K. *The Process of Communication*. New York: Holt, Rinehart & Winston, 1960.

Bluem, A. William. *Documentary in American Television*. New York: Hastings House, 1965.

Bluem, A. William, and Roger Manvell (eds.). *Television: The Creative Experience; A Survey of Anglo-American Progress*. New York: Hastings House, 1967.

Bobker, Lee R. *Elements of Film*. New York: Harcourt, Brace & World, Inc., 1969.

Book, Albert C., and Norman D. Cary. *The Television Commercial: Creativity and Craftsmanship*. New York: Decker Communications, Inc., 1970.

Boutwell, William D. (ed.). *Using Mass Media in the Schools*. New York: Appleton-Century-Crofts, 1962.

Bretz, Rudy. *Techniques of Television Production.* New York: McGraw-Hill, 2nd ed., 1962.

Brown, James Alexander Campbell. *Techniques of Persuasion.* Baltimore: Penguin Books, 1963.

Brown, James W., and Kenneth D. Norberg. *Administering Educational Media.* New York: McGraw-Hill, 1965.

Calder-Marshall, Arthur. *The Innocent Eye: The Life of Robert J. Flaherty.* New York: Harcourt, Brace & World, Inc., 1963.

Callahan, Jennie Waugh. *Television in School, College, and Community.* New York: McGraw-Hill, 1953.

Campbell, James H., and H. W. Hepler (eds.). *Dimensions in Communications Readings.* Belmont, Cal.: Wadsworth Publishing Co., Inc., 1966.

Carnegie Commission on Educational TV. *Public Television.* New York: Harper and Row, 1967.

Chapman, Dave, and Frank Carioti. *Design for ETV: Planning for Schools with Television.* New York: Educational Facilities Laboratories, 1968 ed.

Chu, Godwin C., and Wilbur Schramm. *Learning from Television: What the Research Says.* Stanford, Cal.: Institute for Communications Research, 1967.

Coombs, Don H. *One Week of Educational Television.* Bloomington, Ind.: National Instructional Television Center, 1969.

Costello, Lawrence F., and George N. Gordon. *Teach with Television.* New York: Hastings House, 2nd ed., 1965.

Curran, Charles W. *Screen Writing and Production Techniques.* New York: Hastings House, 1958.

Dale, Edgar. *Audiovisual Methods in Teaching.* New York: The Dryden Press, 3rd ed., 1969.

Dale, Edgar, Fannie W. Dunn, Charles F. Hoban, Jr., and Etta Schneider. *Motion Pictures in Education: A Summary of the Literature.* New York: Arno Press and The New York Times, 1970.

Daly, Charles U. *The Quality of Inequality: Urban and Suburban Public Schools.* Chicago: The University of Chicago Press, 1968.

Diamond, Robert M. (ed.). *A Guide to Instructural Television.* New York: McGraw-Hill, 1964.

Dizard, Wilson P. *Television: A World View.* Syracuse, N.Y.: Syracuse University Press, 1966.

Eastman Kodak Medical Publication. *Medical Infrared Photography.* Rochester, New York: Eastman Kodak Co., 2nd ed., 1st printing, 1969.

Eastman Kodak Scientific Data Book. *Basic Scientific Photography.* Rochester, New York: Eastman Kodak Co. 1970.

Eastman Kodak Scientific Publication. *Photography through the Microscope.* Rochester, New York: Eastman Kodak Co. 5th ed., 1st printing, 1970.

Eastman Kodak Technical Publication. *Ultraviolet and Fluorescence Photography.* Rochester, New York: Eastman Kodak Co. 1st ed., 1st printing, 1968.

Eimerl, Sarel, and Irven DeVore. *The Primates.* New York: Life Nature Library, Time Inc., 1965.

Eisenstein, Sergei. *Film Form and Film Sense.* New York: Harcourt, Brace & Co., 1949.

Elliot, William Y. (ed.). *Television's Impact on American Culture.* East Lansing, Mich.: Michigan State University Press, 1956.

Factual Film, The. (Arts Enquiry), London, 1949.

Fielding, Raymond. *The Technique of Special Effects Cinematography*. New York: Hastings House Publishers, 1965.

Ford Foundation. *Teaching by Television*. New York: Ford Foundation and Fund for the Advancement of Education, 1961.

———. *A Ten Year Report of the Fund for the Advancement of Education: 1951–1961*. New York: The Ford Foundation, 1961.

Friendly, Fred. *Due to Circumstances Beyond Our Control*. New York: Random House, 1968.

Geduld, Harry M. (ed.). *Film Makers on Film Making*. Bloomington, Ind., & London: Indiana University Press, 1967.

Gerlach, Vernon S., and Donald P. Ely. *Teaching and Media: A Systematic Approach*. Englewood Cliffs, N. J.: Prentice-Hall, Inc., 1971.

Gibson, J. J. *The Perception of the Visual World*. Boston: Houghton-Mifflin Co., 1950.

Glick, Ira O., and Sidney J. Levy. *Living with Television*. Chicago: Aldine Publishing Co., 1962.

Glucksmann, Andre. *Violence on the Screen*. London: The British Film Institute Education Department, 1971.

Gordon, George N. *Classroom Television: New Frontiers in ITV*. New York: Hastings House, 1970.

———. *Educational Television*. New York: The Center for Applied Research in Education, Inc., 1965.

Gordon, George N., Irving Falk, and William Hodapp. *The Idea Invaders*. New York: Hastings House, 1963.

Griffith, Richard. *The World of Robert Flaherty*. London: Gollancz, 1956.

Hardy, Forsyth (ed.). *Grierson on Documentary*. Berkeley: University of California Press, rev. ed., 1966.

Haney, John B., and Eldon J. Ullmer. *Educational Media and the Teacher*. Dubuque, Iowa: Wm. C. Brown Co., 1970.

Herman, Lewis. *Educational Films*. New York: Crown Publishers, 1965.

Holaday, P. W., and Stoddard, G. D. *Getting Ideas from the Movies*. New York: The Macmillan Co., 1933.

Hovland, Carl I., Irving L. Janis, and Harold H. Kelley. *Communication and Persuasion: Psychological Studies of Opinion Change*. New Haven, Conn.: Yale University Press, 1953.

Hughes, Robert (ed.). *Film: Book 2, Films of Peace and War*. New York: Grove Press, 1962.

Irving, John A. (ed.). *Mass Media in Canada*. Toronto: The Ryerson Press, 1962.

Jamieson, Ron. *The Troubled Air*. Fredericton, New Brunswick: Brunswick Press, 1960.

Jorgensen, E. S. *A Survey of Instructional Closed-Circuit Television, 1967*. Washington, D.C.: National Education Association, 1967.

Kauffmann, Stanley. *A World on Film*. New York: Dell Publishing Co., 1967.

Kinross, Felicity. *Television for the Teacher*. London: Hamish Hamilton, 1968.

Klapper, Joseph T. *The Effects of Mass Communication*. New York: The Free Press, 1960.

Knight, Arthur. *The Liveliest Art*. New York: The Macmillan Co., 1957.

Larson, Otto N. (ed.). *Violence and the Mass Media*. New York: Harper & Row, 1968.

Lindgren, Ernest. *The Art of the Film*. New York: The Macmillan Co., 1963.

MacCann, Richard Dyer. *Film and Society.* New York: Charles Scribner's Sons, 1964.

MacCann, Richard Dyer (ed.). *Film: A Montage of Theories.* New York: E. P. Dutton & Co., 1966.

Madsen, Roy P. *Animated Film: Concepts, Methods, Uses.* New York: Pitman-Interland, 1969.

Mager, Robert F. *Preparing Instructional Objectives.* Palo Alto, Cal. Fearon Publishers, 1967.

Manvell, Roger (ed.). *Experiment in the Film.* London: Grey Walls Press, 1949.

Manvell, Roger. *Film.* Harmondsworth: Penquin, rev. and enlarged ed., 1950.

———. *The Living Screen.* London: George C. Harrap & Co., 1961.

Mascelli, Joseph V. *The Five C's of Cinematography.* Hollywood: Cine/Graphic Publications, 1965.

Masters, W. H., and V. E. Johnson. *Human Sexual Response.* Boston: Little, Brown, 1966.

May, Mark A., and Arthur A. Lumsdaine. *Learning from Films.* New Haven, Conn.: Yale University Press, 1958.

Mayer, J. P. *Sociology of Film.* London: Faber & Faber, 1946.

McClelland, D. C. *Studies in Motivation.* New York: Appleton-Century-Crofts, 1955.

McGuire, Jeremiah C. *Cinema and Value Philosophy.* New York: Philosophical Library, 1968.

McLuhan, Marshall. *Understanding Media: The Extensions of Man.* New York: McGraw-Hill, 1964.

McVay, Douglas. *The Musical Film.* New York: A. S. Barnes & Co., 1967.

Miller, Lewis, Taby Citbor, and Kanji Hatano. *Adult Education and Television.* London: Unesco, 1966.

Miller, N. E., and J. Dollard. *Social Learning and Imitation.* New Haven, Conn.: Yale University Press, 1941.

Millerson, Gerald. *The Technique of Television Production.* New York: Hastings House, rev. and enlarged ed., 1968.

Murphy, Judeth, and Ronald Gross. *Learning by Television.* New York: Fund for the Advancement of Education, 1966.

Napier, J. R., and P. H. Napier. *A Handbook of Living Primates.* New York: Academic Press, 1967.

Nelson, Lester A. *Towards a Significant Difference.* Washington, D.C.: National Association of Educational Broadcasters, 1969.

Powell, John Walker. *Channels of Learning.* Washington, D. C.: Public Affairs Press, 1962.

Pudovkin, V. I. *Film Technique and Film Acting.* London: The Vision Press and Mayflower Publishing Co., 1958.

Rosenberg, Bernard, and David Manning White (eds.). *Mass Culture: The Popular Arts in America.* Glencoe, Ill.: The Free Press, 1957.

Rossi, Peter H., and Bruce J. Biddle (eds.). *The New Media and Education.* Garden City, N.Y.: Doubleday Co., 1967.

Rotha, Paul. *Documentary Film.* London: Faber & Faber; New York: Hastings House, 3rd ed., 1952.

Rotha, Paul, and Richard Griffith. *The Film Till Now.* New York: Twayne, 1960.

Schramm, Wilbur (ed.). *Mass Communications.* Urbana, Ill.: University of Illinois Press, 1960.

Schramm, Wilbur. *Responsibility in Mass Communication.* New York: Harper & Brothers, 1957.

Schramm, Wilbur (ed.). *The Impact of Educational Television.* Urbana, Ill.: University of Illinois Press, 1960.

Schramm, Wilbur, Jack Lyle, and Edwin B. Parker. *Television in the Lives of Our Children.* Palo Alto, Cal.: Stanford University Press, 1961.

Schwebel, Milton. *Who Can Be Educated?* New York: Grove Press, 1968.

Shaw, Franklin J., and Robert S. Ort. *Personal Adjustment in the American Culture.* New York: Harper & Brothers, 1953.

Siepmann, Charles A. *Television and Education in the United States.* Paris: Unesco, 1952.

Snyder, Robert L. *Pare Lorentz and the Documentary Film.* Norman, Okla.: University of Oklahoma Press, 1968.

Spear, James. *Creating Visuals for TV.* Washington, D. C.: Division of Instructional Services of the NEA, 1965.

Starr, Cecile (ed.). *Ideas on Film.* New York: Funk & Wagnalls, 1951.

Stanford University, Institute for Communication Research. *Educational Television: The Next Ten Years.* Stanford, Cal.: Stanford University Press, 1962.

Steiner, Gary A. *The People Look at Television.* New York: Alfred A. Knopf, 1963.

Sunderlin, Sylvia, and Nan Gray (eds.). *Children and TV.* Washington, D.C.: Association for Childhood Education International, 1968.

Swallow, Norman. *Factual Television.* New York: Hastings House, 1966.

Talbot, Daniel (ed.). *Film: An Anthology.* Berkeley and Los Angeles: University of California Press, 1966.

Thomas, C. A., I. K. Davies, D. Openshaw, and J. B. Bird. *Programmed Learning in Perspective.* Chicago: Educational Methods, Inc., 1963.

Truffaut, François. *Hitchcock.* New York: Simon & Schuster, 1966.

Wainwright, Charles Anthony. *Television Commercials: How to Create Successful TV Advertising.* New York: Hastings House, 1970.

———. *The Television Copywriter: How to Create Successful TV Commercials.* New York: Hastings House, 1966.

Waldron, Gloria. *The Information Film.* New York: Columbia University Press, 1949.

White, David Manning, and Richard Averson. *Sight, Sound, and Society.* Boston: Beacon Press, 1968.

Wolfenstein, Martha, and Nathan Leites. *Movies: A Psychological Study.* Glencoe, Ill.: The Free Press, 1950.

Wykoff, Gene. *The Image Candidates: American Politics in the Age of Television.* New York: The Macmillan Co., 1968.

Articles in Periodicals

Allen, Gerald L. "ETV Stints on News," *Educational Broadcasting Review* (NAEB), Vol. 24, No. 3 (May–June, 1965), pp. 48–50.

Almstead, Francis E., and Raymond W. Graf. "Talkback: the Missing Ingredient," *Audio–Visual Instruction,* Vol. 5 (April, 1960), pp. 110–112.

Blain, Beryl Bruce. "Effects of Film Narration Type and of Listenability Level on

Learning of Factual Information," *Audio-Visual Communication Review,* Vol. 4 (1956), pp. 163–164. (Abstract).

Booth, Ethel. "Public TV Is Where You Find It," *Educational Instructional Broadcasting,* Vol. III, No. 5 (May, 1970), pp. 19–21.

Botden, P. "Introduction to X-ray Television," in *Television in Medical Teaching and Research* by James W. Ramey (Washington D.C.: U.S. Government Printing Office, 1965), pp. 73–74.

Brady, J. P., and E. E. Levitt. "The Relation of Sexual Preferences to Sexual Experiences," *The Psychological Record,* Vol. 15 (1965), pp. 377–384.

————. "The Scalability of Sexual Experiences," *The Psychological Record,* Vol. 15 (1965), pp. 275–279.

Browne, Donald R. "Life Without ETV: A Survey," *Educational Broadcasting Review* (NAEB), Vol. II, No. 1 (February, 1968) pp. 22–26.

Brown, M. "Television as a Tool in Postgraduate and Undergraduate Medical Education," *New York State Journal of Medicine,* Vol. LX, No. 6 (March, 1960), pp. 873–74.

Carpenter, C. R., *et al.* "The Development of a Sound Motion Picture Proficiency Test," *Personal Psychology,* Vol. 7 (1954), pp. 509–523.

Castle, C. Hilmon. "Open-circuit Television in Postgraduate Medical Education," *Journal of Medical Education,* Vol. 38 (1963), pp. 254–260.

Cook, Bruce L. "How Are We Going to Educate 'Em When They Ain't There?" *Journal of Broadcasting,* Vol. XII, No. 2 (Spring, 1968), pp. 137–143.

Graig, Gordon Q. "A Comparison Between Sound and Silent Films in Teaching." *British Journal of Educational Psychology,* Vol. 26 (1956), pp. 202–206.

Darley, W., and A. S. Cain. "A Proposal for a National Academy of Continuing Medical Education," *Journal of Medical Education,* Vol. XXXVI, No. 1 (January, 1961), p. 33.

Douglas, A. "Closed-Circuit Television: One of the World's Greatest Tools in Surgery," in *Television in Medical Teaching and Research* by James W. Ramey (Washington, D.C.: U.S. Government Printing Office, 1965), pp. 60, 112.

Dove, John R., and John L. Marsh. "ETV and the Charge of Depersonalization," *Educational Broadcasting Review* (NAEB), Vol. 26, No. 4 (July–August, 1967), pp. 91–96.

Driscoll, John P. "Can TV Improve College Teaching?" *NAEB Journal,* Vol. 18 (March, 1959), pp. 16, 20.

Dryer, B. V. "Medical School TV Teaching—Three Case Histories," in *Television in Medical Teaching and Research,* by James W. Ramey (Washington, D.C.: U.S. Government Printing Office, 1965), p. 127.

Evans, Richard I. "An Examination of Students' Attitudes Toward Television as a Medium of Instruction in a Psychology Course," *Journal of Applied Psychology,* Vol. 40 (1956), pp 32–34.

Fahs, Ivan J. and Winston R. Miller. "Continuing Medical Education and Educational Television: An Evaluation of a Series for Physicians in Minnesota," *Journal of Medical Education,* Vol. XXXXV, No. 8 (August, 1970), pp. 578, 584, 586.

Foster, Graeme. "LARGE Screen TV at Hagerstown," *Educational Screen and Audio-Visual Guide,* Vol. 43, No. 10438 (October, 1964), pp. 580–582.

Gans, Herbert J. "The Mass Media as an Educational Institution," *Television Quarterly,* Vol. VI, No. 2 (Spring, 1967), pp. 20–37.

Geissendorfer, R. "Color Television Relays of Operations," in *Television in Medi-*

cal Teaching and Research, by James W. Ramey (Washington, D.C.: U.S. Government Printing Office, 1965), p. 113.

Gibson, J. J. "A Theory of Pictorial Perception," *Audio-Visual Communication Review,* Vol. 2 (Winter, 1954), pp. 3–23.

Girdany, B., E. Gaither, and D. Darling. "Large Screen Image Amplification with Closed-circuit Television Employing Television Tape Recorder," *Radiology,* Vol. LXXVII, No. 2 (August, 1961), p. 280.

Gordon, Morton J. "Third Grade Television-Classroom Articulation Program," *Journal of Speech and Hearing Disorders,* Vol. 25 (1960), pp.398–404.

Gosling, J., and D. Anderson. "Television in Teaching Clinical Medicine," in *Television in Medical Teaching and Research,* by James W. Ramey (Washington, D.C.: U.S. Government Printing office, 1965), pp. 29, 30.

Greenhill, Leslie, and Malcolm McNiven. "Relationship Between Learning and the Perceived Usefulness of a Film," *Audio-Visual Communication Review,* Vol. 4 (1956), pp. 255–267.

Groom, Dale. "Television in Postgraduate Education," *Journal of American Medical Association,* Vol. CIIC, No. 3 (October 17, 1966), p. 277.

Hayman, John Luther Jr., and James T. Johnson, Jr. "Exact vs. Varied Repetition in Educational Television," *Audio-Visual Communication Review,* Vol. 11 (1963), pp. 96–103.

Hayt, W. H., Jr. "Notes on Achievements and Limitations of ETV," *Educational Broadcasting Review,* Vol. 23, No. 3 (May–June, 1964), pp. 40–46.

Hedman, Lorraine L., and Elaine Mansfield. "Hospital to Hospital via TV," *American Journal of Nursing,* Vol. LXVII, No. 4 (April, 1967), pp. 808–809.

Hill, Beatrice H., and Francis R. Arje. "ETV Aids Rehabilitation of Ill, Aged, Handicapped," *Educational Broadcasting Review,* Vol. 21, No. 4 (July–August, 1962), pp. 14–16.

Hoban, C. F. "Determinants of Audience Reaction: Status," *Audio-Visual Communication Review,* Vol. 1 (Fall, 1953), pp. 242–251).

———. "Determinants of Audience Reaction to a Training Film," *Audio-Visual Communication Review,* Vol. 1 (Winter, 1953), pp. 30–37.

Holmes, D. "Closed-Circuit Television in Teaching Psychiatry," in *Television in Medical Teaching and Research,* by James W. Ramey (Washington, D.C.: U.S. Government Printing Office, 1965), pp. 60–61.

Hungerford, Arthur. "ETV's Financial Dilemma," *Journal of Broadcasting,* Vol. VIII, No. 2 (Spring, 1964), pp. 133–140.

Hurst, Paul M. Jr. "Learning Sets: Kinescope vs. Film," *Audio-Visual Communication Review,* Vol. 3 (1955), pp. 257–273.

Joiner, Charles W., and Garnet R. Garrison. "ETV Moves into the Courtroom," *Educational Broadcasting Review,* Vol. 21, No. 4 July–August, 1962), pp. 1–5.

Kanner, Joseph H., et al. "Television in Army Training," *Audio-Visual Communication Review,* Vol. 6 (1958), pp. 255–291.

———, and Alvin J. Rosenstein. "Television in Army Training: Color vs. Black and White," *Audio-Visual Communication Review,* Vol. 8 (1960), pp. 243–252.

Keasling, H. H., et al. "Report on the Use of Closed-Circuit Television in the Teaching of Pharmacology," *Journal of Medical Education,* Vol. XXXV, No. 9 (September, 1959), pp. 896–897.

Laurent, Lawrence. "ETV—The Critical Point," *Television Quarterly,* Vol. II, No. 4 (Fall, 1963), pp. 44–48.

Leveridge, L. L. "Preliminary Report of Intramural Television at New York University Medical Center: Experimental Uses of Closed-Circuit Systems," in *Television in Medical Teaching and Research*, by James W. Ramey (Washington D.C.: U.S. Government Printing Office, 1965), p. 129.

Levitt, E. E., and J. P. Brady. "Sexual Preferences in Young Adult Males and Some Correlates," *Journal of Clinical Psychology*, Vol. 21 (1965), pp. 347–354.

———, and R. K. Hinesley. "Some Factors in the Valences of Erotic Visual Stimuli," *The Journal of Sex Research*, Vol. 3 (February 1967), pp. 63–68.

Lumsdaine, A. A. "Audio-Visual Research in the United States Air Force," *Audio-Visual Communication Review*, Vol. 1 (Spring, 1953), pp. 76–90.

Lyle, Jack. "Why Adults Do Not Watch Educational TV," *Journal of Broadcasting*, Vol. V, No. 4 (Fall, 1961), pp. 325–334.

McCarthy, J. F., and J. S. Ritter. "Colored Motion Picture Photography and Black and White Television of the Human Urinary Bladder and Other Interior Body Organs," *Journal of Urology*, Vol. LVIII, No. 5 (November, 1957), pp. 677–79.

McCombs, Maxwell. "ETV Audience Preferences for Information and Culture," *Journal of Broadcasting*, Vol. XII, No. 2 (Spring, 1968), pp. 155–159.

McMahan, Harry W. "New Research Shows the Advantages of Color TV," *Advertising Age* (May–June, 1967), p. 122.

———. "New Techniques in Evaluating TV Commercial Strengths, Weaknesses," *Advertising Age* (November–December, 1967), p. 73.

Meighan, Spence, and Anne Treseder. "Continuing Medical Education Through Television," *Journal of the American Medical Association*, Vol. CC, No. 9 (May 29, 1967), pp. 762, 763, 765, 766.

Meyer, Richard J. "ETV and the Ghetto," *Educational Broadcasting Review* (NAEB), Vol. II, No. (August, 1968), pp. 19–24.

Michael, Donald N., and Nathan Maccoby. "Factors Influencing Verbal Learning From Films under Varying Conditions of Audience Participation," *Journal of Experimental Psychology*, Vol. 46 (1953), pp. 411–418.

Miller, Neal, E. "Social Science and the Art of Advertising." *Journal of Marketing*, Vol. 14 (January, 1950), pp. 580–584.

Moore, F. J., L. C. Hanes and C. A. Harrison. "Improved Television, Stereo, and the Two-Person Interview," *Journal of Medical Education*, Vol. XXXVI, No. 2 (February, 1961), pp. 162–164.

Oestreich, Arthur H. "ETV and You," *Educational Screen and Audio-Visual Guide*, Vol. 46, No. 4. (April, 1967), pp. 26–27.

Palmer, Charles. "Teacher in a Tube," *Educational Screen and Audio-Visual Guide*, Vol. 42, No. 12 (December, 1963) pp. 668–669.

Persselin, Leo E. "Auto-Instructional Technology and the Industry Film Maker," *Business Screen Magazine*, Vol. 24, No. 2 (April, 1963), pp. 48–51.

———. "The Use of Motion Pictures for Automated Instruction," *Journal of the Society of Motion Pictures and Television Engineers*, Vol. 75, No. 9 (September, 1964), pp. 755–766.

Perrin, Donald T. "A Branching Teaching Machine Using Motion Pictures," *Journal of the Society of Motion Picture and Television Engineers*, Vol. 73, No. 9 (September, 1964), pp. 760–764.

Puccio, Dominick, V. "ETV and Industry: The Money Game," *Educational Instructional Broadcasting*, Vol. III, No. 3 (March, 1970), pp. 33–34.

Richards, Victor, and Henry Jacobs. "Television Technics in Graduate Surgical

Education," *American Journal of Surgery,* Vol. C (August, 1970), pp. 153–155.

Roe, Yale. "ETV-Education Is Not Enough," *Television Quarterly,* Vol. I, No. 2 (May, 1962), pp. 50–53.

Rosenstein, Alvin J., and Joseph H. Kanner. "Television in Army Training: Color vs. Black-and-White," *Audio-Visual Communication Review,* Vol. 9 (1961), pp. 44–49.

Ruhe, D. S., *et al.* "Television in the Teaching Development," *Journal of Medical Education,* Vol. VIII, No. 10 (October, 1960), pp. 917, 921–922.

Rumbaugh, Duane M., Austin H. Riesen, and Robert Lee. "Study Guide to Accompany the Film, in *Survey of the Primates*" (New York: Appleton-Century-Crofts, 1970).

Scott, Richard S., and Charles R. Allen. "Cancion de la Raza: An ETV Soap Opera," *Television Quarterly,* Vol. VIII, No. 4 (Fall, 1969), pp. 24–37.

Shaw, Gavin, and Arlene Smith. "Does Medical Television Work?" *Health Bulletin,* Vol. XXVIII, No. 1 (January, 1970), p. 43.

Shepher, John R. "An Experiment in Increasing the Educational Television Audience," *Journal of Broadcasting,* Vol. X, No. 1 (Winter, 1965–1966), pp. 55–66.

Shettel, H. H., *et al.* "An Experimental Comparison of 'Live' and Filmed Lectures Employing Mobile Training Devices," *Audio-Visual Communication Review,* Vol. 4 (1956), pp. 216–222.

Stromberg, Eleroy L. "College Credit for Television Home Study," *American Psychologist,* Vol. 7 (1952), pp. 507–509.

Swain, H. H. "Basic Science Teaching with Television," in *Television in Medical Teaching and Research,* by James W. Ramey (Washington, D.C.: U.S. Government Printing Office, 1965), pp. 34–35.

Ulrich, Roger E. "A Behavioral View of Sesame Street," *Educational Broadcasting Review* (October, 1970).

Vander Meer, A. W. "Color vs. Black-and-White in Instructional Films," *Audio-Visual Communication Review,* Vol. 2 (1954), pp. 121–134.

Warner, R. S., and J. Z. Bowers. "Program of Postgraduate Medical Education," *Journal of the American Medical Association* (April 14, 1956), p. 1306.

Weales, Gerald. "Be Quiet, The Commercial's On," *Television Quarterly,* Vol. VI, No. 3 (Summer, 1967), pp. 23–27.

Yerkes Regional Primate Research Center, *Yerkes Newsletter,* Emory University, June, 1969.

Zuckerman, John V. "Predicting Film Learning by Pre-Release Testing," *Audio-Visual Communication Review,* Vol. 2 (1954), pp. 49–56.

Zworykin, V. W. "Television Techniques in Biology and Medicine," in *Television in Medical Teaching and Research,* by James W. Ramey (Washington, D.C.: U.S. Government Printing Office, 1965), pp. 23, 111.

Formal Reports and Occasional Papers

A. C. Nielsen Company. *What the Ratings Really Mean.* New York: Media Research Division, 1964.

Alexander, Virgil William. "The Contribution of Selected Instructional Motion Pictures to Achievement in Varying School Situations," *Abstracts of Doctoral Dissertations, the University of Nebraska*, Vol. II. Lincoln, Neb.: University of Nebraska, 1950, pp. 146–152.

Allison, Sarah G., and P. Ash. *Relationship of Anxiety to Learning from Films.* Technical Report SDC 269-7-24, Instructional Film Research Program, Pennsylvania State University, Port Washington, L.I., N.Y.: U.S. Naval Special Devices Center, 1951.

American Research Bureau. "A Survey for Immediate Information on the Effects of Sudden Change," *ARB Overnight Television Surveys.* American Research Bureau, 1968.

American Research Bureau. *Research Innovations.* From the ARB 1969 Innovator Awards Program.

American Research Bureau, Inc. *1970 Research Innovations II.* From the ARB Innovator Awards Program.

Amoroso, D. M., M. Brown, M. Preusse, E. E. Wave, and D. W. Pilkey. "An Investigation of Behavioral, Psychological, and Physiological Reactions to Pornographic Stimuli," *Technical Reports of the Commission on Obscenity and Pornography*, Vol. 8. Washington, D.C.: U.S. Government Printing Office, 1970.

Ash, Philip, and B. J. Carlson. The Value of Note-Taking during Film Learning. Technical Report SDC 269-7-21, Instructional Film Research Reports, Port Washington, L.I., N.Y.: U.S. Naval Special Devices Center, 1951.

Ash, Philip, and Nathan Jaspen. *The Effects and Interactions of Rate of Development, Repetition, Participation, and Room Illumination on Learning from a Rear Projected Film.* Technical Report SDC 269-7-39, Instructional Film Research Reports, Port Washington, L.I., N.Y.: U.S. Naval Special Devices Center, 1953.

Birdwhistell, Ray L. *Introduction to Kinesics: An Annotation System for Analysis of Body Motion and Gesture.* Washington, D.C.: Foreign Service Institute, Department of State, 1952.

Boone, W. F. *Evaluation of the U.S. Naval Academy Educational Television as a Teaching Aid.* Annapolis: U.S. Naval Academy (7010 7-26-54): 1954. (Duplicated). (Prepared from abstract in Kumata, Hideya, *Inventory of Instructional Television Research.* Ann Arbor, Mich.: Educational Television and Radio Center, 1956, pp. 38–40.)

Brown, James I. "The Importance of Structured Outside Reading Assignments," *College and Adult Reading*, Vol. 11, Second Annual Yearbook, North Central Reading Association, 1963. (Abstracted in part in *NAEB Journal*, Vol. 21 (March, 1962), pp. 5–7.)

Canadian Broadcasting Corporation, Research, Ottawa. *How Television Audiences Are Measured: A Non-Technical Guide for the Interested Layman.* Toronto, Ontario: CBC Publications Department, 1965.

Carter, Lamore J., Roy B. Moss, and Mamie T. Wilson. *A Comparative Study of the Effectiveness of Three Techniques of Film Utilization in Teaching a Selected Group of Educable Mentally-Retarded Children Enrolled in Public Schools in Louisiana.* [USOE Project No. 272.] Grambling, La.: Grambling College of Louisiana [n.d.]. (Mimeographed).

Cash, Norman E., Pres., Television Bureau of Advertising, Inc. "Television: The Standard of Acceptance." Acceptance speech for the Carta Award, September 9, 1971.

Casper, Wesley. "An Experimental Evaluation of Certain Motion Picture Films in Selected Educational Psychology Classes in Kansas Colleges," *Dissertation Abstracts*, Vol. 16 (1956), p. 1105.

Corman, C. Physiological Response to a Sexual Stimulus. B.Sci. (Hed.) thesis, University of Manitoba, 1968.

Curry, Robert P. *Report of Four Experiments in the Use of Television in Instruction*. Cincinnati: Cincinnati Public Schools, September 1, 1960. (Offset.)

Davis, K. E. and G. N. Braucht. *Reactions to Viewing Films of Erotically Realistic Heterosexual Behavior*. Technical Reports of the Commission on Obscenity and Pornography, Vol. 8. Washington, D.C.: U.S. Government Printing Office, 1970.

——, *Exposure to Pornography, Character, and Sexual Deviance: A Retrospective Survey*. Technical Reports of the Commission on Obscenity and Pornography, Vol. 7. Washington, D.C.: U.S. Government Printing Office, 1970.

Driscoll, John P. *The Effects of Mental Retardation on Film Learning*. USOE Project No. 1 365. Los Angeles: University of California [n.d.]

——. *The Effects of Mental Retardation on Film Learning: A Study to Determine What Type of Instructional Film Experiences Are Meaningful to Children with Mental Retardation Regularly Enrolled in Public Schools*. Los Angeles: University of California, [n.d.]. (Mimeographed).

Duval, D. P., *et al. The Effectiveness, Acceptability, and Feasibility of Technical Training Courses Recorded on Sound Motion Pictures and Slides Plus Tape*. NAVTRADEVCEN Technical Report 364-1, Port Washington, L.I., N.Y.: U.S. Naval Special Devices Center, June, 1960. *Audio-Visual Communication Review*, Vol. 8 (1960), p. 312. (Abstract.)

Elias, J. E. *Exposure to Erotic Materials in Adolescence*. Technical Reports of the Commission on Obscenity and Pornography, Vol. 9. Washington, D.C.: U.S. Government Printing Office, 1970.

Ellery, John B. *A Pilot Study of the Nature of Aesthetic Experiences Associated with Television and Its Place in Education*. Detroit: Wayne State University, January 15, 1959. (Mimeographed.)

Erickson, Clifford G., and Hymen M. Chausow. *Chicago's TV College: Final Report of a Three-Year Experiment*. Chicago: Chicago City Junior College, August, 1960.

Evans, Richard I., Ronald G. Smith, and William K. Colville. *The University Faculty and Educational Television: Hostility, Resistance, and Change. A Social Psychological Investigation in Depth*. USOE Project No. 051. Houston: University of Houston, 1962. (Offset.)

Ford Foundation and the Fund for the Advancement of Education. "The National Program on the Use of Television in the Public School [n.p.], Report of the Second Year 1958–59," NAEB Research Fact Sheet, Series I, 92, *NAEB Journal*, Vol. 20 (July 1961), pp. 1–2. (Abstract.)

Frank, Joseph Henry. "An Evaluation of Closed-Circuit Television for Interceptor Pilot Training," *Dissertation Abstracts*, Vol. 15 (1955), pp. 2060–2061.

Fullerton, Billie J. "The Comparative Effect of Color and Black and White Guidance Films Employed with and without 'Anticipatory' Remarks upon Acquisition and Retention of Factual Information," *Dissertation Abstracts*, Vol. 16 (1956), p. 1413.

Glock, John William. "The Relative Value of Three Methods of Improving Reading-Tachistoscope, Films, and Determined Effort," *Dissertation Abstracts*, Vol. 15 (1955), p. 2072.

Harby, S. F. *Evaluation of a Procedure for Using Daylight Projection Film Loops in Teaching Skills.* Technical Report SDS 269-7-25, Port Washington, L.I., N.Y.: U.S. Naval Special Devices Center, 1952. *Audio-Visual Communication Review,* Vol. I (1953), pp. 291–292. (Abstract.)

Hirsch, Richard S. "The Effect of Knowledge of Results on Learning of Meaningful Material," *Abstracts of Dissertations,* Vol. 27. Palo Alto, Cal.: Stanford University, 1953, pp. 31–33.

Gropper, George L., and Arthur A. Lumsdaine. *An Investigation of the Role of Selected Variables in Programmed TV Instruction.* Studies in Televised Instruction, Report No. 4, USOE Project No. 336, Pittsburgh: Metropolitan Pittsburgh Educational Television Stations WQED-WQEX and American Institute for Research, April, 1961. *Audio-Visual Communication Review,* Vol. 9 (1961), pp. A-52–53. (Abstract.)

Hoban, C. F., and E. B. Van Ormer. *Instructional Film Research, 1918–1950.* Technical Reports: SDC 269-7-19, Instructional Film Research Program, Pennsylvania State University, Port Washington, L.I., N.Y.: U.S. Naval Special Devices Center, December, 1950.

Howard, J. L., C. B. Reifler, and M. B. Liptzin. *Effects of Exposure to Pornography.* Technical Reports of the Commission on Obscenity and Pornography, Vol. 8. Washington, D.C.: U.S. Government Printing Office, 1970.

Hudson, W. "Colour versus Monochrome in a Demonstration Film Used to Administer Performance Tests for the Classification of African Workers," *Journal of National Institute of Personnel Research,* Johannesburg, South Africa, Vol. 7 (1958), p. 128. *Psychological Abstracts,* Vol. 33 (1959), p. 9432. (Abstract.)

Instructional Film Research Program. *Evaluation of the Film: Military Police Support in Emergencies (Riot Control) TF 19-1701.* Technical Report SDC 269-7-52, Instructional Film Research Program, Port Washington, L.I., N.Y.: U.S. Naval Special Devices Center, 1954.

Jackson, Robert. *Learning from Kinescopes and Films.* Technical Report SDC 20-TV-1, Instructional TV Research Reports, Port Washington, L.I., N.Y.: U.S. Naval Special Devices Center, 1952.

Johnson, F. Craig, *et al. An Investigation of Motion Picture Film and the Program Analyzer Feedback to Improve Television Teacher Training.* USOE Project No. 334, Athens, Ohio: Ohio University, April, 1960. (Mimeographed.)

Kale, Shrikrishna Vasudeo. *Learning and Retention of English-Russian Vocabulary under Different Conditions of Motion Picture Presentation.* University Park: The Pennsylvania State College, 1953. (Multilith.)

Katzman, M. *Photograph Characteristics Influencing the Judgment of Obscenity.* Technical Reports of the Commission on Obscenity and Pornography, Vol. 9. Washington, D.C.: U.S. Government Printing Office, 1970.

Kendler, Tracy S., John Oliver Cook, and Howard H. Kendler. "An Investigation of the Interacting Effects of Repetition and Audience Participation on Learning from Training Films." Paper presented to American Psychological Association Convention, 1953. *American Psychologist,* Vol. 8 (August, 1953), pp. 378–379. (Abstract.)

Kinsey, A. C., W. B. Pomeroy, and C. E. Martin. *Sexual Behavior in the Human Male.* Philadelphia: W. B. Saunders, 1948.

Kinsey, A. C., W. B. Pomeroy, C. E. Martin, and P. H. Gehbard. *Sexual Behavior in the Human Female.* Philadelphia: W. B. Saunders, 1953.

Krebs, Robert Edward. "The Effects of Educational Films on Student Perceptions," *Dissertation Abstracts*, Vol. 19 (1957), p. 1030.

Kumata, Hideya. *Attitude Change and Learning as a Function of Mode of Presentation and Prestige of Instructor*. East Lansing, Mich.: Communications Research Center, Michigan State University, 1958. (Mimeographed.)

LeAnderson, Robert Elmer. "A Statistical Analysis of the Contribution of Visual Materials to a unit on Telephone Communication," *Dissertation Abstracts*, Vol. 13 (1953), p. 1115.

Lee, Robert E. *Survey of the Primates, A Motion Picture Script*. The Meridith Corporation, 1970.

LeMaster, Lelan Kenneth. "Filmed Demonstrations with Manual Class Demonstrations vs. Conventional Demonstrations in Introductory Woodwork," *Dissertation Abstracts*, Vol. 23 (1962), pp. 164–165.

Lepore, Albert R., and Jack D. Wilson. *Project Number Two: An Experimental Study of College Instruction Using Broadcast Television*. San Francisco: San Francisco State College, 1958.

Levine, Seymour. "The Role of Motivation in the Effects of 'Active Review' on Learning from a Factual Film." Paper presented at American Psychological Association, 1953. *American Psychologist*, Vol. 8 (August, 1953), pp. 388–389. (Abstract.)

Lumsdaine, A. A., R. L. Sulzer, and F. F. Kopstein. *The Influence of Simple Animation Techniques on the Value of a Training film*. Human Resources Research Laboratories, Report No. 24, April, 1951. *Audio-Visual Communication Review*, Vol. 1 (1953), pp. 140–141. (Abstract.)

MacLennan, Donald W., and Christopher Reid. *A Survey of the Literature of Learning and Attitude Research in Instructional Television*. Columbia, Mo.: University of Missouri, Department of Speech, 1963.

Magnetic Products Division of the 3M Company. *Advertising with Video Tape*.

Mann, J., J. Sidman, and S. Starr. *Effects of Erotic Films on Sexual Behaviors of Married Couples*. Technical Reports of the Commission on Obscenity and Pornography, Vol. 8. Washington, D.C.: U.S. Government Printing Office, 1970.

Martin, Howard S. *The Relative Effectiveness of Teaching Dramatic Understanding and Appreciation as Compared to Conventional Classroom Instruction*. Lincoln, Neb.: University of Nebraska, KUON-TV, and the Nebraska Council for Educational Television, 1961. NAEB Research Fact Sheet, Series 1, 102, *NAEB Journal*, Vol. 21 (1962), pp. 1–7. (Abstract.)

Martin Roberts and Associates, Inc. *Video Tape/Television Film Survey*. September, 1970.

Mayer, Martin. *How Good Are Television Ratings?* A report on the work of the Committee on Nationwide Television Audience Measurements, a joint research group with representatives from the American Broadcasting Company, the CBS Television Network, the National Broadcasting Company and the National Association of Broadcasters.

McIntyre, Charles J. *Training Film Evaluation. FB 254—Cold Weather Uniforms*. Technical Report SDC 269-7-51, Instructional Film Research Reports, Port Washington, L.I. N.Y.: U.S. Naval Special Devices Center, 1954.

McNiven, Malcolm. *Effects on Learning of the Perceived Usefulness of the Material to be Learned*. Technical Report SDC 269-7-54, Instructional Film Research Reports, Port Washington, L.I., N.Y.: U.S. Naval Special Devices Center, 1955.

McTavish, Chester Lynn. "Effect of Repetitive Film Presentations on Learning," *Abstracts of Doctoral Dissertations, The Pennsylvania State College*, Vol. 16 (1954), pp. 333–338.

Mercer, John. *Relationship of Optical Effects and Film Literacy to Learning from Instructional Films*. Technical Report SDC 269-7-34, Instructional Film Research Reports, Port Washington, L.I., N.Y.: U.S. Naval Special Devices Center, 1952.

Miller, J., S. Levine, and J. Kanner. *A Study of the Effects of Different Types of Review and of Structuring Subtitles on the Amount Learned from a Training Film*. Memo Report No. 17, Human Resources Research Laboratories, Bolling AFB, Washington, D.C., March, 1952. *Audio-Visual Communication Review*, Vol. 1 (1953), p. 140. (Abstract.)

Miller, Neal E., *et al. Graphic Communication and the Crisis in Education*. Washington, D.C.: Department of Audio-Visual Instruction, National Education Association, 1957.

Mosher, D. L. *Psychological Reactions to Pornographic Films*. Technical Reports of the Commission on Obscenity and Pornography, Vol. 8. Washington, D.C.: U.S. Government Printing Office, 1970.

Murphy, Francis Eugene. "The Relative Effectiveness of Filmed Introductions to a General Science Motion Picture," *Dissertation Abstracts*, Vol. 22 (1962), p. 3121.

Nelson, H. E., and A. W. Vander Meer. *Relative Effectiveness of Differing Commentaries in an Animated Film on Elementary Meteorology*. Technical Report SDC 269-7-43, Instructural Film Research Reports, Port Washington, L.I., N.Y.: U.S. Naval Special Devices Center, 1955.

Neu, D. Morgan. "The Effects of Attention-gaining Devices on Film-Mediated Learning," *Abstracts of Doctoral Dissertations, The Pennsylvania State College*, Vol. 13, (1951), pp. 414–417.

Peterson, Jack Arno. "The Effectiveness of Selected Motion Pictures in Changing the Beliefs of Nebraska Secondary School Students Relative to the United Nations and Its Activities," *Abstracts of Doctoral Dissertation, The University of Nebraska*, Vol. 11 (1950), pp. 159–164.

Ramey, Dr. James W. *Television in Medical Teaching and Research*. A survey and annotated bibliography: U.S. Department of Health, Education, and Welfare, Office of Education. Washington, D.C.: U.S. Government Printing Office, 1965.

Reid, J. Christopher, and Donald W. MacLennan. *Research in Instructional Television and Film*. Washington, D.C.: United States Department of Health, Education, and Welfare, 1967.

Reifler, C. B., J., Howard, M. A. Lipton, M. B. Liptzin, and D. E. Widmann. "An Experimental Study of Effects." Presented at the American Psychiatric Association Annual Meeting, 1970.

R. H. Bruskin Associates. *The Temptation of Modern Eve*, a survey for CBS Television Stations National Sales, January, 1969.

Rock, Robert T., J. S. Duva, and J. E. Murray. *The Effectiveness of Television Instruction in Training Naval Air Reservists*. Technical Report SDC 476-02-S2, Instructional TV Research Reports, Port Washington, L.I., N.Y.: U.S. Naval Special Devices Center, April, 1951.

Spigle, Irving Samuel. "The Cumulative Effect of Selected Educational Motion Pictures on the Attitudes of High School Boys and the Relationship of Attitude

Changes to Selected Personality and Intelligence Factors," *Dissertation Abstracts*, Vol. 15 (1955), p. 2066.

Southwestern Signal Corps Training Center and Camp San Luis Obispo, California. *Instructor-Student Contact in Teaching by Television*. Training evaluation and research programs, Part IV, Training Research Programs, July 1, 1953. *Audio-Visual Communication Review*, Vol. 3 (1955), pp. 304–305. (Abstract.)

Starck, D., R. Schneider, and H. J. Kuhn. *Progress in Primatology*. Report of the First Congress of the International Primatological Society at Frankfurt. Stuttgart: Gustav Fisher Verlag, 1967.

Stein, J. J. *The Effect of a Pre-Film Test on Learning from an Educational Sound Motion Picture*. Technical Report 269-7-35, Instructural Film Research Reports, Port Washington, L.I., N.Y.: U.S. Naval Special Devices Center, 1952.

The Surgeon General's Scientific Advisory Committee on Television and Social Behavior. *Television and Growing Up: The Impact of Televised Violence*. United States Public Health Service, 1972.

———. *Television and Social Behavior*, Reports and Papers, Vol. III. United States Public Health Service, 1972. Washington, D.C.

Tannenbaum, P. H. *Emotional Arousal as a Mediator of Communication Effects*. Technical Reports of the Commission on Obscenity and Pornography, Vol. 8. Washington, D.C.: U.S. Government Printing Office, 1970.

The Television Bureau of Advertising, Inc. *Low-Cost Television Commercial Production Ideas from Your Own TV Set, as Shown in TVB's Sales Clinics*. A nontechnical guide for viewing commercials. New York.

———. *What You Should Know about Producing Television Commercials*. A report on some basic guide lines to consider when preparing color or black and white commercials. New York.

Tendam, D. J. *Preparation and Evaluation in Use of a Series of Brief Films of Selected Demonstrations from the Introductory College Physics Course. Final Report*. USOE Grant No. 7-12-027.11, Lafayette, Ind.: Purdue Research Foundation, August 31, 1961. (Offset.)

Toffel, George M. *Effectiveness of Instruction by Television in Teaching High School Chemistry in Alabama Schools*. USOE Project Nol 302H. University of Alabama, August, 1971. *Audio-Visual Communications Review*, Vol. 10 1962), pp. A-81–82. (Abstract.)

Vander Meer, A. W. *Effects of Film-Viewing Practice on Learning from Instructional Films*. Technical Report SDC 269-7-20, Instructional Film Research Reports. Port Washington, L.I., N.Y.: U.S. Naval Special Devices Center, November, 1951.

Wagner, Robert Walter. *Design in the Educational Film: An Analysis of Production Elements in Twenty-One Widely Used Non-Theatrical Motion Pictures*. Unpublished doctoral dissertation, Ohio State University, 1953.

Weisgerber, Robert Arthur. "The Effect of Science Motivational Films on the Attitudes of Secondary School Pupils toward the Field of Science," *Dissertation Abstracts*, Vol. 21 (1960), pp. 505–506.

Zuckerman, M. *Physiological Measures of Sexual Arousal in the Human*. Technical Reports of the Commission on Obscenity and Pornography, Vol. 1. Washington, D.C.: U.S. Government Printing Office, 1970.

Index to Film and Television Titles

551

General Index

555

conversion, 323
identification, 325–26
indifference, 323
precipitation, 323. *See also* Educational film, forms and formats; Historical film
Documentary film production, 331–32
mixed. *See* Documentary films, formats
naturalist. *See* Documentary films, forms of
pure, 326
realistic, 319
social action, 319
slice-of-life, 162, 319
story line, 329, 333
subject matter, 318
techniques in dramatic film, 328
television, 87, 124, 280, 341–67
formats, 348–49
classic documentary, 349
mini-documentary, 348–49
subjective first person documentary, 349
forms, 349–358
biographical, 349, 357
digest, 349, 358
dramatized, 349
ethnographic. *See* Ethnographic film
exposé, 349, 352–53
historical complication. *See* Historical film
in-depth, 349, 353–54
information, 349, 357–58
interview, 349, 355–57
live, 349
natural history film, 349, 358, 391–394
news, 349
slice-of-life, 349, 355
functions of, 346–48
sensitive viewer's perception, 346–347
provide a record of our time, 346–348
provide a stimulus, 346–47. *See also* Ethnographic film; Historical film; Natural History film
truth, 329–31
Dolly shot. *See* Cinematography, camera movements
Donald Duck, 290

Double-speed playback. *See* Special effects, electronic
Dubcek, Premier Alexander, 381
Dramatic dialectics, 234–35
Dramatic emphasis. *See* Music, functions of
Dramatic progression, 75, 81
Dramatic structure, 195–218
conflict, 196–200
man against himself, 197
man against man, 197
man against society, 197–200
man against the elements, 197
society against society, 197
emotional appeal, 195–96, 238, 271, 279–80, 385
plot, 200–210, 329
climax, 200, 205
crisis, 200, 202–204
denouement, 200, 205
improvised plot, 215
joining the conflict, 200, 202
obligatory scene, 200, 204
pivotal character, 200–202, 239
reversals of fortune, 200, 203–204
self-delusion, recognition of, 200, 203–204
theme, 200, 236–37, 264, 268–69, 272, 275–76, 278, 281–82, 285, 309–10. *See also* Adaptation, stageplays; Educational film, modified dramatic film; Musical, the
point of dramatic attack, 205–10, 238–239
background of the conflict, 206–207
clues, 209–10
context of the conflict, 206
triggering event, 207
television, 216–18, 269–70, 280–81, 285, 288, 290–91, 295, 304
characterizations, 376
crisis and the commercial, 216–17
guest protagonist, 240–41
joining the conflict, 217
recapitulation, 217
Dramatic unity, 211
Driscoll, John, 489, 491
Dropout of details. *See* Videotape to film transfer
Drug Control Act Amendment of 1965, 352